The Death of the French Atlantic

The Death of the French Atlantic

Trade, War, and Slavery in the Age of Revolution

ALAN FORREST

OXFORD
UNIVERSITY PRESS

OXFORD
UNIVERSITY PRESS

Great Clarendon Street, Oxford, OX2 6DP,
United Kingdom

Oxford University Press is a department of the University of Oxford.
It furthers the University's objective of excellence in research, scholarship,
and education by publishing worldwide. Oxford is a registered trade mark of
Oxford University Press in the UK and in certain other countries

Published in the United States of America by Oxford University Press
198 Madison Avenue, New York, NY 10016, United States of America

British Library Cataloguing in Publication Data
Data available

Library of Congress Control Number: 2019946182

ISBN 978-0-19-956895-6

Printed and bound in Great Britain by
Clays Ltd, Elcograf S.p.A.

For Rosemary and Marianne

Preface: The Death of the French Atlantic?

Until relatively recently, most historians shared the view that the French Revolution was directly responsible for the decline in French commercial fortunes that followed. This was especially true of the French Atlantic and its principal port cities. The last decades of the monarchy were looked back upon rather fondly as the peak years of prosperity, while the Revolution was associated with economic neglect and a damaging indifference to the interests of trade. It was a period when commercial values were decried, the mercantile classes were undermined, and France's colonies were lost to war or revolt. For some of the earliest historians of the port cities, like the nineteenth-century chroniclers Aurélien Vivie and the *abbé* O'Reilly in Bordeaux, an anti-revolutionary, or anti-Jacobin, stance fitted well with their own political views and with their admiration for the work of commercial elites, and they did not hesitate to denounce the Revolution as the source of many of the woes of their own century.[1] While more recent analyses may agree that the revolutionary years spelt disaster, they have been less assured in placing responsibility on the Revolution itself. War has come to be seen as more important than politics in explaining the damage inflicted on the Atlantic, while the role of anti-slavery propaganda (both from abroad and in France itself) has assumed greater significance in forming opinion and turning politicians against what they saw as an immoral trade. It was 'the wars of the Revolution and Empire', in the view of one leading historian, 'the loss of the colonies, the development of an abolitionist morality and the slow elaboration of repressive laws to tackle the illegal slave trade' that condemned it to an irreversible decline.[2]

The opinions of nineteenth-century historians reflected in large measure those of the cities' merchants and commercial elites, who saw themselves as the victims of revolutionary prejudice and Parisian manipulation, and who did not hesitate to speak in apocalyptic terms of the crisis they faced. Any decline in the volume of trade would affect the commercial cities particularly severely, they warned, leaving their quays empty and their dockworkers idle. 'If opinion on the colonies does not change,' insisted the two deputies sent from La Rochelle to the National Assembly in 1792, 'France's trade will be completely lost.' They added, rather plaintively, that a major cause of the current crisis lay in the ignorance of commerce that was

---

[1] Aurélien Vivie, *Histoire de la Terreur à Bordeaux* (2 vols, Bordeaux: Feret et fils, 1877); Patrice-John O'Reilly, *Histoire complète de Bordeaux* (6 vols, Bordeaux: J. Delmas, 1857–8).

[2] Olivier Pétré-Grenouilleau, 'Pour une étude du milieu maritime nantais entre les fins 18ᵉ et 19ᵉ siècles', *Enquêtes et documents* 17 (1990), 52.

shown by the Assembly itself. For, they maintained, 'the people of Paris, and with them members of the National Assembly, have unfortunately no concept of the importance of these precious islands and of the part they play in establishing our national credit'.[3]

The merchants' warning was stark: if Atlantic commerce flagged, the threat of misery and unemployment hung over entire communities, with the direst consequences for the poor and vulnerable. This warning was not new, but it became more strident as the Revolution approached. In 1788, for instance, the Chamber of commerce in Bordeaux had talked of the fragility of trading conditions and had expressed fears that the threatened loss of the city's Parlement would have disastrous effects on the market in luxury goods. Theirs was a deeply conservative and paternalistic view of society, where everything depended on the expenditure of the most affluent. The rich built houses and initiated public works, they argued, and they kept the city's economy vibrant by their consumption, providing the food and housing for ordinary working families. 'As a result, the stonemason, the joiner, the carpenter, the locksmith, the blacksmith, the sculptor, the plasterer, the roofer are all kept in work; money circulates; and it keeps society alive.'[4] With the decline of colonial trade, all this would be lost. A doom-laden pamphlet published in La Rochelle in 1789 pointed out that colonial commerce and local manufacturing were mutually interdependent, and that any reduction in colonial trade would inevitably affect communities in the interior, too. The decline of France's colonies would entail the loss of markets for industrial manufactures and agricultural production across whole swathes of the country, and this would hit workers in communities far beyond the Atlantic littoral. The merchants of La Rochelle emphasized the importance to the wider economy not just of colonial traffic generally, but also, more controversially, of the slave trade.[5] Without it, they implied, their cities would crumble, families would starve, and workers would be forced to migrate back to the countryside from which they had come. The booming Atlantic economy that had promoted their prosperity would die.

This was, needless to say, a gross exaggeration, made with the intention of spreading anxiety and alarm. But in all the Atlantic ports there was a shared sense of apprehension, a belief that the Revolution spelt the end of an era, heralding an uncertain future. Nowhere was this felt more deeply than in Nantes, where the economy was dangerously dependent on slaving and where the interests of family and commerce were often interlocked, whether in the commercial activities of the port or on the plantations of Saint-Domingue, creating frequent family

---

[3] Brice Martinetti, *Les négociants de La Rochelle au 18e siècle* (Rennes: Presses Universitaires de Rennes, 2013), 251.

[4] AD Gironde, Fonds Bigot 8J 703, Chambre de Commerce de Bordeaux, 'Tableau alarmant de la ville de Bordeaux, par un négociant' (Neufchâtel, 1788).

[5] BM La Rochelle, 11877c, 'Précis sur l'importance des colonies, et sur la servitude des noirs, suivi d'observations sur la traite des Noirs' (La Rochelle, 1789).

entanglements between the people of Nantes and refugees fleeing from the Caribbean. Nantes simply could not ignore events in the Caribbean islands, so great was its dependence on trade in slaves and colonial produce. Before the Revolution, the West Indian trade had dominated mercantile life in the city, while after the Revolution the presence of refugees from the Caribbean was a constant reminder of the bonds that had tied the city to the Creoles and their economy. Many could not conceive of their city without the Atlantic trade, and when the Napoleonic Wars were finally over in 1815, Nantes merchants rushed to despatch their vessels to West Africa and to reopen trade routes with the Caribbean.[6] Such over-dependence on one market and on a single form of commerce would prove also to be their undoing.

In the other ports, the dependence on slaving and the Caribbean was less intense. In Bordeaux, for instance, the city's prosperity was spread across a wider range of commercial activities: slaving, of course, in the form of the triangular trade with West Africa and the Caribbean; but also direct trade with the West Indian islands, voyages to India and the East Indies, a valuable entrepôt trade in colonial produce with other parts of Europe, and wine exports to Britain and the Baltic. This gave the city greater flexibility in the face of crisis, and Bordeaux merchants showed more initiative in seeking out new markets in the nineteenth century. But the extent of its economic resilience can easily be over-stated. Over the course of the eighteenth century, a series of naval wars had repeatedly threatened Bordeaux's prosperity, and from 1792 France would again be involved in nearly a quarter-century of warfare. François Crouzet is surely right to underline the fragility of the city's prosperity and the critical importance of keeping open Bordeaux's shipping lanes to the Caribbean. It was based upon structures that invited the jealousy of other European powers and could easily be undermined by war. 'Given the weakness of the French Empire,' he writes, 'an accidental and artificial creation to which public opinion remained largely indifferent, which was not supported by adequate maritime strength and whose economy was tied to the vicious practice of slavery, Bordeaux's prosperity was fragile.'[7] It is a truth that had already been exposed by the Seven Years' War and would be again, though to a lesser degree, in the later 1770s with the war over American independence.

If the claim that the Revolution and the loss of Saint-Domingue would lead to the 'death' of the French Atlantic was a cry of distress, an outraged wail by the cities' merchant elites for more support and understanding, their fears for the

---

[6] Tangi Villerbu, 'Réseaux marchands et chaînes migratoires entre Nantes et la vallée du Mississippi, fin 18ᵉ - début 19e siècle', in Virginie Chaillou-Atrous, Jean-François Klein, and Antoine Resche (eds), *Les négociants européens et le monde: histoire d'une mise en connexion* (Rennes: Presses Universitaires de Rennes, 2016), 64.

[7] François Crouzet, 'La conjoncture bordelaise', in François-Georges Pariset (ed.), *Bordeaux au 18ᵉ siècle* (Bordeaux: Fédération historique du Sud-Ouest, 1968), 323.

future were not ungrounded. The ports did not, of course, die, but the Revolutionary and Napoleonic years went far to destroy France's Atlantic empire and signalled a terminal decline in her Atlantic trade. If the Seven Years' War had resulted in the loss of Canada, the wars of the French Revolution and Empire effectively ended France's presence as a major imperial power in the Atlantic world with revolution in Saint-Domingue and the sale of Louisiana to the United States. A new imperial age would, of course, beckon following the colonization of Algeria in 1830, but it was very different in kind and in geographical impact. Marseille was better placed to profit from the opening up of North Africa; and if Bordeaux's merchants showed some initiative in developing trading links with Africa, the Levant, and the Indian Ocean, the confidence that had inspired an earlier generation had largely evaporated. Some of the port cities sought to industrialize to provide a different kind of employment, especially Marseille and Le Havre, which could turn to a rich and populous hinterland; others, most notably Bordeaux, failed to respond to the challenge of industrialization and increasingly looked back nostalgically on the golden age of colonial trade. From 1823, Marseille's port activity surpassed Bordeaux's, and after 1829 Le Havre, benefiting from its proximity to Paris, had overtaken it as France's principal colonial port. By 1826, indeed, Bordeaux had fallen to fourth among the country's colonial ports, and a mood of pessimism had set in.[8]

In this context, the response of the city's merchant community to France's second abolition of slavery in 1848 was surely eloquent: it was to question the wisdom of the measure, to express the hope that nothing would disturb public order in Martinique, and to plead for financial compensation from the government.[9] They had little enthusiasm for abolition, and saw it as another potential assault on their profitability, an unwanted attack on some of their principal markets and a blow to their economic recovery. And though the city would go on to benefit from the general growth of trade and prosperity that marked the Second Empire, it did not recover its place as a leading commercial port. The number of ships trading out of the Garonne declined, as the sailing ships that were engaged in overseas commerce aged and were not replaced. The sugar refineries closed down, and coastal shipping declined. Only towards the end of the century, with the colonization of Senegal and the opening up of Indochina, did Bordeaux's fortunes show some belated sign of revival.[10]

In Nantes, the sense of decay was greater and more enduring, reflecting the over-dependence of the Quai de la Fosse on the Caribbean and on slaving. The economy of the city, and with it the economies of the smaller ports and towns of

---

[8] André Tudesq, 'La Restauration, renaissance et déceptions', in Louis Desgraves and Georges Dupeux (eds), *Bordeaux au 19ᵉ siècle* (Bordeaux: Fédération historique du Sud-Ouest, 1969), 52.

[9] Christelle Lozère, *Bordeaux colonial, 1850–1940* (Bordeaux: Éditions Sud-Ouest, 2007), 15.

[10] Pierre Guillaume, 'L'économie sous le Second Empire', in Desgraves and Dupeux (eds), *Bordeaux au 19ᵉ siècle*, 197–208.

the Loire estuary, had been built on the slave trade and on the industries that had filled the holds of the slave ships with the textiles and other manufactured goods needed to trade with African kings and other traffickers. There had been little attempt to diversify the city's economy, a task for which the merchants and ship-owners showed no appetite. In the years after 1815, they appealed for government help and too often wallowed in nostalgia for better times. Innovation and recon-version were called for if the city was to flourish in the new industrial world of the nineteenth century. But the commercial elite showed only limited enterprise, with many continuing to associate mercantile wealth with the slave trade. The old merchant families continued to dominate social and economic life in Nantes, resisting change in all its forms, and preventing newcomers to the city from embracing economic diversity. As unchallenged leaders of civic life, they discour-aged innovation, their ideas mired in the previous century, and their continued social dominance meant that the whole city had little choice but to stagnate, too.[11]

The extent of the city's economic decline was clear to all, not least to the merchants themselves, who came to see the nineteenth century as a period of lost opportunity. When, in 1928, the city's Chamber of commerce invited the president of its colonial sub-committee to speak on the subject of Nantes' achieve-ment as a colonial port, he could only contrast the glittering success of the eighteenth century with the misery of the nineteenth, when the sense of decay was so marked that 'it was impossible to avoid the fear that Nantes faced an irreversible decline'. The city's colonial trade had suffered, he claimed, from 'a long and dangerous illness that was brought on by a brusque economic change for which it was in no way prepared'. Even the civic improvements and public works authorized at the end of the nineteenth century had done very little to halt the reversal of its fortunes. Nantes, he now recognized, had taken some very bad strategic decisions. It had remained fixated by the Antilles, and had sought to revive the Caribbean trade at a time when Saint-Domingue was already lost and the slave trade in terminal decline. That could be ascribed to nostalgia for the past and exaggerated conservatism. But the city's problems had not ended there. The century after 1815 had seen a revolution in shipping, with iron-hulled steamships replacing the smaller sailing vessels on the Atlantic, a challenge which Nantes had done nothing to meet, assuming that the Loire, with its shallows and sandbanks, was unable to adapt to the requirements of the age of steam. Commerce had moved elsewhere, and, with the development of sugar beet in the plains of the north and east, demand for the principal product of the Antilles, cane sugar, had fallen away. A mood of pessimism had swept the port. It had seemed, the president concluded, 'that the city had no choice but to die from the effects of

---

[11] Olivier Pétré-Grenouilleau, *Nantes au temps de la traite des Noirs* (Paris: Hachette, 1998), 234.

these economic changes', a view that persisted until the turn of the twentieth century.[12]

But this is not just an economic story, or one of political neglect by a government in the throes of revolution. It is also a tale of moral ambivalence, of a trading community that felt isolated and abandoned in a world where the slave trade had come under increasing attack, and where ideas of liberty and humanity were seen by many to conflict with the economic ambitions of shippers and merchants. Even in the 1780s, humanitarian voices were being raised against the slave trade, demanding its abolition in the name of the rights of man. The French Revolution brought this conflict to a head, spreading humanist ideas not only in Europe, but in the colonies, too, where France responded to slave insurrections by introducing reforms, culminating in 1794 in the abolition, at least temporarily, of both the slave trade and the institution of slavery. And though Napoleon restored slavery to France's colonial possessions in 1802, others took action that changed the moral landscape. Across the Anglo-Saxon world, campaigns for abolition grew in intensity, both in the press and in parliament, leading to the outlawing of the slave trade in Britain in 1807 and in the United States in the following year. In the eyes of many abolitionists, indeed, anti-slavery was the defining moral issue of the day, one that France simply could not ignore. Slaving was widely seen as dishonourable, and, encouraged by the success of the British abolition movements, liberals across Europe pressed with increasing urgency for the trade in African slaves to be banned. In France they would receive encouragement from the government, especially from the July Monarchy, and in 1834 a *Société francaise pour l'abolition de l'esclavage* was founded, publishing a strongly abolitionist periodical and bringing together such leading intellectuals as Lamartine, Odilon Barrot, de Tocqueville, and Victor Schœlcher to form the nucleus of a new pressure group for abolition.[13] In 1848, following another French revolution and more than half a century after the first act of abolition, the slave trade was finally abolished across the French Atlantic, a move that was hailed in France as a victory for republican ideals, the triumph of a liberal and generous French republic.

Over the past half-century, the way in which Atlantic history has been discussed and written has undergone a radical transformation, most critically in Britain and the United States, and since the 1980s that change has affected French historiography, too. When I first stayed in Bordeaux, during yet another revolution in 1968, there was little interest in the slave trade or in its role in the city's history. Bordeaux's eighteenth-century prosperity was discussed in economic terms, seen through the lens of merchant papers and admiralty records, and the last years of the Ancien Régime were quite unapologetically categorized as the

---

[12] Delpuech, 'Nantes port colonial', in Didier Guyvarc'h, 'La construction de la mémoire d'une ville: Nantes, 1914–1992' (thèse de doctorat, Université de Rennes-2, 1994), 639–40.

[13] Bibliothèque Nationale, *Société française pour l'abolition de l'esclavage*, 1–19 (1835–42).

city's golden age, an era of prosperity that had been brought to an abrupt and unfortunate end by the Revolution. 'So much has been written on the eighteenth century as Bordeaux's golden age,' Paul Butel and Jean-Pierre Poussou write when opening their book on everyday life in the city, 'that we hesitate to take up the idea yet again. However, how can we do otherwise since it is such an evident truth?'[14] Of course they were right in many ways: it was a golden age in wealth, urban planning, culture, and good taste. But of the slavery on which these were built there was scarcely a mention; and where the slave trade was talked about, it was presented as another option for merchants in quest of profit, an example of enterprise and risk-taking, an option little different from trading in wine, or spices, or sugar, one that could be alluded to without any sense of moral ambiguity. This was how the merchants themselves saw it, and for years historians saw no reason to differ. In this, they reflected the public opinion of the time and the city's collective memory of the eighteenth century as presented in school textbooks and in displays in its museums and art galleries. In the *Musée d'Aquitaine*, for instance, the region's principal historical museum, little space was devoted to the slave trade, and there was no sense that this was an aspect of Bordeaux's past that required elaboration and explanation to successive generations. In this respect, Bordeaux was in no sense unique. Across France, it would be the later 1990s and the early years of the present century before the slave trade would feature prominently in the public history of Nantes, Bordeaux, Le Havre, or La Rochelle.[15]

The study of the Atlantic, and of slavery and the slave trade in particular, came late to France, where the emphasis on national historiography remained largely intact until the last years of the twentieth century. France's historical memory has seldom given more than a glancing nod to her colonial past or to the impact of her history as a colonial power on French domestic developments. In this respect, the volumes of Pierre Nora's monumental collective work on *Les lieux de mémoire* offer a well-nigh perfect illustration, with just a single chapter devoted to any aspect of France's colonial past—not to the experience of slavery or the economics of the slave trade, but to the Colonial Exhibition in Paris in 1931.[16] In turn, Jacques Godechot's discussion of the Age of Revolutions in the 1960s, while it compared revolutionary movements on both sides of the Atlantic, refused to accept that there was anything to consider beyond two great political revolutions, in the United States and France: there was nothing here on Haiti, or on Africa, or the idea of an Atlantic world that brought the continents together.[17] Indeed, the

---

[14] Paul Butel and Jean-Pierre Poussou, *La vie quotidienne à Bordeaux au 18ᵉ siècle* (Paris: Hachette, 1980), 9.

[15] Renaud Hourcade, *Les ports négriers face à leur histoire. Politiques de la mémoire à Nantes, Bordeaux et Liverpool* (Paris: Dalloz, 2014), 409–60.

[16] Pierre Nora (ed.), *Les Lieux de mémoire* (7 vols, Paris: Gallimard, 1997), vol. 1, 493–515.

[17] Jacques Godechot, *Les révolutions* (Paris: Presses Universitaires de France, 1963).

very notion of an Atlantic world as a single integrated whole, which made such an impression on Anglo-Saxon historians of the eighteenth century—whether American historians of the Haitian Revolution or British scholars working on the British Empire—was slow to take root. In the United States, the first signs of interest in the Haitian Revolution as a subject of scholarship date from the 1940s, with a number of works examining the effects of the revolution on both whites and blacks, as well as the impact of events in Haiti in the United States itself.[18] Perhaps because immigration from Africa and the Antilles was not yet a political question of immediate urgency in France, or perhaps because of France's troubled relations with its colonies in the post-war years, these issues were largely passed over in French school textbooks and were not the subject of any sustained research in French universities until a generation later.[19] The 'Atlantic World' was not yet a recognized field of French historical research.

The change, when it came, was dramatic, reflecting social and cultural concerns in France today, not least the arrival of large number of immigrants from West Africa and the Francophone Caribbean in the years after 1945, and the greater awareness of issues of race and ethnicity that has resulted. It is also a symptom of greater self-awareness on the part of Caribbean and Afro-American scholars and of a greater militancy among members of the immigrant communities themselves.[20] This change has shown itself in many different ways, ranging from demands that their heritage be recognized to claims for financial reparation, and it is also reflected in an upsurge of historical interest in questions of race in France's empire.[21] The history of the French Revolution has been transformed by transnational methodologies, as historians have turned away from analysing France in isolation and have sought to place it in a western, Atlantic, or world context.[22] This in turn has brought the Revolution in Saint-Domingue and its impact on colonized communities across the Atlantic world into much sharper focus. Unlike in the earlier period, events in Haiti are no longer considered a mere codicil to events in Paris, or treated as a response to European ideas; the Haitian Revolution is now seen as a central part of an Age of Revolutions, which, for many in Central and Latin America, would have more immediacy and greater significance than the French Revolution itself. In Ada Ferrer's words, 'the events that

---

[18] Alyssa Goldstein Sepinwall, 'Atlantic amnesia? French historians, the Haitian Revolution and the 2004–06 CAPES exam', *Proceedings of the Western Society for French History*, 2006, 301–4.

[19] Cécile Vidal, 'The Reluctance of French Historians to Address Atlantic History', *Southern Quarterly*, 43: 4 (2006), 153–90.

[20] Françoise Vergès, 'Les troubles de la mémoire: traite négrière, esclavage et écriture de l'histoire', *Cahiers d'études africaines*, 45, cahier 179/180, Esclavage moderne ou modernité d'esclavage? (2005), 1143–78.

[21] David Armitage and Sanjay Subrahmanyam (eds), *The Age of Revolutions in Global Context, c. 1760–1840* (Basingstoke: Palgrave Macmillan, 2010), *passim*.

[22] Frédéric Régent, 'Revolution in France, revolutions in the Caribbean', in Alan Forrest and Matthias Middell (eds), *The Routledge Companion to the French Revolution in World History* (London: Routledge, 2016), 61–76.

shook Saint-Domingue from 1791 to 1804 converted Europe's most profitable colony into an independent nation ruled by former slaves and their descendants.' Its geographic position was critical, and race was now considered central to an international age of revolutions. For 'this new society, born of a process never before contemplated, lay right in the middle of the Caribbean Sea, a short sail from islands ruled by European governors and inhabited, sometimes overwhelmingly, by enslaved Africans'.[23] Its birth was a seminal event across the Atlantic world, spreading fear and racial intolerance among many settler societies, offering hope and inspiration to Africans as much as to the enslaved peoples of South America and the Caribbean.

It is my contention in this book that the history of France's Atlantic ports can no longer be told in isolation from the rest of the Atlantic world. The influence of Bordeaux, or La Rochelle, or Nantes, spread far beyond the west and south-west of France. The towns and cities of the Atlantic region contributed hugely to populating the New World. Large numbers of emigrants flocked to the Americas from all over the West, from Normandy, Brittany, the Pays de Loire, Gascony, Guyenne, and the Basque country. They came as naval officers and colonial administrators, merchants and traders, ships' captains and privateers, and, in increasing numbers, as seamen on slave ships. Many settled in the Caribbean, committing their futures to the Americas and describing themselves as 'American' in official documents and despatches. Men from the region owned slaves, managed sugar plantations, and established trading companies in the Americas from Nova Scotia and Quebec in the north to Martinique, Guadeloupe, Saint-Domingue, and French Guyana in the south. They developed a different lifestyle from the family members they left behind, different aspirations, and more of a frontier mentality. They saw racial difference in a different way, too, in a society where, despite social and legal barriers, those of white and black skin mixed surprisingly freely and where mixed-race children grew up to be free men and women and formed what John Garrigus has called 'the largest, wealthiest and most self-confident free population of African descent in the Americas'.[24] The French Atlantic was not limited to one hemisphere or to France alone. It was a unitary world, held together by common interests and shared outlooks; and in the Revolutionary years it was a political world, too, whose history was influenced by events and pressure groups on both sides of the Atlantic. For many of their inhabitants this was the world to which they felt that they most intimately belonged as they looked increasingly

---

[23] Ada Ferrer, 'Speaking of Haiti: Slavery, Revolution and Freedom in Cuban Slave Testimony', in David Patrick Geggus and Norman Fiering (eds), *The World of the Haitian Revolution* (Bloomington, IN: Indiana University Press, 2009), 223.

[24] John D. Garrigus, '"Sons of the Same Father": Gender, Race and Citizenship in French Saint-Domingue, 1760–92', in Christine Adams, Jack R. Censer, and Lisa Jane Graham (eds), *Visions and Revisions of Eighteenth-century France* (University Park, PA: Pennsylvania State University Press, 1997), 137.

outward from these shores, to the ocean, to France's colonial possessions, above all to the Americas, rather than looking inwards to the towns and villages of the surrounding countryside. This was their identity, and they made no attempt to dissociate from it.

The port cities could not escape from the political influence of the colonies. Slave insurrections in the Caribbean had as much impact on their everyday existence as did republican politics at home or royalist insurrections on their doorstep. Questions of slavery and anti-slavery were not just the subject of abstract debate; they were burning issues that redirected their trade, threatened their investments, and left families scattered across the western hemisphere. In the entangled world of the Atlantic, the close interplay between France and its Caribbean colonies was of critical importance, with the repeated violence in Saint-Domingue affecting the west-coast ports just as much as political decisions taken in Nantes or in Paris defined life in Port-au-Prince or Le Cap. Colonialism was a two-way process. War, revolution and the moral uncertainty over the slave trade—three recurring themes in this book—were the principal elements in a crisis that would destroy France's Atlantic empire, as ships were laid up, firms faced bankruptcy, and colonists fled back to France or moved on to other outposts of the Atlantic world.

With this book, I have sought to write a transnational history as much as a French one, and to follow the traders and merchants of France's Atlantic ports across the ocean, using sources from both sides of the Atlantic (though not, unfortunately, from Haiti itself, where little of archival interest remains). Wherever possible, I have used individual memoirs and testimonies to illustrate what the crisis meant to contemporaries and to show the levels of panic and moral uncertainty that it caused. I have also sought to integrate much of the recent research on slavery, the slave trade, and the public memory of slavery that has been so influential on both sides of the Atlantic, and to bring recent Francophone research to the attention of English-speaking readers. The result, I hope, will be seen as a contribution to the history of the Age of Revolutions that places the Atlantic ports of France in their wider international context and explains the crisis they faced not just at home but across the wider Atlantic world.

Acknowledgements

If I am returning in this book to the Atlantic coast of France, it is with a very different purpose and in a different spirit from my earlier ventures into its history, when my concern was to study the French Revolution as it affected the towns and communities of the south-west. Then my focus was on revolutionary politics and the faction-fighting it embraced, the social divisions within the cities, and the different meanings of republicanism in Paris and the provinces. Commerce played a part, of course. Cities like Bordeaux, Nantes, and La Rochelle found themselves increasingly isolated, accused of egotism for their commercial ambitions, for facing out to the Atlantic rather than inwards towards their agricultural hinterland. It is their role in that global Atlantic world that is my subject here, and it has led me in turn to look out from France to the Americas and France's Caribbean colonies, and to engage with the overarching subject of the slave trade. In doing this I have incurred innumerable debts to friends and colleagues, editors, and readers, which it is a pleasure to acknowledge here.

First and foremost, I wish to thank the three research bodies, in three countries, which have seen fit to support this project at various stages of its development. In France, I was fortunate to enjoy a visiting fellowship at the Institut d'Études Avancées in Nantes, in the spring of 2011, which both allowed me to delve into the archives of Nantes and the Loire-Atlantique, and provided the stimulation and intellectual challenge of a highly diverse community of scholars. To the successive directors of the Institute, Alain Supiot and Samuel Jubé, and to the fellows with whom I had the pleasure to work, I remain deeply grateful. Here in Britain, the Leverhulme Trust awarded me an Emeritus Fellowship (number EM-2015-040) between 2015 and 2017 that enabled me to travel to libraries and archives in France and the United States, and to follow the emigrants from France and Saint-Domingue on their peregrinations across the Atlantic world. Without that support, the later chapters of this book could not have been written. And during the last year, when the greater part of this book was written, I have held a professorship at the State Academic University for the Humanities in Moscow (GAUGN), leading a research group studying responses to French revolutionary ideas in regions of traditional culture in Europe and beyond, supported by a grant from the Ministry of Education and Science of the Russian Federation (number N 14. Z50.31.0045). For their friendship and intellectual stimulation I should like to thank all my colleagues on this project, especially Alexander Tchoudinov and Nikolay Promyslov; they have played a vital part in bringing this book to completion.

To librarians and archivists on both sides of the Atlantic I am indebted for their help and professionalism during what were often ridiculously fleeting visits to their holdings. With their assistance I was able to gain access to private papers in the Archives Nationales (originally in Paris, now at Pierrefitte) and in departmental archives in Bordeaux, Nantes, Rouen, and La Rochelle; to the Chamber of Commerce archive in Marseille; and to the diplomatic papers of the Ministère des Affaires Étrangères, also in Nantes. In the Historic New Orleans Collection I was given access to the Ste-Gême Family Papers, and in the American Philosophical Society in Philadelphia to the Stephen Girard Papers, both of which proved valuable for the history of refugees from Saint-Domingue to the United States; I also found useful material in the holdings of the Library Company of Philadelphia, Tulane University, and the College of Charleston. There have been notable acts of kindness, too. In Basse-Terre in Guadeloupe, the archivist not only opened up the archive to me; she also provided accommodation in an adjoining apartment. Rather closer to home, research for the book leant heavily on the resources of the British Library; I owe an especial debt to the staff of its Reading Room in Boston Spa who have been endlessly patient in tracking down the books and articles I requested.

In the course of research for this book, I have received advice and inspiration from a wide range of fellow historians. In York, I had the good fortune to be able to discuss abolition and the Atlantic slave trade with James Walvin and the historical memory of the slaving with Geoff Cubitt, while Christian Høgsbjerg has proved a tireless guide to the works of C.L.R. James. Jonathan Dalby, who since his move to the History Department at Mona several decades ago has become a specialist in Jamaican history, was a valuable guide in the early stages of the research to materials in the British West Indies. Matt Childs, David Geggus, Nathalie Dessens, and Cécile Vidal all helped me to navigate through sources in the United States; Jeremy Popkin discussed his work on France and her colonies; while Syrine Farhat gave me access to some of her own findings on French *colons* who ended their Caribbean saga in Charleston, South Carolina. In France, I benefited from long discussions on revolution, slavery, and the economy of the Atlantic ports with numerous colleagues, among them I would give special mention to Marcel Dorigny, Éric Saunier, Frédéric Régent, Manuel Covo, Samuel Guicheteau, Pierrick Pourchasse, and Yannick Lemarchand, each of whom brought an individual approach and an enviable knowledge to the table—as well as, many years before, Paul Butel in Bordeaux, in so many ways the pioneer of Atlantic history in France.

If this work is about the place of the Atlantic ports in global history, it is also about the memory of the slave trade in the cities which most profited from it, a memory that is still evolving in the early decades of our own century. Again, my analysis owes much to others who have gone before, as well as to the current mania in France for commemoration and avowal. In Nantes, the publications of the Anneaux de la Mémoire have done much to keep the memory—and public consciousness—alive since their inaugural exhibition in 1992. The museums of the main slaving cities all have permanent displays on the slave trade, and they were happy to answer my questions: in the Musée du Nouveau Monde in La Rochelle, the Musée d'Aquitaine in Bordeaux, and especially the Château des Ducs de Bretagne in Nantes, where Bertrand Guillet and Krystel Gualde did everything possible to facilitate my work. It was most instructive to be able to compare their displays with those in Liverpool and Bristol; while my thoughts on the role of memory were sharpened by working with Étienne François and Karen Hagemann on a volume devoted to war memories of the Napoleonic Wars, as well as with Leighton James and Catriona Kennedy on a research project here in York. As always, it is valuable to be able to discuss with others at workshops and conferences, and I would like to thank those who have invited me to present sections of the book as research in progress: they include, most notably, Matthias Middell and Megan Maruschke in Leipzig, Rafe Blaufarb in Tallahassee, and Timothy Tackett at Irvine. A special word of thanks is due to Ibrahima Thioub, who was a Fellow at the IEA during my time in Nantes, for organizing an excellent short conference in Dakar in 2014 comparing European and African memories—such as they are—of the eighteenth-century slave trade.

At the Press, I have been exceptionally fortunate to have had the most understanding of editors in Cathryn Steele, who kept faith in this project as deadlines came and went and even connived at my desertion to allow me to write a volume on the memories of Waterloo for the bicentenary in 2015. An author remembers such things with gratitude. I would also like to thank the art department at OUP, who have done such an excellent job in redrawing the maps, and the anonymous readers for their acute and very supportive remarks: the book is, I am sure, much better for them. My thanks also go to Michael Broers, who has consistently offered encouragement through sometimes difficult times of his own; and to Godfrey Rogers and Jane Dougherty, who have contrived over the years to make me feel that I still belong in Bordeaux. The book is dedicated to Rosemary and Marianne, who, in York and in London, have somehow survived through it all.

York
March 2019

Contents

List of Maps   xxiii

PART ONE. BEFORE THE STORM

1. The French Atlantic World   3

2. The Port Cities of the French Atlantic   22

3. The Years of Economic Prosperity   41

4. France and the Slave Trade   60

5. Populating the French Atlantic   79

PART TWO. WAR AND REVOLUTION

6. Debating Slavery   103

7. The French Revolution in the Atlantic Ports   124

8. Merchants, Planters, and Revolutionary Politics   147

9. War and Revolution in the Caribbean   166

10. The Saint-Domingue Diaspora   189

11. Economic Stagnation and Decay   211

PART THREE. EMERGING FROM CRISIS

12. The Congress of Vienna and the Politics of Slavery   233

13. The Illegal Slave Trade   250

14. The Slave Trade in Collective Memory   270

   Conclusion   286

Bibliography   291
Index   309

List of Maps

1. France's American Territories in the Eighteenth Century   xxv
   (Gilles Havard/Cécile Vidal, *Histoire de l'Amérique française*, 14)

2. The Ports and River Systems of France in 1789   xxvi
   (*Cahiers des Anneaux de la Mémoire*, 10, 2007, 20)

3. The French Transatlantic Slave Trade in the long eighteenth century,
   1643–1831   xxvii
   (Eltis/Richardson, map 19, p. 33)

4. The Illegal Slave Trade: Slave Voyages from Nantes, 1813–1841   xxviii
   (Eltis/Richardson, map 45, p. 75)

5. The Illegal Slave Trade: Slave Voyages from Bordeaux, 1808–1837   xxix
   (Eltis/Richardson, map 44, p. 73)

6. The ports of Saint-Domingue and their exports in the later eighteenth century   xxx
   (Paul Butel, *Histoire des Antilles françaises, 17e – 20e siècle*, 400)

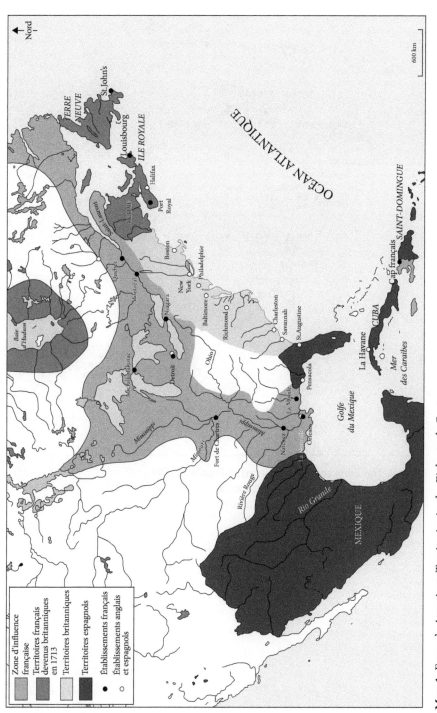

Map 1 France's American Territories in the Eighteenth Century
(Gilles Havard/Cécile Vidal, *Histoire de l'Amérique française*, 14)

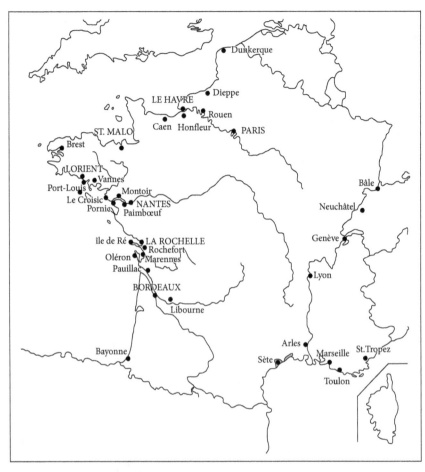

Map 2 The Ports and River Systems of France in 1789
(*Cahiers des Anneaux de la Mémoire*, 10, 2007, 20)

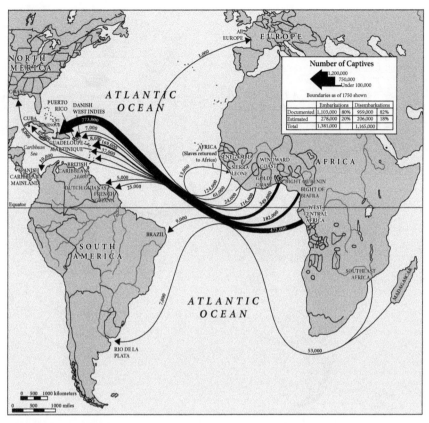

Map 3 The French Transatlantic Slave Trade in the long eighteenth century, 1643–1831
(Eltis/Richardson, map 19, p. 33)

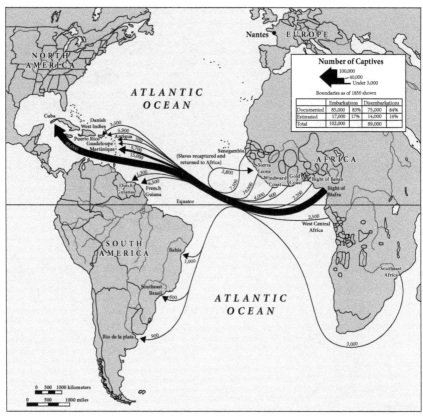

Map 4 The Illegal Slave Trade: Slave Voyages from Nantes, 1813–1841
(Eltis/Richardson, map 45, p. 75)

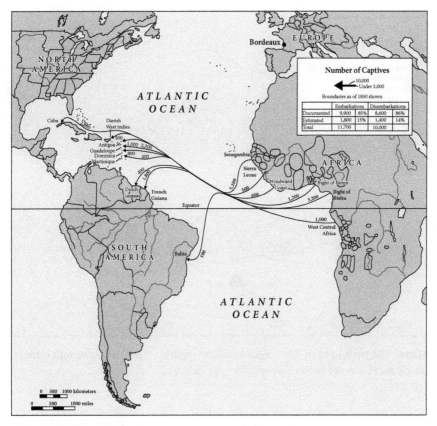

Map 5 The Illegal Slave Trade: Slave Voyages from Bordeaux, 1808–1837
(Eltis/Richardson, map 44, p. 73)

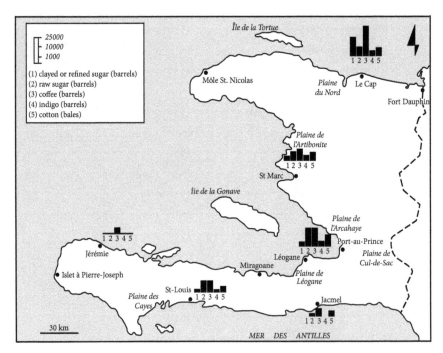

Map 6 The ports of Saint-Domingue and their exports in the later eighteenth century.
(Paul Butel, *Histoire des Antilles françaises, 17e – 20e siècle*, 400)

PART ONE
BEFORE THE STORM

1

The French Atlantic World

The long eighteenth century marked the high point of France's Atlantic empire. Before the reign of Louis XIV, indeed, France had been a relatively minor player, and the Atlantic had been largely the preserve of the Iberian powers, Spain and Portugal, and the territories they controlled in Central and South America. The main interest of European governments in the Americas had been to extract precious metals to enrich their rulers and stock their state coffers. But by the second half of the seventeenth century, the balance of power was shifting, as the Spanish and Portuguese found themselves increasingly challenged by other European states for the commerce of the New World. The traditional quest for bullion gave way to a plantation economy, producing goods like cotton, indigo, sugar, and coffee, which were highly prized in the urban centres of the European world. The Iberian monopoly was first broken by corsairs and interlopers from Britain, France, and Holland; then, little by little, the maritime powers of northern Europe gained access to Caribbean markets, and traders from Britain and France, as well as from mainland North America, challenged the Iberian monopoly.[1] An Anglo-Spanish treaty recognized Britain's occupation of Jamaica in 1670, before, by the Treaty of Ryswick, France was accorded the right to annex the western part of Santo Domingo, which as Saint-Domingue would become the richest European possession in the Atlantic world.[2]

In this way, the North Atlantic was opened up to European settlement, with the maritime powers of north-western Europe—Britain, Holland, and France—extending their influence in the Americas. The eighteenth century was a period of intense colonial rivalry and territorial acquisition, when colonies became one of the principal causes of war between European states, and most especially between France and Britain. Colonies were a major source of both profit and power, and the last decades before the French Revolution were years of intense rivalry over territory, trade, and—increasingly—slaves.[3] In spite of the exhortations of free-market economists like Adam Smith in Britain and Gournay or d'Argenson in France, European governments found it hard to break from ideas of imperial preference and continued to seek competitive advantage from their overseas

---

[1] David Eltis and David Richardson, *Atlas of the Transatlantic Slave Trade* (New Haven: Yale University Press, 2010), 21.

[2] Paul Butel, *Histoire de l'Atlantique, de l'Antiquité à nos jours* (Paris: Perrin, 1997), 143.

[3] Richard Bessel, Nicholas Guyatt, and Jane Rendall (eds), *War, Empire and Slavery, 1770–1830* (Basingstoke: Palgrave Macmillan, 2010), 1–18.

territories. French thinkers, it should be emphasized, had been prominent among the early exponents of laissez-faire economics, with Turgot arguing the need to shift French focus from conquest to commerce and noting that Britain was losing money through its ownership of colonies in North America.[4] But these arguments had a limited impact on public policy. This was a period when the French Crown looked to the Atlantic to obtain the wealth that would secure its political and military power at home, while traders and adventurers from metropolitan France, most especially those from a wide tranche of the Atlantic littoral that stretched from Normandy and Brittany in the north to Gascony and the Bearn in the south, sought to make their fortunes across the ocean, whether from deep-sea fishing off Newfoundland, trapping wild animals for their pelts in Canada, or growing sugar and tobacco in the Caribbean.[5] They did not, of course, get things all their own way, and between the Treaty of Utrecht at the beginning of the century and the end of the Napoleonic Wars, France would be embroiled in a succession of colonial wars, mainly (but not exclusively) with Britain.

The economic potential of the New World could appear limitless, and observers commented on the range of raw materials and of exotic goods that excited consumers across the continent and provided the French Atlantic ports not only with huge import opportunities but also with a lucrative entrepôt trade to the rest of Europe. This was a trade boom that was consumer-led and reflected something of a revolution in European taste. New markets opened up in response to the sudden availability of colonial produce, among them some that encouraged addiction, from coffee and chocolate to sugar and tobacco, the majority of them sourced from the Americas, while fashion and the clothing industry were revolutionized by the availability of cheap cotton.[6] Overall, the commerce in slaves and in colonial goods imported from the Caribbean contributed more than 15 per cent to economic growth in France between 1716 and 1787, meeting a demand that extended across the country and was felt far beyond the Atlantic littoral. Wealthy consumers created a market for semi-luxury products, and the Atlantic merchants were among the first to profit, their business stimulated by the court and public officials in Paris and Versailles. In this respect, in the rather nicely chosen words of Allan Potofsky, Paris served as 'an urban hinterland for the broader Atlantic'.[7]

Of all the foodstuffs produced in the colonies, sugar had the most profound effect on European taste: in France, Susan Pinkard notes 'the array of wafers, biscuits, petits fours and other cakes and pastries that appeared for dessert along

---

[4] Anthony Pagden, *Lords of All the World* (New Haven: Yale University Press, 1995), 192; Andrew Hamilton, *Trade and Empire in the Eighteenth Century Atlantic World* (Newcastle-upon-Tyne: Cambridge Scholars Publishing, 2008), xxiii.

[5] Butel, *Histoire de l'Atlantique*, 143–4.

[6] For the impact of colonial goods on public taste in Britain, see James Walvin, *Fruits of Empire: Exotic Produce and British Taste, 1660–1800* (Basingstoke: Macmillan, 1997), *passim*.

[7] Allan Potofsky, 'Paris-on-the-Atlantic from the Old Regime to the Revolution', *French History*, 25 (2011), 91.

with custards, sweet soufflés, fruits and preserves'.[8] At the same time, the eighteenth century saw a new fashion for coffee houses, especially in London, where they became centres of conviviality and meeting places for the men of letters and the political elite, and for bars and restaurants in Paris and some French provincial cities. In 1804, Louis Prudhomme would claim that eating out had become so normal for Parisians that their city was now home to as many as 2,000 restaurants.[9] While this figure may have been exaggerated for effect, there is no doubt that restaurants, which had been virtually unknown in 1750, were to be found all over the French capital, and that good food and wine were now commonly enjoyed outside the home. There was a social aspect to this, too. Taste was something to be experienced in public, part of a polite sociability that spread across much of urban Europe—and the products of France's colonies contributed mightily to that process.

The key years of French expansion in the Atlantic world were between 1670 and 1730, when France occupied, founded, and settled at least fourteen colonies in the Americas, stretching from Cayenne, next to Brazil on the north-east coast of South America, to Quebec and the valley of the St. Lawrence in modern-day Canada.[10] On the North American mainland, France's other major settlement was in Louisiana, on the Bay of Mexico, a vast and ill-defined territory that stretched back from New Orleans and up the valley of the Lower Mississippi, and would remain French until Napoleon sold it to the United States in 1803. But popular enthusiasm for colonial conquest should not be exaggerated. The country wanted trading posts rather than permanent settlements on the American mainland, and the numbers of emigrants from France to the New World remained disappointingly small, numbering fewer than 75,000 in 1730. But those who did settle in the Americas worked tirelessly to open up the country, as the example of French Canada demonstrates.

In Canada, New France, and the French Acadian territories along the Atlantic seaboard were lands to be exploited, to make men rich, whether as hunters and fur traders doing business with local Native American tribes or as loggers floating timber down the rivers for export back to Europe. French frontiersmen integrated and procreated with local people, much more than settlers from the Anglo-Saxon countries, until *voyageurs* of French extraction dominated the fur trade not just in Quebec but across the whole American West. By the first half of the nineteenth century the ratio of 'Frenchmen' to Americans in the fur trade of the United States was around four to one, the majority being drawn from among the French

---

[8] Susan Pinkard, *A Revolution in Taste: the Rise of French Cuisine* (Cambridge: Cambridge University Press, 2009), 235.

[9] Rebecca L. Spang, *The Invention of the Restaurant: Paris and Modern Gastronomic Culture* (Cambridge, MA: Harvard University Press, 2000), 173.

[10] James Pritchard, *In Search of Empire: The French in the Americas, 1670–1730* (Cambridge: Cambridge University Press, 2004), *passim*.

voyageurs of Western Canada. In 1832, George Catlin described the men working at the American Fur Company's post on the Upper Missouri as being 'nearly all French', while Francis Parkman described the trappers on the North Platte as 'half-savage men...all of Canadian extraction'.[11] Most were half-castes, *métis*, belonging to 'a mongrel race' in which 'the French blood seemed to predominate'. They inhabited a wild, frontier world of trading posts and lumber camps, the world so graphically described in the novels of Annie Proulx.[12] Here traders and settlers made their own societies with little reference to Paris, and, in contrast to the merchants, ship-owners, sailors, and fishermen of the port cities, they looked to the interior rather than to the ocean, lured by the West in their quest for further lands to exploit and natural resources to pillage.

In administrative terms, France's American colonies were widely scattered, and little contact was maintained between them. The islands of the Caribbean were a world apart from the settlements in French Canada, and Paris would seem to have had little notion of building a coherent empire across the Atlantic. At first glance, even France's presence on the North American mainland might appear to lack any strategic purpose. In the years to 1730, for instance, seven separate colonies were established in New France—at Placentia in Newfoundland, Acadia in what is now Nova Scotia, Ile Royale, Louisiana, Illinois, the *pays d'en haut* or Upper Country, and Canada itself, stretching for some 250 miles along the central valley of the St Lawrence River.[13] In wider geopolitical terms, however, this scattered empire made greater sense, stretching like a bow across the interior of the North American continent from Newfoundland to the Gulf of Mexico, an interior defined by the great rivers of the St Lawrence and the Mississippi and linked together by the huge basin of the Great Lakes. Those trekking westwards opened up uncharted territory and cleared forest land for farming. They also discovered the source of the great Mississippi River, from where they followed its course southwards. In 1682, indeed, it was a French expedition, under La Salle, that first canoed the length of the Mississippi down to the Gulf of Mexico.[14] And while the British settled the lands of the thirteen colonies the length of the eastern seaboard, the French, despite their small numbers, threatened to take control of the rich, open lands to the north and west. What they often lacked was a permanent administration and the critical mass of people needed to settle and defend the land, which proved a major impediment to colonization. By the middle of the eighteenth century, settlers from the Anglo-Saxon world outnumbered the French in North America by around ten to one, an imbalance that would prove critical in

---

[11] Leroy R. Hafen (ed.), *French Fur Traders and Voyageurs in the American West* (Lincoln: Nebraska University Press, 1997), 11.

[12] See, for example, Annie Proulx, *Barkskins* (New York: Fourth Estate, 2016).

[13] Pritchard, *In Search of Empire*, 31.

[14] Catherine Armstrong and Laura M. Chmielewski, *The Atlantic Experience: Peoples, Places, Ideas* (Basingstoke: Palgrave-Macmillan, 2013), 9.

determining the future of the continent. But the French did not give up without a struggle.

The roots of their empire can be traced to 1603 and the first voyage of exploration by Samuel de Champlain to what would be New France. Champlain was not just an explorer, though he is primarily remembered as such. He was also a prolific writer and a skilled cartographer, mapping the territories he discovered and assessing their future value to France.[15] Importantly, he was not afraid to treat with the native peoples he encountered. At Tadoussac, around the confluence of the St Lawrence and the Saguenay River, which had been set up as a trading post three years earlier, Champlain signed a peace treaty with the Micmac and other indigenous peoples that would allow the French to establish a durable presence in the region and to dominate the trade in furs and timber. Both sides grasped the opportunity which Franco-Indian cooperation held out for future conquest and, uniquely in the history of Europeans' dealings with the native peoples, both sides saw advantages in the arrangement. In the view of the Canadian historian David Hackett Fischer, the meeting held by Champlain with leaders of the local Native American tribes at Tadoussac in 1603, known in French as the *Grande Tabagie* (or 'Great Feast'), marked the start of an alliance between the founders of New France and three Indian nations from the surrounding region that would establish one of the strongest bonds between Europeans and Native Americans. 'Each entered willingly into the relationship and gained something of value in return. The Indians acquired a potential ally against their mortal enemies, the Iroquois. The French won support for settlement, exploration and trade.'[16] Five years later Champlain founded Quebec, and the settlement of New France began in earnest.[17]

The conquest of the interior would prove long and debilitating, incurring a high cost in human lives. And riches were far from guaranteed. Much of the French presence on the North American mainland took the form of small settlements and isolated trading posts, many of a temporary character, rather than substantial towns and cities. Their first attempts to settle eastern Canada in the sixteenth century had not been filled with promise, with buildings hastily abandoned and would-be settlers forced to return to France. Just like those who came from Britain and other parts of continental Europe, a substantial number of these first settlers belonged to religious minorities, groups fleeing persecution or leaving their homeland in the hope of establishing Christian settlements in the Americas. In Britain, those refugees often belonged to Puritan cults faced with intolerance at home; and in France, too, it was among the Protestant community, those Huguenots threatened with persecution after the revocation of the Edict of Nantes in

[15] David Hackett Fischer, *Champlain's Dream: The Visionary Adventurer who made a New World in Canada* (Toronto: A. A. Knopf, 2008), 5–6.

[16] Ibid., 134.

[17] Gilles Havard et Cécile Vidal, *Histoire de l'Amérique française* (Paris: Flammarion, 2003), 13.

1685, that we find those most attracted to seek out a new life across the Atlantic.[18] Persecution served to reinforce their Protestant identity and their desire to settle on territory removed from the spiritual authority of the Catholic Church. Often they joined existing Protestant communities overseas, where they felt confident that they could integrate and pursue their livelihood, frequently as merchants and traders. Some fled to Protestant Europe—to north Germany, Switzerland, or England—to escape persecution. But others went to the Americas, whether to the British colonies in North America, to Quebec, or to Dutch and Danish colonies in the Caribbean. Others again chose to settle in South Africa. In all, they may have numbered as many as 70,000 of the 200,000 who left France during the seventeenth and early eighteenth centuries, often passing through London or Dublin on their way to the New World.[19]

How far these refugees were driven by religious conscience, is, of course, debatable: many went on to make highly lucrative commercial careers in the New World and took full advantage of the opportunities it offered. And not all left willingly. Some, even in the last decades of the Ancien Régime, used the threat of emigration to put pressure on ministers to grant them toleration, taking advantage of the periodic wars in the Atlantic to pressurize—some would say to blackmail—their own government.[20] They were, they said, prepared to take their families, their wealth, and their labour from France and to settle in what was after 1763 British North America, rather than risk persecution in France, with many planning to set up exclusively Huguenot communities, such as New Bordeaux in the Carolinas, where their religion would be recognized and protected. It seemed a credible scheme, one of a number that were being proposed in these years by their fellow Huguenots. The problem, as so often with French colonial projects, was to find people who were willing to abandon France for a new life in an unknown continent. New Bordeaux was a case in point, its colonists drawn largely from the west and south-west of France. Even as the ship taking the emigrants prepared to leave for the New World, the numbers willing to make the voyage dwindled visibly. What many of them really wanted was not a new life in America, but the promise of religious tolerance at home in France. And if that opportunity presented itself, they were ready to return, or to abandon the project entirely.

Across the eighteenth century, religious persecution accounted for only a small proportion of France's emigrants. The majority were attracted by profit and the promise of wealth, and many saw a greater promise of prosperity in islands off the

---

[18] Jon Butler, *The Huguenots in America: A Refugee People in New World Society* (Cambridge, MA: Harvard University Press, 1983).

[19] Mickaël Augeron, 'Les Huguenots et l'espace atlantique: aux sources d'un riche patrimoine historique et mémoriel', in Mickaël Augeron, Didier Poton, and Bertrand Van Ruymbeke (eds), *Les Huguenots et l'Atlantique, vol 1: Pour Dieu, la Cause ou les Affaires* (Paris: Les Indes savantes, 2009), 27.

[20] Owen Stanwood, 'From the desert to the refuge: the sage of New Bordeaux', *French Historical Studies*, 40 (2017), 11.

American coast. To the north, off Canada, lay rich fisheries close to Newfoundland and Saint-Pierre and Miquelon, which were highly prized by men from La Rochelle, Saint-Malo, and the coastal ports of Brittany and north-west France, and especially, of course, by those who lived in the close-knit fishing communities of the Atlantic and Channel coasts. Like fishermen across Europe, theirs was a dangerous life at the mercy of rocks and currents, which fostered a deep sense of community and interdependence. They were often deeply religious, superstitious about the elements and the workings of fate, communities forged by the sea, their lives punctuated by recurrent tragedy. They had few links with the rural hinterland of their towns and villages, far more with the foreign fishermen whose paths they crossed and whose dangers they shared. For many, the various wars of the eighteenth century had brought new trauma and increased risk, as the men were often impressed into service in the French navy during the war years. The impact on the maritime population could be disastrous, as large numbers of those who were lost to fishing never returned.[21] In Dieppe, it was reported in 1744 that the town had lost 3,000 sailors, many of whom had died on board naval vessels, or on privateers, or in prisons in England.[22] The fishing boats they had sailed on were laid up, often for good, and in some cases ports gave up fishing altogether. For some who returned there were no jobs to go back to, and emigration to the New World must have seemed an attractive option.

It was further south, however, and especially in the Caribbean, that France's eighteenth-century Atlantic empire was concentrated, for it was here that the greatest profits were to be made. By the middle of the eighteenth century, the French had colonized eight islands in the Lesser Antilles or Windward islands: Grenada, Martinique, Marie Galante, Guadeloupe, Saint-Christophe, Saint-Barthélemy, Saint-Martin, and Sainte-Croix.[23] But their greatest prize was Saint-Domingue, which within a few decades had become the epicentre of France's Atlantic economy and the wealthiest colony in the whole Atlantic world, easily outstripping Britain's possessions in Jamaica and Barbados. Crucially, it was a place where Frenchmen were prepared to settle, whether in the open countryside on their sugar plantations or in their town houses amid the relative sophistication of cities like Pointe-à-Pitre and Le Cap, with their clubs and debating societies, their churches and Masonic lodges. Here they tried to replicate the urban culture they had known in Nantes or Bordeaux, and to live the life of provincial notables in a colonial setting. Not everything was ideal, of course. They had to adjust to the Caribbean climate, which could be deadly to Europeans, and many succumbed to

---

[21] Alain Cabantous, *Dix mille marins face à l'Océan* (Paris: Publisud, 1991), 161–206; for a more general discussion of the identity of fishing communities, see Alain Cabantous, *Les citoyens du large: les identités maritimes en France (17ᵉ–19ᵉ siècle)* (Paris: Aubier, 1995), *passim*.

[22] Renaud Morieux, *The Channel: England, France and the Construction of a Maritime Border in the Eighteenth Century* (Cambridge: Cambridge University Press, 2016), 211n2.

[23] Pritchard, *In Search of Empire*, xvii.

the diseases carried by mosquitoes and other tropical insects. But, if these were avoided, the cities of the French Caribbean enjoyed a reputation for elegance and polite society, and life there compared favourably with that in most French provincial towns. Women played an important part in colonial society, and many saw this as a civilizing influence that contrasted with the masculine culture of the American frontier. Creole women were much praised for their elegance and dress sense, and the large number of free women of colour in the cities of Saint-Domingue played a central role in forging Caribbean society.[24]

Those who left France for the islands were seldom venturing into the unknown. They understood that breaking in the soil or setting up in business in the islands would be hard, unremitting work; and it is true that many died relatively young, often before they saw France again. But they went secure in the knowledge that they would find a French community to welcome them in the Caribbean, and that they would discover the benefits of urban civilization when they arrived. These merchants and colonial administrators seldom complained of boredom. They enjoyed levels of comfort and luxury that they could not have aspired to back in France, in a society where they were spared the pain and indignity of manual labour, where they had slaves to serve them in their homes and work for them in the fields. With the passage of time, and with the birth of the second and third generations of Creoles, men who had set out from France as adventurers and soldiers of fortune saw themselves as increasingly divorced from their home land, and as belonging in Saint-Domingue, their country of adoption. They even described themselves as 'Americans'. They had been changed by their experience, and it showed: back home in France, people talked of them with growing reserve, even with a certain moral ambivalence. They had developed, it seemed, their own lifestyle, their own values, and a taste for luxury that marked them out from the people they had left behind in the Old World. In the eyes of many back in mainland France, their spendthrift ways implied frivolity and self-indulgence, and their taste for luxury led to accusations of idleness and decadence.[25]

Part of that moral ambivalence stemmed from the fact that Saint-Domingue, like much of colonial America, was a society built on slavery and on the shipment of black Africans across the Atlantic, through the horrors of the Middle Passage, to cut the sugar cane which, white Europeans had persuaded themselves, was work they were physically incapable of doing in a tropical climate. Originally, in the

---

[24] Dominique Rogers and Stewart King, 'Housekeepers, merchants, rentières: free women of colour in the port cities of colonial Saint-Domingue, 1750–1790', in Douglas Catterall and Jodi Campbell (eds), *Women in Port: Gendering Communities, Economies, and Social Networks in Atlantic Port Cities, 1500–1800* (Leiden: Brill, 2012).

[25] John Shovlin, *The Political Economy of Virtue: Luxury, Patriotism and the Origins of the French Revolution* (Ithaca, NY: Cornell University Press, 2006), 42–3.

seventeenth and early eighteenth centuries, the French had attempted to populate their sugar islands through voluntary engagement, principally in the port of La Rochelle, but by 1717 it was becoming clear that it was well-nigh impossible to persuade young French workers to commit themselves to labour in the plantation economy; conditions were simply too hard, the heat and humidity enervating. And as merchants turned increasingly to African slave labour for the colonies, they lost all interest in other forms of engagement or indentured labour, until in 1774 a royal decree stipulated that it was no longer necessary to sign on French workers or to pay men to populate the Antilles. Abruptly, the system of engagement was abandoned.[26] Like the planters on Saint-Domingue, the French Atlantic ports became more intensely dependent on the slave trade in order to profit from the fruits of empire.

The move from engagement to slavery was not achieved without dissent, however, since by the end of the Ancien Régime slavery had become more morally questionable, as men educated in enlightened ideas increasingly challenged institutions, talked about liberty and equality, and argued over human rights. How far could the system of slavery, or the huge profits France made through the use of slave labour, continue to be morally justified, even in the eyes of its own people? For how long could the merchant houses and landed estates, the factories and charitable institutions which derived profit from slavery continue to escape scrutiny for their actions and their investments? If the slaves remained far away, concealed from French eyes by 2,000 miles of ocean, what of the slave trade itself, when the ships consigned to carry their human cargoes left from the Loire or the Garonne for the west coast of Africa, crewed by Bretons or Basques or Gascons who would dock in the port cities of the Atlantic coast before returning home to their villages with tales of their adventures in exotic parts? Did their lips remain sealed? Could Frenchmen deny all responsibility for human trafficking, or was the lure of profit sufficiently strong to blind them to the moral incongruity of the trade? In the course of the eighteenth century, French merchants sent out more than 3,000 ships to the African coast in search of slaves, and transported more than 1 million black Africans to the slave markets of the New World. The toll on human life was a deadly one. Between 100,000 and 200,000 of the captives died before they reached the Caribbean, in addition to more than 10,000 French sailors who lost their lives on slaving voyages.[27] It was hard to remain blind to such horrific losses, or to provide a moral justification for human trafficking on this scale. Yet before the second half of the eighteenth century, these questions were

---

[26] Christian Huetz de Lemps, 'Engagement et engagés au dix-huitième siècle', in Paul Butel (ed.), *Commerce et plantation dans la Caraïbe, 18ᵉ–19ᵉ siècles* (Bordeaux: Presses Universitaires de Bordeaux, 1992), 66–9.

[27] Robert Louis Stein, *The French Slave Trade in the Eighteenth Century: An Old Regime Business* (Madison: Wisconsin University Press, 1979), xiii.

seldom discussed. Abolitionism would emerge only later as a political issue, as part of the democratic impulse of the period we know as the Age of Revolutions.[28]

Saint-Domingue intrigued and fascinated the French. The eighteenth century was a golden age of travel literature, when writers and intellectuals were swept by a passion for the exotic and the Orient, and this curiosity drew them to France's overseas colonies, too.[29] Among eighteenth-century writers on Saint-Domingue, the best known was himself a Creole, Moreau de Saint-Méry, who at the age of nineteen had left his native Martinique to pursue legal studies in Paris before setting out in 1775 to make his fortune, like so many others, in Saint-Domingue. Here he proved himself to be a jurist of some distinction, a leading member of the masonic lodge and a self-proclaimed son of the Enlightenment; the planters were highly litigious, and the young lawyer became a wealthy man.[30] In 1785, at the age of thirty-five, he was elected to the Council of Le Cap, in 1789 played a limited role in the first months of the Revolution, and throughout his life would retain a passion for the island and its people. But he remained a figure of deep contradictions. Though liberal on particular issues—on the status of free men of colour, for instance—he was also, in revolutionary terms, a deeply conservative, if not an openly reactionary figure who after a few months changed his allegiance and joined the Club Massiac, the organization most closely aligned to the interests of the rich planters in the Caribbean. In this, he illustrated better than most the fundamental dilemma of the *colon* and colonial administrator, forced to choose between accepting a new sort of society on the one hand and maintaining colonial authority on the other.[31] The violence that followed drove him into emigration in the United States, and in 1797, from exile in Philadelphia, he published the first volume of his great work on Saint-Domingue—his *Description topographique, physique, civile, politique et historique de la partie française de l'isle Saint-Domingue*. This was the fruit, he said, of around fourteen years' work, packed with administrative and religious detail and containing telling comment on the climate, culture, and character of the population. A second volume followed in the next year, and a classic of French literature was born, a book that set out to explain exactly what most clearly distinguished the French colonists of Saint-Domingue.[32]

---

[28] See, for instance, Joanna Innes and Mark Philp (eds), *Re-imagining Democracy in the Age of Revolutions: America, France, Britain, Ireland, 1750–1850* (Oxford: Oxford University Press, 2013).

[29] There is a burgeoning literature on Orientalism, both in France and the English-speaking world. Most influential is Edward Said, *Orientalism* (London: Routledge, 1979).

[30] David Geggus, 'Moreau de Saint-Méry et la Révolution de Saint-Domingue', in Dominique Taffin (ed.), *Moreau de Saint-Méry ou les ambiguïtés d'un créole des Lumières* (Fort de France: Société des amis des archives et de la recherche sur le patrimoine culturel des Antilles, 2006), 129.

[31] Dominique Taffin, 'Introduction', in Dominique Taffin (ed.), *Moreau de Saint-Méry ou les ambiguïtés d'un créole des Lumières*, 7.

[32] Moreau de Saint-Méry, *Description topographique, physique, civile, politique et historique de la partie française de l'isle Saint-Domingue*, Paris, 1796–7, reprinted in 3 volumes, eds. Blanche Maurel and Etienne Taillemite (Paris: Société de l'Histoire des Colonies Françaises, 1958).

In the *Description topographique*, French readers could find information on every aspect of colonial life. They read about the conditions of the soil in the different parts of the island, the extent of landholding, the level of church attendance, the population of every commune, and the numbers of slaves that each man held. But what the book sought to do above all else was to explain to the French something of the grandeur of Saint-Domingue, a colony which, until the unremitting violence unleashed by the French Revolution, had been, Moreau claimed, the envy of the European world. The riches of the island were described in alluring detail, but so were the frequent tensions that had developed with successive waves of immigration from Europe— especially tensions between those who had been born in Saint-Domingue, the Creoles, and those who had come more recently from France, bringing different demands and expectations. Many of the new arrivals had served as soldiers in the wars and had gone on to own land and oversee plantations. But they found it hard to break into the society of Creoles, those who had been there for a generation or more and who suffered problems of a different sort. Moreau talks of the temptations of luxury and idleness, of the destructive pleasures of gambling, of oversexed appetites which drained away the robust physical health of youth, of the passivity and self-indulgence that came with being served by others at all times. These, he believed, could have a detrimental effect on their physical strength and expose them needlessly to sickness and disease. Moreau goes so far as to imply that their premature youth and the abuse of alcohol and sexual pleasure help explain the high death rates and the proneness to suicide among the Creole population.[33] Reading the *Description*, it is hard to avoid the conclusion that Moreau commented on Creole society less from the standpoint of a fellow Creole than through the eyes of a French outsider who had become increasingly critical of the island's society and seemed detached from the attitudes he observed.

The eighteenth-century French Empire was not, of course, confined to the Atlantic; the colonies there were part of a wider, global economy that stretched as far to the east as to the west. France had also established a presence in the Indian Ocean, and though she had entered the race for India rather later than either the British or the Dutch, by the mid-eighteenth century France had established outposts across the Indian Ocean. The first steps in opening up Asian trade to French commerce, taken by Colbert in the 1660s, had hardly been encouraging, as the original flotation of a French East India Company, the Compagnie des Indes Orientales, was seriously undersubscribed.[34] But Colbert was eager to establish a government-protected company that would enjoy a

---

[33] Ibid., 39.
[34] Glenn J. Ames, *Colbert, Mercantilism and the French Quest for Asian Trade* (DeKalb: Northern Illinois University Press, 1996), 22–6.

monopoly of the Asian trade, to be run in accordance with his mercantilist principles, and the Company benefited from the many favours and privileges that the monarchy could bestow. In 1665, it was granted a fifty-year monopoly on French trade in the Indian and Pacific Oceans, a region stretching from the Cape of Good Hope to the Straits of Magellan. It was also granted a concession in perpetuity for the island of Madagascar, as well as for any other territories it might conquer in the Indian Ocean. It had some notable successes in its early years, setting up successful ports on the islands of Bourbon (today's Réunion) and Île-de-France (Mauritius), and established a number of important trading ports on the Indian mainland, most notably at Pondichéry and Chandernagore on the east coast and Mahé on the west.[35] The government involved itself in the struggle for trading posts, backing the aggressively expansionist policy of the Governor-General, Joseph-François Dupleix, in the 1740s, which inevitably brought the French into conflict with the British and the Dutch. This was not an issue that could be left to commerce. Colonial trade was a matter for the state, and for the military, too.

In India, as in other colonial spheres, France suffered severe losses during the Seven Years' War which provided encouragement to those reformers, like André Morellet, who advocated free trade and opposed company monopolies. They bore some responsibility, indeed, for forcing the French East India Company into liquidation in 1769.[36] Its buildings and property were seized by the state in return for paying off the Company's debt, and its monopoly privileges were abolished. For a brief period, French India was opened up to commercial competition, but investment declined along with the number of voyages to the East Indies from French ports. Morellet's victory proved short-lived.[37] In 1785, four years before the outbreak of the French Revolution, the monarchy reconstituted the Company with a share capital of 40 million *livres*, and restored its monopoly, if only for a fixed term of fifteen years. Though this allowed for the injection of large sums of money into French trading operations in India, it proved of short duration and did little to appease the fears of the French community in the sub-continent. They were alarmed by other developments in colonial administration which suggested that the French government was losing interest in the colony. The shift of the capital to Port-Louis on Mauritius, the withdrawal of the last European troops from French India, and the decision in 1787 not to rebuild the damaged fortifications of Pondichéry all suggested a reduction in government support and weakened the colony's defensive capacities in the face of Indian or British

---

[35] The most authoritative recent history of the *Compagnie des Indes* is Philippe Haudrère, *La Compagnie française des Indes au 18e siècle, 1719-1795* (2 vols) (Paris: Les Indes savantes, 2005).

[36] André Morellet, *Mémoire sur la situation actuelle de la Compagnie des Indes* (Paris, 1769).

[37] Anoush Fraser Terjanian, *Commerce and its Discontents in Eighteenth-century French Political Thought* (Cambridge: Cambridge University Press, 2013), 147–50.

aggression.[38] When, in 1790, the revolutionaries abolished all commercial mon-opolies and opened up East Indian trade to independent merchants, the Company could not cope with the effects of competition. It collapsed ignominiously four years later, its reputation tarnished by corruption, bringing the Jacobin leader Georges Danton down with it in what was probably the biggest corruption scandal of the Revolutionary years.[39]

In contrast, the Atlantic economy emerged from the pre-Revolutionary years on a buoyant note. Between 1716–20 and 1784–88, the quantity of goods shipped in and out of France's Atlantic ports trebled; their value—without taking account of inflation—increased five times, a figure that far outstripped the growth figures of British ports across these years.[40] An increasing proportion of that trade was with France's overseas colonies, especially with her transatlantic possessions; indeed, France's North American and Caribbean trade across these years rose by a factor of ten. Commercial optimism grew apace, especially during the last years of the Ancien Régime, when, with peace signed in 1783 to end the War of American Independence, commercial shipping again enjoyed freedom of the seas. By the outbreak of the Revolution in 1789, French commerce had reached record levels, with the consequence that many merchants had redirected their shipping operations to the Antilles and began to dream of a future of limitless growth, with their port cities booming and employing ever more workers as crewmen and stevedores. Sugar, indigo, rum, molasses, and the myriad products of France's overseas colonies held out the promise of ever-growing wealth and prosperity, and of the social esteem which such wealth brought to successful merchant houses. Increasing numbers of merchants, lured by the promise of quick returns on their investments, fitted out ships for the Atlantic crossing, and especially for the Caribbean. There was a buzz about the quaysides of Bordeaux, Nantes, and Le Havre that exuded confidence and prosperity.

But rapid colonization brought risks, too. For the individual merchant the profits of a trading season could be jeopardized by misfortune, by a shipwreck, or the loss of a crew, or the seizure of a ship by pirates and corsairs. It was a period of flux, when ambitious young merchants could hope to find a place among the elite, but when a number of established merchant companies were ruined or faced bankruptcy. There were other threats, too. The cost of colonial expansion, to both the government and the tax-payer, had been immense, drawing France into a succession of costly wars that had drained the country's reserves and contributed

---

[38] Mike Rapport, '"Complaints lost in the wind"—French India and the crisis of the absolute monarchy: a global dimension?', in Julian Swann and Joël Félix (eds), *The Crisis of Absolute Monarchy: France from Old Regime to Revolution* (Oxford: Oxford University Press, 2013), 223–4.

[39] Albert Mathiez, 'Un procès de corruption sous la Terreur, l'affaire de la Compagnie des Indes', *Annales Révolutionnaires*, 13 (1921), 516.

[40] François Crouzet, 'Angleterre et France au 18ᵉ siècle: essai d'analyse comparée de deux croissances économiques', *Annales: Economies, Sociétés, Civilisations*, 1966, 261.

to the fiscal crisis in 1787 and 1788, which made political reforms unavoidable and nudged the country towards revolution. In part, of course, this can be explained by the refusal of the privileged orders to accept that they should be taxed. However, it was France's involvement in war, not least her ill-advised entry into the War of American Independence in 1778 to pursue her colonial rivalry with Britain, that finally threatened the monarchy with bankruptcy. The finances of the state were always precarious, though in normal circumstances they could be managed and massaged through resort to a variety of credit mechanisms. But a succession of wars had put this balance in jeopardy, and the cost of credit rose steeply. The five years of war between 1778 and 1783 cost the French exchequer more than 1 billion *livres*—more than twice the annual revenue of the state[41]—and left the Controller-General with a budget where more than half the revenue generated was spent on servicing the national debt. Since this required unpalatable political reforms, reforms which Necker's false optimism in his budget statement of 1781 had appeared to render unnecessary, the administration was faced with a political stalemate at a time when the demands on the exchequer continued to rise. For the fiscal crisis could not be divorced from political crisis. In John Shovlin's words, the political economy of France cannot be explained—and could not be solved—by fiscal measures alone. It was necessarily 'at the confluence of old regime political culture and the institutional structures of the fiscal-military state'.[42]

In the peacetime years after 1783, France still needed to maintain a standing army to defend her position in Europe; to renew her fleet if she was to remain competitive with the Royal Navy; and to pay the costs of protecting French global commerce. France tried to do all these things, seeming oblivious to the consequences. Like Britain and Spain, she engaged in an ambitious shipbuilding programme to try to make good the losses in war, but this was an arms race she could ill afford. The French were not deterred, however, launching thirty-eight new ships of the line in the ten years after 1783, to Britain's forty-four and Spain's twenty-three.[43] Given France's position in the world, this construction programme cannot be seen as excessive,[44] but it was economic folly. The interest rates offered by international creditors were unsparing, putting the French government at a cumulative disadvantage when compared to her competitors. While the Dutch government could access credit at an interest rate of 2.5–3 per cent, and Britain at 3–3.5 per cent, investors were charging France a much higher rate (between 4.8 and 6.5 per cent). These higher interest rates made investment in

[41] Peter McPhee, *Liberty or Death: The French Revolution* (New Haven, CT: Yale University Press, 2016), 38.

[42] Shovlin, *The Political Economy of Virtue*, 152.

[43] Jonathan R. Dull, *The Age of the Ship of the Line: The British and French Navies, 1650–1815* (Lincoln: University of Nebraska Press, 2009), 119.

[44] Jonathan R. Dull, *The French Navy and American Independence: A Study of Arms and Diplomacy, 1774–1787* (Princeton, NJ: Princeton University Press, 1975), 336.

French debt attractive to foreign investors who could not get a similar return in their domestic markets. But for the French there was a cost. 'The convergence of growing wealth, growing needs and growing supplies of international capital,' concludes Lynn Hunt, 'made it possible for the French to borrow themselves into bankruptcy.'[45]

The years of optimism could not last. By the early 1790s, France's merchant community would be embroiled in political disputes about privilege and monopoly which risked pitting them against the Revolution in Paris, even as the stability and profitability of transatlantic trade were once again undermined by foreign war. In retrospect, the years between the end of the War of American Independence in 1783 and the declaration of war on France's principal colonial rival, Britain, ten years later proved something of a false dawn, bearing a promise of colonial prosperity that would never be fulfilled and tempting many merchants into overinvestment and bankruptcy. For the same decade that marked the high point of France's colonial trade was to herald the near-collapse of the country's Atlantic empire. The speed of the decline in commercial activity was quite startling, replacing the mood of optimism in the merchant community with a deep-seated sense of insecurity. Between 1789 and 1792, for example, there were 152 slave voyages out of Nantes; but the number of ships involved in the trade each year fell steadily, from forty-six at the beginning of the Revolution to only six four years later.[46] Waterfronts that had only recently resounded to the bustle of docks and shipyards and the clamour of crews leaving for the Caribbean had fallen ominously silent. The Atlantic ports that had, a few years before, pointed France towards a glorious commercial future based on transatlantic exchange had now, it seemed, been unstuck by internal turmoil and foreign war. What, many asked, had gone wrong? And was the Revolution to blame?

In fact, appearances in the last years of the Ancien Régime were deceptive. If the French emerged from this period on an unprecedented high, the eighteenth century as a whole had not spelt unbroken prosperity or colonial success. If it was to be successful, trade required a sustained period of peace and international stability to allow ships to be fitted and crewed, voyages to be planned, and transatlantic crossings to be made in relative security. Wars imperilled all these things, and the eighteenth century had been a century of war, war that had too often been waged over colonies and the Atlantic trade routes.[47] The War of the Spanish Succession, at the beginning of the century, had been a conflict over

---

[45] Lynn Hunt, 'The Global Financial Origins of 1789', in Suzanne Desan, Lynn Hunt, and William Max Nelson (eds), *The French Revolution in Global Perspective* (Ithaca, NY: Cornell University Press, 2013), 33.

[46] Nathalie Touzeau, 'Etude des expéditions négrières nantaises sous la Révolution Française (1789–93) au temps des droits de l'Homme' (2 vols, mémoire de maîtrise, Université de Nantes, 1993), 2, 4–6.

[47] Geoffrey Plank, 'War and Warfare in the Atlantic World', in D'Maris Coffman, Adrian Leonard, and William O'Reilly (eds), *The Atlantic World* (London: Routledge, 2015), 275.

access to the commercial wealth of the Spanish empire in the Americas, and Britain had emerged from it with important concessions. The next colonial war—in 1739—was a consequence of Britain's determination to hold on to these privileges, and, rather ominously, it started in the Americas. In the same way, the Seven Years' War was, outside of continental Europe, a global war between Britain and France over colonial possessions, one which Britain, with its parliamentary institutions and tax structures, was better equipped to wage. The City of London was already proving its worth as a source of cheap and reliable borrowing for governments facing the extreme, exceptional costs that waging war entailed, whereas the French had no such resource, and were thrown back on the markets of Amsterdam and Antwerp, as well as London itself, to raise the sums that their war effort required. The Bourbons also lacked the tax base of the British Crown, the foundation on which the fiscal-military state was built.[48] By the end of the eighteenth century, a strong fiscal base, combined with established networks of private contractors, was seen as increasingly necessary for any ruler bent on pursuing a successful campaign of colonial warfare. The lack of such a base placed France at a permanent disadvantage every time a naval or colonial war threatened.

For geopolitical reasons, France had no choice but to fight on both land and water, to raise large continental armies to combat attacks from Austria or Prussia at the same time as constructing a navy that could match Britain at sea. This proved a costly imposition, and one which almost certainly doomed France's military ambitions from the start. It is a supposition that France's later involvement in colonial conflicts—whether with Britain in the War of American Independence after 1778 or with the United States in the so-called 'Quasi War' of 1800—did nothing to dispel. Yet France, it might seem, had little choice, as she needed to be able to defend her colonies and her place in international trade. And that was not easy, as commercial rivalries extended across the globe. According to the French government's own secret estimates, in 1788 France dominated trade in the Caribbean, Spain enjoyed the lion's share with South America, Britain had a slight edge in trade with the newly independent United States, and the British and Dutch far outstripped the French in trade with China and India.[49] If world trade was developing rapidly, the European trading nations were developing strengths and weaknesses, and these would increasingly inform their commercial strategies. For France, the waters of the North Atlantic seemed the most remunerative and among the most propitious. It was there to be conquered.

The relatively short period of colonial prosperity that France experienced after 1783 was exceptional even within the prism of the eighteenth century. It was the fruit of a rare victory over Britain at sea, the consequence of France's cripplingly

[48] John Brewer, *The Sinews of Power: War, Money and the English State, 1688–1783* (Cambridge: Cambridge University Press, 1990).

[49] See Desan et al., *The French Revolution in Global Perspective*.

expensive and ultimately misguided decision to take part in the War of American Independence. On the colonial front, the American War was simply the latest of a long series of conflicts, and one of the few where the French had emerged with tangible gains. It was undertaken, indeed, largely to gain back a little of the prestige lost in 1763. By the terms of the Peace of Paris, the French had had to cede their major possessions in mainland North America, India, and Senegal in West Africa. Quebec and her other Canadian possessions were handed over to Britain and Louisiana to Spain. Senegal had to be sacrificed, which had been a major source of West African slaves for the sugar plantations for the Caribbean, many shipped through the island of Gorée which the British had seized in 1758.[50] France's only consolation—and it was a significant one—was that she had been allowed to retain her sugar islands in Guadeloupe, Martinique, and especially Saint-Domingue, which had proved by far the most profitable of her colonies. To preserve Saint-Domingue, France's leaders were fully prepared to cede Canada to Britain: at the time, it seemed a price worth paying in order to secure the 'pearl of the Antilles' and to maintain France's presence in the Caribbean.

Why was Saint-Domingue deemed so valuable as to justify the cession of sucha huge and potentially wealthy land-mass as Canada? In part it is because eight-eenth-century Frenchmen had little reason to appreciate Canada's future poten-tial. The country remained seriously under-populated by Europeans, and appeared little more than a series of settlements along the St Lawrence River with trading posts for trappers in the hinterland beyond. The geopolitical possi-bilities of a territory that could link east to west and follow the Mississippi down to its mouth in Louisiana were only poorly understood. Besides, in commercial terms Canada seemed of little value compared to the eye-watering riches of the Antilles. In 1789, Saint-Domingue produced half the world's exports of coffee and sugar; it accounted for two-thirds of the goods imported to Europe from all France's colonies, and produced twice as much income for France's royal coffers as Spain's richest colony, Mexico. It was also the most heavily populated of the Caribbean sugar islands: Britain's most developed colony in the West Indies, Jamaica, produced only about a third of the sugar grown in Saint-Domingue and had only about half the population. Seen from this perspective, it is easy to understand why Paris was so reluctant to lose Saint-Domingue, or why many in Paris were prepared to accept the loss of Canada without demur.

Yet with the benefit of hindsight, even that calculation proved problematic. The French Atlantic world was more mutually dependent, and more inextricably entangled, than many contemporaries realized, as the loss of Canada and subse-quently of Louisiana would undermine France's ability to supply and provision her possessions in the Caribbean. The principles governing France's relations with

---

[50] Cyr Descamps, 'Gorée au temps de la Compagnie des Indes, 1718–1758', in *Lorient, la Bretagne et la traite, 17e–19e siècles: Cahier de la Compagnie des Indes*, 9/10 (2006), 202–3.

her colonies were long-established and were supposedly to the advantage of both the colonies and the mother country. Mercantilist policies made the colonies entirely dependent on France and French produce; and the primary purpose of islands like Saint-Domingue was, as Manuel Covo has insisted, to engage in capitalist agriculture and farm lucrative crops like sugar and coffee that could not be produced in Europe; this was the very basis of the rationale for slavery. Under the terms of the *Exclusif*—the regulations that governed trading relations between France and her overseas colonies during the Ancien Régime—France had enjoyed a monopoly over the colonial produce of its possessions overseas, leading in principle to a situation where France would import the entire crops of sugar, rice, or indigo and either use them for her own consumption or take advantage of free ports on the French mainland to re-export them, free of import duty, to customers across Europe. In return, France would supply the colonies with the basic commodities they needed and which they could not grow on their own soil—everything from corn and wine to timber and fish, much of it carried in French ships on their return voyages from ports like Bordeaux and Le Havre to the Caribbean.

Much, but not all: traditionally the French had brought some of this produce, and heavier goods like timber, from French North America. The Peace of Paris took away this option, and it proved a real challenge to provision the colonies, especially in years of war when the shipping lanes to and from the Antilles risked being cut. At such times it was customary to allow neutral vessels to break the national monopoly and import goods to the colonists, while smugglers, ever-present in the waters off the Americas, could be assured of good business.[51] After 1763, indeed, those defending France's mercantilist laws came under increasing pressure from reformers and those advocating a free market in colonial goods, and saw this as a possible way to combat British ambitions in the Americas. French trade could be strengthened, they argued, through such collaborations, without incurring the costs of establishing a formal empire. France could also aspire to a share in the lucrative American trade that had been thrown open through Britain's loss of her thirteen colonies.[52] Thus we find that by the end of the Ancien Régime, the *Exclusif* was rarely enforced to the letter as neutral ships increasingly became involved in colonial commerce, with the new United States the principal benefi-ciary. In 1785, for instance, American ships were allowed to trade directly with the entrepôt ports of Pointe-à-Pitre and Basse-Terre in Guadeloupe, and foreign merchants were authorized to import some foodstuffs, primary materials, and animals into the colony on the same terms as French traders. By 1788, a new

---

[51] Manuel Covo, 'Baltimore and the French Atlantic: Empires, Commerce and Identity in a Revolutionary Age, 1783–1788', in Adrian Leonard and David Pretel (eds), *The Caribbean and the Atlantic World Economy: Circuits of Trade, Money and Knowledge, 1650–1914* (Basingstoke: Palgrave Macmillan, 2015), 89.

[52] Ibid., 90.

pattern of trade had emerged, with the port of Basse-Terre alone seeing 304 ships take on cargoes. Of these, only forty-two were French; one was Danish, four Dutch, and forty-eight British—with the others, 209 in all, being registered in the United States.[53] Even without the Revolution, France's traditional position in the Caribbean—as, indeed, in the Indian Ocean—was coming under pressure, and many were persuaded that as the century drew to a close, it was Britain, and not France, that looked best placed to assume the role of a truly global power.

[53] 'Arrêts et ordonnances portant sur le commerce entre la Guadeloupe et la métropole', in Françoise Koest, *La Révolution à la Guadeloupe, 1789–1796* (Basse-Terre: Archives Départementales, 1982), 'La Guadeloupe en 1789'.

2

The Port Cities of the French Atlantic

The opening up of the Atlantic world to trade and settlement heralded a century of growth and increasing prosperity for France's west coast ports, whose geographic position made them obvious points of departure for the New World. Like Lisbon and Cadiz to the south, or Bristol and Liverpool in England, they were eager to take advantage of the many opportunities that came from colonial trade, including physical expansion, rapid population growth, and exceptional levels of investment.[1] Not all ports, of course, benefited to the same degree, and not all showed the same enthusiasm for the new colonial markets that were opening up. Fitting out ships for the long voyage to the Antilles took substantial amounts of capital incurred a high degree of risk, especially during the many wars that broke out between Europe's colonial powers in the course of the century. Fortunes could be lost as well as won. In the smaller ports, there were often insufficient numbers of merchants to share the investment in Atlantic voyages and thus reduce the risk of loss and bankruptcy, as was the norm elsewhere. Or a port would find itself geographically disadvantaged, too far from the Atlantic or too close to the enemy's navy in times of war. Dangers lurked. From Norman ports like Rouen and Honfleur a captain had to steer his vessel past the mud banks of the Seine estuary and through the hostile waters and prevailing westerlies of the English Channel before passing Cap Finisterre and moving out into the ocean. So from Marseille, ships had to escape the Mediterranean through the Straits of Gibraltar—a favoured lurking-place for Barbary pirates—before setting course for West Africa or the Caribbean. In wartime, of course, these problems became more marked as the sea routes were littered with English privateers eager to profit from every lapse in the vessels' defences. The practice of using corsairs to attack commercial shipping was long-established in England, where it had been turned to both military and commercial advantage since the wars with Spain in the late sixteenth and early seventeenth centuries.[2]

---

[1] For an analysis of the 'golden age' of slaving in Britain, see Kenneth Morgan, *Bristol and the Atlantic Trade in the Eighteenth Century* (Cambridge: Cambridge University Press, 1993), 128–51; also, by the same author, 'Liverpool's Dominance in the British Slave Trade, 1740–1807', in David Richardson, Suzanne Schwarz, and Anthony Tibbles (eds), *Liverpool and Transatlantic Slavery* (Liverpool: Liverpool University Press, 2007), 14–42.

[2] Nicholas Kyriazis, Theodore Metaxas, and Emmanouil Economou, 'War for profit: English corsairs, institutions and decentralised strategy', *Defence and Peace Economics*, 29 (2018), 335–51.

The slave trade formed an important part of Atlantic commerce, but its importance varied from city to city, while a port's involvement in slaving could change rapidly across time. In the years between 1642 and 1807—from the time when northern Europe began to supplant Spain and Portugal in organizing slave voyages until the first major abolition, in Britain—France was a major player in the slave trade, transporting some 1,188,000 black Africans to the New World. But hers was never a dominant position. In these years, French ships carried only about a third of the number of slaves transported by Britain (3,247,000) and Portugal (3,061,000), and no French port ever came near to challenging Liverpool's predominance in the trade. Nantes was the most successful across the whole of the century, carrying nearly half a million slaves from West Central Africa and the Bight of Benin, the vast majority to Saint-Domingue.[3] Other ports flourished over shorter periods, or had more concentrated periods of activity. Le Havre, for instance, was the first port of any importance to turn to trading in African slaves, and it was one of the last to renounce slaving; but the voyages it fitted out were not spread equitably across the century and were heavily concentrated in the last years of the Ancien Régime.[4] Bordeaux only figured among the leading slave ports after about 1750. And La Rochelle, which had been the second most successful slaving port in France, saw its share of the trade decline after 1788, during the very period when other ports were enjoying high returns.[5] Each port city responded in its own way to the challenges of Atlantic commerce, and to the problems of finding credit and managing risk. Some gave it up altogether.

As time passed, it seemed that it was the smaller ports that lost out in the struggle for Atlantic dominance. Local circumstances differed from one town to another, though all the smaller towns complained of the fierce competition they faced from their larger neighbours, from ports able to offer more generous credit terms or better placed to take advantage of economies of scale. Lorient is a case in point. It had, as we have seen, become heavily dependent for its wealth on the monopoly of the East Indian trade enjoyed by the Compagnie des Indes after it moved its headquarters and the bulk of its activity there from Nantes in 1733. This did not exclude it from the slave trade, however, as the Company had incorporated the old Compagnie d'Afrique in 1719 and continued to fit out slave ships for Africa for a further fifty years. But the level of its slaving activity declined, especially after periods of maritime warfare. Between 1719 and 1769, it sent 151 slave ships out of Lorient; thereafter it largely left the trade to private shippers, who sent a further twenty-five vessels from Lorient between 1764 and 1790.[6] In Saint-Malo, too, merchants' interest in the slave trade tended to be spasmodic,

[3] Eltis and Richardson, *Atlas of the Transatlantic Slave Trade*, 59.
[4] Ibid., 56.   [5] Ibid., 56.
[6] Nolwenn Picote, 'Lorient, la Compagnie des Indes et la traite', in *Lorient, la Bretagne et la traite (17ᵉ–19ᵉ siècles)*, 33.

reflecting the varying profitability of their other commercial ventures; and after 1769, left without the assurance provided by Company backing, few of Saint-Malo's merchants were prepared to risk major investment in slaving. Trade with the Indian Ocean seemed to offer higher returns and less risk, and the ending of the Company's monopoly provided the merchants with the freedom and commercial opportunity they desired. In the last twenty years before the Revolution, they placed more and more of their capital in the east, especially in trade with India and China.[7]

Marseille expanded its trade with the West Indian islands in the last decades before the Revolution, until by 1789 it had become the second port in France for exchanges with the Antilles. The years from 1790 to 1792, before war broke out again, saw more ships fitted out in the city for the colonial trade than at any other moment in the eighteenth century. But Marseille, a long-established Mediterranean port with commercial links in North Africa and the Levant, never became wholly dependent on the Atlantic, or over-exposed to the vagaries of the slave trade. While it was reinvigorated by the opening up of the Atlantic shipping lanes, its merchants continued to develop trade with the Levant; this diversity would prove to be a considerable source of strength when crisis struck in the Caribbean. As Charles Carrière has shown, in the last years of the Ancien Régime commerce with the Caribbean colonies accounted for 23 per cent of Marseille's activity compared to 44 per cent for Bordeaux. Similarly, the re-export of colonial produce accounted for 11 per cent of total business in Marseille compared to 30 per cent in Bordeaux.[8]

Others faced more intractable problems. Bayonne's potential for growth was restricted by the presence of a huge sandbank across the mouth of the Adour, which excluded larger ships and forced others to wait at anchor in the roads before entering the harbour, some for as many as sixty or eighty days. By the 1780s, Bayonne was also dependent on its newly won free port status if it was to have any success in luring trade from its rivals along the north coast of Spain, Bilbao, and San Sebastian. It was a forlorn cause: Bayonne would see its commerce drain away and its population fall steadily across the century, from 15,000 in 1715 to 11,000 in 1764 and fewer than 10,000 by the mid-1770s.[9] Its participation in the Atlantic slave trade dwindled, too, with only eight merchants involved and nine voyages fitted out between 1741 and 1792. They were not helped by the tendency, common to all the Atlantic ports, to use larger vessels for slaving, which led to the disappearance of the smaller boats of between fifty and eighty tons in favour of

---

[7] Alain Roman, 'Les représentations de la traite à Saint-Malo (18e–20e siècles)', in *Lorient, la Bretagne et la traite (17e–19e siècles)*, 163.

[8] Charles Carrière, *Négociants marseillais au 18e siècle* (2 vols, Marseille, 1973), vol. 1, 65–7.

[9] Pierre Hourmat, *Histoire de Bayonne, vol.1 Des origines à la Révolution Française* (Bayonne: Société des sciences, lettres et arts, 1986), 491–2.

large ocean-going ships of 250–300 tons.[10] It was a trend that could not but benefit the major port cities such as Le Havre, Nantes, and Bordeaux, with their larger merchant houses and easier access to credit and investors.

To the north, the smaller ports of southern Brittany and the Loire estuary—Pornic, Paimboeuf, Le Pouliguen, or Bourgneuf—were increasingly drawn into the slipstream of their bigger neighbour, Nantes, serving as feeder ports to the Atlantic trade.[11] Even larger ports up the Breton coast, like Vannes, which had fitted out their own transatlantic voyages and had invested in the slave trade, lost out in competition with their bigger neighbour. As the eighteenth century drew to a close, the merchants who traded successfully with the Caribbean and the Americas were increasingly concentrated in four cities: Le Havre to the north, and Nantes, Bordeaux, and La Rochelle on France's west coast.

Each port exploited its strengths and its value to the expanding colonial population of the Americas, who remained highly reliant on food and other basic commodities imported from France. The Atlantic ports were not only key points of entry for colonial products into France; they were also, necessarily, the source of goods passing in the other direction, in particular the agricultural cereals and industrial staples which were in constant demand in the colonies. For this purpose, geography was everything, as the shippers were dependent on the cities' hinterlands for the foodstuffs and raw materials their customers required. Some Atlantic ports were better sited than others from this perspective. Le Havre, for instance, benefited from its position at the mouth of the Seine, along which goods for export were channelled; its proximity to Paris meant that it could easily access goods manufactured in the capital; and it also had, in Lower Normandy, a flourishing agricultural hinterland on which to draw. The port's status had grown rapidly since the early eighteenth century, when it was still principally a centre for deep-sea fishing: on a list of the leading merchants drawn up in the 1680s, all but five had concentrated their energies on catching cod in the Atlantic shoals and off the coast of Newfoundland, while overseas trade, credit, and insurance facilities had been more widely available upstream in Rouen.

Rouen enjoyed other advantages, too. It was the administrative centre for Normandy; it was home to a range of industries, not least in textiles; and it was an important banking centre.[12] But by the mid-eighteenth century, Le Havre's fortunes had changed dramatically. The relationship with Rouen was more one of competition, the two cities vying with each other for commercial privileges and markets, and Le Havre increasingly challenging Rouen's established position

---

[10] Jacques de Cauna and Marion Graff, *La traite bayonnaise au 18ᵉ siècle: Instructions, journal de bord, projets d'armement* (Pau: Éditions Cairn, 2009), 17.

[11] Olivier Pétré-Grenouilleau, *Nantes: histoire et géographie contemporaine* (Plomelin: Palantines, 2003), 96.

[12] Pierre Dardel, *Commerce, industrie et navigation à Rouen et au Havre au 18ᵉ siècle* (Rouen: Société libre d'émulation de la Seine-Maritime, 1966), 107–39, 147.

among the merchant elite. In particular, merchants abandoned fishing to concentrate their investment in the colonial trade, and from the mid-1780s expanded their interest in the African slave trade.[13] Other, smaller, ports close to the Seine estuary fared markedly less well. Honfleur, which some had earlier regarded as a serious rival to Le Havre at the mouth of the Seine, served rather as a feeder port, taking responsibility for much of the traffic upriver to Rouen and beyond, and taking over from Le Havre as the principal centre for cod-fishing in the Seine estuary. By the eve of the Revolution, the fishing families who had figured among the richest entrepreneurs in Le Havre a hundred years earlier had either given up fishing or had moved elsewhere. The merchant houses of Le Havre were more interested in the profits to be made from trade in colonial produce.[14]

This new interest in colonial commerce and eagerness to get involved in slaving did not pass unremarked. By the 1780s, the commercial newspapers of Nantes and Bordeaux began to see Le Havre as a serious rival to their domination of the Atlantic, leading them to fear for their own future prosperity. In their view, Le Havre had that precious advantage with which they could never compete: it was the gateway to Paris, which was the unchallenged centre of consumption for luxury goods, with more than a third of the purchasing-power of the entire country and a metropolitan lifestyle no other city could match.[15] A study of Le Havre's merchant elite suggests that they left little to chance, that over the course of the century they developed a coherent commercial strategy, maintaining partnerships with merchants in other ports, choosing an appropriate legal structure for their business, and establishing a high standard of bank credit to tide them over in difficult times. The liberalization of trade in 1784 provided them with an opportunity to expand their trading activities, but, significantly, the nature of their commerce did not change. The big merchant families were discerning, and they knew their business world. They made alliances with third parties to get round blockades; they maintained a prudent balance between the slave trade with West Africa and direct commerce between France and the Caribbean; and they re-exported the colonial goods they imported to their traditional destinations in Scandinavia and the Baltic.[16] By the last years of the Ancien Régime, Le Havre was solidly established as the third slaving port in France, behind Bordeaux and Nantes. It was clearly a rival to be taken seriously.

Yet Le Havre remained a small town, provided with modern, elegant buildings that impressed the visitor, yet strangely cramped on a site dominated by its military defences, the ramparts and citadel built for Louis XIV by Vauban. This

---

[13]   Ibid., 61.

[14]   Jean Meyer, 'Les paradoxes du succès havrais', in André Corvisier (ed.), *Histoire du Havre et de l'estuaire de la Seine* (Toulouse: Privat, 1983), 78–81.

[15]   Ibid., 75–8.

[16]   Edouard Delobette, 'Ces « Messieurs du Havre » : Négociants, commissaires et armateurs de 1680 à 1830' (thèse de doctorat, Université de Caen, 2005), 513–14, 710.

undoubtedly had the effect of limiting its potential for growth in the early part of the eighteenth century at a time when the bigger maritime cities of the Atlantic coast were expanding rapidly. Le Havre had been conceived as a military town, and in the eighteenth century it still maintained a strong military presence, even if it had never really developed into the major naval port and dockyard that Louis XIV had dreamt of founding. If it had a weakness as a port city, it was the constant threat of silt blocking access to the biggest ocean-going vessels, a threat that became more troubling as it launched itself into the colonial trade in the last years of the Ancien Régime. But that colonial trade implied change: expansion and population growth, much of it drawn from the surrounding countryside and from other coastal towns in Normandy, most notably Dieppe. Successive censuses in the eighteenth century show a town whose population was rising steadily, if not dramatically, from around 12,780 inhabitants in 1723 to 14,653 in 1763 and more than 18,000 in 1787, as opportunities opened up to those who made their living from ships and the sea. The ramparts were finally breached to build new suburbs on land beyond Vauban's planned city—a move that, after decades of overcrowding on its fifteen-acre site, finally allowed Le Havre to satisfy more of its commercial and maritime potential.[17] The years immediately before the outbreak of the Revolution represented something of a boom for the city, and for the triangular trade with West Africa and the Caribbean in particular.

Though the rate of population growth in Le Havre was by no means exceptional across the eighteenth century—it was dwarfed by figures in Bordeaux, Nantes, and Marseille—not all colonial ports benefited equally from the boom years. For La Rochelle, in particular, the eighteenth century was a period of relative decline after years of growth and prosperity. From the sixteenth century the port's merchants and sea captains had thrown themselves into Atlantic trade, scouring the Americas from Newfoundland to Brazil, and establishing a capitalist network that encompassed Paris and the major French ports, as well as England, the United Provinces, and Spain.[18] But this era of prosperity had come to an abrupt end with the Revocation of the Edict of Nantes in 1685, which ended a hundred years of toleration for Protestants in the city. The result had been an exodus of some of the city's most dynamic Protestant merchants, and with their departure the Protestant dominance in the Chamber of commerce was ended. Wars also caused disruption from which La Rochelle never recovered, while other problems soon presented themselves. Although La Rochelle was a well-established port with longstanding connections across North America, its geographical location was less ideal than it seemed; the narrowness of the old port and its tendency to silt up meant that larger vessels could not access it at low tide. And, unlike the Bordelais

---

[17] André Corvisier, 'La part des réalités quotidiennes', in Corvisier (ed.), *Histoire du Havre et de l'estuaire de la Seine*, 107–14.

[18] Jean-Michel Deveau, *La traite rochelaise* (Paris: Karthala, 1990), 17.

with its rich vineyards, the Saintonge and Aunis were regions of relatively poor soil that did not produce the wheat or cereals needed to provision the islands; the wines they produced were of mediocre quality, and much of the coastal land was given over to salt marshes.[19]

Overseas trade declined over the century as the economy weakened, and if it was still a specialist colonial port on the eve of the Revolution, it operated on a much more modest scale, with only thirty-four ships registered at or departing from the port in 1787 compared to 116 in Nantes, 119 in Le Havre, 146 in Marseille, and 245 in Bordeaux. Even Lorient boasted more shipping movements than La Rochelle.[20] Its modest commercial position was reflected in demographic weakness, too. Whereas the second half of the seventeenth century had seen a rapid growth of population, the new century brought decline, with more people leaving than arriving. From 25,000 inhabitants in 1700, La Rochelle's population fell to 20,000 by 1728, and stood at only around 17,250 on the eve of the Revolution.[21] This decline was both absolute and relative as other ports continued to grow and to attract migrant labour. Nantes was now two and a half times its size, Bordeaux five times. And if La Rochelle still had wealthy merchant families who built fine town houses in the old city, they were few in number, and they could not hide the fact that the port was no longer prosperous enough to provide a magnet to the dispossessed of the rural West. Even in the early part of the century, it was difficult to deny that the city's prosperity was unhealthily dependent on the enterprise of a handful of individuals, or to ignore the fact that a golden age that had numbered it among the premier ports of France now lay well in the past.[22]

Down the coast, the naval port of Rochefort fitted out some twenty slaving expeditions to the West African coast, almost exclusively in the years after 1770. But it had no claim to being a major colonial port, and, significantly, very few local people were involved in these ventures. Rochefort, like the other naval dockyards of Toulon and Brest, had no tradition of commercial slaving, or, more generally, of fitting out vessels for the colonies. It was a naval arsenal, its activity dominated by the needs of the navy and financing from the state; and state officials played a disproportionate part in organizing and financing these expeditions. Indeed, although naval vessels were seldom permitted to be used for commercial voyages, it is clear that there were occasions when ships of La Royale were authorized to carry out slaving missions on behalf of merchant houses, most notably at those moments when French colonies had reported a dearth of labour and when the government was actively encouraging the slave trade. In 1768, for instance, a naval

[19] Marcel Delafosse, 'Le solide 17e et le brillant 18e siècle', in Marcel Delafosse (ed.), *Histoire de La Rochelle* (Toulouse: Privat 1985), 196.

[20] John G. Clark, *La Rochelle and the Atlantic Economy during the Eighteenth Century* (Baltimore, MD: Johns Hopkins University Press, 1981), 27.

[21] Ibid., 4.

[22] Brice Martinetti, *Les négociants de La Rochelle au 18ᵉ siècle*, 27.

vessel, *Le Salomon*, stripped down to maximize its cargo space, was loaned by the Duc de Praslin on the King's behalf to a merchant from La Rochelle to sail to Cayenne with a cargo of slaves. Similarly, in 1771 and 1786, two naval vessels stationed in Rochefort, *L'Expérience* and *Le Pérou*, were lent to merchants to pursue the royal aim of assisting colonization. Both were authorized to carry slaves to France's Caribbean colonies; in exchange, part of the hold space was set aside for the king's use. In the hold of *L'Expérience*, for instance, were goods loaded on the king's account for use in Gorée.[23] These voyages may not have made a major contribution to the pre-Revolutionary slave trade. They did, however, bestow a degree of respectability on a type of trade whose morality was coming to be questioned.

In contrast, eighteenth-century Bordeaux thrived on colonial traffic. The Atlantic trade brought to its merchants a period of unparalleled commercial success, reaching its zenith in the last years before the Revolution, leading to a new confidence and civic pride that was reflected in bold town planning and proud public buildings. But Bordeaux's wealth and regional prominence did not depend on trade alone, nor was its urban elite restricted to the merchant classes. It was the capital of a province, seat of an archbishopric, and home to a royal *intendant* and to one of the country's thirteen *parlements*. It was, in other words, an important centre of both administration and justice, a city to which people brought civil cases from all over the South-west and where a powerful legal fraternity was clustered. And unlike Le Havre or La Rochelle, Bordeaux was home to a substantial number of local nobles, many of whom would divide their time between the spacious town houses they had built in the city and their wine-growing estates in the Médoc or Entre-Deux-Mers. There was old money in Bordeaux as well as new; and these legal and professional elites, as much as the rich merchants, helped ensure that the city enjoyed a varied and sophisticated cultural life, whether through its learned societies, like the Académie and the Musée, or through the plays presented in its lavish new theatre, the Grand Théâtre, designed by the architect Victor Louis in 1779 and for many the very epitome of Bordeaux's cultural pretensions. Money was lavished, too, on the construction of elegant squares and boulevards, and on the opening of a public park (the Jardin Public), investments in public space that showed the pride the new commercial elite took in their city and its amenities. But the benefit that accrued was not that of the wider community; every decision taken was carefully calculated to serve the mercantile interest of the elite. As the *Intendant* wrote in 1746 when announcing the investment in the new park, it had a commercial benefit, too, since its presence on the edge of the Chartrons would encourage lucrative deal-making. 'In a

---

[23] Christophe Cadiou-Quella and Céline Mélisson, 'Enseigner l'histoire de l'esclavage à partir des ressources locales: les expéditions négrières de Rochefort', in Mickaël Augeron and Olivier Caudron (eds), *La Rochelle, l'Aunis et la Saintonge face à l'esclavage* (Paris: Les Indes savantes, 2012), 311–14.

commercial city,' he noted, 'we must see a garden like this as necessary, or at least very useful, to commerce, since merchants will often have occasion to meet and will broker a greater number of business transactions: in this way it will serve as a second stock exchange, one that will be used in the evenings.'[24]

If merchants invested in public spaces, they also built opulent new houses in suburbs like the Faubourg du Nord and the Chartrons, *hôtels* distinguished by their classically formal design, their construction in stone, and the fastidious concern for detail that was shown in the use for decoration of wrought iron railings and sculpted masks (or *mascarons*). That concern for detail was visible on the inside of many of these homes, too, which are characterized by their sweeping staircases and sumptuous interior design.[25] What is striking is the concern of so many merchants to build their monument in stone, to invest the profits of trade in real estate and the security it offered. The Bordeaux merchant François Bonnaffé bought some twenty houses in the city over his career, in addition to four properties in the wine-growing lands of the Ambès peninsula. In the course of making these acquisitions, Bonnaffé spent more than 1 million *livres*.[26] In Nantes, too, merchants indulged in speculative building, with some developments, like those in the Île Feydeau or the Quartier Graslin, requiring a capital investment of more than 1 million *livres*.[27] In both cities, speculation flourished, often encouraged by governors and *intendants* eager to capitalize on their new-found wealth. But Bordeaux was the principal beneficiary, as Nantes was handicapped by its lack of administrative and judicial institutions and by the continued resistance and prejudice with which its plans were met by the provincial estates. As a consequence, Bordeaux's speculative frenzy lasted forty-six years, compared to twenty-eight in Nantes.[28]

Bordeaux's strength lay in the diversity of its trade and especially in the wealth of its winegrowing hinterland. Its merchants sold the wines of the South-west across the world, sending them to the Americas in substantial quantities as well as to its traditional European markets in Britain, Ireland, Holland, and, increasingly, Scandinavia and the Hanseatic ports. There were also more local markets, many of served by smaller barques and flat-bottomed boats that distributed Bordeaux wines within France, along river networks to the interior and to Brittany and the West. In this way, Bordeaux's merchants maintained links with local distributors and created solid circuits between Bordeaux and Brittany, often setting out

[24] Jean-Claude Perrot, 'Urbanisme et commerce au 18e siècle dans les ports de Nantes et Bordeaux', in Centre d'histoire économique et sociale de la Région Lyonnaise, *Villes et campagnes, 15e–20e siècles* (Lyon: Presses Universitaires de Lyon, 1977), 208.

[25] François-Georges Pariset, 'Le Bordeaux de Boucher et de Tourny', in Pariset (ed.), *Bordeaux au dix-huitième siècle*, 581–6.

[26] Bertrand Guillot de Suduirant, *Une fortune de haute mer: François Bonnaffé, un armateur bordelais au 18e siècle* (Bordeaux: Confluences, 1999), 166.

[27] Perrot, 'Urbanisme et commerce au 18e siècle dans les ports de Nantes et Bordeaux', 208.

[28] Ibid., 194.

from the smaller ports of the Gironde estuary, like Blaye and Bourg, which were positioned closer to the vineyards.[29] This diversity was what most clearly distinguished Bordeaux's position within the Atlantic economy, and it would prove a source of stability in a region continually buffeted by the ravages of war. Unlike Nantes, the merchants never became over-tied to a single trade, or a single destination. Bordeaux boasted the largest port facilities in Europe on the eve of the Revolution, with more than two-thirds of the ships leaving for foreign destinations—3,009 out of 4,215 between 1785 and 1789—sailing to ports in northern Europe.[30] This diversity proved crucial in explaining the city's commercial dynamism. 'The greatest originality of Bordeaux,' insists Paul Butel, 'was to be ... the principal marketplace for trade with the Baltic.'[31]

The eighteenth century proved to be a period of unprecedented growth, when the prosperity of Bordeaux attracted migrant labour from all over the South-west, as well as merchants, ships' agents, insurers, and importers from across northern Europe and a large number of artists, architects, and town planners from Paris. From a population of around 45,000 in 1700 the city grew exponentially—to 60,000 in 1747 and more than 110,000 according to the census of 1790, a figure that made it the third city of France behind Paris and Lyon. In the process, Bordeaux had developed from being a regional capital, attracting workers from its immediate hinterland, to being a pole of attraction for migrants from across a much wider area, including men and women from towns and villages in the catchment areas of other cities, like Toulouse, Poitiers, or Limoges. Immigrants were attracted by the possibility of employment, in the docks and on ships, of course, but also in ancillary trades like sail-making and bottle-manufacture, in the building trade, in transport, shops, and warehouses. Bordeaux by the second half of the eighteenth century was much more than a commercial port; it was a regional centre of note, a magnet for lawyers and professional men as well as artisans and workers. Some came, of course, as migrants always have, as a result of harvest failures of joblessness at home. But increasingly they came because Bordeaux attracted them, a city that had grown into 'a remarkable and complex tissue of activities, populations and quarters', a diversity born of confidence and commercial success.[32]

Nantes enjoyed less diversity, its economy being more tightly tied to Atlantic trade and especially to the colonies in the Caribbean. Its freedom of choice was limited. It did not have the same options as Bordeaux. It lacked the rich vinicultural hinterland, for Loire wines were less prized than clarets in the markets of

---

[29] Hiroyasu Kimizuka, *Bordeaux et la Bretagne au 18ᵉ siècle. Les routes du vin* (Rennes: Presses Universitaires de Rennes, 2015), 134–8.

[30] Paul Butel, *Les dynasties bordelaises de Colbert à Chaban* (Paris: Perrin, 1991), 66–7.

[31] Paul Butel, *Les négociants bordelais, l'Europe et les Îles au dix-huitième siècle* (Paris: Aubier, 1974), 23.

[32] Jean-Pierre Poussou, *Bordeaux et le Sud-ouest au 18ᵉ siècle: croissance économique et attraction urbaine* (Paris: Éditions de l'EHESS, 1983), 34.

England and northern Europe. It could not aspire, as Bordeaux could, to provide the colonies with the grain and flour for their daily needs; on the Loire there was no equivalent of the great flour mills at Tonneins and Marmande. As a result there were limited possibilities for Nantes to engage in direct trade with the colonies, the *commerce en droiture* that saw Bordeaux ships taking agricultural and industrial goods from France to supply the colonists in return for cotton, tobacco, indigo, and the other products of the plantations. Thus, very early in the century, the city's merchants made what they saw as an obvious choice: to invest in slaving and the triangular trade with West Africa and the Caribbean. Nantes was a pioneer here, building between 1707 and 1721 a clear dominance over other Breton slaving ports like St Malo and Lorient, and establishing important connections with both the planters in the Antilles and traders in West Africa. If the following decades marked a period of consolidation when they faced stiff competition from other French ports, by mid-century, Nantes merchants established their predominance in the slave trade, a position they largely maintained until the Revolution. But it was not easy: these were years blighted by war, first the War of the Austrian Succession, then the Seven Years' War, years when few others were prepared to risk so much and when the Bordelais, in particular, sought succour in more traditional European markets. Only in the final years of the Ancien Regime, when Le Havre and Bordeaux flexed their commercial muscles and expanded their Atlantic operations, did Nantes merchants finally see their dominant position in the slave trade threatened by the competition of other slaving cities. Over the eighteenth century, they had bought nearly 450,000 slaves on the west coast of Africa, and with more than 1,400 slave voyages were responsible for 42 per cent of the French slave trade.[33] The fruits of their industry were to be seen in the streets around them.

Nantes enjoyed very impressive growth over these years, doubling in population between the end of the seventeenth century and the Revolution from around 40,000 to 80,000, and acting as a magnet for migrants from across the west of France.[34] If the port was heavily dependent on the West Indian trade, so, too, was Nantes' industrial base. In the shipyards along the Loire, workers built the large, heavy commercial ships needed for the Atlantic crossing and the slave trade. And the city's textile industry, which employed thousands in spinning and weaving cotton, found a lucrative market in the West Indian islands where they sold the brightly coloured *indiennages* that were so highly prized in planter society (though we should not forget that they were also sold to rich French families for their town houses and rural châteaux). The production of these fabrics, with their bold designs and highly coloured patterns, was a specialism of the city, which had nine factories devoted to their production and which at their peak provided

---

[33] Pétré-Grenouilleau, *Nantes: histoire et géographie contemporaine*, 82–92.
[34] Ibid., 101.

employment for more than 2,000 workers; in 1785, the inspector Watier de Nantes estimated that they turned out around 70,000 pieces each year.[35] On the other hand, there is little to suggest that Nantes benefited directly from the importation of cane sugar and other colonial products, at least in the industrial sphere. The sugar that was landed at the port was transported to Orleans and other towns in the interior for processing; it was not processed in Nantes itself.

As in Bordeaux and other port cities, part of the wealth that was created by trade was invested in real estate and reflected in the fabric of the city: the Bourse and the new theatre that was opened at the very end of the Ancien Régime—the Théâtre Graslin—are suggestive of a highly developed civic pride and concern for urban planning. In particular, a new merchant quarter grew up in what had been the outskirts of a city still clustered around the cathedral and its medieval heart: the Quai de la Fosse and the Île Feydeau. And though at the beginning of the century, Nantes merchants were unable to compete with their Bordelais counterparts in matters of wealth and elegance, by 1742 the city authorities were engaged, encouraging merchants to demolish houses along the Quai, contributing half the cost of construction, and insisting that the houses be rebuilt to a clear architectural design and be aligned to the river. On the Île Feydeau, too, though merchants proved hostile to any idea of homogenization and sought to reflect their status and personality in the facades of their new homes, development provided the city with a new and elegant *quartier* that was a reflection of the taste and values of the merchant community. It helped to attract younger merchants and ship-owners new to the city and to integrate them into the commercial fabric of the city. Of those who built new houses along the Quai de la Fosse between 1718 and 1780, it has been shown that twenty-three were merchants, the architecture of their homes a reflection of their social aspirations. But few of them—no more than 8-9 per cent—came from established Nantes families or could claim to represent old money. These merchants were, in the great majority, a migrant population, men attracted to Nantes by the opportunities it offered for commerce and profit. Around 44 per cent of them came from the surrounding regions, Brittany, the Loire valley, and the West of France; the remainder came from other parts of France or from elsewhere in Europe, or else they were returning to France from the islands.[36] Nantes was not only a major port of departure for the Caribbean; it also welcomed back many of those returning to France from the New World, among them hundreds of Acadians from Quebec after the Peace of Paris in 1763.[37]

---

[35] Samuel Guicheteau, *La Révolution des ouvriers nantais. Mutation économique, identité sociale et dynamique révolutionnaire, 1740–1815* (Rennes: Presses Universitaires de Nantes, 2008), 34–5.

[36] Yannick Soufflet, 'Les négociants nantais et l'architecture: le Quai de la Fosse, 1735–55' (mémoire de maîtrise, Université de Nantes, 2003), 40.

[37] Gabriel Debien, 'Les exilés acadiens après leur départ du Poitou', *La Revue du Bas-Poitou et des provinces de l'Ouest*, 2 (1972), 150–1.

If the eighteenth century was a golden age for Atlantic commerce, it was also an age of tourism and travel, when the rich and curious began to visit new places, taste exotic foods, explore historical ruins, and fantasize about the past. For many members of the English nobility and gentry, it marked the high point of a Grand Tour that offered the opportunity to travel and experience other cultures, a Tour that might take in many different regions and cities, but which had its heartlands in Italy and France. Within France, attention was, of course, most concentrated on Paris and the monuments surrounding it, notably the royal palace at Versailles and the great houses of the Île-de-France. But as the century advanced, so people's curiosity widened to encompass visits to provincial cities and the coastal spa towns of the Mediterranean.[38] Travel guides were published which further stirred the curiosity of the traveller and gave shape to his journey, and, among France's myriad places of possible interest, the port cities of the Atlantic coast could not fail to attract the interest of greater numbers of visitors.[39] They came to see places they had heard of or read about; many were prepared to be impressed and to admire. Travel opened their minds and was reflected in a vogue for travel literature, mainly in the form of personal narratives, giving accounts of places visited and wonders observed.[40]

By the second half of the eighteenth century, the most notable feature of these accounts is the emphasis they placed on the cities' physical appearance and the quality of their fabric. They admired the public buildings and monuments, noting the clearance of congested slums to make way for open spaces and elegant town-houses. In Nantes and Bordeaux, what most impressed visitors was the speed of their expansion and renewal.[41] Some could not hide their astonishment, especially after long wars which, they imagined, would have crippled France's economy and disrupted its merchant shipping. Richard Hopkins, visiting in Brittany in 1749, had not expected to be confronted with all the symptoms of commercial prosperity that he saw in Nantes, and, as a patriotic Englishman, he could barely hide his dismay. He was, he said, 'much surprised and indeed sorry to see so much appearance of wealth and commerce, the more so when from many hands I was assured that there was not a merchant in the town who had not lost almost all their vessels in the war'. But if they had, they had not lost their fortunes, as the ships were all insured in London, so that it was the London market that had taken the hit. Instead, 'in every river, in every seaport town, nay in every ditch, they are

---

[38] See, for instance, Aimé Dupuy, *Voyageurs étrangers à la découverte de l'ancienne France, 1500– 1850* (Paris: Club du Livre d'histoire, 1957).

[39] Louis Desgraves, *Voyageurs à Bordeaux du dix-septième siècle à 1914* (Bordeaux: Mollat, 1991), 11.

[40] Matthew Binney, *The Cosmopolitan Evolution: Travel, Travel Narratives and the Revolution of the Eighteenth-century European Consciousness* (Lanham, MD: University Press of America, 2006), 141. The same theme is developed in Anthony Pagden, *European Encounters with the New World* (New Haven, CT: Yale University Press, 1993).

[41] Desgraves, *Voyageurs à Bordeaux*, 135.

building to restore, rather than increase their commerce above what it was at the beginning of the last war'.[42] With the return of peace, Nantes would again be ready to compete at sea with Bristol and Liverpool.

The surprise was all the greater for those travellers who had had to labour through mud and ill-made roads in the surrounding countryside to reach their destination. The huge contrast between the wealth of the city and the squalor of the villages and hamlets through which they had passed could not but impress them. In France, as throughout much of Europe, it was a contrast that was often expressed by references to what contemporaries saw as the symbols of civilization, a contrast which they described in terms of wealth and poverty, cleanliness and dirt. There was so little that appealed to the traveller in rural areas, where he was met with a succession of rutted roads, inadequate communications, poor harvests, and miserable inns in the villages through which he passed. In this, the reflections of foreign travellers in France differed little from those of Frenchmen when they travelled abroad. The countryside always seemed dark and impoverished, its inhabitants rude and vaguely threatening. So it would be for the French soldiers who travelled to Spain during the Peninsular War, or for Germans when first they laid eyes on rural Poland. The territory they passed through seemed backward and impoverished, a world away from Paris or Berlin.[43] Like all Europeans, they passed judgement on the lands they travelled through and compared them with what they had left at home. For those who came from cities, that comparison could often be unflattering, and the sight of poor rural farmsteads and failed crops only convinced them that they were in a world of mud and filth, misery and underdevelopment. Few found much in the countryside that was worthy of their attention or consideration.

For many travellers to France, Paris was, of course, the yardstick by which other towns were judged, and mostly they were doomed to disappoint. Market towns often seemed to share the misery of their rural hinterlands, and were dismissed as provincial backwaters, far removed from enlightenment and civilization. Even provincial capitals, despite the roles they played in administration and the law, attracted little praise. The English agronomist Arthur Young, on his travels through France in 1787, 1788, and 1789, did not restrict his comments to agriculture and animal husbandry, the subjects on which he could exercise real expertise. He deplored the misery he found in provincial cities, too: of Limoges, he commented, no doubt with some justification, that 'it is ill-built, with narrow and crooked streets, the houses high and disagreeable',[44] while Rouen was 'ugly,

---

[42] Jeremy Black, *France and the Grand Tour* (Basingstoke: Palgrave Macmillan, 2003), 141.

[43] Nicolas Bourguinat and Sylvain Venayre (eds), *Voyager en Europe de Humboldt à Stendhal: Contraintes nationales et tentations cosmopolites, 1790–1840* (Paris: Nouveau Monde Éditions, 2007).

[44] Paul Gerbod, *Voyages au pays des mangeurs de grenouilles: La France vue par les Britanniques du 18e siècle à nos jours* (Paris: Albin Michel, 1991), 28.

stinking, close and ill-built', and 'full of nothing but dirt and industry'.[45] Whatever local prominence these cities might enjoy in Normandy or the Limousin was an irrelevance; to Young they symbolized that misery and lack of technological awareness which were to be equated with backwardness, a lack of enlightenment and civility, and an absence of civilized values. He was an unapologetic advocate of modernization, critical of the values of the local elites and of their stubborn refusal to break with the past.

The inequalities that he witnessed in France seemed especially shocking. Young held forth at length on the baleful effects of noble and ecclesiastical privilege on the prosperity of the nation, and repeatedly condemned the depths of poverty in which the majority of the inhabitants lived. To one of his hosts he commented, rather accusingly, that 'his province of Brittany seemed to me to have nothing in it but privileges and poverty'.[46] For an English agronomist accustomed to see drainage schemes, enclosures, and crop rotations as the requisites of modern agriculture, much of what greeted him in France seemed wasteful and undercapitalized, ensuring that the land would not produce the quantities of grain needed to feed the population and virtually guaranteeing the annual round of undernourishment and seasonal migration which so characterized many regions of the country. Of course, Young was not a neutral observer of French farming methods; indeed, it is often difficult to avoid the impression that he wrote with an assumption of superiority that came naturally to a prosperous gentleman farmer from the Home Counties immersed in the philosophy of his age. Everything he saw tended to be compared—and generally compared unfavourably—to the comfortable life he had left back home in Bradfield.

And yet the port cities of the Atlantic coast proved a startling exception to this perception of a France that was perpetually backward and impoverished. The architecture was often formal, the buildings of stone; they were new, capturing current classical fashion in architectural design. Young's first impression of Nantes, for instance, was one of surprise and satisfaction. Barely had he pulled out of the marshy *landes* of the Loire estuary than he was in the city, and the contrast astounded him. In the rural hinterland, he had found little sign of agricultural improvement, little evidence that farmers had learned anything from the experience of the past century. Even the most basic rules of crop rotation seemed foreign to them. 'Pare and burn,' he scoffed, 'and sow wheat, then rye and then oats. Thus it is forever and ever! The same follies, the same blundering, the same ignorance; and then all the fools in the country said, as they do now, that these wastes are good for nothing!'[47] But what really shocked him was not the backwardness of Breton agricultural methods, for which he had little respect, but

---

[45] Arthur Young, *Travels in France during the Years 1787, 1788 and 1789* (Cambridge: Cambridge University Press, 1929), 113.
[46] Ibid., 131.   [47] Ibid., 132.

the fact that these antiquated practices were still to be found less than three miles from the commercial metropolis that was Nantes, where life was cultured and sophisticated. Young went to the new, lavishly appointed theatre: it was, he proclaimed, 'twice as large as Drury Lane and five times as magnificent', adding that 'within all is gold and painting'. He also took time to admire some of the city's other public buildings. 'The town has that sign of prosperity,' he remarked, 'of new buildings, which never deceives. The quarter of the Comédie is magnificent, all the streets at right angles and of white stone. I am in doubt whether the Hôtel de Henri IV is not the finest inn in Europe.'[48] His enthusiasm contrasts sharply with the contempt he showed for the miserable provision that he found for travellers in many other French provincial cities. But almost everything he was shown in Nantes seemed to command his interest. He was particularly impressed by the city's library, or *chambre de lecture*, an institution which, he discovered, was frequently to be found in France's trading ports. It was 'what we should call a book-club that does not divide its books, but forms a library'. He went on to describe the comfort that awaited its subscribers: 'There are three rooms, one for reading, another for conversation, and the third is the library; good fires in winter are provided, and wax candles.'[49] All this Young found to his taste, though he cannot forbear from adding one crucial reservation. 'What a miracle,' he sighs, 'that all this splendour and wealth of the cities of France should be so unconnected with the country!'[50] It was an unease that many Frenchmen shared.

In Bordeaux, Young also found a city that oozed prosperity and lavish consumption, and where planners and speculators were executing the most remarkable works of urban renewal, laying out new squares and central quarters that would transform the appearance of the city. He does not stint in his praise. 'The quarter of the Chapeau Rouge,' he notes, 'is truly magnificent, consisting of noble houses, built, like the rest of the city, of white hewn stone.' He admired the Place Royale, with an equestrian statue of the King at its heart; and he praised the plans that had been prepared for a whole new quarter, with some 1,800 houses, that was to be built along half a mile of the river bank where the old Château-Trompette still stood. As for the city's theatre, Young shared the view of Bordeaux's inhabitants that it was 'by far the most magnificent in France'. The superlatives do not stop there: he heaps praise on building after building, only expressing some reservations about the appearance of the Quay along the Garonne, 'which is respectable only for length and its quantity of business, neither of which, to the eye of a stranger, is of much consequence, if devoid of beauty'. Overall, however, he makes no secret of the positive impression which the city has made on him. 'Much as I had read and heard of the commerce, wealth and magnificence of this city,' he opines, 'they greatly surpassed my expectations. Paris did not answer at

[48] Ibid., 133.   [49] Ibid., 134.   [50] Ibid., 132.

all, for it is not to be compared to London; but we must not name Liverpool in competition with Bordeaux.'[51] It was a sentiment with which, he could be sure, the city fathers of Bordeaux—proudly aware of the cultural potential and commercial dynamism of their city—would not hesitate to concur.

Young's opinion of Bordeaux was widely shared by his contemporaries. Outsiders declared themselves to be impressed by both the levels of investment and the good taste of Bordeaux's merchant community. In 1783, the young François de la Rochefoucauld, son of the philanthropist Duke of La Rochefoucauld-Liancourt, took time off from his studies to undertake his own Grand Tour of the Midi. In Bordeaux, he admitted to being dazzled by the style and elegance of the architecture and by the activity of the port. 'The Chartrons', he wrote, 'is one of the most beautiful suburbs in all of Europe', stretching for several miles along the Garonne 'until you get tired passing between fine houses and a forest of masts, for there are places where you cannot see the river'. To his eyes the houses that lined the quays were 'almost all fine', built of dressed stone and to a standard height. He had, he confessed, seen nothing so beautiful in either Lyon or Marseille, while, when talking of Bordeaux's public buildings, he added that 'overall, the luxury of the buildings in Bordeaux was as impressive as anything he had seen in Paris'.[52] From a Parisian there could surely be no higher praise.

Foreign visitors came from across Europe, attracted, no doubt, by the commercial opportunities which the city offered, and most were unstinting in their praise. Whether it was the Swedish merchant, Hallman, the English Mrs Craddock, or the German Madame de la Roche, the impressions they recorded of the city were universally favourable, seeing in Bordeaux an outpost of urban civilization that reassured and surprised them, offering them both material comfort and—at least for some—levels of intellectual stimulation which they had not expected.[53] Hallman, in a letter to the Swedish botanist Carl Linnaeus, emphasized the dazzling opulence of the city and the huge sums spent on meals and balls by Bordeaux's merchant elite. Expense, he marvelled, was never spared, adding—perhaps with a touch of exaggeration—that for the average *négociant* it was nothing to serve a dinner with seventy or eighty dishes on the table.[54] Mrs Craddock, for her part, remained largely unaffected by intellectual matters; she enjoyed concerts and the theatre, appreciated luxury, and limited her comments to questions of urban elegance, or the wealth and conspicuous consumption of leading merchants and

---

[51] Ibid., 67.

[52] Jean Marchand (ed.), *Voyages en France de François de la Rochefoucauld, 1781–83* (Paris: Honoré Champion, 1938), 111–12; Paul Butel and Jean-Pierre Poussou (eds), *La vie quotidienne à Bordeaux au 18e siècle* (Paris: Hachette, 1980), 30–1.

[53] Maurice Meaudre de Lapouyade, 'Impressions d'une Allemande à Bordeaux en 1785', *Revue historique de Bordeaux*, 4 (1911), 168; Paul Courteault, 'Bordeaux au temps de Tourny d'après un correspondant de Linné', *Revue historique de Bordeaux*, 10 (1917), 134.

[54] Butel and Poussou, *La vie quotidienne à Bordeaux au 18e siècle*, 263.

their families.[55] Madame de la Roche was the most observant of the three. She was a woman of some education who had read the works of the *philosophes* and liked to see Bordeaux as the city of Montaigne and Montesquieu. Though she was German, from near Mannheim, she knew Bordeaux well as a friend of the Bethmann family, Frankfurt merchants who had established themselves in Bordeaux and to whom she made regular visits. Bordeaux did not disappoint here. She spent several years in the city, tightly integrated into the merchant aristocracy, and got to know Montesquieu's château at Labrède and the Montesquieu family. Hers were more than the casual scribblings of a passing tourist; she viewed the city through the eyes of its merchant elite.[56]

What impressed these visitors was less the city's historical monuments than the Bordeaux of the eighteenth century, the streets and squares that had been built during the previous decades to accommodate the merchant community, and which seemed to express the city's commercial dynamism and to epitomize a civic pride which only prosperity could bestow. This pride was not confined to the commercial elite. It extended to high society, to ballrooms and concert halls, art and theatre. Bordeaux was a cosmopolitan city, with, in particular, a well-established German merchant community; it was curious, noted the young Arthur Schopenhauer when he visited the city in 1804, to hear so much German spoken. For him it was a symptom of a more general cultural sophistication and love of the arts. The Grand Théâtre, he thought, was a 'sumptuous' building, 'massive, superb', the roof 'supported by magnificent columns surrounded by arcades and decorated with twelve statues'. But his enthusiasm was somewhat dimmed when he had seen the play. 'It is astonishing,' he confided, 'that a town like Bordeaux does not have better actors.'[57]

Other west-coast ports made a less favourable impression on the visitor, one that was often vitiated by a sense of economic stagnation. At Lorient Arthur Young was more concerned with the inadequacy of the hostelry where he had to stay and the poor stabling provided for his mare. The town's commerce was in decline following the loss of the East India Company monopoly under Louis XVI. Yet he still has words of praise for the port, and willingly concedes that 'the town is modern, and regularly built, the streets diverge in rays from the gate, and are crossed by others at right angles, broad, handsomely built, and well paved'. It was a Company town, which meant that it had been logically planned, while the large warehouses built by the Company to store the produce of the Indies gave the port true distinction: 'they are', Young notes, 'of several storeys, and all vaulted in stone, and of vast extent'; they 'speak', he adds, of 'the royal munificence from

---

[55] Paul Courteault, 'Les impressions d'une Anglaise à Bordeaux', *Revue historique de Bordeaux*, 4 (1911), 9–23.

[56] Desgraves, *Voyageurs à Bordeaux*, 53–4.

[57] Desgraves, *Voyageurs à Bordeaux*, 110–14.

which they arose'.[58] And in Bayonne, though he is aware that silting has caused problems at the mouth of the harbour and that trade is not booming as it had earlier in the century, it is again the fabric of the city rather than the sluggishness of its commerce that holds his attention. 'Bayonne,' he says, 'is by far the prettiest town I have seen in France; the houses are not only well built of stone, but the streets are wide, and there are many openings which, though not regular squares, have a good effect.' He is particularly impressed by the view from the bridge and the appearance of the houses that fronted the river. The promenade, shaded by trees against the hot summer sun, elicits his particular praise, and Bayonne's women are 'the handsomest I have seen in France'. Unlike in the towns of the interior, where 'hard labour destroys both person and complexion', they were 'clean and pretty', with 'the bloom of health' on their cheeks.[59] The ports along the Atlantic coast were privileged indeed, their inhabitants enjoying levels of education and culture denied to those whose lives were spent in the small administrative and clerical centres that characterized so much of provincial France.

Young was undoubtedly the most analytical of the many visitors to the west coast ports, and the writer who left the fullest account of his impressions. However, he was not alone in admiring the architecture of these commercial cities, or of expressing some astonishment at the levels of prosperity he observed. But could that prosperity last? In particular, could it survive ten years of revolution and maritime war, when trade was increasingly disrupted and merchant ships were left at the mercy of English privateers prowling the Atlantic sea lanes? Nothing was less certain. Under the Revolution, the inflow of visitors dried up as repression increased and tourists stayed away. But at the beginning of the nineteenth century, encouraged by the truce in the war that was heralded by the Peace of Amiens, visitors began to return. Within a year, nearly 20,000 British travellers came to France, resuming the tradition of the Grand Tour that had been brutally interrupted by the revolution. Some came to the commercial cities of the West, though few left diaries or memoirs to reflect their feelings or leave behind their impressions. Those who did tended to talk of the Revolution as a tragedy, its consequence the decline and ruin of commercial trade and the cities that depended on it. They noted the appearance of neglect and desolation around the docks and talked of the damage done to local industry. Port cities that had prospered on the back of Atlantic commerce now seemed to face only decay, with their docks idle, their industry in decline, and their population shrinking. Foreign merchants who passed through registered their shock that so much prosperity and culture should have been lost in such a short period of time. By 1800, they were already looking back nostalgically on a world they had lost.

---

[58] Young, *Travels in France*, 129.   [59] Ibid., 62.

3

The Years of Economic Prosperity

Contemporaries did not hesitate to contrast the prosperity of the Ancien Régime with the decay of the revolutionary years. They painted a picture of the eighteenth century as an age of opportunity, when the Atlantic ports had become by-words for commercial success and the quaysides resonated to the cries of dock workers and stevedores filling the holds of ships setting out for the Indies. But all that, they insisted, was now lost. A golden age had been swept away, leaving merchants ruined, ships idle, and the domestic economy of thousands of families destroyed. In the nineteenth century, investment would be diverted elsewhere, to the booming textile towns of the north of France and the coal- and iron-rich provinces of the east. The people of the west and south-west felt neglected, and this led to an outpouring of nostalgia for the monarchy that goes far to explain Bordeaux's enthusiastic embrace of the Bourbons after 1814 and the continued fascination of historians and collectors in the city for the Restoration period which followed.[1] The monarchy was praised for its encouragement of enterprise, for the naval protection it had provided for the merchant community, and for a colonial policy that had opened up European markets for colonial products. All this, it seemed, had been lost in the chaos of the revolutionary decade.

Taken over the century, commercial growth in the port cities of France's Atlantic coast certainly looks impressive, especially in the decades leading up to the French Revolution. Of course there were discrepancies among them. Not all grew at the same rate, or experienced the same boom years; not all attracted the same entrepreneurial spirit, or showed the same taste for risk. But the general picture is clear: the century saw an expansion in Atlantic commerce that was reflected in higher profits, greater port activity, higher tonnages and volumes of trade, and which—albeit briefly—saw the wealthiest of the port cities, Bordeaux and Nantes, grow at a faster rate than Paris itself. So in the West Indies, against a backcloth of general expansion, volumes of trade with France fluctuated. The century saw a relative decline in the importance of Martinique compared to its Caribbean neighbour, Guadeloupe, and, more importantly, a spectacular rise in the position of Saint-Domingue among France's Caribbean sugar islands. Sugar was the most profitable of all colonial products, the one that revolutionized taste

---

[1] Jacqueline Du Pasquier, *Raymond Jeanvrot, une passion royaliste: naissance d'une collection bordelaise* (Bordeaux: Musée des arts décoratifs, 2007).

not only in France but throughout the European world.[2] It lay at the heart of the
plantation economy, but that does not mean that the colonies were primarily
rural, or that the sugar plantation was the centre of Caribbean social life; for
France's West Indian colonies also produced a flourishing urban culture, especially during the key growth years of the second half of the eighteenth century.[3] In
particular, Saint-Domingue's two main cities, the commercial city of Cap Français
(more commonly known as Le Cap) and the administrative capital of Port-au-
Prince, were urban centres of some size and importance. By 1789, Le Cap
numbered around 15,000 people and provided the link to the outside world for
some 170 sugar estates and 274 coffee plantations; Port-au-Prince was perhaps
half that size. Both had the range of amenities, and much of the ambience, that one
might find in a major provincial French town. As David Geggus explains, 'with an
uneasy mixture of military and civil government, large theatres, Masonic temples,
billiard halls, bathhouses, a fine colonial highway, and growing though recent
systems of fountains and aqueducts, the two towns were quite distinctively
French.'[4] They were also recognizably urban, places where a Frenchman from
the metropole could expect to find the amenities he needed for a civilized lifestyle.

Both Le Cap and Port-au-Prince were cities in the throes of rapid growth
during the last twenty years of the Ancien Régime, a growth that was reflected
in the new quarters that were being opened up and the houses that were con-
structed in the city centres and in suburbs stretching back toward the mountains.
These houses were often of a single storey, especially in Port-au-Prince where
people had lurid memories of the destruction caused by earthquakes at regular
intervals across the century (there had been five earthquakes in all, in 1701, 1713,
1734, 1770, and, most terribly, in 1751, when more than half the city had been
razed to the ground). Many of the new buildings were built of wood and to a
colonial design, with covered galleries leading to internal courtyards where people
could meet to socialize, offering some protection from the hot tropical sun. The
more luxurious of them would be equipped with wells from which dwellers could
pump drinking water, another prerequisite of a comfortable lifestyle in the
Caribbean.[5] Such houses represented a rich investment and could command
substantial rents; they were not built for the more modest inhabitants, who were
increasingly forced to live farther out from the centre of the cities. A study of
notarial records has allowed Paul Butel to identify the groups with money in Le

---

[2] Jean Meyer, *Histoire du sucre* (Paris: Desjonquères, 1989), *passim.*

[3] Anne Pérotin-Dumon, *La ville aux îles, la ville dans l'île: Basse-Terre et Pointe-à-Pitre, Guadeloupe,
1650–1820* (Paris: Karthala, 2000), 13–16.

[4] David Geggus, 'The Major Port Towns of Saint-Domingue in the Later Eighteenth Century', in
Franklin W. Knight and Peggy K. Liss (eds), *Atlantic Port Cities: Economy, Culture and Society in the
Atlantic World, 1650–1800* (Knoxville: University of Tennessee Press, 1991), 87–92.

[5] Philippe Loupès, 'Le modèle urbain à Saint-Domingue au 18e siècle: la maison et l'habitat au Cap-
Français et à Port-au-Prince', in Paul Butel and L. M. Cullen (eds), *Cities and Merchants: French and
Irish Perspectives on Urban Development, 1500–1900* (Dublin: Trinity College, 1986), 165–79.

Cap, the groups who were capable of paying high rents for their housing and who would benefited most from the boom years from 1740 to 1780. Among those renting prime properties or who owned the capital necessary for purchase were merchants (unsurprisingly), lawyers (for the legal process was particularly onerous in the Antilles), staff in the colonial administration, and plantation owners who chose to invest part of their profit in urban real estate. Free men of colour figured prominently among them, a sign of their increasing wealth and greater social aspiration. Also significant were the purchases of townhouses by absentee owners, often plantation owners who had left their plantation in the hands of an estate manager to return, or retire, to France.[6]

So in Guadeloupe, city life was sufficiently varied and sophisticated to appeal to men who had been raised in France, and they came in many different roles: as merchants, ships' chandlers, shopkeepers, tradesmen, or colonial administrators. It had not always been so: Basse-Terre had been founded as a fortified trading post, which by the second half of the eighteenth century, thanks mainly to the expansion of trade within the Americas and the maintenance of strong cultural ties with France, had developed a discrete urban culture of its own. Its raison d'être remained, of course, that of every colonial port, as a service node for the Atlantic economy; but, as Anne Pérotin-Dumon shows, it was not purely through its trading function that it had grown and developed its particular urban contours. Basse-Terre was shaped by the waves of immigration it received, both white and black, from France and from Africa; by the needs of military defence and colonial administration; by the different requirements of colonial trade in war and peace; and by the range of crafts and trades to which it was home.[7] By the end of the Ancien Régime, the city not only had schools and medical facilities to cater for the health and education of the inhabitants, but also boasted shops that sold fine clothes and jewellery, carpets and furnishings, paintings and decoration. It offered inns and meeting halls, theatres and masonic lodges, printing presses and bookshops. From 1775, the island had a regular newspaper in the form of the *Gazette de la Guadeloupe* and published various periodicals and almanacs. These were features of other Caribbean islands, too, in both the British and the Hispanic world, creating a creole culture that was shared by its different inhabitants and had at its root an Atlantic world that was united by colonial commerce and a taste for urban civilization.[8]

Back in France, trade with Saint-Domingue had become by the end of the Ancien Régime the single most important source of commercial wealth for the

---

[6] Paul Butel, 'Le modèle urbain à Saint-Domingue au 18ᵉ siècle: l'investissement immobilier dans les villes de Saint-Domingue', in Butel and Cullen (eds), *Cities and Merchants*, 149–51.

[7] Anne Pérotin-Dumon, 'Cabotage, Contraband and Corsairs: The Port Cities of Guadeloupe and their Inhabitants, 1650–1800', in Franklin W. Knight and Peggy K. Liss (eds), *Atlantic Port Cities: Economy, Culture and Society in the Atlantic World, 1650–1800*, 58.

[8] Pérotin-Dumon, *La ville aux îles, la ville dans l'île*, 640.

ports of the Atlantic coast.[9] But it was not the only source, as Bordeaux's success makes clear. Ships sailing from the Gironde estuary traded with cities in Germany and the Baltic, with Spain and Portugal, with Ireland, Scandinavia, and beyond. Bordeaux merchants had commercial contacts and agreements with shippers and agents in ports across Europe, while merchants from across the continent flocked to Bordeaux to establish a commercial presence in the city. Bordeaux had a rich hinterland, which provided the port with exports of grain, flour, and wine, as well as more particular regional specialities like prunes from the Agenais.[10] Its merchants had long grown affluent on the profits of the wine trade, especially with markets in northern Europe that had been developed since the late Middle Ages and would continue to flourish across most of the century. But it was the opening up of the Atlantic world during the eighteenth century, and the expansion of commerce with France's possessions in the Antilles in particular, that transformed Bordeaux from a regional port within Europe into a centre of world trade with lucrative investments on both sides of the Atlantic. By the second half of the eighteenth century, a major part of the port's exports of wine and flour was being despatched to the Caribbean to serve the needs of a fast-growing colonial population, a market that Bordeaux was uniquely well-positioned to capture. The tonnage of the goods exported increased dramatically over the century: for wines, for instance, it increased from an average of 1,800 tons in 1713–14 to 27,700 tons in 1787–9. In terms of value, the figures are equally impressive. In 1788, Bordeaux exported to Saint-Domingue alone wines worth around 4.5 million *livres* and flour worth 4.8 million.[11] These products filled the holds of ships on their long voyage westwards and helped ensure the profitability of the return trip. They go far to explain Bordeaux's dominant position in direct trade with the islands and the seeming reluctance of many merchants to send their vessels to the African coast.

The heterogeneity of Bordeaux's merchant community, and the prominent part played by foreign merchants in the business of the port, can be seen as a symptom of economic dynamism, of a community seizing the advantages offered by colonial trade. And over the century colonial traffic did increase dramatically, though Bordeaux appeared relatively slow in exploiting the opportunities offered by the Caribbean, and reluctant to move out of more traditional markets in pursuit of West Indian riches. The fact that it was new and often foreign-owned companies that first traded with Martinique, Guadeloupe, and Saint-Domingue betrays a

---

[9] Paul Butel, *Les négociants bordelais, l'Europe et les Îles au dix-huitième siècle* (Paris: Aubier, 1974), 31–5.

[10] Christian Bouyer, *Au temps des Isles: les Antilles françaises de Louis XIII à Napoléon III* (Paris: le Grand Livre du mois, 2005), 177.

[11] Jean-Pierre Poussou, 'Le dynamisme de l'économie française sous Louis XVI', *Revue économique*, 40 (1989), 970; Paul Butel, 'La croissance commerciale bordelaise dans la seconde moitié du 18e siècle' (Lille: Service de reproduction des thèses de l'université, 1973), 210.

certain prudence among established merchants in the port, who continued to rely on their profitable markets for wine in northern Europe. It was not until the second half of the century, and particularly after the Seven Years' War, that Bordeaux became a major Atlantic port. Nantes was the port most prepared to embrace risk, staking all on the Americas, while Bordeaux's merchant elite preferred to spread their activity across Europe and the world. The eighteenth century saw commercial vessels setting out from Bordeaux for many parts of the globe, among them India, the East Indies, and China. After 1783, there was a cautious enthusiasm for trade with the new United States, though the majority of the ships coming into Bordeaux from American ports were American, not French.[12] By this time the Caribbean, and especially Saint-Domingue, was clearly seen as the most lucrative destination for Bordeaux's high-seas fleet. Yet even in the last years before the Revolution, when Bordeaux's stake in the Caribbean trade was at its peak, its share was little different from its share in French colonial trade as a whole: in 1789, the city fitted out some 40 per cent of French shipping leaving for Saint-Domingue, and around a third of those arriving back from the islands.[13]

If Bordeaux flourished in these years, it was because it succeeded in establishing itself as a centre for the lucrative entrepôt trade between France's American colonies and the European continent. Colonial traffic almost tripled between 1749 and 1788, from some 36,000 tons to more than 87,000 tons when measured by weight. When expressed in the value of colonial goods imported, that growth was even more impressive, rising from a figure of 20 million *livres* before 1750 to 163 million twenty years later, with tobacco from the southern United States complementing the sugar, coffee, and indigo imported from Saint-Domingue. Bordeaux's fortunes cannot, however, be measured by colonial imports alone. The city's wealth stemmed also from the re-export of colonial produce to large parts of northern Europe, a trade which was largely undertaken by ships of other European countries: British, German, Danish, and Dutch. Much of this trade passed through Amsterdam, then later through Hamburg and the Hanseatic ports; and Bordeaux merchants had been pioneers in trade with Russia, conducted through St Petersburg and Archangel.[14] By the later eighteenth century, indeed, Bordeaux had become home to a substantial colony of immigrants from Hamburg and other Baltic ports who were engaged in the re-export of colonial produce to their own countries. Among them were the commercial agents who represented Hanseatic merchant houses, some of whom, like J.-J. Bethmann, were to become successful

---

[12] Silvia Marzagalli, *Bordeaux et les Etats-Unis, 1776–1815. Politique et stratégies négociantes dans la genèse d'un réseau commercial* (Geneva: Droz, 2015), 62.

[13] François Crouzet, 'Le commerce de Bordeaux', in Pariset (ed), *Bordeaux au dix-huitième siècle*, 223.

[14] Peter Voss, 'Le commerce bordelais et la route d'Arkhangelsk à la fin du dix-septième siècle', in Silvia Marzagalli and Hubert Bonin (eds), *Négoce, ports et océans, 16ᵉ–20ᵉ siècles* (Bordeaux: Presses Universitaires de Bordeaux, 2000), 135–47.

merchants in their own right.[15] These two forms of commerce—a colonial trade dominated by native Bordeaux merchants and a European trade that was largely devolved to foreign shippers—grew apace and were mutually supportive, together generating the commercial dynamism on which Bordeaux's growth was largely dependent.[16]

That dynamism was reflected in the heterogeneity of Bordeaux's merchant elite, composed as it was of Protestants, Catholics, Christians, and Jews. In religious terms, Bordeaux was a notably tolerant city, prepared to integrate outsiders and free from the heritage of religious acrimony that had been engendered by the Wars of Religion and which was so evident in La Rochelle. If some had been born in the city, others had migrated there from across the commercial world, from Germany, the Baltic, England, Ireland, Spain, and Portugal, as well as from towns and cities across France. Protestants, it is true, were not admitted to public office under the Crown and had become accustomed to conceal their religious feelings following the revocation of the Edict of Nantes. But after mid-century, when there was no prohibition on worship or expressions of Protestant identity, individual Protestants could choose how to react. If they were strongly committed to their families and to achieving commercial success, not all cared deeply about the religion of their forefathers. Some rallied to the Protestant faith and attended religious services; others showed a marked indifference, or participated with discretion.[17] What united them far more was their focus on the commercial opportunities which their presence on the Bordeaux waterfront afforded and the need to defend these against outside competition. In 1789, for instance, when a meeting of the entire mercantile community was called by the city's Chamber of commerce, more than 500 turned up, men of different religious groupings and national identities, all equally concerned about the implications for their fortunes of the revolution that was being prepared.[18]

The colonies of foreign merchants in Bordeaux were replicated by colonies of French merchants elsewhere in Europe who formed commercial networks of their own, often based on national and friendship groups. In London, for example, there was an important French presence among City traders, many of them Protestants and Jews who had links with the co-religionists in Bordeaux and who could provide them with valuable contacts in London's commercial circles. Religious affinity certainly appears to have been a significant factor in forging these friendships. A good example is Theodore Thomas, a Protestant and the

---

[15] François Crouzet, 'La croissance économique', in François-Georges Pariset (ed), *Bordeaux au 18e siècle*, 215.

[16] Paul Butel, 'Le trafic européen de Bordeaux, de la Guerre d'Amérique à la Révolution', *Annales du Midi*, 78 (1966), 41.

[17] Séverine Pacteau de Luze, *Les protestants de Bordeaux* (Bordeaux: Mollat, 1999), 111.

[18] AD Gironde, C4438, 2 March 1789; Alan Forrest, *The Revolution in Provincial France. Aquitaine, 1789–1799* (Oxford: Oxford University Press, 1996), 21.

commercial agent through whom the leading Bordeaux merchant, Jean Pellet, worked to raise funds on the London market. When Pellet travelled to London, he would often stay with his commissioners: they became friends, much more than just business associates, and they provided an entrée into London's commercial circles. By 1739, Thomas had risen to be the managing director of a London insurance company that did much of its business in Bordeaux. He was also related by marriage to wealthy figures in the English financial world, where banking and insurance companies could offer better terms than their counterparts in Paris. The links between merchant houses in Bordeaux and financiers in London were a major element in the financial structures the city relied upon at the end of the eighteenth century.[19]

Though Nantes' position as a major port was not in doubt in the eighteenth century, its fortunes were less assured than those of Bordeaux, in part because its reliance on the slave trade, and on the heavy, less manoeuvrable ships which slavers used, made it more exposed to attack by enemy warships in times of war. At the beginning of the century, Nantes' status, even within Brittany, was unremarkable: it was the second port of Brittany for overseas trade, considerably behind Saint-Malo, which enjoyed an outstanding period of prosperity between around 1680 and the end of the War of Spanish Succession in 1715. But the opening up of the colonial market had brought dramatic expansion as Nantes benefited from the explosion of demand for sugar, tobacco, and other colonial products, and by 1730 it had become the most important commercial port in France. But this proved short-lived. By the eve of the Revolution, Nantes had regressed, and though it was still a major slaving port, the other forms of commerce that had sustained it had declined. By 1789, Bordeaux had established a clear lead, as the figures for the value of trade in each port make clear. Bordeaux enjoyed 41 per cent of French commerce by value, compared to 18 per cent for Nantes and 17 per cent each for Le Havre and Marseille.[20]

The statistics of commercial voyages from Nantes in the second half of the century have been closely analysed by Jean Meyer. He notes that during periods of warfare at sea the activity of the port would suddenly fall away, only to resume with increased vigour once peace was signed. Between the Treaty of Augsburg and the outbreak of the Seven Years' War, for instance, levels of trade were maintained with around sixty or eighty voyages *en droiture* each year: the figures for 1752, 1753, and 1754 were seventy-eight, eighty-three, and seventy-nine respectively. The outbreak of war caused the number of departures to collapse, with only one voyage out of Nantes in 1761 and three the following year. Yet, almost as soon as peace was announced, trade picked up again. From only three voyages in 1762,

[19] Paul Butel, 'Armateurs bordelais et commissionnaires londoniens au 18e siècle', *Revue historique de Bordeaux et de la Gironde* (1974), 152, 161.

[20] Crouzet, 'Le commerce de Bordeaux', 204.

activity rallied so that there were sixty-six in 1763 and 110 the following year. Though figures rose and fell from year to year, the general trend was maintained, of profitable trading conditions in the peacetime years of the early 1770s, followed by a slump in the American War (though never on the same scale as the virtual wipe-out of the early 1760s), then recovery, or at least a partial recovery, after 1783. By the end of the monarchy, however, Nantes' relative position in Atlantic trade had weakened, and Meyer argues that the apparent ease with which the port recovered after each period of war was deceptive, as the losses suffered were such that merchants were forced to change their priorities and to abandon parts of their activity. Fishing was largely left to Saint-Malo after mid-century, while Nantes' contribution to privateering expeditions during the second half of the century was of little importance. Scarcely a dozen ships were fitted out as corsairs during the whole of the Seven Years' War, while in the War of American Independence the number was only three.[21] If the American War did not decimate Nantes' Atlantic trade to the same degree as the Seven Years' War, the reprise afterwards was less imposing, too. Recovery was proving ever more difficult.

War and peace were the principal determinants of maritime activity in Atlantic waters during the eighteenth century, and with good reason. Almost as soon as war was declared, Britain profited from its naval strength to blockade the French coast and cut off the principal shipping channels, and the French ports began to suffer serious losses of ships, cargoes, and crews. Merchants, ships' captains, and insurers alike took fright, and responded by cutting back on colonial voyages. In Bordeaux, for instance, where 154 vessels had sailed for the Americas in 1754 and another 147 in 1755, the statistics thereafter tell a story of fear, caution, and diminished activity: 103 departures in 1756, thirty-eight in 1757, then four and eight in 1758 and 1759. Ships stayed in port to avoid capture or sinking; so the reduced number of sailings could expect to be reflected in a smaller number of losses. The figures for Nantes in the Seven Years' War bear this out. The largest number of vessels lost—twelve—was recorded early in the war, in 1757. Thereafter numbers dropped to single figures: nine Nantes ships were lost in 1758, two in 1759, five in 1760, and then only a solitary vessel in each of 1761 and 1762.[22] With few vessels leaving port, there were scant pickings for the frigates of the Royal Navy or for the privateers of the English Channel coast.

For most of the eighteenth century, Nantes' merchant community had shown an almost stubborn spirit of particularism and a distrust of central authority that was constant from the reign of Louis XIV to the Revolution. This spirit was especially evident over the question of collective representation and in their reluctance to create a chamber of commerce like those in other commercial cities.

[21] Jean Meyer, *L'armement nantais dans la deuxième moitié du 18ᵉ siècle* (Paris: SEVPEN, 1969), 82–9.

[22] Patrick Villiers, 'Le commerce colonial pendant la Guerre de Sept Ans', *Enquêtes et documents*, 17 (1990), 32.

Chambers of commerce were established, and actively encouraged, by the King, whose decree of 1701 authorized their creation in all major port cities. The advantages were spelt out in the decree. The chambers, it was stated, could represent merchant interests through a single body; they would allow them to speak with a collective voice; and they provided the community with a simple structure and the funding they would require. Other commercial cities had responded favourably, Lyon setting up its chamber in 1702, Rouen and Toulouse in 1705, La Rochelle in 1710, Lille in 1714, and the monarchy had made it clear that any application from Nantes would be approved. But Nantes demurred, insisting that it be allowed to retain its old (and many would say archaic) system of *juges-consultes*, on the grounds that this was a guarantee of their autonomy from outside interference. As late as 1791, in an address to the city council, the merchants stood by their position. They had, they said, never been forced into any form of corporation, nor were they subject to any direct ministerial regulation, as other towns had been that had set up a chamber of commerce. In truth, they said, choosing their words carefully to assuage the revolutionary authorities, though they had been pressurized many times to fall into line by a succession of royal ministers, 'the merchants of this city have always rejected the idea with that liberty and energy which they maintained under the former despotism, protected by those rights which at the time we were pleased to call provincial privileges'.[23] Theirs was a spirit of defiance that betrayed a deep-seated distrust of authority and a fear of change. It was an attitude that also affected their approach to commerce and to the trading conditions brought on by war. The merchants felt that they had a lot to lose, and much to defend.

The eighteenth century had not only brought prosperity to the west-coast ports; it had also conferred unprecedented prestige on an elite of merchants, ship-owners, and insurers who had established themselves as a sort of commercial nobility, respected for their style and consumerism as much as for the profits they generated. Established merchant families were not only looking after their profits; they were also concerned to maintain their social pre-eminence and their place in urban society. Though they were careful to avoid flaunting their wealth, they lived in large houses, maintained country estates, were leading figures in the commercial and cultural life of their town, and they did not want to run the risk of imperilling their social position by courting dishonour or bankruptcy. They thought and acted as a social elite, as men who might aspire, in the most favourable conditions, to be granted titles of nobility by the king, to live nobly on their country estates in rural Brittany, along the Loire valley, or in the vineyards

---

[23] AD Loire-Atlantique, L-A 6JJ 36, minutes of the Société d'Agriculture et de Commerce, 21 December 1791; Maurice Quénet, 'Le Général du commerce de Nantes: Essai sur les institutions corporatives coutumières des négociants au 18ᵉ siècle (thèse de doctorat, Université de Nantes, 1973), 22–5.

of the Médoc. For by the mid-eighteenth century there was nothing about commercial activity that would disqualify them from holding noble titles, and there were in all the great Atlantic ports a handful of merchants—a 'noblesse commerçante' or 'noblesse d'affaires' in the language of Guy Richard[24]—who could lay claim, at least in a personal capacity, to all the privileges of nobility. It was in Rouen that their number was highest, with fifty-five of the 165 merchants of the town claiming nobility in 1785; Bordeaux's capitation rolls of 1777 listed thirty-one *anoblis* out of a merchant population of 455; in La Rochelle, Le Havre, and Marseille their numbers were much lower and the desire for social elevation and privilege less evident.[25] They were in many ways an incoherent grouping, some emerging from the local bourgeoisie, others—most notably in Bordeaux— scions of an international merchant community. But the fact that some were to be found in all the principal Atlantic ports is evidence of the status that wealthy merchants now enjoyed and of the social heights which economic success could bring.

The bonds that tied the merchant elite to the local aristocracy were not all one-way, the result of purchase or ennoblement for service to the king by merchants whose coffers were bulging from the profits of trade. For if merchants might seek the respectability that came with a noble lifestyle, some at least among the nobility aspired to make their fortune from commerce. During the eighteenth century there had been a long and sometimes bitter debate between those who believed that the nobility's function was to fight and serve the king, and whose who, like Voltaire, castigated the French aristocracy for showing an open contempt for trade and admired the way the younger sons of British peers openly embraced capitalism.[26] The Enlightenment sided strongly with the modernizers, culminating in 1756 in the publication, in both Paris and London, of the abbé Coyer's uncompromising tract on *La noblesse commerçante*, which castigated the aristocracy for their profligacy and demanded that they start to make a useful contribution to France's economy.[27] Coyer's book could not have been more explicit in contrasting commercial enterprise and aristocratic torpor. Its frontispiece depicted an impoverished nobleman about to board the merchant ship that would take him to future riches, looking down on the coat of arms and titles of nobility that he would leave behind. What good, he asked, could be served by such baubles, by what he now saw as a heap of useless glory?[28]

---

[24] Guy Richard, *Noblesse d'affaires au 18e siècle* (Paris: Armand Colin, 1974), *passim*.
[25] Ibid., 93–5.
[26] William Doyle, *Aristocracy and its Enemies in the Age of Revolution* (Oxford: Oxford University Press, 2009), 50.
[27] Gabriel François Coyer, *La noblesse commerçante* (London and Paris, 1756).
[28] Martha L. Keber, *Seas of Gold, Seas of Cotton: Christophe Poulain DuBignon of Jeckyll Island* (Athens, GA: University of Georgia Press, 2002), 1–2.

His book pointed to a very different future. And as the century progressed, and more and more nobles turned their hand to commercial activities to boost their fortunes, so the longstanding prejudices against commerce began to fade as the threat of public humiliation through *dérogeance* was withdrawn. From 1669, indeed, commerce on the high seas had been specifically excluded by royal edict from the general prohibition on noble mercantile activity.[29] For many, whether younger sons who were unlikely to inherit the family estates, impoverished *hobereaux* barely able to make ends meet, or young nobles driven by social ambition and economic aspiration, the lure of Atlantic commerce proved too strong to resist. Though the stigma of commerce dissolved only gradually and many nobles continued to profess their distaste for commerce, noble culture was changing. Others saw little reason to abandon the wealth of transatlantic commerce to commoners now that shipping and insurance had become respectable areas of activity. Only retail trade and inshore navigation were forbidden as a cultural change took place that allowed nobles to reinvent themselves as capitalists, merchants, and entrepreneurs.[30]

Across the region, some nobles responded by investing in trade and commerce. The gravitational pull towards the Atlantic port cities was strong throughout the West and was especially marked in Brittany, a region with large numbers of impoverished nobles and a high proportion of poor and unyielding agricultural land. Brittany was a land of sailors and ships' captains where the sea played an important part in the lives of the community, where the small ports of the Breton coast had provided both the French navy and the merchant marine with their officers and crews for many generations. The sea and seamanship were in Breton blood, and for the merchants and ship-owners of eighteenth-century Nantes, the hinterland of Brittany was a valued source of seamanship on which they liberally drew as the prospect of Atlantic wealth opened invitingly before them. Nobles were not immune to the call of commerce—or, indeed, of empire, as some joined the mercantile community in sending their sons not just to Nantes, but on to the cities of the French Caribbean, to Pointe-à-Pitre, Basse-Terre, Port-au-Prince, Le Cap, or Les Cayes. For many of them poverty was the determinant factor, the destiny from which, despite their noble status, there was no escape at home in Brittany. They belonged to what Martha Keber describes as the 'impoverished gentry', whom respectability and social status impeded from gaining the levels of family income they required. Though social hierarchies were loosening, she argues, they had few choices. 'Their station in life limited them to the professions of law, the military and the church, yet noble descent counted for little without the

---

[29] *Édit portant que les nobles pourront faire le commerce de mer sans déroger à la noblesse. Vérifié en Parlement le 13 août 1669* (Paris, 1669).

[30] Guy Chaussinand-Nogaret, *The French Nobility in the Eighteenth Century* (Cambridge: Cambridge University Press, 1985), 84–116.

money and patronage to establish a young man in an acceptable profession. As a result,' she concludes, 'many well-born men languished on their estates, dependent on the productivity of their tenants, and fell year by year closer to penury.'[31] A minority, doubtless chosen from among the more enterprising and impatient among them, headed for Nantes to answer the call of the sea.

But it is perhaps too tempting to equate prosperity with the Ancien Régime as a system of government or with the eighteenth century as years of unbroken harmony. For if across the century there were periods of dazzling commercial success, there were also deep troughs that saw profits slump and rows of merchant ships lie idle. By the mid-century, it is true, France's Atlantic outreach seemed unchallengeable. In the early 1750s, the Breton and Norman ports still controlled the Newfoundland fisheries and the Canada trade, while the market in colonial produce with the West and East Indies was booming. It was easy to be optimistic about the future. But the French faced serious competition in these markets, and not only from Britain. Holland had acquired colonies in the Petites Antilles, while Denmark's Guinea Company had also established a foothold in the Caribbean in the islands of Saint-Jean and Sainte-Croix and had built sugar refineries in Copenhagen from which to supply much of the Baltic.[32] As for Britain, which was less concerned with European dynastic issues than France and arguably more commercial in its approach to foreign policy, it fought a succession of wars as much for trade and colonial expansion as for political advantage within Europe. In what became a keenly fought contest for imperial dominance, France's colonial possessions were prizes to be seized and haggled over as a precondition for peace. During the frequent periods of conflict, colonies were no longer seen as a peripheral issue; they had become a *casus belli* in their own right. In wartime many commercial houses stopped sending cargoes across the Atlantic, and trading conditions deteriorated to the point where one historian can suggest that all transatlantic commerce, and the slave trade in particular, had become 'incompatible with the state of maritime war'.[33]

Commercial growth was not steady and measured, but spasmodic, determined by external circumstance and by France's capacity to keep her sea lanes open in the face of repeated blockades and raids on commercial shipping. Given Britain's naval supremacy, there were limits to what the French navy could do to defend its interests, and during long periods the government found itself unable to respond in any meaningful way to British acts of aggression. During the war of the Austrian Succession, for instance, the French naval minister, Maurepas, lacked the resources to offer meaningful resistance and was able only to send out small

---

[31] Keber, *Seas of Gold, Seas of Cotton*, 12.   [32] Bouyer, *Au temps des Isles*, 60.
[33] Karine Perraud, 'L'armement maritime nantais en période de guerre: étude de la traite et de la course' (mémoire de maîtrise, Université de Nantes, 1999), 225.

squadrons of patrol vessels and the occasional frigate to patrol the French coast. If Britain determined to attack France's colonial possessions, there was little the French navy could do to deter her. Indeed, such was Britain's naval superiority that any French response could be little more than symbolic.[34]

Over the century, wars with Britain were increasingly focused on the colonies, as the British targeted France's overseas possessions and sought to weaken her grip on empire. In India, in the Caribbean, and off the African coast, British ships sought to intercept French merchant shipping and to seize or destroy French settlements and trading posts. During the Seven Years' War, for instance, the British navy effectively established British dominance of the Atlantic. In 1759, Britain seized Guadeloupe and held it for four years. In 1762, France's other island in the Lesser Antilles, Martinique, fell. And though these islands were returned to France under the terms of the Treaty of Paris in the following year, this concession came at a price. In order to retain her colonies in the Caribbean and her share of the lucrative sugar trade, France had to renounce control of most of her possessions in North America and lost territories in India and the Indian Ocean. France, in other words, emerged from the War with her colonial strength undermined and her reputation in the Atlantic world greatly diminished. It took a costly intervention on the side of the Americans in the War of American Independence to regain her Caribbean colonies and to restore her credibility as a major player in the West Indian trade.[35]

Commercial prosperity was a by-product of peace. The evidence here speaks for itself. In periods of peace French shipping prospered, with increasing numbers of vessels and a vastly larger tonnage involved in Atlantic commerce. When, on the other hand, France was at war—and most especially when she was engaged in a naval war with Britain—that growth slowed or was dramatically reversed. In each of the three major maritime wars with Britain—the War of the Austrian Succession, the Seven Years' War, and the War of American Independence—levels of colonial commerce slumped as merchant ships became legitimate targets for enemy corsairs and privateers, licensed by their governments to carry arms and seize commercial prizes. Corsairs were not free to do as they pleased: they were authorized—and to a degree regulated—by governments to act in their national interest. In the case of France, they were subjected to a series of rulings that were laid down in a royal ordinance on the navy dating back to 1681, and which would result in the issue of a *lettre de marque*, needed if their activity were to be legalized. The corsair had to obtain royal authorization for each individual voyage, to be confirmed in writing by the local admiralty, and to leave a caution of 15,000 *livres tournois*, to be guaranteed by a merchant of solid reputation. In return they were given royal permission to fire on and capture other vessels, but they could not

---

[34] Ibid., 9–10. [35] Bouyer, *Au temps des Isles*, 61.

attack indiscriminately. They were limited to taking the ships of enemy states, and the authorization lasted only for the duration of the war. Moreover, their activities and their manning levels were monitored by the authorities. Where a ship's captain was armed with a *commission en guerre*, he had to take on at least double his normal crew so as to be able to man the ship's guns, to board enemy vessels, and to steer any captures back to port. There the prize had to be declared to the port authorities, and it would be thoroughly searched to ensure that the ship really did belong to an enemy power. Only then could it be sold, along with its cargo, and only then was the owner of the privateer, along with his captain and crew, able to share the profits of the voyage.[36] It was a perilous enterprise that incurred high risks and loss of life. These profits were far from guaranteed.

Privateering was a long-established weapon of European warfare, and its legitimacy was recognized by all seafaring nations. In peacetime, of course, it was outlawed, and was seen as indistinguishable from piracy; but in wartime even the most respectable merchants might sign up for privateering voyages, looking to the capture of an enemy cargo on the high seas as a profitable alternative to a long voyage to the Americas or the west coast of Africa. It could also be portrayed as a patriotic gesture, depriving the enemy of vital supplies and cutting off the sea routes to their colonies. In the *grande guerre de course* of the late seventeenth and early eighteenth centuries—and most notably during the Nine Years' War of 1688–97 and the War of the Spanish Succession—the most famous French corsairs, men like Jean Bart and Duguay-Trouin, became national heroes, and their expeditions into the Western Approaches out of Dieppe, Dunkerque, and Saint-Malo posed a constant threat to British shipping.[37] Saint-Malo, in particular, with a population of 20,000, was a classic *cité corsaire*, from where privateers roamed the oceans, from Guinea and the Caribbean to Chile and Peru and the fisheries of Newfoundland. In coastal communities, they were far from being peripheral figures drawn from a criminal underclass. Rather, they were civic leaders, men of wealth who commanded high social status and who often moved from winning notoriety as corsairs to serving as officers of the King's navy. Besides, their activities were much prized since they brought prosperity to their entire community.[38]

The exploits of French corsairs were widely admired and celebrated in literature and in occasional memoirs. The most famous text of the period, by the seventeenth-century corsair Alexandre-Olivier Oexmelin, was first published in Amsterdam in 1678 before being translated into German, Spanish, English, and

---

[36] Daniel Binaud, 'Note sur les corsaires de Bordeaux de la fin du 17e siècle à 1815', in Silvia Marzagalli (ed), *Bordeaux et la marine de guerre, 17ᵉ–20ᵉ siècle* (Bordeaux: Presses Universitaires de Bordeaux, 2002), 121.

[37] Michel Vergé-Franceschi, 'Les Bart: une dynastie d'officiers-généraux de la Marine Royale', in Silvia Marzagalli and Hubert Bonin (eds), *Négoce, Ports et Océans*, 371–87.

[38] J.S. Bromley, *Corsairs and Navies, 1660–1760* (London: Hambledon, 1987), 279–80.

French over the following decade.[39] Oexmelin, who had been born in Honfleur and who enjoyed a colourful career as a privateer on the Île de la Tortue, captured the imagination of his readers with tales of bravery, temerity, and defiance of the authorities that were, he implied, a part of everyday life in the seas of the French Caribbean. As he described them, his characters were brazen and fearless, carefree buccaneers who lived and died with their sword in their hand. They inspired admiration, not fear, and became natural heroes for succeeding generations of young men with a taste for adventure, appealing to the wild and untamed instincts of the young, to an exotic world of danger, empire, and the sea.

France was not, of course, alone in turning to privateering: it was the resort of every maritime nation, a hallmark of every colonial war. Like piracy, privateering was endemic in the colonial world of the Caribbean and the Americas: indeed, it was an essential part of the economy of port cities like Basse-Terre in Guadeloupe, where coastal trade, contraband, and privateering were interrelated activities, each with an essential place in the economy of the port.[40] Indeed, when the British captured Basse-Terre during the Seven Years' War, one of the main benefits that accrued from the capture was the destruction of a greatly feared nest of corsairs.[41] In wartime merchant ships were routinely fitted out for privateering and used indiscriminately by the British, French and Spanish authorities as well as by the United States in the War of 1812. In Martinique and Guadeloupe, however, European governments could exercise little direct control, and privateering, like smuggling, was largely the resort of local people. Privateering had a long pedigree in the region: the islands of the Lesser Antilles were especially feared by commercial vessels from Europe, for whose arrival corsairs would customarily lurk in wait. French merchants viewed the activities of corsairs with a degree of ambivalence. For some merchants privateering was a means of survival during the war years; but for others it was the cause of crippling financial losses. Those who continued to send their ships to the Americas ran huge risks, as commerce had become something of a gamble. For those merchant ships that did get through and escape the attentions of British privateers, the rewards were, of course, considerable. But not all got through, and ships' captains and merchants risked losing everything in pursuit of these gains. Convoys to and from the Caribbean were routinely attacked at sea. Ships were boarded, commandeered, burned or sunk. Return cargoes from the Antilles were seized and sold by their captors. Crews risked being seized, tried and imprisoned in England. In 1778, the first year in which France was involved in

---

[39] The most recent edition of this work is Alexandre-Olivier Oexmelin, *Les flibustiers du Nouveau monde: histoire des flibustiers et boucaniers qui se sont illustrés dans les Indes*, introduction by Michel Le Bris (Paris: Phébus, 1996). For a brief history of the book in its various editions, see Bouyer, *Au temps des isles*, 274–7.

[40] Anne Pérotin-Dumon, 'Cabotage, Contraband and Corsairs: the Port Cities of Guadeloupe and their Inhabitants, 1650–1800', in Knight and Liss (eds), *Atlantic Port Cities*, 58.

[41] Ibid., 66.

the American War, 110 ships of her merchant marine were seized or sunk by enemy privateers while on the high seas.

The results were easy to foresee. A number of established firms faced ruin as a consequence of corsair attacks, while others were tempted to abandon their commercial activities entirely until peace was restored in 1783. For some merchant houses, indeed, these years only confirmed their worst fears about the shipping lanes of the Atlantic, which they saw as a source of danger more than of opportunity. The larger Bordeaux houses had initially been slow to send vessels to the islands, wary of a form of commerce that tied down large sums of capital and which in wartime incurred high levels of uncertainty. Their natural aversion to risk often returned. Earlier in the century, indeed, it had taken a sea-change in their approach to risk before some of the principal names in the port were persuaded to invest in voyages to the Caribbean or to get involved in the slave trade. Many did so prudently, buying shares in voyages rather than fund entire cargoes, or spreading their exposure to risk by investing in a number of voyages in the same season. In wartime, when losses were being posted daily at the Bourse, they were often among the first to pull back.[42]

Others chose to gamble, to turn themselves to the uncertain profits of privateering, seeking commissions from the French government and investing in new ships better fitted to this form of trade. Sending merchant ships unescorted to the islands had become too risky, and they felt they had little choice. Insurance rates soared and with them the capital costs of commercial voyages to the Americas, and their crews found themselves forced to take up arms if they were to avoid what they saw as the inevitability of capture and loss. In every war from the Nine Years' War in the late seventeenth century to the War of American Independence a hundred years later, levels of commercial activity fell away as French vessels were taken as prizes by British warships, with their crews either killed or taken as prisoners to England. In the Seven Years' War alone, Nantes lost around 115 ships to British privateers, with some of the larger merchants losing as many as five of their vessels. Three merchant houses claimed to have suffered to the tune of more than a million *livres*. This partly reflected a concerted British campaign against French merchant shipping, and partly the refusal of the French government to provide naval protection for the sea lanes. The result was a disaster for the port. In the three years from 1756 to 1758, thirty-seven of the 104 ships that left Nantes for the Caribbean were captured, while those plying the triangular trade between Nantes, West Africa, and the Americas suffered even more grievously. Of a total of twenty-eight departures, no fewer than fifteen, more than half the total, were lost. When Nantes began to recover, it was through the increased use of neutral shipping and a change of government policy on convoys.[43]

---

[42] Butel, *Les négociants bordelais, l'Europe et les îles au 18ᵉ siècle, passim*.
[43] Perraud, 'L'armement maritime nantais en période de guerre', 17–22.

In each of these wars, the French Atlantic ports lost large tonnages of shipping and recorded dramatic reductions in their commercial activity. Privateering was seen as a form of warfare as much as a mechanism for trading in commercially perilous circumstances, and in each war merchant houses took individual decisions as they made their own calculations about what would be a tolerable level of exposure to loss. Merchants clubbed together to spread risk at times when there were no realistic or affordable rates of insurance on offer. And many did refit ships more customarily used for commercial voyages with the cannon required if they were to succeed as privateers. The numbers varied from war to war, but in each of the wars of the eighteenth century their number ran into hundreds. The figures for Bordeaux alone make salutary reading: here 221 *lettres de marque* were issued in the course of the War of the Spanish Succession, 150 in the War of the Austrian Succession, 169 during the Seven Years' War, reaching an unprecedented 412 in the War of American Independence.[44] The names of the ships, their owners, and their captains were all recorded in the admiralty's ledgers.[45] If Bordeaux merchants suffered losses to British privateers, they responded in kind, despite the costs that were involved. Captains invested their own money in the hope of sharing in the large profits which a successful privateering voyage always promised, but also because their normal commercial activities had become too risky.

Successful corsairs could easily become local, even national, heroes. In some French ports, and most notably in Saint-Malo, there were long-established traditions of privateering which were seen as both legitimate and honourable, traditions to which the government could turn in moments of national emergency.[46] Here corsairs were honoured as patriotic figures who had stood up to the enemy and protected the honour and reputation of their communities. Notable among them in the early years of the century was Robert Surcouf de Maisonneuve, who had captained the corsair *L'Aimable* during the wars of Louis XIV. His great-grandson, also called Robert, was born in 1773 and grew up in the family tradition; he, too, would serve as a corsair and would go on to satisfy his love of adventure and his hatred of the English in a series of daring attacks on British shipping during the Revolutionary and Napoleonic Wars. Surcouf captained corsairs around the Channel coast and in European waters, but also, more successfully, in the Indian Ocean, where he harassed and captured East Indiamen on their return from the East laden with treasure. Before he died in 1827 he captured more than forty prizes, built a huge personal fortune from trade, and was rewarded by his government with the Legion of Honour. Like Jean Bart, Surcouf was widely admired, the adventurous hero of popular imagery during the nineteenth century

---

[44] Binaud, 'Note sur les corsaires de Bordeaux de la fin du 17ᵉ siècle à 1815', 123.

[45] Daniel Binaud, *Les corsaires de Bordeaux et de l'Estuaire: 120 ans de guerres sur mer* (Biarritz: Atlantic, 1999), 279–91.

[46] Alain Roman, *La saga des Surcouf: mythes et réalités: une famille de marins, de corsaires et de négociants à travers deux siècles de l'histoire d'un port* (Saint-Malo: Cristel, 2006).

and even the subject of a comic opera (*Surcouf*) by Robert Planquette in 1887.[47] Today there is a street named after him in Saint-Malo, where his statue was funded by public subscription and inaugurated on the Quai de Dinan in 1903. The capital also boasts a street named in his honour. Yet not everything he did was honourable. Like many corsairs, he was a man of the sea prepared to make his fortune by any means available, and after the Napoleonic Wars in 1815 he would be one of the most prominent figures to invest in the illegal slave trade with Africa and the Caribbean, a fact that is largely erased from public memory today.[48]

Surcouf was not alone in acquiring riches through privateering: others, like Léonor Couraye of Granville, became local notables through *la course*, acquiring a manor house in the hinterland of the town and living in the style which his wealth permitted. Privateering did not, however, present any guarantee of profit or glory, and many eschewed it. Down France's Atlantic coast, indeed, only Bayonne stood out as a centre of privateering, its seamen preying on English ships as they slipped in and out of Spanish and Portuguese ports. Over the century, it would be the smaller vessels fitted out along the English Channel, taking advantage of their manoeuvrability and their captains' knowledge of the tides, that would inflict the greatest damage on the enemy and bring home the richest prizes. But generally, the effectiveness of privateering as a weapon of war declined in the second half of the century. Saint-Malo offers a perfect example, with its privateering voyages during the American War reduced by half since the Seven Years' War. This may seem curious, in that privateers were also operating in the Caribbean, where the French found powerful allies in American corsairs like the legendary John Paul Jones. But for many the risks simply seemed too great, and they preferred to stand back and wait for peace to be restored.[49]

The lesson of the eighteenth century seems clear: that if French merchants could contemplate the future with a degree of optimism and equanimity, and in many cases amass huge fortunes from their commercial activities, their prosperity was not assured and was always threatened by the onset of war. Atlantic trade demanded open seaways and the defence of France's colonies from attack and capture, assurances that could not be given once war had been declared and when all the European states along the Atlantic seaboard were pursuing their ambitions for conquest in the colonial sphere. Britain was the main threat, but not the only one, as Holland, Denmark, and Spain continued their quest for wealth in the Americas, and the peace on which commerce relied was regularly disrupted across the century. In 1789, the outbreak of revolution in France undoubtedly added a

---

[47]   Robert Planquette, *Surcouf: Opéra-Comique en 3 Actes et un Prologue* (Paris, 1887).

[48]   Elodie Le Garrec, 'La place de la Bretagne et des Bretons dans la traite illégale française, 1814–1831', in *Lorient, la Bretagne et la traite: Cahier de la Compagnie des Indes*, 9/10 (2006), 121.

[49]   Michel Aumont, 'La guerre de course française et atlantique sous Louis XV et Louis XVI, 1744–1783', in Gilbert Buti and Philippe Hrodĕl (eds), *Histoire des pirates et des corsaires, de l'Antiquité à nos jours* (Paris: CNRS Éditions, 2016, 294–8).

new element of disruption which few merchants welcomed. But, whatever these merchants may have said during the following decade, initially at least the Revolution had little effect on business confidence. There was no sudden recession in 1789, or in 1790 or 1791, the years of constitutional monarchy and of the early revolutionary reforms. It was in 1792 that the merchant community really began to suffer, following two developments that were far more ominous for commerce: the first signs of revolutionary insurrection in Saint-Domingue as civil rights were extended to free men of colour, and the declaration of war, first on Prussia and Austria in 1792, then on Britain in the spring of 1793. The wars that followed would disrupt commerce for nearly a quarter of a century and would upset the established order not just in Europe but across the globe: in Egypt and elsewhere in North Africa, in India, and ultimately in places as far distant as Java.[50] For the Atlantic ports the twin forces of war and anti-slavery had been unleashed, forces that would go far to destroy the Atlantic economy on which they relied.

---

[50] Desan et al., *The French Revolution in Global Perspective*, 1.

4

France and the Slave Trade

Before the end of the seventeenth century, French ships had played little part in the Atlantic slave trade. Indeed, until about 1673 Dutch vessels probably carried more slaves to France's Caribbean sugar islands than the French themselves, and French slavers made little progress in non-French markets. Others forged ahead. Spain and Portugal were the nations most involved in slaving, while Britain's slave trade expanded rapidly in the late seventeenth century. However, after the War of the Spanish Succession, this changed rapidly. From 1713, when the monopoly of the Guinea Company was ended, French ports invested seriously in slave voyages, supported by the Crown through generous subsidy schemes. Indeed, by the eve of the Revolution, foreign companies were registering their ships in France so that they might profit from them. The transformation was dramatic. Between 1716 and 1793, French vessels transported more than 1 million Africans to the Americas, and during the fifteen years to 1793 they were carrying an average of 24,000 slaves each year.[1] Slavery lay at the heart of a production system that supplied Europeans with increasing quantities of sugar, coffee, and indigo; and the French Empire, far more than the British, relied on slave labour for its continued prosperity. The French Atlantic became, in Silvia Marzagalli's words, 'more centred on West Indian production, less diversified, and less integrated than the British Atlantic'. This left it more vulnerable to fluctuations in trading conditions and less able to adapt to changes in the Atlantic world.[2]

This in turn led some merchants to turn to slaving in preference to less remunerative forms of colonial trade. Direct commerce with the Caribbean was profitable only if there was cargo for the outward journey, since the principal purpose of the voyage was to bring colonial goods back to France, to feed the voracious European market for sugar and other colonial produce. Captains seldom had difficulty in filling their holds for the trip back from the islands; indeed, the needs of the planters were such that they were under pressure to build ever bigger ships to transport their cargoes. But finding a full cargo for the journey from France was a more difficult problem, especially for ships coming out from

---

[1] David Eltis and David Richardson, 'A New Assessment of the Transatlantic Slave Trade', in Eltis and Richardson (eds), *Extending the Frontiers: Essays on the New Transatlantic Slave Trade Database* (New Haven, CT: Yale University Press, 2008), 26–7.

[2] Silvia Marzagalli, 'The French Atlantic world in the seventeenth and eighteenth centuries', in Nicholas Canny and Philip Morgan (eds), *The Oxford Handbook of the Atlantic World, 1450–1850* (Oxford: Oxford University Press, 2011), 250.

the Loire. Nantes vessels often made the outward journey to the Caribbean very lightly laden, their cargoes too small to cover the costs of the voyage, far less to register a profit. And once there, the captains had to find freight for the return voyage, and pay for it in hard currency. If they could not raise sufficient money from the sales of the goods they arrived with, this raised further financial problems for the owners, who were tempted to turn instead to slaving. Many, indeed, were convinced that only by investing heavily in the slave trade could they hope to recoup their original outlay, since the margin between the price of sugar and coffee in Saint-Domingue and the price at which they could sell it back in France was seldom sufficient of itself to provide a satisfactory return.[3]

This trend was particularly marked in the years after the American War, when the competition between French ports became intense. Nantes, of course, as the leading slave port across much of the eighteenth century, resumed slave voyages after the lean years of the war, but it was not alone in looking to the slave trade to resolve the challenges it faced. The ports of the Seine estuary, especially Le Havre and Honfleur, resumed the triangular trade with obvious relish. In the years leading up to the Revolution, indeed, Le Havre risked becoming dangerously over-dependent on slaving at a time when merchants elsewhere looked to diversify their activities, especially into the Indian Ocean.[4] Other ports also saw the slave trade as an opportunity for short-term profit in the post-war world. Between 1783 and 1792, Bordeaux became, briefly, the leading slaving port in France, knocking Nantes off a pedestal which it had occupied for most of the century.[5] Marseille merchants also became more deeply involved in slaving in the years after the War of American Independence, though on a modest scale, sending no more than eight expeditions a year to the coast of West Africa.[6] And in La Rochelle, which fitted out 13 per cent of French slaving voyages over the century, the years after the American War saw an increasing dependence on the triangular trade, to the point where slaving accounted for 58 per cent of the vessels it despatched outside France.[7] Prices were high as the planters sought to increase their labour force after years of poor supply, and those who supplied them with slaves were tempted to take full advantage.

---

[3] Robert Stein, 'The profitability of the Nantes slave trade, 1783–1792', *Journal of Economic History*, 35 (1975), 780.

[4] Edouard Delobette, 'La traite négrière dans la croissance atlantique havraise du 18e siècle', in Éric Saunier (ed.), 'Villes portuaires du commerce triangulaire à l'abolition de l'esclavage', *Cahiers de l'histoire des mémoires de la traite négrière, de l'esclavage et de leurs abolitions en Normandie*, 1 (2008), 55.

[5] Jean Mettas, *Répertoire des expéditions négrières françaises au 18ᵉ siècle* (2 vols, Paris: Société française d'histoire d'Outre-Mer, 1978–84).

[6] Gilbert Buti, 'Commerce honteux pour négociants vertueux à Marseille au 18ᵉ siècle?', in Saunier (ed.), 'Villes portuaires du commerce triangulaire à l'abolition de l'esclavage', 209.

[7] Brice Martinetti, 'Les résistances du négoce rochelais à la première abolition de l'esclavage: les apports des correspondances', *Revue du Philanthrope*, 4 (2013), 155.

For merchants and commissioners, slaving was a commercial investment like any other. Few acknowledged any moral qualms about buying and selling their human cargoes, and in the course of the eighteenth century, the richest and most respectable merchant families engaged in the trade at times when there were profits to be made. Where they held back, it was generally for commercial rather than moral or religious reasons. The monarchy regulated the slave trade and itself extracted profit from it. In the early years of the century, the King had taxed the trade, levying a tax of ten *livres* on every slave transported to the West Indies. Then, in 1776, when it was thought necessary to relaunch slaving in a bid to compete more effectively with Britain, the monarchy offered inducements to merchants to encourage them to engage in slaving, offering a *prime* of fifteen *livres* for every African safely landed in the islands. After the end of the American War, the sums involved were hugely increased, until by 1786 merchants would earn 160 *livres* for every slave who disembarked in Martinique or Guadeloupe, and 200 *livres* for all those taken to Guyana and the southern part of Saint-Domingue.[8] These sums not only help to explain the surge in the slave trade after 1783; they also, by indicating the King's tacit approval for slaving, gave the trade an unexpected air of respectability. Who could be deterred by moral considerations if, as it seemed, the King himself had no such compunction?

A small number of merchants did admit to being affected by the moral doubts that were being expressed in society at large. In Bordeaux, a city that took pride in a cultural heritage that included both Montaigne and Montesquieu, there was some public disquiet about the morality of the slave trade and the assault on the dignity of man which it implied.[9] Some questioned the source of the city's newfound riches; a few even called for the trade to be abolished. But such voices were still relatively rare and they had little practical effect. Doubts might be raised in debates in Bordeaux's two learned societies, the Académie and the Musée, where many leading *négociants* were members, but they did little to deter those who wanted to trade; and as soon as the American War was over, some of the most notable merchants in the port, men like Gradis, Saige, Baour, Balguerie, and Nairac, rushed to fit out new expeditions to West Africa. Those who desisted, or who continued to send their vessels to the Caribbean *en droiture*, did so because they knew that these voyages would still return a handsome profit. They were not moralists. They were men who prided themselves on their pragmatism and for whom slaving remained an option whenever commercial conditions demanded it.

---

[8] Bertrand Guillot de Suduiraut, *Une fortune de haute mer: François Bonnaffé, un armateur bordelais au 18ᵉ siècle* (Bordeaux: Confluences, 1999), 72.

[9] Jean Mondot (ed.), *L'esclavage et la traite sous le regard des Lumières* (Bordeaux: Presses Universitaires de Bordeaux, 2004); Jean Mondot and Catherine Larrère (eds), *Lumières et commerce: l'exemple bordelais* (Berne: Peter Lang, 2000).

Slaves, it was clear, were just another commodity to be bought and sold by men who judged every voyage by a single yardstick, that of profit. They were a cargo, the property of the merchant for the period of the voyage, and it is clear that their humanity bought no special consideration. Some said as much in print, like the merchant and *maire-échevin* of Le Havre, Dubocage de Bléville, who wrote that he saw no distinction between slaves and the other products, like coffee or rubber, which filled the holds of his company's ships.[10] To the modern ear this materialism can seem rather shocking, and the merchants' indifference to the fate of their slaves brutal and callous. But to contemporaries it was unexceptional. The La Rochelle merchant Pierre-Jean Van Hoogwerff offered a telling insight into what was a widely held attitude in the merchant community when he assessed the success of the most recent voyage of his slave ship, *L'Aimable Suzanne*, to Africa and Le Cap.[11] He congratulated himself on its profitability, achieved, he believed, against the odds, since the ship had suffered an outbreak of smallpox that had killed a hundred Africans. For him this was not a human tragedy, merely an inconvenience that had lost him a great deal of money. The voyage had been very good, he said unhesitatingly; but for 'that unhappy level of mortality' he had no doubt that it would have been 'superb'. The welfare of his slaves, it is clear, did not unduly concern him.

Yet in other respects Van Hoogwerff was not a cruel man. His correspondence shows a deep concern for his family, not least for his youngest child, Betsy, who suffered from chronic ill-health and who was a constant source of family anxiety. As a caring father, it is touching to see that he even named one of his slave ships after her: *La Nouvelle Betsy* made several triangular trips in the years before the Revolution. He was a religious man, too, like many of the leading merchants in La Rochelle, a practising and seemingly devout Protestant who on several occasions invoked his Protestant God to ask for good health or the safe return of his cargoes.[12] Indeed, religion and the liberties of Protestants would seem to have been important to him, conscious as he was of past persecutions, and he wrote to his brothers and sister elsewhere in Europe to tell them of the rights that French Protestants had won. They had built a new church in La Rochelle, he said, they could get married by their Protestant pastors, while their infants would be baptized by the Catholic priest to ensure their legitimacy. Tellingly, his detailed and enthusiastic account of these Protestant liberties followed closely on his unemotional reference to the slave deaths on his ships.[13] The one mattered to him; the other did not.

---

[10] Hervé Chabannes, 'Entre prise de parole et occultation: les intellectuels havrais, la traite des Noirs et l'esclavage', *Revue du Philanthrope*, 4 (2013), 146.

[11] Vanessa Martin, *Pierre-Jean Van Hoogwerff: chronique d'une ascension sociale à La Rochelle, 1729–1813* (Paris: Association pour le développement de l'histoire économique, 2002), *passim*.

[12] Brice Martinetti, *Les négociants de La Rochelle au 18ᵉ siècle*, 167.

[13] AD Charente-Maritime, 4J 2848, 'Lettres particulières de Pierre-Jean Van Hoogwerff, négociant à La Rochelle, 1784–1805', letter sent to his sister in Edinburgh, 22 April 1789.

The expansion of the plantation economy on Saint-Domingue and the islands of the Lesser Antilles meant that there was a seemingly insatiable demand for slaves, and where French ships did not supply them, others would step in to satisfy that demand. The rewards for transporting several hundred Africans from Senegambia to the Caribbean were always tempting, even for the most scrupulous. And with the government actively rewarding those who fitted out their vessels for slaving voyages, the risks they incurred could seem more acceptable, too. For risks there undoubtedly were, that ran far beyond the dangers that derived from war and enemy privateering, dangers which were shared by all merchant shipping on the Atlantic. Slave voyages were particularly long and hazardous. Crews were afflicted by fevers and a range of deadly tropical diseases between the coast of Africa and the Caribbean. In Africa itself, ships' captains had to negotiate with duplicitous merchants and local princes, ready to cheat and defraud them, and face the possibility of long months spent in protracted negotiations, of ships becalmed in African waters, of sick and rebellious slaves, of crewmen mutinying against the conditions on board or absconding at the first opportunity to sell their services to a rival. There was nothing certain, nothing guaranteed about the returns they would make. But the opportunity to fill their holds with able-bodied Africans seemed to many an easy solution to the problem of finding an outbound cargo, and if they were lucky, there were huge profits to be made. Jean Meyer has pointed to some of the best returns from Nantes slave voyages in the years immediately before the Revolution; in 1785 one ship returned a 100 per cent profit, another in 1784 chalked up 110 per cent, a third, in 1789, an eye-watering 120 per cent. A storm-free crossing, a cargo free of disease, a rapid turn-around on Gorée island, and success would follow. This was the prospect that enticed so many to set sail westwards.[14]

It is clear from these statistics that high profits could be, and sometimes were, made from a single slaving voyage. But the conditions had to be right and the firm's luck had to hold if such margins were to be achieved, and most historians are agreed that returns of 100 per cent were wholly exceptional. Hugh Thomas illustrates this by citing what he terms an 'ideal voyage, the voyage of which merchants dreamed'. In 1783, the Nantes firm of Giraud and Raimbaud sent a 150-ton slaver, *La Jeune Aimée*, on a voyage to Angola and from there to Saint-Domingue. They had bought the vessel for the voyage at a cost of 6,000 *livres*, and when account is taken of other expenses—the crew, cargo, and food and drink for the voyage, presents for the slave-traders, and the equipment needed to sail across the Atlantic—the costs incurred before they had even crossed the harbour bar were already high. When the sum paid for the cargo of 264 slaves is added, they had spent around 156,000 *livres* before they turned west towards the Americas.

[14] Jean Meyer, *L'armement nantais*, 394–411; Stein, 'Profitability', 782.

All this required capital and credit before a single *livre* had been earned or any business had been concluded. On this particular voyage, the investors got their reward. When the slaves, along with some other cargo stacked in the hold, were sold in Le Cap, they raised more than 366,000 *livres*—a profit of some 135 per cent on outgoings.[15] But there was nothing typical about the voyage. The ship reached the Americas in an unusually fast time. It did not encounter storms or hurricanes to hamper its progress. It was not delayed off the African coast by prolonged negotiations with African merchants. The slaves arrived in good condition instead of being decimated by fevers. And the prices they fetched at auction in the Caribbean were unusually high. All the conditions were in place to earn record returns.

But equally, things could go disastrously wrong, as the experience of another Nantes slaving firm shows. The family firm of Orry de la Roche had been successful merchants in the port; and they had engaged in a succession of unspectacular voyages, resulting in small to middle-sized commercial operations, in the period immediately before the War of American Independence. However, their business suddenly faced a series of overlapping problems. Orry's family finances suffered a blow in 1776 when his ship, the *Télémaque*, was wrecked at sea, just at the moment when war in the Atlantic made it impossible for him to recoup his losses by sending out other vessels. He found himself forced to abandon his major activity, fitting out ships for the islands, in favour of domestic trade, and his profits suffered a disastrous collapse; indeed, in 1783 he had to pull out of the colonial market entirely. Five years later, the firm had no choice but to declare bankruptcy, and although Orry did resume some business dealings after 1788, the years of prosperity were behind him. He was a victim of the vicissitudes of the slave trade and of its capital demands on the merchant community, and, like many others, he lacked the robust financial base necessary to sustain his company through periods of dearth and misfortune.[16]

Owning and fitting out slave ships incurred heavy costs which not all were able to sustain. Engaging in the slave trade was impossible without considerable capital outlay before the ship even sailed, and this necessitated an easy access to credit which the slave ports could not command. The Paris banking system was not as developed as its counterpart in London, and local banks were in decline across the eighteenth century, making it difficult to obtain any privileged terms of credit. Indeed, Paris banks were only too well aware of the risks posed by the slave trade, and interest rates tended to reflect this: in 1786, for instance, one Nantes merchant house, the Chaurands, had to pay a rate of 10 per cent—double the current market

---

[15] Hugh Thomas, *The Slave Trade: The Story of the Atlantic Slave Trade, 1440–1870* (London: Weidenfeld and Nicholson, 2015), 442.

[16] Hervé Landais, 'Une famille de négociants armateurs dans la seconde moitié du 18e siècle : les Orry de la Roche' (mémoire de maîtrise, Université de Nantes, 1992), 42.

rate—in order to unlock the funds they needed to finance their trade.[17] But the part played by Paris finance houses was modest, in contrast to the role of City banks in the affairs of Bristol or Liverpool. In eighteenth-century France, banks routinely lent only a proportion of the merchant's costs, often no more than 20 per cent of what was required, forcing him to look to different sources of finance, in his home port or through investments in the plantations, if his venture was to succeed. The decision to lend owed much to personal confidence—of the kind that could only be established through family links, through a presence on the Chamber of commerce, or through freemasonry— and it varied according to the prominence of the merchant and his commercial record in past voyages. Credit, in other words, was as much about confidence in the person raising the loan, his standing and reputation, as it was about monetary calculation, a judgement that could be applied equally to modern capitalism in general.[18] Marriages between merchant families were common, and were a source of credit as well as of wealth. When Honoré Chaurand married the daughter of a leading Nantes trader, Marie Portier de Lantimo, for instance, he gained more than her hand in marriage. He was integrated into the inner circle of Nantes merchants, as a result of which he started taking shares in vessels outfitted by other Nantes commercial houses before going on to outfit vessels in his own name.[19] Marriage was an important commercial investment, too, though its value might not extend into wartime. Indeed, when war was declared or there was a grave threat to the safety of commercial shipping—as happened in 1792—and banks refused to lend at all, the result was the almost total cessation of slaving in any form.[20]

A successful slave voyage required more than credit. It required sturdy ships, capable of resisting the Atlantic swell and large enough to transport hundreds of captives in their holds. It demanded a high level of seamanship in treacherous waters, a skilled captain, and a degree of good fortune, if the voyage were to succeed. The choice of captain was especially critical given the range of respon- sibilities that fell on his shoulders. He had to take all the key decisions that affected the management of the ship, from loading and distributing its cargo to its preparation for sea; he had charge of the cargo while at sea and was responsible for the sale of the goods on board and the purchase of slaves during trading in Africa. In short, quite apart from his navigational skills, a good captain had to have commercial expertise, accounting skills, and an ability to impose rigorous discipline and manage a crew that could be insubordinate and close to mutiny

[17] Stein, *The French Slave Trade*, 116.

[18] Antoine Lilti, 'Le pouvoir du crédit au 18e siècle, histoire intellectuelle et sciences sociales', *Annales: Histoire, Sciences Sociales*, 70, 4 (2015), 958.

[19] Albane Forestier, 'A "considerable credit" in the late eighteenth-century French West Indian Trade: the Chaurands of Nantes', *French History*, 25 (2011), 52.

[20] Edouard Delobette, 'Mercure et Sosie', *Revue du Philanthrope*, 6 (2015), 54, 56–64.

over a lengthy and often difficult voyage. For this reason, the choice of crewmen for the voyage was often left to his sole discretion.[21]

An experienced captain with knowledge of Atlantic currents and trading conditions was much prized. Experience did not necessarily translate into age, however. The Atlantic was a young man's world, and captains were often quite young, with an average age in the years 1763–78 of thirty-seven in Bordeaux and just thirty-two in Nantes. Many made only one slaving voyage, for to survive, a captain needed to be physically strong and enjoy good health—and a little luck as well. Death rates among captains were high, from fevers and tropical diseases or as a result of shipwrecks or slave insurrections on board. Christophe Grovellet calculates that during these years, whereas Le Havre lost only four captains from its slaving fleet (or 5.3 per cent of the total), Bordeaux lost six (9 per cent), Saint-Malo six (12.8 per cent), La Rochelle eight (at 16.7 per cent, the highest losses proportionally), and Nantes twenty-one (or 9.8 per cent of a much larger total).[22] But for those who did return, the slave trade could bring unimagined riches and, with it, social esteem.

Slave ships demanded larger numbers of crewmen than other merchant vessels, and they remained at sea for much longer, incurring high seas and gale-force winds as well as the extreme heat of equatorial Africa. And as the century progressed, the leading slaving ports all required ever greater numbers of seamen. Nantes, for instance, was calling on the services of up to 5,500 men to crew its ships in the years up to the Revolution, many of them for slave voyages. Where, we may ask, were such unprecedented numbers of sailors to be found, men with the experience and the physical strength to handle a slave ship where nautical skills had to be matched by a capacity to contain possible rebellions on board? The circumstances of each port differed considerably. Nantes, with its long tradition of seafaring, provided a high percentage of the men needed to crew its ships, as many as 40 per cent of all those who signed on for slaving voyages; of the rest, a substantial number came from the smaller ports of the Loire estuary and from coastal villages in Brittany.[23] By way of contrast, the parishes of Le Havre closest to the port provided surprisingly few recruits in the second half of the century, with the consequence that slaving captains had to look further afield for crews—initially to Saint-Malo, then to other ports in Normandy, especially Honfleur and Rouen.[24] In Bordeaux, the recruitment pattern was different again, reflecting the city's wide catchment area across the west and south-west of France. From a

---

[21] Christophe Grosvallet, 'Les capitaines négriers bordelais entre 1763 et 1778', *Institut aquitain d'études sociales, bulletin*, 76 (2001), 66–9.

[22] Ibid., 56–7.

[23] Murielle Bouyer, 'Les bassins de main d'œuvre des équipages négriers nantais au 18e siècle', *Revue du Philanthrope*, 6 (2015), 149–54.

[24] Éric Saunier and Florian Caillot, 'Le recrutement des équipages de navires de traite havrais au 18e siècle', *Revue du Philanthrope*, 6 (2015), 171–2.

sample of slaving vessels sailing for the Caribbean in 1774, Éric Saunier concludes that the crews came principally from three regions: Guyenne to the south of the city, the Saintonge to the north, and, through Bordeaux's strong trading connections with the region, Brittany. Bretons would seem to have manned slave ships from across the Atlantic littoral and beyond. Indeed, what is most striking is how few of those who manned Bordeaux's slave expeditions came from the city itself.[25] Unlike Nantes, Bordeaux had a diversified economy with the consequence that its sons did not need to go to sea.

Such was the lure of profit that many merchants were undeterred by the dangers and hardships involved. Those who engaged in the slave trade were well aware that their enterprise was of value to the nation, and they sought out the prerogatives and commercial privileges which they saw as their due. In particular, they valued the laws that gave them privileged access to colonial markets. In 1766, in response to a ministerial query about what would help to restore the slave trade at a moment when its future seemed threatened, the Nantes merchants insisted that their exclusive right to trade in slaves be maintained 'by an express and irrevocable law' and that foreign vessels be excluded from taking slaves into French colonies. They also wanted unlimited rights to re-export colonial goods free of all tariffs and demanded to be exempted of taxes and duties on all materials used to build, fit out and stock vessels leaving the city to engage in the slave trade. For them, there was nothing discreditable about their form of commerce, and they were adamant that the risks they took should be recognized and their work generously remunerated.[26] Repeatedly, in petitions and correspondence, merchants talked of their exposure to financial loss and the unpredictability of the slave trade as a source of profit.

There were certainly high stakes to play for, and the fact that different voyages reported contrasting fortunes might seem to favour the view that fitting out a ship for *la traite* represented something of a gamble. If occasional slaving voyages, like the ones cited above, resulted in a profit of 100 per cent or more, others ended in disaster or brought minimal returns on the capital invested.[27] Moreover, there were years when merchants gave up slaving entirely because it had become too risky or because other forms of commerce brought a quicker return.

Few merchant houses kept commercial records detailed enough to allow for any consistent comparison, but the most important one to do so, Chaurand *frères* in Nantes, reflects the unpredictability of the slave trade, even in years when it was not threatened by war at sea or by a blockade of the French coast. Slave ships had to be smaller and more manoeuvrable than other Atlantic cargo vessels if they

[25] Éric Saugéra, *Bordeaux, port négrier, 18ᵉ–19ᵉ siècles. Chronologie, économie, idéologie* (Paris: Karthala, 1997), 221; Bouyer, 'Les bassins de main d'œuvre des équipages négriers nantais', 149n.

[26] Gaston-Martin, *L'ère des négriers, 1714–1774* (Paris: Karthala, 1993), 418–19.

[27] Jean Meyer, 'Le commerce négrier nantais, 1774–92', in *Annales: Economies, Sociétés, Civilisations*, 15 (1960), 121.

were to transport their cargo of Africans to the Americas without heavy loss of life and to escape the attentions of pirates and corsairs.[28] It followed that few merchants risked sending vessels to the Bight of Africa during periods of war, even at times when ships were still trading with the islands *en droiture*. In practice, slave voyages were limited to peacetime only, with the consequence that, as soon as a war ended—as was the case with the American War in 1783—there was an explosion of activity in Nantes and the other slaving ports, as merchants jostled to get their vessels to sea early while high demand ensured a good return. They knew that the favourable trading conditions would not last, and that the price of slaves in the Antilles would soon fall. It was imperative that they recruit crews, fit out their ships, and purchase goods for the outward voyage as expeditiously as possible.

Robert Stein has examined the profitability of twenty-one slave ships fitted out by the Chaurands between 1783 and 1792, which together accounted for twenty-six expeditions to Africa and the islands, or about 7 per cent of all slaving expeditions in these years. Their very mixed results show that profits were far from being guaranteed, with only ten of the ships registering a clear profit—six of them of 20 per cent or more—across the period. On the other hand, six of the ships studied suffered substantial losses in these years, while one just about broke even. Four others, still trading when payments from Saint-Domingue planters ceased in 1792, saw their profit undermined by the outbreak of war and by insurrection on the island. In other words, though there were substantial profits to be made, they could not be taken for granted. Those who engaged in the slave trade understood that they were gambling, and that, even if the odds seemed stacked in their favour, they had to insure against possible disaster. Slaving was not a panacea for commercial uncertainty.[29] It called for higher investment and initial expenditure, and therefore greater exposure to loss if a ship were wrecked or captured. If they were to succeed in the slave trade, merchants had to have sufficient assets to be able to sustain such losses, and many failed.

Fitting out a slave ship required a higher level of investment than did direct voyages to the Americas, and, since the bulk of the trade fell to independent merchants after the demise of company trading in mid-century, that generally involved seeking out loans and raising new capital. This would cause difficulties for smaller merchant houses, which often enjoyed less credit with the banks and had less chance to spread risk across a number of voyages. The exact cost of a slaving expedition depended, of course, on the size of the ship and the value of the cargo; but as a general rule, it seems that merchants spent two to three times as much in preparing and fitting out a *négrier* as they did for a direct expedition to the Caribbean. Merchants found the capital they needed in a number of ways.

[28] James Walvin, *A Short History of Slavery* (London: Penguin, 2007), 70.
[29] Stein, 'The profitability of the Nantes slave trade', 784.

The most traditional, and the cheapest, way would be to raise it privately, from family members or other traders who were prepared to buy a part-share in the voyage. Merchants would help one another out in this way, spreading their exposure over a number of different ships and slaving trips. But the ambitions of Nantes and Bordeaux merchants could not always be met in this way, and they increasingly had to seek loans from beyond their own port or their friends on the Chamber of commerce. The slave trade found its capital in a variety of ways, from regional, national, and international investors.[30] In Bordeaux, sources of finance varied greatly and evolved in the course of the century, as family networks in other ports and in the Caribbean allowed for the more efficient financing of expeditions. A network of brothers, cousins, and sons would take a share in fitting out the slave ships. Though based in France, they often owned sugar plantations in the islands which would be supplied by the ships on their outward journey and whose production would then provide cargo for the return; they would also help finance the voyage by business dealings with other colonists.[31] Religious communities also provided welcome sources of finance for colonial trade, with Protestant and Jewish merchants able to look to their co-religionists—both in France and across Europe—for sources of credit. Protestant merchants benefited, for instance, from investment from Holland and Switzerland. The firm of Jean-Jacques Bethmann had associates in Geneva, and Baux, Balguerie in Geneva and Mulhouse, providing useful sources of additional capital for their slaving adventures.[32]

For some the problem was not just the lack of capital for investment, but a lack of currency with which to make purchases, as the Atlantic economy expanded exponentially in these years. This was especially true of Marseille, which not only faced the challenge of a rapid explosion of colonial traffic but also maintained its traditional Mediterranean trade with the Barbary Coast and the Levant. Here merchants faced a different kind of problem. In the Levant in particular, they were forced to buy with cash while they were obliged to sell on credit, which created serious cash-flow problems. The merchant community found itself increasingly starved of foreign currency at a time when it was having difficulty meeting the needs of its growing domestic market in French currency, which the small mint in Aix was unable to satisfy. As a consequence, merchants turned to another form of commerce, importing *piastres* from Spain and the Americas and establishing Marseille as a major entrepôt for currency, which it would export onwards to the cities of Central and Eastern Europe, to Milan, Vienna, and the Levant. This trade contributed to Marseille's commercial prosperity in the last years of the Ancien Régime and helped it to maintain its economic dominance in the

---

[30] François Renault and Serge Daget, *Les traites négrières en Afrique* (Paris: Karthala, 1985), 86.
[31] Butel, *Les négociants bordelais*, 194–5.
[32] Herbert Lüthy, *La banque protestante en France* (2 vols, Paris: SEVPEN, 1959–61), vol. 2, 666n.

region. Between 1785 and 1790, for one company, Roux, the trade in currency was worth as much as 28 million *livres*.[33]

Fitting-out costs varied hugely from voyage to voyage and from ship to ship; indeed, the ultimate success of the voyage would depend greatly on the skills and perceptions of the outfitter. Of the twenty-six ships sent by the Chaurands after 1783, for instance, the costs varied between 180,000 and 460,000 *livres*, costs which had to be recovered before any profit was made on the voyage.[34] These often began with the purchase of a suitable ship and the charges incurred in converting it for use as a slave ship. For the ship's owners would seldom engage exclusively in slaving; commercial shipping had to be flexible, and even on a slave voyage the ship had to serve very different purposes in the various stages of its journey: from the French port to West Africa with objects to trade, across the Atlantic on the Middle Passage with a cargo of slaves, and then the return to France when its hold would be stuffed with goods for the European market. Often the ship was bought for a single voyage and sold on after its return. The ship *Le Joujou*, for instance, left Bordeaux in September 1788 for Angola, before continuing to Saint-Domingue and returning to Bordeaux. It had been bought from a local shipbuilder for 12,000 *livres*, a sum that included the provision of an iron boiler—the ubiquitous *chaudière à nègres*—used to heat the slaves' rations on board.[35] Preparing the vessel for an ocean-going voyage and providing the wooden planks needed to convert the hold to receive its cargo of slaves was another major capital expense, one that involved more than 500 working days for carpenters and other tradesmen. The cost of the conversion came to nearly 4,300 *livres*. Then there were the bills for ironworkers, sail makers, rope makers, stevedores, and all the other workmen whose expertise was needed to make the ship seaworthy and to prepare it for the slave trade. The crew had to be recruited and paid three months in advance of the ship's departure. Surgical equipment had to be bought to prepare for medical emergencies on board. There were also the costs of pilots' fees before the ship could nose its way down the Garonne. None of this came cheap. A basic insurance policy was bought for 2,217 *livres*, making the total cost of fitting out and preparing the voyage in excess of 50,000 *livres*.[36]

Then there was the cargo, the first of the cargoes that would reflect the different stages of the life of the ship as it ploughed onwards on its slaving voyage. When it left Nantes or Bordeaux, the ship would be loaded with goods for the African market, to be traded when the ship arrived off Gorée, Ouidah, or the Angolan

---

[33] Ferréol Rébuffet and Marcel Courdurié, *Marseille et le négoce monétaire international, 1785–90* (Marseille: Chambre de commerce et d'industrie de Marseille, 1966), 166; see also Charles Carrière and Michel Goury, *Georges Roux de Corse: L'étrange destin d'un armateur marseillais, 1703–1792* (Marseille: Éditions Jeanne Lafitte, 1990).

[34] Stein, 'The profitability of the Nantes slave trade', 785–8.

[35] For an image of the *chaudière à nègres* on a Nantes slave ship, see Bernard Guillet, *La Marie-Séraphique, navire négrier* (Nantes: Musée d'Histoire de Nantes, 2009), 97.

[36] AM Bordeaux, S1, Compte de l'armement du navire *Le Joujou*, mis en mer le 8 septembre 1788.

coast, as well as with the essentials for the Atlantic crossing, including considerable supplies of food and drink for the officers, crew and, of course, the slaves they would take on board when they reached Africa. For the Frenchmen on board—especially for the officers' table—this involved a considerable variety of victuals: there are receipts for salt beef, dried cod, ham, flour, sugar, butter, cheese, oil, some vegetables, and spices.[37] Officers and crew members crew also drank copiously during the voyage: all slave ships were stocked with red and white wines, brandy and spirits, as well as some beer. The *Joujou*, for instance, was laden with alcohol to the value of more than 3,200 *livres* when it sailed out of port.[38] For the slaves, the ship carried ample supplies of beans and rice, a diet that did little to protect them against scurvy and the other forms of onboard sickness that blighted many slave voyages. These goods were purchased in port, before the ship sailed and, in the case of Nantes, acquired from across a hinterland that stretched from Brittany to the Pays de Loire, where towns like Tours and Cholet were notable beneficiaries of the trade with West Africa.[39]

When they left the French coast, slave ships carried cargoes for several different markets and destinations. In Africa they would sell guns, ammunition and textiles of various kinds; in Saint-Domingue the market was for flour, fine wines, and industrial products from France and Europe. They also took care to carry the sorts of goods that African kings and princes would accept as presents, an essential part of the ceremonial surrounding trade in Africa. And they could not leave port without taking on board the equipment they might need to defend the ship from attack and to carry out emergency repairs in the event of a storm. So ships' logs reveal a host of equipment which all ships' captains deemed essential. They included a range of spare parts for the ship: sails, ropes, anchors, nails, replacement masts, candles, and firewood. They also carried a range of weaponry to use in the event of an attack or at the first sign of rebellion from the slaves in the hold: there were cannon and firearms, gunpowder and bullets.[40] There were always rich supplies of firearms on slave ships, to be used as presents for African traders, as merchandise to sell to planters and privateers in the Caribbean, or as means of self-defence against raiders, pirates, and mutinies by the slaves in the hold.

The captain had to decide where along the African coast to drop anchor, and, by the same token, how best to trade. His company might have long-established connections with African merchants, or seek the patronage of a local king or prince: hence the need to plan the journey, its trade and its gifts, with such care.

---

[37] Aka Kouamé, 'Les cargaisons de traite nantaises au 18e siècle. Une contribution à l'étude de la traite négrière française' (thèse de doctorat, Université de Nantes, 2005), 9.

[38] AM Bordeaux, S1, Compte de l'armement du navire *Le Joujou*.

[39] Aka Kouamé, 'Les produits des pays traversés par la Loire dans les cargaisons négrières nantaises au 18e siècle: une approche à partir des archives des armateurs et de la chambre de commerce', *Cahiers des Anneaux de la Mémoire*, 16 (2015), 103–11.

[40] Kouame, 'Les cargaisons de traite', 10.

But he might also adjust to the current trading conditions he found when he reached Angola or the Bight of Benin: the presence of other ships, of rival vessels from other ports and other countries, could cause costly delays, force up prices or threaten supply, while there were various prejudices about the health, physical strength, and moral character of the slaves that issued from the various African nations. Some were singled out as being prone to fever and disease, given to psychological ailments, or feared for their explosive and insurrectionary character. A prospectus from the 1760s raising capital for three voyages out of Le Havre and Honfleur shows the care that went into planning the ships' arrival off the African coast. It was proposed to trade to the north of the Gold Coast, between six and ten degrees latitude north, though few French ships had previously gone there. Yet that part of the coast, it was maintained, could have decided advantages for the French: the climate was less oppressive and the voyage less laborious; certain colonial goods were easier to trade; and it was possible to find supplies of food for the slaves which were both cheap and of good quality, food that was familiar to them and would not cause the stomach disorders that so often occurred in Angola and other parts of Africa. The financier who had launched the operation held out the prospect of a profit of more than 318,000 *livres*.[41]

Few would deny that the slave trade was a tough, highly competitive business that allowed for few concessions to moral scruples or human frailties. The traders' aim was to complete the voyage as quickly and efficiently as possible, avoiding profitless months spent at anchor off the African coast, conducting business with their African suppliers as swiftly as possible before setting sail with their human cargo across the Atlantic. Trade was usually conducted at one of the main *comptoirs* established along the West African coast, Ouidah, in the early part of the century, and later at Porto Novo or Badagry.[42] Those sold into captivity had often been taken prisoner in the many wars that scarred the history of West Africa in these years, in many cases with the express aim of selling them for profit. Of slaves transported to Saint-Domingue on French vessels, the majority came from two regions: from West Central Africa, the largest single source, and from the Bight of Benin, where many were Yoruba, victims of wars between Oyo Yoruba and the king of Dahomey, who would leave a strong cultural and religious legacy in Haiti.[43] Accessing these *comptoirs* was not easy, however, as it required considerable navigational skills and a certain measure of good fortune. There were few natural harbours, while the sea along the entire coast of the Bight of Biafra enjoyed a fearsome reputation. The presence of a sandbar and heavy surf

[41] Hervé Chabannes, 'Les Havrais et la traite des Noirs dans le haut de la Côte d'Or du sieur Amand Le Carpentier', *Revue du Philanthrope*, 4 (2013), 172–8.

[42] Brigitte Kowalski, 'Acquérir les bois d'ébène : les comptoirs de traite sur la Côte d'Esclaves', in Saunier (ed.), 'Villes portuaires du commerce triangulaire à l'abolition de l'esclavage', 104–9.

[43] Kevin Roberts, 'The Influential Yoruba Past in Haiti', in Toyin Falola and Matt D. Childs (eds), *The Yoruba Diaspora in the Atlantic World* (Bloomington: Indiana University Press, 2004), 177–9.

posed a danger to ships approaching the coast, and strong easterly currents presented an added peril. Traders and missionaries repeatedly commented on the frequent delays that were caused by storms and adverse currents in West African waters, where ships had to anchor off the coast and their crews use canoes to reach the shore to trade. Yet the currents and sandbanks were critical to the growth of the slave trade, since they created a navigable lagoon system linked to rivers that ran far into the interior. Many of those who were sold into slavery had been transported to the coast along these river networks.[44]

The trade with Europeans involved complex rituals of exchange, and, like their British and Spanish competitors, French slave ships came well-equipped, loaded with the brightly coloured textiles, rolls of cloth, handkerchiefs, hats, guns, powder, iron bars, and alcohol that were the usual staples of trade, the goods favoured by African kings, princes, and slave masters.[45] But it was not all about trade. There were also ceremonials to be gone through and presents to be offered before exchanges could begin. The journal of one French slave ship, the *Guerrier*, which sailed out of Nantes in 1790 for West Africa, is especially instructive in this regard. It gives an account of a voyage to the Guinea coast, and describes the approach that was adopted by the captain as he arrived off Bany, anchoring offshore and—if, as with the *Guerrier*, he had a small ship—going immediately to meet the king, who was the principal supplier of slaves to visiting vessels. The ceremony, it was understood, started with present-giving; nothing would be achieved until he had opened the presents for the King's wives—'a good side of salted beef, around twenty pounds of biscuit, and an agreed amount of brandy'. Then the captain would press for the trading session to begin, as nothing could be purchased until the King solemnly performed the opening ceremony. But more was to follow. When the King came on board with his counsellors and his retinue, salt beef and biscuit should be prepared; 'only the king and the principal princes are admitted to the banqueting table; the others should eat on the bridge', where, the captain added, 'due care should be taken to supervise them as they like to steal'. In the evening it was the captain's turn to go ashore to visit the King and his court. Once more there was a ritual to be followed before any bargain could be struck. The captain must begin by asking about the captives whom they had acquired that day, and then offer presents. 'The value of the presents offered to each courtier should reflect the number of captives whom, we believed, they were capable of delivering.'[46]

Only then could they get down to business. The journal went on to enumerate the trading that was concluded, day by day, over the next six weeks—two slaves

[44] Caroline Sorensen-Gilmour, 'Slave-trading along the lagoons of south-west Nigeria: the case of Badagry', in Robin Law and Silke Strickrodt (eds), *Ports of the Slave Trade (Bights of Benin and Biafra)* (Stirling: Centre of Commonwealth Studies, University of Stirling, 1999), 84.

[45] AM Bordeaux, S1, 'Marchandises données en traite pour six captifs', 20 May 1791.

[46] AD Loire-Atlantique, 1J679, Journal de traite du navire 'Le Guerrier' de Nantes, 1790.

purchased here, three there—with a detailed listing of the articles that were traded in return and of the further presents that were needed to facilitate each deal. These mostly seem to have been for the King, but it is clear that there were other palms that needed to be greased, too: those of African merchants, slave-traders, princes, and courtiers, all those who could facilitate the transaction. When the ship's holds were filled and trading was completed, the captain knew that there were other formalities still to complete which no slaving captain could overlook. Presents had to be distributed once again if the ship were to hope for a friendly welcome in future. The King had to be given what the captain calls 'his customary presents when trading closes', which he then lists: they include a cannon, caps and hats for the men who row his barge, and normally a stock of guns (though on this occasion he had run out of guns and so substituted other goods as his present). Presents had also to be given to the men who had worked on his ship during its weeks at anchor, and—on this voyage—to the captain of a Liverpool slave ship who had come to his aid by lending him some crew members in an emergency. West Africa, and with it the slave trade, was fuelled by a gift culture which a slave captain would ignore at his peril. When trading was finished, he noted that his supplies were exhausted: the goods that remained were valued at no more than 188 *livres*, along with a barrel and a half of brandy worth a further seventy-five *livres*.[47]

Once the slaves had been loaded on board, the most dangerous section of the triangular voyage began, the notorious 'Middle Passage' between the African coast and the Americas, generally, in the case of French vessels, to Guadeloupe, Martinique or the ports of Le Cap and Port-au-Prince in Saint-Domingue. The hell that was the hold of a slave ship has been described in graphic terms, and the fetid air and squalid conditions below deck blamed for the spread of scurvy, fevers, typhoid, diarrhoea, vomiting, and the myriad illnesses that caused so much death and suffering during the crossing.[48] The slave ship was essentially a cargo vessel, its hold crudely adapted for its human cargo by the insertion of a second deck some three or four feet beneath the bridge on which children and those of small stature could be stacked with a bare minimum of air to breathe. Even the main section, where the fully grown adults lay, was only four or five feet high, so that they could sit up only with difficulty. It was in these confined spaces that several hundred slaves would be chained together in twos, often completely naked, so as to reduce their mobility. To avoid such physical and psychological damage as would lead to their loss or reduce their value at auction, it was imperative to provide fresh air and exercise. On the majority of slave ships, the captives were unshackled and taken on deck for exercise between their two daily meals, between nine in the morning and five in the afternoon. Men and women remained strictly

---

[47] Ibid., folio 10.
[48] Jean-Philippe Platel, 'La santé à bord des navires négriers de Bordeaux au 18ᵉ siècle' (diplôme d'état de docteur en médecine, Université de Bordeaux-2, 1988), 68–81.

segregated, and while they were on deck they would be closely supervised by the crew, who were often armed to avert any sign of mutiny or rebellion. For, however putrid the air the slaves breathed, the captain's aim was to get as many as possible of them to America unharmed. The slaves were regularly washed in sea water, their mouths cleaned, their hair and nails cut—all in a bid to ensure that what was for the ship's owner a valuable cargo was not lost or damaged during the crossing.[49] A captain who lost a substantial part of his cargo would be held accountable by the *armateur* back in France; and in the most extreme cases, where slaves had been beaten to death or thrown overboard to the mercy of the sharks, he might find himself answerable to the admiralty and French justice.

Sometimes there was little the crew could do to preserve the lives of slaves who were determined to escape the misery of life on board or the prospect of the plantations that lay ahead. Self-harm and self-mutilation were regular occurrences on board; there were also numerous reports of suicides, both attempted and successful, when an opportunity presented itself. Indeed, in his *Dictionnaire universel de commerce* of 1743, Jacques Savary listed the principal methods of suicide employed by slaves during their shipment to the Americas. All involved violence, though of very different kinds: going on hunger strike, deliberately choking by swallowing their tongue, smashing their skull against the side of the ship, and—undoubtedly the most common method—jumping overboard into the sea. Especially when this occurred in mid-Atlantic, it cannot be seen as an easy option, and few, of course, survived. The witnesses called by the Admiralty of Nantes in one such case in 1740 admitted to being shocked by what they had seen. Two slaves who had thrown themselves into the sea together were seen by the rest of the crew as they battled with sharks in the water. 'Straight away, part of our crew jumped into the ship's boat to try to save them, others threw planks and ropes from the ship's deck, but it was all in vain, and they were devoured by the fish before our very eyes.'[50]

Violence was endemic on board all ships in the eighteenth century, and seamen expected to be treated brutally at times: it was part of the culture of maritime communities that a captain could order physical punishments to impose discipline on board, indeed that it was necessary for the safety of the ship that he should do so. But violence was probably at its most unforgiving on slave ships because they were at sea for such long periods with so many human beings packed into a small space—violence towards the slaves, of course, which was unremitting, but also violence towards crewmen, whether in the form of floggings carried out on board ship or of the many fights recorded between crew members themselves.

---

[49] Guy Saupin, 'La violence sur les navires négriers dans la phase de décollage de la traite nantaise, 1697–1743', in Mickaël Augeron and Mathias Tranchant (eds), *La violence et la mer dans l'espace atlantique, 12ᵉ–19ᵉ siècle* (Rennes: Presses Universitaires de Rennes, 2004), 202–3.

[50] Ibid., 204.

Many of the men were drained of strength by the hot climate and the tropical maladies to which they were subject, but they often received scant sympathy from the officers, who were wont to mistake lethargy for idleness and malingering, and punish them accordingly. There was nothing exceptional about violence and ill-treatment of this kind; rather it was a daily event to which the young and sickly were especially exposed, as they were punched or flogged by sadistic officers for the slightest misdemeanour. In the view of Alain Cabantous, beatings of this kind could almost be classed as an initiation rite for the young crewman.[51] But it helped to turn many slave voyages into a living hell, for the crew as much as for the slaves. And since they, unlike their cargo, had no market value, there is little doubt that, as a ship struggled to reach its destination in Saint-Domingue, their welfare was given the lowest priority. The voyage of the Nantes slaver *La Georgette* in 1788 may be an extreme case, but it is a salutary one which goes far to explain the frequent instances of mutiny on slave vessels. Of the thirty-five crewmen who had been taken on board in Nantes, only nineteen survived to reach Saint-Domingue the following year. And their Calvary did not end there. They were in such poor physical condition that all but four of them had to be taken immediately to hospital for treatment.[52]

What the ships' owners feared most was a slave rebellion on board, which could lead to the seizure of the ship or the death of crew members. Although the incidence of rebellion fell in the course of the century, the danger of a slave revolt remained sufficiently great that it alarmed both captain and crew. Indeed, Serge Daget estimated that, of the 3,134 slaving voyages undertaken by French ships, 138 (or 4.4 per cent) incurred a slave rebellion in some form, and though that number had declined to around 2 per cent by 1790, that still constituted a tangible threat.[53] Of course, these statistics can only be read as crude averages. Vessels sailing out of Nantes recorded significantly higher figures across the century, with seventy-four revolts on its 1,424 slaving expeditions, or a rate of 5.1 per cent. Just why Nantes, the principal slaving port, should have fared so much worse than the other ports is not clear, though Philippe Haudrère has suggested that it may be down to the avarice of those captains who sought to increase profits by piling their slaves more tightly into smaller spaces, making for conditions on board that were even more penal and finally became intolerable.[54] While this may explain some of

---

[51] Alain Cabantous, *Le vergue et les fers: mutins et déserteurs dans la marine de l'Ancienne France* (Paris, 1984), 68.

[52] Vincent Bugeaud, 'La violence sur les navires négriers: une approche à partir de l'exemple nantais au 18ᵉ siècle', in Éric Saunier (ed.), 'Villes portuaires du commerce triangulaire à l'abolition de l'esclavage', *Cahiers de l'histoire et des mémoires de la traite négrière, de l'esclavage et de leurs abolitions*, 1 (2009), 132.

[53] These statistics are taken from Jean Mettas, *Répertoire des expéditions négrières françaises au 18e siècle* (2 vols, Paris: Société française d'histoire d'Outre-Mer, 1978, 1984).

[54] Philippe Haudrère, 'La révolte des esclaves à bord des bâtiments négriers français au 18ᵉ siècle: essai de mesure', in Augeron and Tranchant (eds), *La violence et la mer dans l'espace atlantique*, 191–2.

the rebellions, especially those that took place in mid-ocean, it does not explain them all. The rebellions mostly took place off the coast of Africa before the crossing had even begun. Slaves broke loose to throw themselves into the sea, to run back on to African soil, to escape a fate of which they were already conscious and which they feared more than death itself. Figures suggest that as many as 75 per cent of rebellions took place while the ship was still in African waters, compared to 24 per cent at sea, and a paltry 1 per cent once it had reached the Caribbean.[55] If they were acts born of desperation and despair, they were also political acts by Africans unwilling to accept that they would be separated forever from their people and their continent. Those who did go, and who completed their journey to the New World, did not forget Africa; they took their memories and their culture with them, and these would do much to determine their attitudes to the French, to their work on the plantations, and to slavery itself.

[55] Ibid., 193.

5

Populating the French Atlantic

The slave trade, in France as in all the slaving nations of the Atlantic, had grown out of a conviction that white men could not work in the intense heat of the Caribbean and that Europeans were uniquely exposed to the fevers that period-ically decimated their numbers. It was a claim repeated almost mechanically in the pamphlets published by the pro-slavery lobby and by the chambers of commerce of the Atlantic ports. Africans, they had convinced themselves, enjoyed a stronger physical constitution and were better acclimatized to the ravages of tropical diseases: they could therefore endure hard physical labour under the boiling suns of the West Indies to a degree that Europeans could not hope to do. For some, this contrast was part of a wider problem: how to explain negritude, how to give meaning to skin colour. It was a question that fascinated theologians and philosophers alike, and the eighteenth century tended to look for an explanation in nature, to see the colour of a man's skin as a direct reflection of his exposure to heat. This might not seem entirely satisfying as an explanation, as there were no black-skinned peoples native to the Americas, even in regions close to the Equator, but many authors persisted in voicing this view. The French naturalist and cosmologist Georges-Louis Leclerc, comte de Buffon, maintained in 1777 that winds and altitude were also relevant determinants. He argued that it was 'the excessive heat that is encountered in some countries of the world' that made for black skin colour, and that such heat is not to be found in mountainous countries like Peru or the interior of Africa. Hence 'it is on the west coast of Africa, the countries from which slaves were exported to the New World, that are to be found men of the blackest complexion'.[1] From this it followed logically that Benin, Senegal, and the Bight of Guinea were among the best places in Africa to trade in slaves.

The forced migration of millions of Africans to the slave plantations of the American South, the Caribbean, and Central and South America was undoubtedly the most brutal part of the movement of peoples across the Atlantic world, but Frenchmen were affected, too, as imperial conquests brought new scope for trade and travel between continents and hemispheres. Like Britain, eighteenth-century France had a global presence, even if, as a result of a series of wars, her outreach was increasingly curtailed as the century progressed. Her empire offered

---

[1] Jean Ehrard, *Lumières et esclavage: l'esclavage colonial et l'opinion publique en France au 18e siècle* (Paris: Sofédis, 2008), 107.

economic, administrative, and military opportunities to people who would never previously have dreamt of crossing the ocean in search of wealth and security for their families. France's eighteenth-century world stretched from the Americas to the Levant and from the Caribbean to the East Indies, and her merchants, seamen, planters, administrators, craftsmen, and soldiers criss-crossed that world to an unprecedented degree. Not all were rich. In the Caribbean islands, the less affluent could find a niche and prosper, and even former indentured servants went on to own land.[2] Back in Europe, the Atlantic achieved a new familiarity and immediacy in everyday life. In French ports local people mingled with ships' captains and crews recently returned from exotic overseas parts; and, as consumers, they became accustomed to the delights of sugar, coffee, tobacco, and the produce of foreign climes. Elizabeth Marsh, the heroine of Linda Colley's global narrative of the British Empire, may not have had a precise French equivalent: she did, after all, live an exceptional life even for Britain, passing seamlessly from Jamaica, where she was born, to London, then to Menorca and Marrakesh, then on to the Cape and Rio, before finally following her husband to India, where she died of cancer, in Calcutta, at the age of only forty-nine. But she illustrates perfectly the global character of the eighteenth century colonial world, and, more generally, of European empires. 'Elizabeth Marsh's existence coincided with a distinctive and markedly violent phase of world history, in which connections between continents and oceans broadened and altered in multiple ways. These changes in the global landscape repeatedly shaped and distorted Elizabeth Marsh's personal progress.' Hers is, Colley insists, 'a global story'.[3] It is one that would have found instant resonance across France's overseas empire.

The Atlantic world was built around human mobility. The belief that tilling Caribbean soil was an activity that must be reserved for Africans had developed only gradually, with the consequence that it was only around the mid-eighteenth century that white Europeans were finally supplanted by African slaves as labourers on West Indian plantations. In the late seventeenth and early eighteenth centuries, in contrast, it was largely Frenchmen who had laboured in the Caribbean heat, and during the first decades of France's presence in the Antilles there had been repeated migrant voyages from France, and especially from the regions of the west and south-west that formed the hinterland of the great Atlantic ports. Those who left were drawn from a wide spectrum of trades and professions, some paying their own way, others sailing as *engagés*, their passage paid in return for a period of contracted labour once they had reached the islands. Some of the migrants were merchants set on enriching themselves and on exploiting the

---

[2] Philip Boucher, 'The French and Dutch Caribbean, 1600–1800', in Stephan Palmié and Francisco A. Scarano (eds), *The Caribbean: A History of the Region and its Peoples* (Chicago: University of Chicago Press, 2011), 225.

[3] Linda Colley, *The Ordeal of Elizabeth Marsh: How a Remarkable Woman Crossed Seas and Empires to become Part of World History* (London: Penguin, 2007), xix.

growing market for colonial produce. But most were men of modest means, who could not find the price of their ticket but who were imbued with ambition and a sense of adventure. They were recruited with government support, and in the first years of the scheme, from 1699, volunteers were not hard to find.[4] They would sign a sworn contract before a notary, accepting to work for three years for *colons* who, in return, paid for their passage. Those who sponsored them did so out of the myriad motives that underpinned the imperial dream. Like their British counterparts, they hoped through migration to ensure imperial and domestic security and to strengthen the French economy; they held out the prospect of social betterment to the poor and vulnerable; but they were primarily concerned to ensure profits for themselves through higher productivity and cheap labour.[5] They were not philanthropists.

The practice of *engagement* had begun at a time when the government was anxious to populate its Caribbean islands with Frenchmen, and voluntary engagements of this kind—of those who became known as *les trente-six mois*—continued until 1772, when the scheme was finally abandoned. By then the planters had no need for their services. They had turned to slave labour, which both made the scheme unnecessary and discouraged French workers from accepting any form of legal commitment that would equate their labour with that of slaves.[6] For the French workers, their status as free men was a key part of their identity and self-esteem. But the planters and merchants also resisted the temptation to enslave white men for the plantations, despite the higher costs involved in seeking their labourers from Africa. And though they generally believed their own propaganda about the need for African labour to resist the Caribbean heat, climatic arguments were only part of their rationale for engaging in the slave trade with West Africa. They also shared in a more general European culture that found the idea of enslaving fellow-Europeans repugnant. There was a cultural element in this that was almost ideological, and from the time of the earliest colonization in the sixteenth century there had been no serious effort to enslave fellow Europeans, whether the poor from their own society or prisoners captured in war. 'In a fundamental sense,' concludes Seymour Drescher, 'early modern Europeans were culturally inhibited from enslaving each other, while uninhibited from, and even encouraged to, enslave others.'[7] Even the most impoverished of white men,

---

[4] Christian Huetz de Lemps, 'Engagement et engagés au 18e siècle', in Paul Butel (ed.), *Commerce et plantation dans la Caraïbe, 18ᵉ–19ᵉ siècles* (Bordeaux: Presses Universitaires de Bordeaux, 1992), 66.

[5] Marjory Harper and Stephen Constantine (eds), *Migration and Empire* (Oxford: Oxford University Press, 2010), 21.

[6] Jacques de Cauna, *L'Eldorado des Aquitains: Gascons, Basques et Béarnais aux Îles d'Amérique, 17ᵉ–18ᵉ siècles* (Biarritz: Atlantica, 1998), 123–5.

[7] Seymour Drescher, 'White Atlantic? The Choice for African Slave Labour in the Plantation Americas', in David Eltis, Frank D. Lewis, and Kenneth L. Sokoloff (eds), *Slavery in the Development of the Americas* (Cambridge: Cambridge University Press, 2004), 36.

once settled in the French Caribbean, enjoyed personal freedom and the status that went with it.

But the years of *engagement* left their mark on the Caribbean economy. Substantial numbers of poor whites had left France for the islands, with many electing to stay on after their legal commitment was over. Some became *habitants* in their turn, clearing ground for cotton or sugar cane, and, after several good harvests, employing their own slaves to spare themselves the hard manual labour of tilling the soil.[8] Others stayed as seamen, artisans, or small shopkeepers. They had been chosen for the skills that they brought to a community that was sorely in need of them, and they played an important part in building a diversified French community in the Caribbean. They had just one thing in common. They enjoyed a privileged status that distinguished them from the slave majority, and they cherished it.

The presence on the islands of Frenchmen of different classes and social outlooks is important in explaining the relative complexity of Creole society. The French who settled in Saint-Domingue—as in the Petites Antilles—were not simply a governing and plantation-owning elite. They came from all classes of society. In a study of the *rôles d'armements* of the port of Nantes, Corinne Janin has concluded that in the fifty years before engagements were abandoned, some 4,435 men embarked in Nantes to seek their fortunes in the New World.[9] The majority of these were young: the law stipulated that they must be aged between eighteen and forty, but the overwhelming majority were under twenty-five, sometimes well under: the high number who declared their age as eighteen (556 in her sample) makes one suspect that younger men were falsely claiming to be eighteen so as to be admitted to the scheme. Many came from Nantes and its immediate hinterland, though among these were men who had journeyed to the city with the express purpose of signing their engagement. Beyond the city, two regions stand out as suppliers of colonial labour: Brittany, where most men came from the textile towns of the interior, and the Loire valley, most notably Anjou, where, by contrast, the majority came from farms and rural villages. The number of Breton sailors leaving through Nantes for the islands was consistently low, perhaps because they were drawn to other ports of departure, like Saint-Malo, or perhaps because there was enough work to be had at home. Along the Loire valley, Tours, Angers, Saumur, and Orleans were active centres of emigration, towns which were regular stopping points for river craft and where significant numbers were employed in the sugar refineries that treated the raw sugar imported from the islands through Nantes.[10] Most had skills that would be of value in the New

[8] De Cauna, *L'Eldorado des Aquitains*, 98.
[9] Corinne Janin, 'Les engagés pour les Antilles à partir des rôles d'armement nantais, 1722–1772' (mémoire de maîtrise, Université de Nantes, 1971), 3.
[10] Ibid., 21–5.

World: they had worked with wood and metal, in the building trades, or as textile or leather workers.

A similar pattern can be observed in all the west-coast ports which sent engaged men to the Antilles. Jean-Pierre Poussou, who has examined departures from Bordeaux between 1713 and 1787, concludes that two-thirds of those emigrating through the port came from the south-west, and that, more generally, around 40 per cent of all emigrants from France in these years came from the south-western quarter of the country. Bordeaux itself produced significant numbers of those who sought to make a new life in the islands, with the Charentes and the Pyrenees not far behind.[11] Again, not all were native to their port of departure. Many had travelled from the towns and villages of the interior to claim their passage from Bordeaux, from across a broadly defined region that included the Agenais, the Rouergue, the Albigeois, and the Toulousain.[12] Bordeaux served as a magnet for all those who, whether through poverty or ambition, set out to make their fortune in the New World.

By far the most popular destination for the *engagés* was Saint-Domingue. From Nantes, for example, 2,642 men embarked for Le Cap or Port-au-Prince over these years, compared to 1,265 for Martinique (the second most popular destination), and only 201 for Guadeloupe.[13] Not all were employed on the plantations that spread over the plains and the lower slopes of the mountains; many joined the administrators and merchants who settled in the cities, flourishing urban centres that reminded them of the provincial France they had left behind. These towns had grown rapidly, often in spectacular style, during the second half of the eighteenth century. Each had its style of life and its distinctive elite. Thus, if the French administration, answerable to the Intendant and General, was concentrated in Port-au-Prince, Le Cap was home to a dynamic merchant community, as powerful a group here as they were in Nantes or Bordeaux. They needed space to talk and plot deals, and from 1761 the city was endowed with its own Chamber of commerce, just like any French port city of this period.[14] Smaller towns had a more specialized role. Fort-Dauphin was a fortified town on the frontier with the Spanish part of the island, while Jacmel, Jérémie, and Saint-Marc were all important centres of maritime trade.[15] But all were recognizably urban. For a young man plucked from one of the cities of western France, the urban texture of the

[11] Jean-Pierre Poussou, 'L'immigration européenne dans les îles d'Amérique', *Voyage aux Îles d'Amérique* (Paris: Archives Nationales, 1992), 45–53; De Cauna, *L'Eldorado des Aquitains*, 106.

[12] Christian Huetz de Lemps, 'Engagements et engagés au 18ᵉ siècle', *Commerce et plantation dans la Caraïbe* (Bordeaux: Presses Universitaires de Bordeaux, 1992), 65–70; De Cauna, *L'Eldorado des Aquitains*, 106.

[13] Janin, 'Les engagés pour les Antilles à partir des rôles d'armement nantais, 1722–1772', 60.

[14] Moreau de Saint-Méry, *Description de la partie française de l'Isle Saint-Domingue*, vol. 1, 318.

[15] Jacques de Cauna, 'Architecture coloniale: Haïti, des richesses à découvrir', *Art et Fact: Revue des historiens de l'art, des archéologues, des musicologues et des orientalistes de l'Université d'État à Liège*, 7 (1988), 59.

Caribbean provided reassurance and familiarity, while the major cities offered many of the cultural facilities of metropolitan France: libraries, reading circles, masonic lodges, and—perhaps the most popular form of entertainment in the Caribbean—theatres with resident troupes of players. Moreau de Saint-Méry, who himself had headed one of the lodges in Le Cap, laid special emphasis on freemasonry as a source of sociability in the city. Of the Lodge 'L'Amitié', he wrote fondly that it was situated in the outskirts of the city, close to where it merged with the countryside. 'Here we had the benefit of being able to hold lodge meetings with the doors wide open, without fearing being watched by non-believers, which is an inestimable advantage in a hot climate.' He added that he had attended a large number of its meetings and had witnessed generous acts of charity 'which provide a fitting response to those who argue that the lodge does nothing useful; it provides the opportunity for us to meet, an opportunity that is so rare in Saint-Domingue'.[16]

Some met to discuss politics and public affairs, taking advantage of the arrival of ships from France to keep abreast of events in Europe. To this end a learned society, the *Cercle des Philadelphes*, was established in Le Cap in December 1784, which would develop into one of the principal philosophical societies of the age. Its membership was divided into three distinct classes that took account of the floating nature of colonial society: there were resident associates, who lived in Le Cap and its immediate hinterland; colonial associates, who were based elsewhere in the islands; and national or foreign associates, drawn from the transient population of French and foreign merchants who came and went with the merchant marine. But their constitution stated firmly that only the resident members, whose number was limited to twenty at any time, could direct the work of the society or elect its office-holders.[17] In its purpose and social composition, the Cercle closely resembled the academies and learned societies of its day. Its members were men of substance: besides a few merchants, they were drawn primarily from among the 'grands blancs' of colonial society, planters, government officials, magistrates, and members of the liberal professions. Many were also freemasons. They would seem to have been especially interested in botany and the challenges of agriculture in the tropics, a subject that made regular appearances on the agenda of its fortnightly meetings. Outside of its meetings, the Cercle had many of the trappings of a gentlemen's club, providing its members with a library, a cabinet to study the physical sciences, and a botanical garden. It offered an entrée into polite society and held out the promise of intelligent and cultured conversation.[18]

---

[16] Moreau de Saint-Méry, *Description de la partie française de l'Isle Saint-Domingue*, vol. 1, 434.

[17] American Philosophical Society, Pam. V. 1101–14, *Statuts du Cercle des Philadelphes* (Le Cap, 1785).

[18] Blanche Maurel, 'Une société de pensée à Saint-Domingue, le «Cercle des Philadelphes» au Cap Français', *Revue Française d'Histoire d'Outre-mer*, 48 (1961), 234–66.

But it was at the theatre that colonial society most often congregated to relax and be entertained. The theatre had social value too, as a brochure published in 1774 made clear: it provided distraction to merchants and tradesmen alike and encouraged a degree of social integration. 'If theatre is useful in Europe where there are many other means of distraction and relaxation,' it argued, 'it is even more indispensable in the colonies where there is nothing but this single establishment.' The author was not only thinking of entertaining the population; he was also concerned with public order in a town with a large population of artisans and single men. 'Experience shows us that since the opening of the theatre in this city there have been many fewer quarrels and incidents because people of different social groups come together to watch plays.'[19] It could not but meet with the approval of the town's police and militia.

In Le Cap, the first theatre was opened in 1740, and it soon proved too small for the needs of an expanding city. As a result, a second theatre was inaugurated in 1766: it was lavishly appointed, with fine plasterwork and tastefully decorated *loges* for the Intendant and other civic leaders, and it impressed Moreau de Saint-Méry. It could, he noted, hold 1,500 spectators, which was a telling indication of the city's cultural ambition. Yet demand for seats far exceeded supply, with the consequence that in 1784 the building underwent further improvements, including the addition of a third row of *loges*. Unlike many provincial theatres in France, it could afford to maintain a resident troupe of around twenty actors, the majority of whom had come out from France to work in Le Cap. But Moreau admits to being impressed more by the building than by its levels of comfort. The sun's heat only exaggerated by the stuffiness of the theatre, he observed, with the narrow corridors perennially short of fresh air because of the impact of surrounding buildings.[20] Across the island, other cities followed Le Cap's example. In the new capital of Port-au-Prince, despite its exposure to the ravages of earthquakes and hurricanes, a hall for plays and spectacles was seen as a priority; the first theatre was opened in 1762, though it quickly had to be replaced as the entire city was razed to the ground in the terrible earthquake of 1770.[21] The fact that the theatre was replaced within a few years illustrates the high priority it commanded in Creole society.

The Creoles had a reputation for enjoying dance and spectacle. The *beau monde* of Saint-Domingue gave lavish balls and attended performances of theatre and dancing wherever they were presented, and by the end of the 1780s theatres had been built throughout the island, even in the smaller urban centres like Saint-Marc, Léogâne, Jacmel, Les Cayes, and Jérémie, while travelling troupes of players

---

[19] 'Mémoire concernant le spectacle de la Ville du Cap', in Jean Fouchard, *Le théâtre à Saint-Domingue* (Port-au-Prince: Imprimerie de l'État, 1955), 15–18.
[20] Moreau de Saint-Méry, *Description de la partie française de l'Isle Saint-Domingue*, vol. 1, 360.
[21] Fouchard, *Le théâtre à Saint-Domingue*, 45–6.

went on tour, performing for a couple of nights in smaller towns where their arrival created ripples of excitement. In 1786, for instance, a troupe of Italian actors performed in Anse-de-Veau, and in 1790 a dance troupe in La Croix-des-Bouquets.[22] Tastes were eclectic, ranging from vaudeville to opera and plays by Molière, Racine, Beaumarchais, or Marmontel. There were also performances of works by Voltaire and Rousseau.[23] For exiles from the metropole, it was all so reassuringly French, a reminder of the Francophone culture they had left behind. But Creole drama could be innovative, too, reflecting the interests and tensions of Saint-Domingue society. It is surely no accident that playwrights and theatre directors from the island would play a prominent role in promoting Francophone theatre in New Orleans during the first half of the nineteenth century.[24]

Saint-Domingue's reputation for gaiety and urban sophistication was not undeserved and it helped attract migrants to the island who had few links with trade or the plantation economy. The career of Albert Simon is instructive in this regard. Simon was a relatively junior official in France, who had held minor administrative posts in the customs houses of Metz and Bar-le-Duc, before moving to Marseille, where he seems to have developed a taste for life in the colonies. After the death of his wife he decided, at the age of thirty, to try his luck in Saint-Domingue, spurred on by the customary colonial dream of lands and riches. But when he got there, in December 1784, he found few openings in trade and turned instead to his other skill, as a musician, taking a post as second violin at the Comédie in Port-au-Prince. From there he maintained a regular correspondence with his brother-in-law, Mathurin Henry, in Lorraine, from which it becomes clear that the brash commercial ambitions he had once harboured were not to be realized. Simon would remain a member of the orchestra until his death, and he seems to have become satisfied with his role, admitting to Henry that he had no regrets about coming to America and that 'I will be well satisfied if, after ten years here, I can retire to Lorraine with savings of 20 to 30,000 livres'. His wish was not to be granted, however, as he died a few years later, most probably a victim of the violence and murder that swept the island in 1791. His fellow musicians played in a concert in his memory, staging the first production of a Gluck opera in Saint-Domingue to raise money for his family.[25]

Like Simon, most of those who left France for the islands were economic migrants, lured by dreams of wealth and prosperity. But relatively few—certainly

[22] Ibid., 117–19.   [23] Ibid., 220.

[24] Juliane Braun, *Creole Drama: Theatre and Society in Antebellum New Orleans* (Charlottesville: University of Virginia Press, 2019), 11–41.

[25] Jacques Cauna and Richard Beckerich, 'La Révolution de Saint-Domingue vue par un Patriote', *Revue de la Société haïtienne d'histoire et de géographie*, 46/161 (1989), 2–4.

of those who paid their own fares and arranged their own passage—did so as idle speculation. Merchants sent their agents, their traders and not infrequently their sons to represent their interests in the colonies, and they could spend years in the Caribbean, purchasing and deal-making to further their company interests. Others combined the roles of merchant and planter, or encouraged their younger brothers to work plantations, seeing the twin roles of *armateur* and *habitant* as complementary in the dynamic of capitalism. They were part of a family enterprise, united in a single belief that, for Frenchmen in the eighteenth century, colonial trade and slavery represented the key to wealth-creation and social ascension. Given the cost of fitting out a slave voyage, this was not an option available to all. It required savings and considerable outlay, through inherited wealth or the help of friends or the capacity to raise funds cheaply. And it was, as we have seen, imbued with risk. But so strong was the attraction of the Atlantic, and so exciting the dreams that it conjured up, that many were tempted to take that risk, and invest their fortunes, and those of their families, in the sugar islands. Some had come from relatively humble backgrounds, seeing the Caribbean as a means of establishing their fortunes; others were established merchants who looked to profit from sugar and tobacco; others again were sons of noble families, often of the poor nobility of regions like Brittany, who saw in the Antilles a means of restoring their fading family finances. But they all had one thing in common—a determination to share in what Olivier Pétré-Grenouilleau has aptly dubbed a 'machine of dreams'.[26]

Studies of emigration from Nantes to the Caribbean show that the majority of those who bought plantations regarded their holdings in Saint-Domingue or in the Lesser Antilles as extensions of their business interests and of the property they held in France. They were taking a commercial decision, often as part of a broader family strategy after previously investing in privateering and in colonial trade.[27] Not all succeeded; in the years before the Revolution, particularly, there were complaints about the prices they were being offered for colonial goods and the low returns on their investments. The hard work involved in maintaining a sugar plantation with its mill and sugar refinery could seem thankless. As one *colon* wrote back to his wife in Poitou in 1788, he had had to bring in new slaves, buy mules, build a new mill, and replace the boilers used to prepare the sugar, all in the course of a single winter, in order to pay off his debts back in France. In his words, 'I thought this work far beyond my strength, but with patience I shall get there.'[28] Like so many pioneers, he was determined not to give up.

---

[26] Olivier Pétré-Grenouilleau, *L'argent de la traite: milieu négrier, capitalisme et développement, un modèle* (Paris: Aubier, 1996), 32–41.

[27] Natacha Bonnet, 'L'investissement colonial au 18e siècle: l'exemple de quatre plantations sucrières à Saint-Domingue', *Entreprises et Histoire*, 52 (2008/3), 46–55.

[28] Chevalier de la Barre to Madame de la Barre, 31 August 1789, in Gabriel Debien, *Un colon sur sa plantation* (Dakar: Université de Dakar, 1959), 111.

Such were the profits to be made from sugar that many remained undeterred by what they regarded as short-term problems. The example of those who had preceded them offered encouragement and inspiration, for during the previous century many merchants and ships' captains had invested in refineries and bought plantations in the hope of making a quick fortune, and few had been disappointed. It seemed a logical form of investment which complemented their shipping interests, the plantation producing the sugar and indigo that would fill the holds of the merchants' ships on their return journey to France. In 1775, for instance, the wealthy Le Havre merchant Stanislas Foäche built himself a sugar mill in Môle Saint-Nicholas on Saint-Domingue to exploit the sugar cane fields which he owned in the surrounding area. By the time of the Revolution, Foäche was employing some 550 slaves and had accumulated a considerable fortune, less because of the high quality of his sugar, Moreau suggests, than because his *sucrerie* was equipped with a water mill on a nearby river, while others in the area were still dependent on mills powered by oxen.[29] Continuous production was virtually guaranteed. For the *armateur*, the act of acquiring the *sucrerie* was primarily a means of spreading risk and protecting himself from the hazards of the Atlantic and the vicissitudes of war.

There was nothing demeaning about owning a plantation, or owning slaves, for that matter, nothing that could threaten a family with disgrace or social degradation—even in the case of a noble family. Nobles had strict notions of what constituted correct behaviour and they knew what activities would incur rejection or disapproval in the society they frequented. And though buying and selling slaves might seem to the modern mind a less than honourable pursuit, noble families were among the largest slave-owners on Saint-Domingue, and they were untroubled by questions of honour and status. Natacha Bonnet discusses four planters from Anjou who crossed the Atlantic and who successfully combined the roles of *seigneurs* in western France and planters in the Caribbean. They had very different family histories, four distinct social profiles, in spite of their claims to nobility. The Pays de Lathan were a family that had risen from the bourgeoisie of the Sarthe and had been ennobled early in the century; the Galbaud du Fort were from Nantes, a family whose background lay in the *noblesse de robe*; the family of Le Chauff de Kerguenec belonged to the Breton rural nobility; whereas the Stapletons were of old Irish aristocratic stock. None of them felt any shame in owning a sugar plantation. Indeed, Bonnet finds that, between Anjou and Saint-Domingue, they evolved a family strategy as they looked to construct their family fortunes and—in some cases—to acquire *anoblissement* in the process. Certain of them had been office-holders in Anjou and had been in the service of the King. They were all well educated, with private libraries, and they

---

[29] Moreau de Saint-Méry, *Description de la partie française de l'Isle Saint-Domingue*, vol. 2, 14

made sure that their children were well educated, too. But, equally, she finds that they had no difficulty in transferring their lifestyle and their interests to their plantation and to make money from slavery.[30]

Since 1669, French nobles had been permitted to engage in overseas commerce, and from 1681 to build and fit out ships for trade on the high seas. And by the mid-eighteenth century, those merchants who invested in the Caribbean were among those who bought titles of nobility. Some made their money from slaving and from trade with the Antilles; others bought land on Saint-Domingue where they owned slave plantations and sugar mills. Laffon de Ladebat, for instance, was a prominent Bordeaux slave-trader who from 1764 transported around 4,000 negroes from West Africa to the Caribbean; he also owned around 2,000 acres of land on Saint-Domingue and was unapologetic in his pursuit of slaving. He was rewarded in 1774 with letters of nobility and his passport to membership of the second estate.[31] Laffon was only one of several Bordeaux merchants whose fortunes were based on the slave trade and whose position among the city's elite was sealed by ennoblement. And the merchants were not alone. A considerable number of the magistrates who sat on the Bordeaux Parlement also invested in the plantation economy and became slave-owners. Among them, Pocquet de Lilette spent the major part of his life in Martinique; Lamolère and Prunes regularly travelled back and forward to their Caribbean plantations to manage their affairs; and the president of the Parlement, Dupaty, owned one of the richest *habitations* on Saint-Domingue, a property estimated to be worth almost 1.5 million francs by the eve of the Revolution.[32] But it was not only his great wealth that Dupaty owed to Saint-Domingue; he owed much of his social standing, too, to his colonial connections. Whereas other presidential families had unimpeachable noble titles going back to the sixteenth century, he risked being seen as something of an *arriviste*. His third-degree nobility was relatively undistinguished; but he benefited from strong colonial connections, his father and his grandfather having been counsellors on the sovereign council of Cap Français.[33]

Those who migrated to the Caribbean were willing to work, to invest, and to take risks to succeed; they also shared a common desire to establish their lineage, to set up the next generation. To that end, most maintained regular correspondence with family members back in France, and some criss-crossed the Atlantic many times during their careers. Pierre Letestu, from Honfleur, described himself as an '*armateur, capitaine de navire* and *planteur*' whose career oscillated between

---

[30] Natacha Bonnet, 'Seigneurs et planteurs, entre Ouest Atlantique et Antilles: quatre familles du 18e siècle' (thèse de doctorat, Université de Nantes, 2006); Bonnet, 'L'investissement colonial au 18e siècle', 46–55.

[31] Michel Figeac, 'La noblesse aux Antilles: l'exemple bordelais', *Bulletin du Centre d'histoire des Espaces Atlantiques*, 8 (1998), 90–1.

[32] Ibid., 94–6.

[33] William Doyle, *The Parlement of Bordeaux and the End of the Old Regime, 1771–1790* (London: Edward Arnold, 1974), 19.

the two shores of the Atlantic. But his loyalties did not weaken: he was a businessman first and foremost, and he died in the town where he was born, in Dieppe.[34] In this he was surely typical. Families were often split by the decision to leave for the colonies, and few planters wished to leave France forever or to abandon the wives and parents they had left behind. Among those sailing from Nantes who came from Poitou, for instance, Gabriel Debien distinguishes several discrete groups. The majority, of course, were first-time emigrants; they accounted for around four-fifths of those who sailed in the later eighteenth century. They sailed alongside *colons* who had returned to France for family reasons or on business, and who were now going back to their workplace. Others were officers in the King's army, returning to the Caribbean to rejoin their garrison or to manage their plantation: a number of army officers, generally still young, had taken wives in the colonies and had bought property, sugar mills, or plantations, in Saint-Domingue or Guadeloupe. Some, following their army service, made a new career among the sugar cane groves of the Antilles and became *colons* in their turn. Others left—and it is a feature of emigrant communities across the world— for social and economic reasons, ranging from poverty and a lack of opportunity at home to disillusionment, family disputes, and boredom with village life.

Not all the passengers on ships bound for the Caribbean were men. The passenger lists also contain the names of women, mostly wives leaving France, alone or with their children, to join their partners in the Caribbean.[35] Some went with their husbands to take up posts in the islands, whether in the army, the French administration, or a trading house in Le Cap or Basse-Terre. For families accustomed to move from posting to posting this was a necessary stage in their lives, though the children would often be sent home to France for schooling. In merchant families, too, it was not uncommon to move with one's family to the Caribbean, as the societies of the islands and of merchant houses in the cities of western France were tightly interconnected. The case of Jeanne-Eulalie Lebourg was in no way exceptional. Her husband was a colonial merchant in Nantes, Jacques Millet, who after his marriage in 1773 retired from a life at sea captaining one of his father's merchantmen to manage the family plantation in Saint-Domingue. He and his young wife sailed from Nantes together with their baby of seven months. But she lasted only seven years in the Antilles before returning to France, leaving her husband behind. Creole society did not suit her, she explained to her sister some years later. There were aspects of colonial life, especially for wives, to which she had found it difficult to adjust, not least the islands' well-founded reputation for libertinage. She noted that 'the women here are almost all

---

[34] AD Calvados, F 5545, Fonds Letestu, correspondence between Pierre Letestu and his son-in-law, starting in 1767.

[35] Gabriel Debien, 'Poitevins partis par Nantes pour les Antilles, 1772–1791', *94ᵉ Congrès national des sociétés savantes* (Pau, 1969), histoire moderne, t. 2, 463–70.

very gallant, but gallant in a scandalous way. They no doubt measure their qualities by the number of their lovers and the publicity they can command.' And affairs could scarcely be kept secret in a society which loved to gossip, where houses had few alcoves and closets to which they could withdraw, and where they could always be spied on by their slaves.[36]

Affairs and sexual conquests were an accepted part of life in the Antilles, and, however much planters insisted that their main interest was to further their family fortunes, this did not make them any more faithful to partners back in France. The baptismal records in Le Cap and Port-au-Prince make frequent reference to illegitimate births and to the liaisons that were established between French planters and African women. These were often slaves or former slaves who worked as housekeepers and domestic servants, roles in which they gained privileges denied to those working in the fields, and who had less restricted access to their colonial masters. Casual sex and rape were frequent on the plantations, where slaves had little recourse against their masters, and slave women were frequently thought of as easy game by Frenchmen removed from the civilizing constraints of family life. For slave women, moreover, living with their master was also a way of buying their freedom from slavery. The process of creolization involved a certain fluidity in relations between the races, resulting in the birth of mulatto children who, as free people of colour, would go on to play a vital part in the multi-tiered racial structure of the Antilles. Sometimes the *colons* would marry their black mistresses; on other occasions they would simply live together, and we find them listed as the beneficiaries of their wills, often many years later.

A good example of this pattern of behaviour is Aimé-Benjamin Fleuriau, one of the most successful of La Rochelle's colonial merchants in the eighteenth century.[37] He left for Saint-Domingue in 1730 at the age of twenty-one to join his uncle's trading house, and would spend a quarter of a century on the island before returning to La Rochelle a very wealthy man. For much of this period he lived at La Croix-des-Bouquets with a woman variously described in official papers as either a 'ménagère' or 'négresse libre', and almost certainly one of his former slaves. Between 1740 and 1748 she bore him at least eight children, who were all duly baptized in the local church at Cul-de-sac. But he was not finished with procreation. On his return to France in 1755, and thinking of the future of his business, he took up with another woman, Marie-Anne-Suzanne Liège, twenty-three years his junior, whom he married in the following year and with whom he had six children, all born between 1758 and 1766. On his death it was she took

---

[36] Gabriel Debien, 'Une Nantaise à Saint-Domingue', *Revue du Bas-Poitou et des Provinces de l'Ouest*, 6 (1972), 413–14, 435.

[37] Jacques de Cauna, *Au temps des Isles à sucre: Histoire d'une plantation de Saint-Domingue au 18e siècle* (Paris, 1987).

control of his business on Saint-Domingue, though she ran it entirely from France, never bothering to set foot on the island.[38] His mulatto children were not forgotten, however. They were remembered in his will, and the two eldest, both girls, accompanied their father when he returned to France and spent the rest of their lives in La Rochelle, close to the family home. They saw their father marry, watched on as their six half-brothers and sisters were born, and remained on amicable terms with their new family. Fleuriau kept in touch with his children on Saint-Domingue, too, or with the two sons who survived. In 1777, he made a gift of four slaves to his elder son, Jean-Baptiste, who was described in the legal papers as a '*mulâtre libre*, living in Port-au-Prince'. By the time of Fleuriau's death in 1785, Jean-Baptiste had predeceased him, but Paul, his younger son, was left 26,000 *livres* in his will, and a similar sum was left to the next generation, to the sons and daughters of Jean-Baptiste.[39] Fleuriau, like so many others, had become a Creole: to his mind race did not define relationships in the way it still did to many in metropolitan France.

Life in the Caribbean was often hard and dangerous for one's health: men might grow old before their time and succumb to tropical diseases, and as they grew older, many lived in fear of an uncertain future, apprehensive lest they face a slave rebellion or die in an epidemic of yellow fever. Their correspondence was filled with their fears and anxieties, which they relayed to their families back in France. Unsurprisingly, health was a major topic of conversation. Their letters often told of sickness and disease, offered reassurances about the health of sons and daughters, and inquired desperately after the health of parents in France. The letters of Pierre-Jean Van Hoogwerff are typical in this regard. Every letter returned to issues of health, most especially that of his beloved daughter Betsy, for whose welfare, as we noted in an earlier chapter, he cared deeply.[40] Betsy appears to have been in a state of chronic ill-health, not helped, one must assume, by the ravages of the Caribbean heat. Although she was a young adult by the time his correspondence begins—in 1784 she would have been twenty years old—he writes of her as he would of a young child, a girl with the mental age of an infant who required of him a constant care and attention he was ill-equipped to provide. Van Hoogwerff, a slave-trader from La Rochelle who still saw himself as part of a Dutch extended family, wrote regularly about Betsy's condition to his brothers in the Hague and St Petersburg and to his sister, married to another merchant, William Stuart, in Edinburgh. These letters are infused with a genuine humanity, a Protestant conscience, and a concern for family matters. Yet in commercial matters he could appear hard and uncaring, not least about the welfare of the Africans in his employ. Writing in 1789, he notes that, of his two slave ships, one had earned

---

[38] Jacques de Cauna, *Fleuriau, La Rochelle et l'esclavage: trente-cinq ans de mémoire et d'histoire* (Paris: Les Indes savantes, 2017), 80–6.
[39] Ibid., 93.   [40] See Chapter 4, page 63.

nothing from its latest voyage, while the other, *L'Aimable Suzanne*, had performed much better, 'trading at a profit far beyond our hopes'; the voyage can be regarded as a good one, he adds rather casually, 'despite the fact that a hundred negroes died of smallpox during the crossing'.[41] For the caring Christian that he was, their deaths were a matter of little import.

Where plantations were owned by men from the west and south-west of France, their owners tended very frequently to look to their home regions for agents, factors, and others whom they had to trust with large sums of money and heavy responsibilities, often when they themselves were thousands of miles away. Distance posed a threat to their fortunes, as did political turmoil and the uncertainties of war and peace. In a letter of 25 June 1768, Dominique Clérisse notes that he has been unable to access the funds he required for his marriage because 'his fortune was too far distant, and in a country that is subject to too many great revolutions in wartime'.[42] It was comforting to do business with people close at hand, fathers and sons, agents and ship-owners back in France, preferably in the familiar settings of Bordeaux, Nantes, or Le Havre. Like soldiers and sailors on campaign, the owners of habitations in the Caribbean would reflect on the world they had left behind and their loved ones back home. Colonial life, too, could evoke a sense of loss, a spirit of nostalgia, and for many it was a matter of importance to keep these links alive. When they wanted to enquire after the health of their families, to consult with insurers or business partners, or to hire a crew for their next voyage, it was often to their home port that they wrote or to a ship heading home that they entrusted their mail. Home was, for many, still back in France, in those west-coast towns and cities where they had lived their adolescent years, where they still had close ties of family or friendship and to which many dreamt of returning when their working lives were over. This emotional pull is not peculiar to those from the west coast of France, of course; it is an almost universal characteristic of colonial societies, one that was to be found in every corner of the British Empire.[43] Transatlantic communication was always a two-way process, with messages about commerce, family illness, and life and death crossing the ocean in both directions.

Some plantation owners chose to return to France before old age set in, and to run their estates from afar, entrusting the day-to-day transactions to a factor or estate manager back in the Caribbean. They might do so for health reasons, or to invest their profits in property, or to send their children to French schools. But it

---

[41] AD Charente-Maritime, 4J 2848, letter-book of Pierre-Jean Van Hoogwerff, letter to his sister, 22 April 1789.

[42] CAOM, 95 APOM/2, Letter-book of Gilles Clérisse, letter to Dominique Clérisse in Bayonne, Paris, 25 June 1768.

[43] Alexia Grosjean, 'Returning to Belhelvie, 1593–1875: the impact of return migration on an Aberdeenshire parish', in Marjory Harper (ed.), *Emigrant Homecomings: The Return Movement of Emigrants, 1600–2000* (Manchester: Manchester University Press, 2005), 229.

was not easy to maintain control from a distance of several thousand miles, and those who returned often complained of lax management, sliding profits and poor productivity from the slaves. To manage effectively called for regular exchanges of papers and detailed accountancy if the owner was to remain in charge: he needed full lists of the slaves he owned, their ages, their functions, and their state of health; in addition, just as important for the owner of an *habitation*, he must keep abreast of fluctuations in sugar and indigo prices, and details of market trends, slave prices, and animal and crop disease. Absenteeism only worked if the owner was prepared to put in long hours and commit himself to hard work, and if he was lucky in his choice of agent and in the passivity of his slaves. Louis Drouin, for instance, having already established his position as one of the most prudent *négociants* trading with Saint-Domingue, bought two plantations near Saint-Marc, a town which he already knew well. This knowledge engendered trust and enabled him to leave the day-to-day running of the estate to others while he returned to Nantes. But he was careful not to lose control of his assets, appointing several people to represent his interests at all times and establishing a clear chain of command and responsibility. He might not be there in person, but his agents knew that they had to report to someone else, and no one was allowed too great autonomy of action.[44]

Another example of estate management at distance is the sugar plantation on Guadeloupe owned jointly by Jacques Reiset, who held the post of *receveur-général des finances* back in Rouen, and his cousin Xavier, who lived in Guadeloupe and maintained a frequent correspondence on the business affairs of the *sucrerie* in the decades after 1822.[45] As a result, the older man, in France, was able to study the regular lists he received of the slaves on their plantation, the majority *cultivateurs*, but including some who were employed as sugar-refiners, with their ages and state of health, the number of children among them, the number aged sixty and over, those who were in poor health.[46] He also received regular notes from his agent on the plantation, Giraud, with information about the prospects for the year: such matters as the state of the harvest, the price that could be obtained for sugar in Le Cap, any legal problems that had to be settled in court, and details of the purchase and sale of slaves. Giraud was keen to reassure him, and Jacques Reiset's replies suggest how much he relied on his agent's financial prudence. Occasionally, though, the news conveyed was more alarming and jolted the older man's confidence. In 1822, Giraud informed him of the 'catastrophe', as he calls it, which had befallen the neighbouring island of Martinique, where a hundred

---

[44] Laure Pineau-Defois, 'Un modèle d'expansion économique à Nantes de 1763 à 1792: Louis Drouin, négociant et armateur', *Histoire, économie et société*, 23 (2004), 387–8.

[45] For these papers, and especially the regular communication with his agent see CAOM, Fonds Privés (FP), 170 APOM.

[46] CAOM, FP. 170 APOM 4, *feuilles de recensement* for slaves on the Habitation Reiset, forms submitted annually from 1822.

escaped slaves, living in the mountains, had joined up with criminal elements to attack the plantations on the plain below, leaving around ten people injured and three dead. Giraud commented ominously that this sort of violence 'necessarily threatens the existence of all whites living in the Antilles'.[47] His fears were widely shared by *colons* across the French Caribbean, with many recognizing that theirs was a society living on borrowed time and that the revolutionary insurrection that had swept Saint-Domingue in the 1790s could at any moment undermine their well-being, too.

As the decades passed, the trading routes between France and the Caribbean saw more and more Frenchmen abandon their Creole lifestyle and return to France, usually by way of the same Atlantic ports through which they had travelled west in their youth. The more successful among them returned as wealthy men, their fortunes made, and with money to hand that they could invest back in France. Like the merchants on the Île Feydeau or along the quays of the Chartrons, many of the rich *colons* sought to buy handsome town houses or domains in the region of their birth, often decorating them with textiles, paintings, mahogany furnishings, and carved clocks to remind them of the luxury they had once enjoyed. During their exile in the Antilles, many had shown signs of a nostalgia for the France they had left behind; now, in their surroundings and in their choice of interior décor, they harked back to another world, to the rich colours and the exotic landscapes of the Caribbean.[48] Maps of the islands and prints of sugar plantations, watercolours of Caribbean landscapes, images of slaves at work in the fields or of slave girls in domestic service, scenes depicting African music-making and dance, and brightly coloured *indiennes* with traditional floral motifs were the very stuff of colonial taste.[49] The returned *colons*, like the colonial merchants and ship-owners who had been their partners in Atlantic commerce, did little to hide their wealth or disguise their taste for luxury. As in imperial Britain, the ripple effects of their wealth were felt in towns and villages across the west of France, places far beyond the merchant quarters of Nantes or Bordeaux. They returned as notables, men with money to spend who were prepared to enjoy the status and lifestyle that their wealth permitted. But if they brought prosperity to their wider communities through their lavish consumption, their wealth might also have aroused jealousy and some resentment.

But as the journal of one *colon* who had returned from Martinique would make clear, the France they returned to sometimes caused them bitter disappointment, and left some dreaming lovingly of the colours of the Caribbean countryside and

[47] CAOM, FP, 170 APOM 5, letter from Giraud in Guadeloupe to Jacques Reiset in Rouen, enclosing a letter written about the troubles in Martinique, 22 November 1822.

[48] See the catalogue of the exhibition 'Regards sur les Antilles: Collection Marcel Chatillon' (Bordeaux: Musée d'Aquitaine, 1999).

[49] Délie Muller, 'La constitution d'une collection et son inventeur averti, Marcel Chatillon', ibid., 16–17.

the plantation life they had left behind. Pierre Dessalles, it is true, belonged to a slightly later generation: he was a planter in Martinique from 1806 until the middle of the nineteenth century, troubled years when the opportunities available to white settlers were changing. But he was unashamedly nostalgic for his Caribbean island and the Creole lifestyle it had allowed him. Like many *colons*, he was a political conservative and a practising Catholic, and in his journal he reveals his goals, his family ambitions, and the practical and moral standards to which he feels a planter should adhere. With time he had become more Creole than French in his attitudes and prejudices, and, once back in France, he did not hide his admiration for the relaxed and informal manners of the Antilles. He regarded his investments in Martinique as more vital to his family interests than his properties in France; above all, he resented the fact that his children no longer treated him with respect. Indeed, there is much to suggest that he felt repelled by what he saw as the affectation of Paris. He felt oppressed by its materialism, its competitive consumer culture. 'How I miss my plantation in Martinique,' he would sigh, before calling it by name: 'Where is La Nouvelle Cité? How I would love to be there!'[50]

Those crossing the Atlantic to Europe were not all Frenchmen making their way back home; nor were they all Europeans, as the declarations of ships' captains to the admiralty in the principal slaving ports of the Atlantic coast reveal. From the late seventeenth century, indeed, it had been quite common for ships' captains to return to France with black slaves whom they employed as cooks, valets, and domestic servants. The Code noir only applied in the colonies, and once on French soil slaves could and did claim their freedom from any form of servitude. But the government was not consistent in its application of the freedom principle: in some cases manumission was made conditional on payment, while in others slaves were arbitrarily returned to their masters in the colonies. Some further codification was clearly required, and an edict of 1716 tried to establish the conditions on which slave-owners could bring their slaves to France without fear of losing them. But confusion ensued. The edict was not registered in the Parlement of Paris, and as a consequence slaves coming to France found themselves condemned to a 'legal limbo' that could only be settled in the courts.[51] As the number of court cases mounted, moreover, and slaves continued to claim their freedom in French law, the attitude of the executive hardened and the stipulations imposed became more and more restrictive. In 1777, the entry of black people into France was forbidden altogether, with anyone who allowed them to land at a French port liable to a fine of 3,000 *livres*, and the slave sentenced to deportation

---

[50] Elborg Forster and Robert Forster (eds), *Sugar and Slavery, Family and Race: The Letters and Diary of Pierre Dessalles, Planter in Martinique, 1808–1856* (Baltimore: Johns Hopkins University Press, 1996), 10–11.

[51] Sue Peabody, 'There are no Slaves in France': *The Political Culture of Race and Slavery in the Ancien Régime* (Oxford: Oxford University Press, 1996), 22.

on the first available ship.[52] But soon it became clear that the new law—which drew little distinction between freedmen and slaves—was easy to evade. Slaves were often allowed to land in France without submitting to the registration process, just as the Church reported a large increase in the number of interracial marriages. There is no doubt that the number of black men and women landing on French soil continued to rise.[53]

According to official figures, there were seven French cities which in 1777 housed more than fifty people of other races (though it must be acknowledged that some of these may have been short-term residents, those newly landed from colonial ships but bound for other parts of the kingdom). Besides Paris, to which many domestic servants were taken, the major Atlantic port cities unsurprisingly headed the list: Nantes with 338 residents and Bordeaux with 310, principally from the Caribbean, and Lorient with 132, largely from India and the East Indies. Following behind were the other Atlantic slaving ports: Le Havre (ninety-eight), La Rochelle (seventy-four), and Marseille (fifty-three). While most of their arrivals came on commercial ships, naval vessels also brought in black immigrants and refugees from slavery: Brest was home to around thirty-five and Rochefort to a further thirty.[54] Not all people of colour were slaves: among those settling in France were black soldiers who had served in the colonial regiments and former slaves who had been freed by their masters, either as a reward for their services or in their wills. In the Généralité of Bordeaux, for instance, the admiralty records show that ninety-four free blacks were living in the area, almost equally divided between men and women.[55] But these are official figures which generally under-estimate the number of immigrants. Over the century, Alain Croix suggests that the total number of people of colour who landed and settled in Nantes may have reached around 1,500.[56] Others were born in France, the sons and daughters of former slaves who had returned with their masters to France. In the parish of Saint-Nicolas in Nantes—the parish that included the merchant quarter of the Quai de la Fosse—the birth rate in the black community far exceeded the death rate. Between 1680 and 1792, parish records reveal that there were 266 baptisms compared to ninety-eight burials, a proportion far in excess of two to one.[57]

Indeed, for those walking along the docks in Nantes, Bordeaux and a handful of other coastal ports, the sight of Africans—generally young, male, and well-attired,

[52] Alain Croix (ed.), *Nantais venus d'ailleurs: Histoire des étrangers à Nantes des origines à nos jours* (Rennes: Presses Universitaires de Rennes, 2007), 108.

[53] Peabody, 'There are no Slaves in France', 121–36.

[54] Pierre H. Boulle, *Race et esclavage dans la France de l'Ancien Régime* (Paris: Perrin, 2007), 179.

[55] Marcel Koufinkana, *Les esclaves noirs en France sous l'Ancien Régime, 16ᵉ–18ᵉ siècles* (Paris: L'Harmattan, 2008), 110.

[56] Croix (ed.), *Nantais venus d'ailleurs*, 108–9.

[57] Erick Noël, 'Gens de couleur à Nantes et à Bordeaux au 18e siècle: mise au point, bilan et perspectives', in Éric Dubesset and Jacques de Cauna (eds), *Dynamiques caribéennes: Pour une histoire des circulations dans l'espace atlantique, 18ᵉ–19ᵉ siècles* (Bordeaux: Presses Universitaires de Bordeaux, 2014), 81.

and often in the company of their masters—had become commonplace, with the consequence that their presence on French soil would have caused little surprise. They were no longer slaves, but artisans and domestic servants, highly valued by their masters and clients, often seen as providing docile and cheap labour. Many had trades: statistics from the admiralty of Nantes show that among men the highest numbers were of cooks, wigmakers, and barrel-makers; among women, dressmakers, washerwomen, and nurses to small children.[58] Some married, in exceptional cases to white women, before settling in either their port of entry or, quite frequently, in Paris. As domestic servants, they impressed by their appearance and by a suggestion of exoticism, and—like Amerindians and the servants brought to France from the East Indies—they were a source of prestige and pride to those who employed them.[59] Some entered France on repeated occasions, passing freely back and forth across the Atlantic as crewmen on ships sailing either directly to the Caribbean or on triangular slaving voyages by way of Africa. In the nineteen years between 1770 and 1788, for instance, we know of twenty-four 'persons of colour', one of them a woman, who embarked on ships at La Rochelle as crew members. Thirty of the ships leaving La Rochelle in these years had one or more black crewmen, some still enslaved, but the majority free and paid wages for their labour. Ships' captains had few qualms about employing black cooks and seamen on slaving voyages, and their presence on board was deemed to be quite natural. Some, used as interpreters, had language skills that were uniquely valuable on triangular voyages to the west coast of Africa.[60] All were, first and foremost, experienced sailors.

Watching smartly dressed Africans going about their daily work, the citizens of the west-coast ports would have had little cause to associate them with the slaves who had endured the miseries of the Middle Passage or the cruel indignities of the plantations. The slave ships that took on their cargo at Bordeaux or Paimboeuf—the Loire at Nantes was too shallow to allow them to dock in the city—gave no hint of their future use: no slaves were ever brought to France, and the ships themselves were cargo vessels like any other, taking on a mixed cargo for their Atlantic voyage. Those in the know might recognize the bright textiles being hoisted aboard or note the presence in the cargo of firearms and gunpowder. But it was only once the ship was at sea, and safely distant from the French coast, that the tell-tale signs would appear. Carpenters would insert another deck, an *entrepont* between the actual deck and the bottom of the hold, that doubled the

---

[58] Koufinkana, *Les esclaves noirs en France*, 63–4.

[59] Mickaël Augeron, 'Des esclaves et des domestiques amérindiens à La Rochelle au 18e siècle', in Mickaël Augeron and Olivier Caudron (eds), *La Rochelle, l'Aunis et la Saintonge face à l'esclavage* (Paris, 2012), 182.

[60] Olivier Caudron, 'S'insérer dans une société de Blancs: destins de «gens de couleur» à la Rochelle et dans sa région, 18e – début 19e siècle', in Dubesset and de Cauna (eds), *Dynamiques caribéennes*, 90–2.

ship's capacity and allowed slaves to be chained on two separate levels during the crossing. Only then was the vessel transformed from the innocent cargo vessel it had appeared to be into a *négrier*, a ship specially designed to transport its human cargo. Once the slaves were sold, often on board in the harbour at Port-au-Prince or Le Cap, it was quickly transformed again for the return voyage, its new cargo the sugar, rum, and colonial produce that were so greatly prized in Europe. When the last slave had been auctioned, the ship once again became an innocent trader. The scaffolding holding the extra deck was dismantled along with the barrier that had been inserted to prevent the slaves from rioting. The wood that had been used to build them was sold, the bars and chains were removed, and all trace of its use as a slave ship was destroyed.[61] As a result, when the ship finally sailed back up the Loire or the Garonne, its mission accomplished, the people of France's port cities had no reason to feel queasy about the nature of its commerce or to question the source of their city's prosperity. There was nothing on deck or in the hold of the vessel that to suggest the human suffering it had witnessed. It was a simply another merchant ship returning from a profitable voyage to France's colonies.

[61] Bertrand Guillet, *La Marie-Séraphique, navire négrier* (Nantes: Musée d'histoire de Nantes, 2009), 117.

PART TWO
WAR AND REVOLUTION

6

Debating Slavery

Those who sent ships to Guinea and the Bight of Biafra felt under increasing attack from another quarter in the eighteenth century, from abolitionist writers and pamphleteers who professed themselves outraged by the immorality of the slave trade and denounced slaving as a crime perpetrated against fellow human beings. Slaving had not been an issue of much moral debate in earlier centuries, but the huge growth in the scale of the trade, combined with a heightened moral conscience in the wake of the Enlightenment, resulted in a growing unease in some quarters about the morality of making huge profits through buying human beings and selling them into slavery. Those who shared these moral qualms found inspiration in the new-found humanism of the eighteenth century and in the writings of some Enlightened authors, most especially Raynal, Voltaire, and Montesquieu. But we should be clear: there was no agreement among contemporaries about the rights and wrongs of the slave trade. What we are witnessing is growing concern over the issue, and public discussion of whether those condemned to slavery should enjoy the same rights as others. Was humanism to be reserved for Europeans alone, a prerogative of white races? Or was liberty a fundamental right of all human beings, a right that was denied when Africans were bought and sold and treated as chattels? Could slavery be made compatible with the dictates of reason? By the end of Louis XV's reign, these questions were being asked not only by French *philosophes* but by intendants, colonial governors, and government officials.[1] They were aware of the evils of the slave trade and sought ways to ameliorate the conditions of its victims, asking repeatedly the same question: was the system capable of reform?

Philosophical debate on slavery in the eighteenth century ranged over a wide range of topics: the equality of human beings in the eyes of God, the meaning and significance of negritude, the supposed qualities of different races, and what was coming to be seen as the civilizing mission of white Europeans across the globe were all proposed and debated. Not all were opposed to slavery. Some, indeed, were quite vehement in its defence, arguing from ideas of racial difference and questioning the universality of the rights of man. The reluctance to endorse abolition is not difficult to comprehend, since the system which was under attack

---

[1] Jean Tarade, 'Is Slavery Reformable? Proposals of Colonial Administrators at the End of the Ancien Régime', in Marcel Dorigny (ed.), *The Abolitions of Slavery: from Léger Félicité Sonthonax to Victor Schœlcher, 1793, 1794, 1848* (Oxford: Berghahn, 2003), 101–2.

as being contrary to the dictates of Reason and Justice was also the source of the material prosperity on which they all depended for their well-being.[2] Even philosophers could not afford to be entirely unworldly. Behind many of the arguments posited in defence of slavery, Montesquieu detected traces of European self-interest and self-aggrandizement which he pilloried in the most sardonic tones. 'The peoples of Europe,' he wrote in *L'Esprit des Lois*, 'once they had exterminated those of America, had to enslave those of Africa so that they could use them to clear such a great expanse of territory.'[3] For him it was a moral issue, a simple question of right and wrong. Elsewhere he wrote that he was not surprised that Negroes 'painted the devil in a dazzling white and their gods black like coal'.[4] It was, he felt, a just representation, one that condemned the crimes of the colonists and reflected their everyday experience of white rule. Abolitionists would continue to quote him and to look to him for inspiration and moral guidance.

But Montesquieu's concern with the slave trade, his belief that it was one of the major moral issues of the eighteenth century, was not typical of the French Enlightenment. The expression of indignation about the ill-treatment of African slaves remained rare in the writings of enlightened authors, whose concerns were generally with problems closer to home or with more abstract approaches to the question of liberty. For many *philosophes*, as for their followers, mankind was everywhere in chains, and there was nothing qualitatively different about African slavery that merited their interest.[5] Nor was there much economic criticism of slavery. The Physiocrats, though opponents of imperial preference and vigorous exponents of free trade, did little to question the economic basis of slavery, which seemed to them to be, in Philippe Steiner's words, 'everyday common sense' and a guaranteed source of cheap labour for the plantations. If there was a debate, it was about the relative economic benefits of slave and free labour. But, again, the argument had little to do with Africans' rights. It focused on how best colonial trade might be organized to accelerate the development of the French economy and how it might help to resolve the increasing disparity between France and Britain.[6]

Some did, however, join Montesquieu in openly challenging men's right to own or to trade in others. Rousseau, for instance, observed approvingly that in the state of nature slavery did not exist, since everyone was his own master and was not beholden to others.[7] He argued in general terms, without any particular reference

---

[2] Yves Benot, 'Diderot, Pechmeja, Raynal et l'anticolonialisme', in Roland Desné and Marcel Dorigny (eds), *Les Lumières, l'esclavage, la colonisation* (Paris: La Découverte, 2005), 107.

[3] Ehrard, *Lumières et esclavage*, 151.   [4] Ibid., 152.

[5] Daniel P. Resnick, 'The Société des *Amis* des Noirs and the abolition of slavery', *French Historical Studies*, 7 (1972), 561.

[6] Philippe Steiner, 'Slavery and French Economists, 1750–1830', in Dorigny (ed.), *The Abolitions of Slavery*, 134.

[7] Jonathan Israel, *Radical Enlightenment: Philosophy and the Making of Modernity, 1650–1750* (Oxford: Oxford University Press, 2001), 274.

to Africa or the Caribbean, concluding that slavery was an abrogation of rights, so that 'the words "slavery" and "right" are contradictory, they cancel each other out'.[8] He, too, believed—as did Diderot—that no man can rightly be considered to be born into slavery, just as no parent has the right to sell his children. Such ideas would be, they argued, against the laws of nature. Condorcet was equally forth-right in his condemnation of the institution of slavery, arguing in 1781, in his *Réflexions sur l'esclavage des Nègres*, that the time had come for France to move towards the progressive elimination of slavery from her colonies.[9] In the same vein, the abbé Raynal, in his *Histoire des Deux Indes*, maintained that no man has the right to sell himself into slavery in what was necessarily an inequitable deal in which he receives nothing and sacrifices everything. Raynal, as a priest, turned to theology to support his case, arguing that any man 'belongs to his first master, God, from whom he can never be freed'.[10] Raynal's work was not only a cry of protest against slavery; it was also a study of networks and communications between Europe and the Indies, east and west. Its importance lies in the influence it was able to exercise. Though the work was forgotten and disavowed in the nineteenth century, it was widely read in its own time, and among its readers were philosophers, statesmen, and creative writers from across Europe and the Amer-icas.[11] A once largely forgotten writer, he is now once again studied and analysed, this time from the viewpoint of the history of global exchange.[12]

For most Frenchmen, however, Atlantic slavery seemed a marginal issue, not an everyday concern, and this is reflected in the philosophers of the day, who devoted far more space in their writings to French institutions, justice and administration, than they did to slavery. And when they did talk about slavery, they often did so in a dry analytical way that did little to appeal to popular emotions and seemed divorced from contemporary problems. The plantations of the Americas or the horrors of the Middle Passage could seem very distant to a debate conducted around Montesquieu's critique of slavery in Ancient Rome, and French intellec-tuals seldom discussed it in immediate or human terms.[13] For many in France, as for Americans like Thomas Jefferson or George Washington on the other side of

[8] Jean-Jacques Rousseau, *The Social Contract* (London: Penguin, 1968), 58.

[9] Joachim Schwartz (pseudonym, Marie-Jean-Antoine-Nicolas Caritat, Marquis de Condorcet), *Réflexions sur l'esclavage des Nègres* (Neuchatel, 1781).

[10] Edward Derbyshire Seeber, *Anti-slavery Opinion in France during the Second Half of the Eighteenth Century* (Baltimore, MD, 1937), 67–8.

[11] Hans-Jürgen Lüsebrink and Manfred Tietz (eds), 'Lectures de Raynal: l'«Histoire des Deux Indes» en Europe et en Amérique au 18ᵉ siècle: actes du colloque de Wolfenbüttel', *Studies in Voltaire and the Eighteenth Century*, 286 (1991), *passim*.

[12] Cecil Courtney and Jenny Mander, 'Introduction', in Cecil Courtney and Jenny Mander (eds), *Raynal's Histoire des deux Indes: Colonialism, Networks and Global Exchange* (Oxford: Voltaire Foundation, 2015), 6.

[13] Matthias Middell, 'France, the Abolition of Slavery, and Abolitionisms in the Eighteenth Century', in Damien Tricoire (ed.), *Enlightened Colonialism: Civilization Narratives and Imperial Politics in the Age of Reason* (Basingstoke: Palgrave Macmillan, 2017), 249–50.

the Atlantic, there was no contradiction between slave-ownership and revolution-ary or humanitarian views of society at large.

Even in the pages of the *Encyclopédie* the issue of slavery is discussed principally in abstract terms, with the emphasis placed on past civilizations, with Egypt and Rome given greater prominence than present-day colonial society. Moreover, what is said about the slave trade is curiously neutral in tone. The entry on 'Negroes' acknowledges that there is a substantial commerce in Africans, and that negroes form 'the principal source of wealth of the inhabitants of the islands', but it is reluctant to condemn it. There is some discussion of their strengths and weaknesses as field workers, of where 'the best negroes' were to be found—Cape Verde, Angola, Senegal—and of the different routes by which they come to be enslaved. Here the article placed much of the responsibility on the Africans themselves. Some, it was suggested, sold themselves of their own free will to local kings and princes in order to escape famine and misery in Africa; others had been taken prisoner in wars between local kings and tribes. And, once in the Caribbean, where they would become the responsibility of their new masters, the picture that is painted is one of almost unbelievable paternalism. Humanitarian-ism combined with self-interest to ensure that they were well treated: for the first ten days in the colonies, we are assured, they are well fed, rested, and given sea baths to prepare them for work, while the masters who bought new slaves were obliged to instruct them in Christianity. At the same time, those slaves who had already settled on the plantations would reassure them, tell them what was expected of them, and 'explain to them that they had been bought to work, and not to be eaten, as some of them imagined when they saw that they were being well fed'.[14]

Discussion of the trade in eighteenth-century France was usually couched in deeply utilitarian terms: whether the slaves were well looked after, whether their rights were being breached, or whether it would be possible to manage the sugar plantations without some form of forced servitude. The abolitionists had no economic arguments to offer, and, since there were few philosophical principles at stake, even committed humanists seem to have viewed the question with a culpable indifference. If there was a new scientific interest in issues of race, it was directed at other questions: explaining why men were born with skins of different colours, understanding the nature of negritude in an age which believed it had refuted earlier theological explanations and could find answers in science.[15] Biologists and naturalists turned to these questions, too, often concluding, like Buffon, that if all human beings had a similar constitution, if they shared the same

[14] Diderot and d'Alembert, *Encyclopédie, ou Dictionnaire raisonné des Sciences, des Arts et des Métiers*, entry on 'Nègres', vol.11, 76–80.

[15] Muriel Brot, 'La couleur des hommes dans l'*Histoire des deux Indes*', in Sarga Moussa (ed.), *L'idée de «race» dans les sciences humaines et la littérature, 18ᵉ et 19ᵉ siècles* (Paris: L'Harmattan, 2003), 91.

interests and the same sources of pleasure, then the differences between the 'varieties of the species', differences in stature, physiognomy, skin colour and customs, must be explained by accidental, external factors such as heat and climatic conditions. As a naturalist, he believed that human beings could and should be studied like any other living creatures, and concluded that 'the human race is not composed of radically different species', but of men of common origins who had been marked by differences in climate, diet, disease, and life-style.[16] Buffon and Voltaire agreed on this point; they also appeared to agree on the intrinsic cultural supremacy of the white race, a common supposition in what was a very Eurocentric literature.[17] In the same vein, travellers set out on scientific voyages to visit foreign lands and exotic cultures, writing up accounts of their travels and of the peoples they encountered. For Volney, for instance, an inveterate traveller and orientalist, there could be no assumption of equality between different races: race was a subject for scientific research and anthropological inquiry, a means of building an understanding of the rest of humanity. He had the good grace to admit that Reason alone could not achieve this, since 'we reason too much in accordance with our own ideas, and not sufficiently in accordance with theirs'.[18]

The arguments often lacked sensibility and emotional depth. They did not appeal to the sympathies of the reader or express a sense of shared suffering. As Jean Ehrard has pointed out, everyday life in France was often brutal and violent; in Alsace and other parts of the east forms of serfdom still lingered on; and justice was enforced through cruel and exemplary punishments, carried out in public places before crowds of baying onlookers. Executions were staged as public spectacles, the pain and suffering quite deliberately dramatized, as a deterrent, of course, but more critically as a harsh reminder of the power of the state.[19] No one who witnessed the drawing and quartering of Damiens on the Place de Grève in Paris in 1759 would have been shocked by the tortures perpetrated on the bodies of slaves in the Antilles. He was not only to die for attempted regicide; he was to suffer, as an example to others:

> On a scaffold that will be erected there, the flesh will be torn from his breasts, arms, thighs and calves with red-hot pincers; his right hand, holding the knife with which he committed the said parricide, burnt with sulphur; and on those places where the flesh will be torn away, poured molten lead, boiling oil, burning

[16] Buffon, 'De l'homme', in Silvia Marzagalli et al. (eds), *Comprendre la traite négrière atlantique* (Bordeaux: SCÉRÉN-CRDP Aquitaine, 2009), 228.

[17] José-Michel Moureaux, 'Race et altérité dans l'anthropologie voltairienne', in Moussa (ed.), *L'idée de «race»*, 46.

[18] Simone Carpentari Messina, 'Penser altérité: les «races d'hommes» chez Volney', in Moussa (ed.), *L'idée de «race»*, 117.

[19] Pieter Spierenburg, *The Spectacle of Suffering: Executions and the Evolution of Repression from a Pre-industrial Metropolis to the European Experience* (Cambridge: Cambridge University Press, 1984), 43.

resin, wax and sulphur melted together; and then his body drawn and quartered by four horses, and his limbs and body consumed by fire... [20]

Against the background of such state-sponsored cruelty, how could people be expected to react to mundane acts of everyday cruelty, the beatings and hangings that were meted out to insubordinate or runaway slaves? In any case, this was not the dominant image of Caribbean slavery. 'In contrast to these accustomed horrors,' Ehrard explains, 'in Versailles, Paris or the great ports along the Atlantic, colonial exploitation offered its most smiling face.' What people encountered at court and in Parisian salons 'was not its drivers brandishing their whips' but 'beautiful women toying with little black boys dressed in red'.[21] The image of negritude and the reflection of the Caribbean that were most familiar to French-men were carefully sanitized.

What seems lacking in most French writings on the slave trade is any expres-sion of the enthusiasm or moral outrage that are to be found in the English abolitionists of the day, like William Wilberforce or Thomas Clarkson, little sense that opposition to the slave trade might one day mobilize public opinion in France or become a popular political cause in its own right. Indeed, when the abolitionist movement in France did become more militant and started to win over the public, it was often to English publications that it turned, overseeing their translation into French and citing their authors—particularly Clarkson—as pioneers and leaders of liberal opinion. Anti-slavery as a moral cause did not arouse the same level of indignation in Catholic France as in Protestant England, and where members of the clergy did comment on the slave trade in the port cities of western France, it was usually without any hint of condemnation. In 1765, for instance, the *abbé* Jacques-Olivier Pleuvri published a history of Le Havre which enjoyed consider-able success. His coverage of the eighteenth century dismissed the slave trade in half a page within a chapter on the city's commerce, treating it without emotion as an unexceptional part of mercantile life. Nothing about it caused him to express any repugnance or seemed to prick his clerical conscience.[22]

This lack of moral concern is not easy to explain. In France, those professing Christian beliefs played a full part in profiting from the slave trade, and there was little discernible difference between Catholics and Protestants, with both commu-nities deeply implicated. Did it matter that France was at least nominally a Catholic state? While Britain, the United States, and other Protestant countries seemed prepared to give a lead on abolition, most Catholic states showed no desire

---

[20] This graphic description, drawn from a contemporary account (*Pièces et procedures du procès fait à Robert-François Damiens*, published in Paris in 1757) is famously reproduced in Michel Foucault, *Discipline and Punish: The Birth of the Prison* (New York: Vintage Books, 1995), 3.

[21] Jean Ehrard, 'Slavery before the Moral Conscience of the French Enlightenment: Indifference, Unease and Revolt', in Dorigny (ed.), *The Abolitions of Slavery*, 112.

[22] Hervé Chabannes, 'Entre prise de parole et occultation: les intellectuels havrais, la traite des Noirs et l'esclavage', *Revue du Philanthrope*, 4 (2013), 146.

to intervene. Perhaps it was because the great Catholic nations of Iberia, Spain and Portugal, were so deeply involved in the slave trade, and saw their interests threatened by abolition. Or perhaps it was because the Pope did not get round to condemning slavery until 1839, by which time, of course, the issue had ceased to be so contentious.[23] But even then it is clear that politics continued to cloud the Vatican's judgement, with Rome insistent that it could not be seen to defer to British pressure and that a proper condemnation would only result if, and only if, Britain requested it in concert with a Catholic power.[24] The case for abolition was not couched, as it was in England, in religious terms or on a specifically Christian basis, appealing to spirituality and emotion, but was expressed, as we have seen, in the elitist philosophical language of the Enlightenment. The clerical authorities in France largely refrained from comment. They either approved of the institution of slavery, or else simply kept quiet, leaving a void for others to fill, with the consequence that the movement for religious anti-slavery evolved only slowly, largely after Napoleon's reinstitution of the slave trade in 1802 or through the activities of organizations like the *Société de la morale chrétienne*.[25] But that did not really take off until the 1820s. Until that time, the French Church would appear to have offered little by way of moral leadership. Even during the debates on American independence, inspiration for anti-slavery often seems to have originated in England.[26] Non-conformists, and especially the Society of Friends, the Quakers, had a disproportionate part to play.[27]

Clarkson himself was not a Quaker, though he established strong connections with Quaker networks, which were vital to his activism and to his success in mobilizing a mass movement against the slave trade.[28] He would attribute much of the popularity which he enjoyed in Britain to what he called the influence of 'religious progress', and particularly to the growth of Protestant groups like Methodists in the cities of the north of England. Even Britain's slave ports, like Bristol and Liverpool, could galvanize abolitionist sentiment, with large crowds turning out to hear abolitionist speeches—and that despite the fact that the livelihoods of many in these cities depended on the prosperity that colonial

---

[23] Apostolic letter *In supremo apostolates*, 3 December 1839.

[24] Paul Kielstra, *The Politics of Slave Trade Suppression in Britain and France, 1814–48* (Basingstoke: Palgrave MacMillan, 2000), 198–9.

[25] Marie-Laure Aurenche (ed.), *Le combat pour la liberté des Noirs dans le Journal de la Société de la Morale Chrétienne* (2 vols, Paris: L'Harmattan, 2011). The Society was one of the few specifically Christian organizations in France to play an active role in the campaign against the illegal slave trade after 1820.

[26] Marie-Jeanne Rossignol, 'The Quaker Anti-slavery Commitment and How it Revolutionized French Anti-Slavery through the Crèvecoeur-Brissot Friendship', in Brycchan Carey and Geoffrey Plank (eds), *Quakers and Abolition* (Urbana-Champaign: University of Illinois Press, 2014), 180–93.

[27] James Walvin, *The Quakers: Money and Morals* (London: John Murray, 1997), 126–8.

[28] Dee E. Andrews and Emma Jones Lapansky-Werner, 'Thomas Clarkson's Quaker Trilogy: Abolitionist Narrative as Transformative History', in Carey and Plank (eds), *Quakers and Abolition*, 194.

commerce bestowed. Support for abolition came from all classes of society, not least from industrial workers in the midlands and the north. 'To Christianity alone,' said Clarkson, 'we are indebted for the new and sublime spectacle of seeing men and women go beyond the bands of individual usefulness to each other; of seeing them associate for the extirpation of private and public misery; and of seeing them carry their charity, as a united brotherhood, into distant lands.'[29] Of course, as a committed Christian himself, he may have exaggerated the importance of religious faith in explaining the growth of abolitionism as a popular cause. And politicians in England were more accustomed to look to the Scriptures than they were in France (though it is worth noting that in Britain, pro-slavery campaigners also cited the Bible in support of their claims).[30] But where religious leadership was absent, as in France, it seems undeniable that the campaign remained rather low-key and that popular enthusiasm of the kind that was seen at English abolitionist rallies simply failed to materialize.

Clarkson enjoyed an unusual level of popularity and exposure in France, and not just because he was a well-known English abolitionist. He had, among the English anti-slavery campaigners, a unique knowledge of the French Antilles, and he had admirers in France and throughout the French Caribbean. More importantly, perhaps, he was a superb publicist for the abolitionist cause. Before, during, and after the Revolution he argued against the slave trade and persisted in his demand that the slaving nations examine their consciences and press ahead with abolition. His argument was as much a religious as a political one. He saw abolition as a potent symbol of Britain's Protestant morality, and he clamoured for action, unwilling to be 'answerable for the guilt' of doing nothing.[31] But what appealed most strongly to abolitionists in France was the moral tone of his writings, the insistence that abolition was not only a dictate of Reason but a cry from the heart and a response to the suffering of Africa. Clarkson did what no French abolitionist had done: he made his cause a religious crusade, presenting it as a litmus test of Christian faith. His Society for the Abolition of the Slave Trade, founded in London in 1787, not only lobbied parliament for abolition. It also conducted research of its own which helped to expose the iniquities of the trade, research that was as relevant to France as it was to Britain and which would be fed into France's own abolitionist campaign. In 1789, for instance, Clarkson was able to answer questions sent to him by Mirabeau on behalf of the *Amis des Noirs*, questions about the means that the French used to enslave Africans and about

---

[29] Christopher Leslie Brown, 'Christianity and the Campaign against Slavery and the Slave Trade', in Stewart J. Brown and Timothy Tackett (eds), *The Cambridge History of Christianity, vol. 7, Enlightenment, Reawakening and Revolution, 1660–1815* (Cambridge: Cambridge University Press, 2006), 517.

[30] Michael Taylor, 'British proslavery arguments and the Bible, 1823–1833', *Slavery and Abolition*, 37 (2016), 139–58.

[31] Ellen Gibson Wilson, *Thomas Clarkson: A Biography* (Basingstoke: Macmillan, 1989), 125.

their condition before the arrival of the slave ships. He had a deep understanding of the question because he had built up a network of correspondents to whom he could turn. To Mirabeau he passed on information regaled to him by Geoffrey de Villeneuve, who had served for two years as aide-de-camp to the French Governor of Gorée in Senegal. He was better informed about French slaving than the foremost anti-slavery campaigners in Paris.[32]

Clarkson researched into the conditions in which the slaves were kept, investigating the dimensions and deck plans of slave ships sailing out of Liverpool in a bid to expose the demeaning conditions in which human beings were piled up on board. The result was what became perhaps the most effective single piece of propaganda against the slave trade, a plan of the slave ship *Brooks*, supposedly to scale, showing the dimensions of the ship and the way in which the slaves were piled on top of one another for the duration of the Atlantic crossing. It did not matter that the drawing may have lacked accuracy: it made a powerful appeal to the emotions, conveying something of the claustrophobia felt by the captives and suggesting that the heavy mortality during the voyage was linked to the way in which so many human beings were stuffed into an enclosed space. The image of the *Brooks* became instantly memorable. It had, says Marcel Chatillon, a 'directness of gaze' and a terrible sense of dramatic suffering the few pictures could equal, and in both Britain and France it became an iconic reminder of the cruelty and barbarism of the slave trade.[33] In England it helped to sway opinion in parliament and in the country. In France it was reprinted by anti-slavery activists, not least by the newly established *Société des Amis des Noirs* in 1788 which valued the evidence of the English abolitionists all the more highly as no such research had been done on the slave trade in France; indeed their first wave of leaders had not even visited the slave plantations of the Caribbean.[34] In the following year, Clarkson launched a coordinated campaign in Paris to try to win over the National Assembly, sending across 1,000 prints showing the cross-section of the slave ship with a comprehensive text in French, and though they did not sway a majority in the Assembly, they helped win over a number of prominent deputies to the cause of abolition, among them the *abbé* Grégoire.[35] By then abolition had become a truly transnational cause.

Political debates conducted through pamphlets and the press were followed keenly in the provinces and in French colonies overseas, where arguments about the rights and wrongs of the slave trade had a particular resonance. Bordeaux, for

---

[32] Françoise Thésée, 'Au Sénégal, en 1789: Traite des nègres et société africaine dans les royaumes de Sallum, de Sin et de Cayor', in Serge Daget (ed.), *De la traite à l'esclavage: Actes du Colloque International sur la traite des Noirs* (2 vols, Nantes: Centre de recherche sur l'histoire du monde atlantique, 1988), vol. 2, 222–4.

[33] Marcel Chatillon, 'La diffusion de la gravure du *Brooks* par la Société des *Amis* des Noirs et son impact', in Daget (ed.), *De la traite à* l'esclavage, vol. 2, 136–7.

[34] Resnick, 'The Société des *Amis* des Noirs and the abolition of slavery', 560.

[35] Chatillon, 'La diffusion de la gravure du *Brooks*', 141.

example, had every reason to take an interest in the question of slavery, and in the questions of rights and ethnicity which it raised. And it had the intellectual infrastructure to do so. The city's elite was not restricted to *négociants* and *armateurs* whose professional activities brought them into daily contact with the slave trade; it also contained liberal nobles, men of letters, and a powerful legal fraternity whose concern for the law naturally engaged with questions of rights and liberties. They had, moreover, multiple opportunities to meet and discuss ideas, including—in the city of Montaigne and Montesquieu—the philosophical ideas that were current at the time. By the outbreak of the Revolution, public affairs were being discussed in various overlapping institutions, as well as in the newspapers, pamphlets, and ephemeral publications that abounded in the 1780s. Men met socially in cafés and masonic lodges, in the Chamber of commerce, and in learned societies like the Académie de Bordeaux and the recently founded Musée. Most of these bodies had a fixed membership from whom they levied subscriptions; they were not open to all comers. But for that reason they were places where one could meet with like-minded people and discuss political matters in a relatively secure and harmonious atmosphere.

The most venerable intellectual society in the city was the Académie of Bordeaux, which had received its letters patent from Louis XIV in 1713 and continued to meet regularly throughout the century to discuss scientific, moral, and medical issues that were deemed to be of topical interest. The Académie brought together men from different legal estates and professions, though the dominant group were undoubtedly the *parlementaires*, men who shared a natural interest in the law and politics. This was, of course, the group to which Montesquieu himself belonged— in 1721 he spoke urging a greater spirit of intellectual inquiry[36]—and both he and Montaigne figured prominently on the Académie's programme. But membership was not restricted to any intellectual clique or to the legal profession. Rather, its meetings brought together large swathes of the city's elite: between 1713 and 1793, Charles Higounet identified 175 of its members, of whom fifty-six were nobles, thirty-two held offices under the Crown, thirty-two were clergy, and sixty-eight were bourgeois, among them a cluster of members of the medical profession.[37] There were, however, few merchants among its membership. They preferred to foregather in the Chamber of commerce, where both public debates and private conversations were closely tied to economic and commercial questions, leaving the questions of slavery and human rights to those with a legal training.

It was largely to fill this void and to provide the merchant families of the Chartrons with intellectual debate and stimulation that the Musée was founded in

---

[36] Pierre Barrière, *L'Académie de Bordeaux, centre de culture internationale au 18ᵉ siècle, 1712–92* (Bordeaux: Bière, 1951), 10.

[37] Louis Desgraves and Charles Higounet, 'La vie intellectuelle et musicale', in François-Georges Pariset (ed.), *Bordeaux au dix-huitième siècle*, 79.

1783. The Musée did not cater for the traditional elite of Bordeaux, the *parlemen-taires* and legal patriciate of the city. A membership list published in 1787 noted the high number of merchants (27.8 per cent of the total) and lawyers (20.6 per cent), with a further 16 per cent drawn from royal officials, 'les officiers nobles de justice et de finance'. It included some of the leading merchants in the city, men with wealth and status such as Bonnaffé and Cabarrus, Dutasta and Laffon aîné, Nairac and Ravezies. The Musée was the also forum where many of the future Girondins and of those who would make their mark on the city's revolutionary politics plotted, networked, and served their political apprenticeship.[38] To take just one example, Marguerite-Élie Guadet, who would go on to be a founder member of the city's principal republican club and to serve the Gironde in the Legislative Assembly, first spoke at the Musée.[39] Two other future deputies, Vergniaud and Gensonné, also attended. In the years up to 1789, its members debated a wide range of matters linked to commerce and to the Antilles, and they were surely fully aware of the moral dilemmas involved. Yet—and despite the fact that several of its members are known to have engaged in the slave trade, Laffon de Ladebat and Paul Nairac among them—slavery was not a subject that figured greatly on the Musée's agenda. This can only suggest that their silence was tactical, and that no one wished to disturb the calm and decorum in which the members took such obvious pride. It also signals the varied functions of the Musée, which was not primarily a debating society for the politically aware but a society in which men and women of taste could learn new skills or take their ease. If intellectual discussion was important to them, so were the arts, literature, and particularly music. It offered courses in modern languages, in mathematics, and in practical crafts.[40] It also promoted concerts. Between 1784 and 1793, the *Journal de Guienne* advertised some seventy-five concerts in the Musée, many of them featuring leading musicians of the day and making a major contribution to the cultural life of the city.[41] Its members went to be entertained as well as to be educated.

The Académie, in contrast, did devote a considerable amount of attention to the question of negritude, though, as a scientific society, its members showed more interest in biological than in political or economic issues. They were well aware of the presence of black men and women in their city, and they understood the degree to which Bordeaux's prosperity was reliant on slavery. During much of the century, abolitionists did not make themselves heard at meetings, and the main

---

[38] Maïté Bouyssy, 'Le Musée négrier', *Lumières*, 3 (2004), *L'esclavage et la traite sous le regard des Lumières*, 109–10.

[39] BM Bordeaux, MS 829(3), Musée de Bordeaux, list of members for 1784 and of officers for 1788.

[40] Musée d'Aquitaine, *Bordeaux au 18ᵉ siècle: Le commerce atlantique et l'esclavage* (Bordeaux: Musée d'Aquitaine, 2010), 31.

[41] Michel Hild, 'Les concerts à la fin du 18ᵉ siècle d'après le *Journal de Guienne*', in Patrick Taïeb, Jean Gribenski, and Natalie Morel-Borotra (eds), *Le Musée de Bordeaux et la musique, 1783–93* (Rouen: Publications des Universités de Rouen et du Havre, 2005), 123–37.

focus of debates was the appearance and skin colour of Africans and the meaning that should be attached to their pigmentation. In this they were, of course, following a well-trodden path, in line with the concerns of scientists in Paris and other cities; but the interest they showed in the question also reflects the concerns of local notables in Bordeaux and its surrounding region. One of the major activities of the Académie was the setting of an annual essay competition, open to the public, on a selected theme, and it is interesting how regularly questions of trade and colonization recur. The Academicians looked for scientific analysis, and valued ideas that were founded on personal experience or medical diagnosis. Equally, they distrusted ideas that were presented as theological truth. This was shown in the judging of the competition of 1741—when no prize was finally awarded—on the subject of 'what causes the colour of Negroes'. Of the seventeen entries, the judges preferred the submissions that based their argument on experience or observation, even if none of the arguments proposed convinced everyone. They quickly discarded those that talked of Africans as the descendants of Cain or which depended for their force on Biblical citation. They were also divided on the more 'scientific' explanations. Some propounded the fashionable argument that skin colour was determined by climate; others veered in the direction of nineteenth-century racial theories, claiming that there were incontestable genetic differences between white and black, though they were careful to avoid suggesting any hierarchy between races.[42]

Freemasonry flourished in all the Atlantic port cities, the lodges providing a meeting-place for merchants, investors, ships' captains, and the many men who derived their living from the sea. The diversity of the maritime communities undoubtedly contributed to the popularity of the lodges, for in most of the ports the commercial elite contained men who had been attracted there by the trading opportunities they offered, men from different provinces of France and from across Europe, men of different religious creeds and none, men whose commercial activities meant that they were often on the move, mixing with people from different countries and with different thoughts and ideas. For many the lodges, with their traditions of freethinking, offered the perfect environment to meet others of like mind, as well as a place to welcome visitors who were members of lodges elsewhere. Some had especially strong ties with the merchant community: in Nantes, for instance, four of the city's five lodges on the eve of the Revolution had a high merchant membership.[43]

Lodges also, it has been suggested, embraced traditions that made them especially accessible to those who worked at sea; in the words of two recent scholars of

[42] Marie Bové, 'Mémoires présentés à l'Académie de Bordeaux au 18e siècle: «La cause de la couleur des nègres»', *Institut Aquitain d'Etudes Sociales, bulletin*, 76 (2001), 144–74.

[43] Jean-Marc Masseaut, 'Les milieux négriers et la franc-maçonnerie à Nantes', in Cécile Révauger and Éric Saunier (eds), *La Franc-maçonnerie dans les ports* (Bordeaux: Presses Universitaires de Bordeaux, 2012), 207.

the subject, 'by marrying festivity and reflection, and by favouring initiation rites and mutual help, the lodge was in effect upholding values which were those of seafaring communities'.[44] It was perhaps especially valuable to those, like the Protestants of La Rochelle, who were discouraged from worshipping freely in their congregations. But it was also useful for merchants seeking to build friend-ships and associations with planters in the Caribbean, and, since they were often among the leading merchants in their respective ports, the *négriers* made full use of them. They corresponded with merchants and plantation owners in their sister lodges on Saint-Domingue, while in their own lodges they promoted leading slavers to positions of trust and responsibility. In Le Havre, a slave ship fitted out in 1787 was named *Le Franc-maçon* in a clear sign that there was no incompatibility between slaving and lodge membership, while ships from other Atlantic ports carried the names of masonic lodges or masonic symbolism (*La Parfaite Union, La Concorde, L'Amitié, Les Vrais Amis*). In Nantes in the 1780s, lodges specifically listed a member's profession as 'négrier' on the certificates they issued to allow them to be received in lodges elsewhere.[45] Freethinking clearly did not exclude slave-trading or profiteering from human misery, and there was no shame involved if one advertised one's participation in the trade to others.

The bodies which most directly spoke for the merchant community, however, were the chambers of commerce, and it is here that the collective voice of colonial traders was most stridently heard. The chambers had mostly been established during the eighteenth century, and they would remain the principal spokesmen for mercantile interests until their abolition, as privileged corporations, in 1791. Privileged they undoubtedly were in the eyes of the revolutionaries; yet it is difficult to argue that they were not representative of the trading community, bringing together a large number of those who sailed, fitted out, and financed colonial commerce. They also took responsibility for making political submissions on behalf of the merchants. In Bordeaux, when the merchants were asked to draft a *cahier de doléances* in the spring of 1789 in advance of the meeting of the Estates-General, it was the Chamber that called a meeting of all the '*négociants-armateurs, assureurs, banquiers* et *commissionnaires*' working in the city, all those who cooperated in fitting out ships for the Antilles. The meeting was well attended: the register of the Chamber contains 509 names, including eleven listed as 'négociants juifs', Jewish merchants who as yet did not enjoy full civil rights but who, as major players in the port, were respected and listened to.[46] The Chamber

---

[44] Cécile Révauger and Éric Saunier, 'Introduction', *ibid.*, 11–12.

[45] Eric Saunier, 'Les francs-maçons français, la traite des Noirs et l'abolition de l'esclavage: bilan et perspectives', in Jacques de Cauna and Cécile Révauger, *La société des plantations esclavagistes. Caraïbes francophone, anglophone, hispanophone: regards croisés* (Paris: Les Indes savantes, 2013), 143.

[46] AD Gironde, C 4438, Chambre de Commerce de Guienne, 'Répertoire contenant les noms de MM les négociants-armateurs, assureurs, banquiers et commissionnaires, convoqués à l'Assemblée qui doit avoir lieu, le 2 mars 1789, dans l'Hôtel de la Bourse'.

would prove a forceful mouthpiece for mercantile interests in the months that followed. In 1789, interestingly, it placed great emphasis on free trade and the abolition of company privileges; and it demanded the suppression of the various dues and taxes that fell on wine exports. However, it was silent on the question of slavery.[47]

One possible explanation for this silence is that, with the Revolution approaching, the Chamber was reluctant to expose itself to obloquy by coming out in support of the slave trade, even if the interests of many of its members were dependent upon it. Another is that it was genuinely divided on the issue, and that the writings of the Enlightenment and the debates in Bordeaux had altered the moral compass of at least a part of its membership. A third reason can be found in the strength of the conflicting lobbies to which the Chamber was exposed. As the months passed, it found itself caught between the demands of its members in France and the increasingly insistent calls for support from traders and planters in the Caribbean, many of whom retained close ties with family back home. Trade quickly gained the upper hand. Pamphlets circulated freely between the various chambers and city authorities in France, and a stream of petitions and protests arrived on returning ships from the Caribbean as the planters of Martinique, Guadeloupe, and Saint-Domingue piled moral pressure on their partners back home. In their eyes, justice was on their side. The planters had become victims of slave violence and aggression at the very moment when liberty, that most revolutionary of ideals, was being preached in France. They embraced liberty with alacrity, but not in the political sense that the Assembly intended. They thought rather of liberty from state intervention, the liberty to trade freely and exploit others in the name of profit.[48]

Unease among the merchant community was already growing in 1788—unease about the future of the colonies, of course, but also about the threats to prosperity which they saw all around them. A pamphlet of March 1788, for instance, talks of a decline in economic activity and a general malaise in Bordeaux. It was written by a merchant from eastern France and printed in Neufchatel, a merchant who knew the city's reputation and had come expecting to find a booming port and full employment. He declared himself to be both disappointed and disturbed by what he saw. The rich bustling market he had expected to find had been replaced by tepid trading and half-empty docks. Bordeaux, more than Lyon, had suffered as a result of the Eden Treaty of 1786 with England, which had opened the French market to mass-produced English manufactures at a time when French domestic industry was still undercapitalized and in need of protection. The pamphlet

---

[47] AM Bordeaux, AA 26, cahier de doléances de la ville de Bordeaux, sent to the Assemblée du Tiers Etat de Guienne, 6 April 1789.

[48] Hélène Sarrazin, 'Comment peut-on défendre l'esclavage?', Institut Aquitain d'Études Sociales, bulletin, 76 (2001), 182.

expressed dismay that the terms of the treaty were entirely in England's interest.[49] The great fairs had declined; the surety of lenders had been sacrificed, with debtors 'insolently' ignoring their debts; unemployment had risen; construction had ground to a halt; and since there were reduced levels of money in circulation, landlords had been unable to rent their rooms. The city, in short, was facing, even before 1789, the reality of a downward spiral, an economic recession. Even when we allow for the author's strongly pro-Bourbon prejudice, his reflexions would have made uncomfortable reading for many in Bordeaux. The golden goose of colonial commerce was, it seemed, threatened by yet another downturn in a trade on which they had, perhaps rather unhealthily, come to depend.[50] And though the writer no doubt exaggerated the level of his alarm, his words confirmed the worst fears of many who traded on the Bordeaux waterfront. Merchants across the Atlantic world regarded the Revolution's commercial policies with disquiet and not a little concern for the future of their colonial markets.

That does not necessarily mean that all merchants were entirely self-consumed, or that none expressed reservations about the morality of the slave trade. Some showed an awareness of the wider picture, and even of the political, economic and social problems which slavery posed. They understood that there were contradictions between the liberties they were claiming for themselves and those, the most fundamental, which they continued to deny those they enslaved.[51] Even the ships' captains who sailed for Africa and bought and sold their human cargoes could betray signs of humanity, indications that they, too, shared some of the moral doubts that were gaining support in humanist circles. Joseph Crassous, born in La Rochelle and son of a royal notary, was attracted from a very young age to life at sea, and, having failed to be accepted as an officer cadet in the navy, he threw himself eagerly into life in the merchant marine, sailing out of his home port on merchant vessels to the Caribbean. In 1772, on his return to La Rochelle, he was appointed as first lieutenant on the slaver *Le Roy Dahomet*, sailing to the coast of Guinea, and then on to Le Cap. In the course of this voyage, Crassous kept a very detailed ship's log, which allows us not only to follow the day-by-day progress of the voyage but also to read some of his reflections on what he was witnessing. In it he described the raiding parties on the African coast and suggests that European slavers—he singles out the Dutch in particular—were deliberately fomenting conflict among African nations so as to lay their hands on more captives. Though common knowledge today, it seems to have surprised and appalled the young

---

[49] For a contemporary British view of the treaty, see 'A short vindication of the French treaty, from the charges brought against it in a late pamphlet, entitled, A view of the treaty of commerce with France, signed at Versailles, Sept. 28, 1786, by Mr. Eden' (London, 1787).

[50] AD Gironde, Fonds Bigot, 8J 703, Chambre de Commerce de Bordeaux, 'Tableau alarmant de la ville de Bordeaux, par un négociant (Neufchâtel, 1788).

[51] Jean Tarrade, 'Les colonies et les principes de 1789: les assemblées révolutionnaires face au problème de l'esclavage', in Tarrade (ed.), *La Révolution Française et les colonies* (Paris: L'Harmattan, 1989), 9–33.

Frenchman that Africans would sell their own brothers and sisters into slavery in this way. 'How surprising it is,' Crassous argued while his ship was anchored off the Guinea coast, 'to see men sell their liberties, their lives, and their fellow citizens as blindly as do these miserable blacks. Passions, passions and ignorance – what damage you inflict on humankind!'[52]

In the most exceptional cases, men who were themselves heavily involved in trade and shipping—and even in slaving—lent open support to the abolitionist cause. Among the most prominent of these was André-Daniel Laffon de Ladebat, whose family had made its fortune from fitting out vessels for the navy in Bordeaux; he campaigned against the slave trade in the last years of the Ancien Régime and was soon won over to the ideals of the early Revolution. Between 1788 and 1792, he produced a flurry of speeches and pamphlets condemning the slave trade. The most influential of these was read at the Académie in the city, of which Laffon was an enthusiastic member, pressing on his audience the urgent need for slave emancipation. It was the fault of Europeans, he told his fellow academicians, that 6 million Africans had been forcibly deported from their homes in the greatest forced migration of people in modern times. In condemning this injustice, he did not spare either France or those who had been charged with its government. They were responsible for so much that was wrong, he reminded them, most especially for despoiling a continent in pursuit of profit. 'We have depopulated and demeaned Africa', he declared, to satisfy greed and ambition; and it was not only Africa that had been wronged. 'America, devastated, has folded under the yoke of our tyranny. We have established slavery there even although religion proscribed it in our own climes.' This was, he believed, morally indefensible, one of the most heinous of the 'crimes to which cupidity draws us', and he poured scorn on the economic justifications so often heard for the maintenance of slavery.[53]

But his was undoubtedly a minority voice among the merchant community of the Atlantic ports, whose fortunes were so deeply enmeshed with the profits of the slave trade. Nowhere was this more evident than in La Rochelle, whose Huguenot merchants had turned with enthusiasm to slaving after the loss of Canada in 1763, a loss that harmed their port more than any of their competitors. The slave trade had become more and more important for the prosperity of the city as other forms of trade declined, until in the 1780s the number of slave ships leaving the harbour constituted 58 per cent of all shipping leaving for foreign destinations.[54] Between the Peace of Paris and the early Revolution, a new generation of *négociants* fitted out 202 *négriers* for West Africa; in the same period, seven merchants from La

---

[52]   Alain Yacou, *Journaux de bord et de traite de Joseph Crassous de Médeuil: De La Rochelle à la côte de Guinée et aux Antilles, 1772–76* (Paris: Karthala, 2001), 99–100.

[53]   AD Gironde, 8J 707, Laffon de Ladebat, 'Discours sur la nécessité des moyens de détruire l'esclavage dans les colonies', adresse à l'Académie de Bordeaux, 25 August 1788.

[54]   Jean-Michel Deveau, *La traite rochelaise* (Paris, 1990), 44.

Rochelle, five of them Protestants, purchased plantations on Saint-Domingue, living and working in the Caribbean while retaining family connections and business partnerships in their home city.[55] The merchant communities on the two shores of the Atlantic remained closely linked, communicating regularly on trading matters as well as about family affairs. As a result, the Chamber of commerce in La Rochelle was kept keenly aware of the interests of the *colons*, and, as in other merchant communities, there was always a temptation to side with them against the 'incorrigible' philanthropists whom it was only too easy to deride as intellectuals, outsiders, Parisians, men ignorant of the ways of trade.

An anonymous pamphlet of 1789 tried to respond to what it called 'the cry of humanity and philosophy against the enslavement of negroes', and denounced those who would make the removal of slaves from Africa into a moral fault.[56] 'Slavery', exclaimed the writer, 'this word produces the effect on philosophers that Circe's liquor produced on the companions of Ulysses', making them blind to the reality of the Africans' lot once they were settled on the plantations. At this point, the pamphlet indulges in the sort of eulogy of the *colons* and the paternalism of the plantation economy which had become a commonplace of pro-slavery literature.

> It is almost always the case that a feeling of pity stirs the hearts of the *colons* as strongly as the self-interest which, they would have us believe, is a crime. They are freed from the double slavery to which fate had condemned them, both in their country and in the ship which had brought them to the colonies. They are housed, they are clothed in a manner that fits the climate, they are allowed to rest and to acclimatize for six months before they are put to work.[57]

In short, the *colons*, men like themselves, can be trusted to treat the Africans well since it is in their interest to do so.

Pragmatism in merchant eyes meant two things; an awareness of the political and moral climate in which they lived, and a clear understanding of where the country's interest lay. For most merchants in the Atlantic ports, that also meant a commitment to the colonial regime. The argument was primarily about the economy—about profit, of course, but also about the jobs they created and the wealth that flowed into France from the colonies. A pamphlet published anonymously in La Rochelle in 1789 put the commercial case forcibly, emphasizing that France's aim in founding its colonies had been 'to procure through the consumption of the planters greater industrial and cultural activity in metropolitan France, and to furnish the mother country, in return for the goods it sent out, with

[55] Brice Martinetti, *Les négociants de La Rochelle au 18e siècle* (Rennes: Presses Universitaires de Rennes, 2013), 233.

[56] AD Gironde, MI 80004/41, «Mémoire sur l'affranchissement des nègres et en épigraphe quod vidi, testor»; Hélène Sarrazin, 'Comment peut-on défendre l'esclavage?', *passim*.

[57] Sarrazin, 'Comment peut-on défendre l'esclavage?', 175–7.

produce it could exchange with foreign countries that would bring greater benefits than the manufactures and production of the mother country itself. But more than exports and imports were at stake. Without its colonies, the pamphlet continued, France would have little use for its merchant marine, which in turn would strip away the naval strength it needed to protect its coasts and fisheries. Without its colonies, in matters of foreign policy France risked being completely dominated by Great Britain and would lose its political influence in Europe. Without its colonies, industry would lose vital markets and workshops; factories would close, agriculture would be impoverished, and jobs would be lost, among them many of the 25,000 men employed as sailors and seamen. The picture would be grim, indeed: a picture of decline and economic desolation that would impoverish families and bring joy only to France's rivals. All this, the author implied, would surely be sacrificed should the slave trade be abolished or slavery ended. It was, he insisted, in the economic interest of all to resist all calls for emancipation.[58]

The chambers of commerce were not slow to mobilize as the Revolution approached and they watched the threat of abolition grow. Their attitude was defensive in the face of what they saw as a potential disaster: the complete collapse and destruction of the colonial system on which their prosperity was dependent. They were temperamentally conservative, seeking to save the status quo from assault, wherever that assault might originate. And they increasingly identified a double threat. One was commercial, and lay in the desire of some planters to sell to the highest bidder and to free the islands from the obligation to sell to France or through the good offices of French merchants. The other was humanitarian, the threat that was posed by abolitionists and the anti-slavery lobby. There was recognition that merchant and planter interests did not always correspond, and more than one attempt to find a compromise that would serve the interests of both France and the Antilles. Pamphlets and addresses denounced fraud and tax evasion; others railed against connivance with the British which was prejudicial to France. Both the demands of the planters and those of the merchants demonstrated legitimate cause for complaint, and, as the chief judge of the commercial court in Nantes acknowledged, cried out for a settlement that brought benefits to both. Some at least recognized the need for progress and compromise.[59]

From this it followed that the commercial cities had every reason to cooperate, to share their fears and anxieties, and to lobby the National Assembly as a single interest group. Petitions were circulated from town to town and from chamber to chamber in a bid to strengthen their authority by speaking with a common voice.

[58] BM La Rochelle, 11877 C, 'Précis sur l'importance des colonies et sur la servitude des Noirs' (La Rochelle, 1789), 1–12.

[59] AD Loire-Atlantique, 1 ET A 27, 'Mémoire sur la nécessité d'unir de la manière la plus avantageuse les intérêts des Colonies et du Commerce et celui des Colons et des Commerçants, par M. Joubert du Collet, Juge en chef du Consulat de Nantes, 20 novembre 1789'.

Often the enemy they picked out was the liberal elite, those who spoke for the *Amis des Noirs* and who made common cause with the black population. In the early months of the Revolution, their anger was focused on the campaign to offer full civil rights to men of colour, to the mulattoes who were already free but who did not yet enjoy full citizenship. A document that circulated in 1789 among the cities of the West attempted to define the terms in which all merchant communities might make common cause on the issue. They should engage in a frontal attack on the *Amis des Noirs*, 'those men who for two years have been disrupting all our colonies, who spread in a host of writings and in the public prints the idea that the National Assembly will only succeed in bringing peace to the colonies by granting to men of colour the rights of active citizens'. Such a measure, in the merchants' view, would lead to universal disorder, for the system of subordination on which the colonial system was built 'cannot exist without an intermediary class between that which is engaged in the work of the plantations and that which can be called upon to administer public affairs'.[60] Colonialism, they believed, could not survive without such inequality. And the prosperity of the west-coast ports could not outlive the fall of France's colonial empire.

This led them to make a further allegation, that those factions that sought to deny the principle of ethnic inequality were not true liberals or sons of the Enlightenment, but men of treasonable intent, men in the pay of foreign governments who had an interest in undermining French prosperity, possibly for their own gain. At the top of the list of suspects, as ever, was their main commercial rival, Britain, the country which was responsible for circulating so many abolitionist tracts in the pre-revolutionary years, and which was France's principal rival along the north Atlantic shipping lanes. Nantes' loss, it was assumed, must necessarily be Liverpool's gain, especially in the wake of the Eden Treaty which was widely blamed for slowing French economic growth, again to Britain's long-term advantage. There was no altruism in England's desire to abolish the slave trade, they insisted. Abolition was yet another weapon in a cynical English assault on France's colonial possessions, an assault that already extended across a number of fronts, and the first months of the Revolution did nothing to reassure them. In particular, they were concerned that the National Assembly would cease to offer protection to the colonies or to provide resources for their defence. The Assembly had decreed that 'the French nation renounces all wars made for the purpose of conquest, and that it will never deploy its forces against the liberty of any people'.[61] That might seem to rule out any return to the foreign policy aims of the eighteenth century, to redefine the very function of war. Did it, they wondered, leave French

---

[60] AD Loire-Atlantique, 1 ET A 27, 'Bases d'après lesquelles doivent être rédigées les adresses des Communes des villes maritimes de Commerce et des Manufactures du Royaume à l'Assemblée Nationale', n.d.

[61] *Archives Parlementaires*, première série (1789–1800), vol. 15, pp. 661–2.

territories exposed to attack? The decree made no provision for the defence of essential interests, and, declared the merchants of Nantes in a collective address to Paris, 'it has not disarmed England, which, we have no doubt, aspires to exercise a despotism over the seas and over commerce'. Merchant communities had long memories, and they remembered the serious losses they had suffered at British hands during the Seven Years' War. Once more their colonies seemed particularly vulnerable: 'our merchant vessels sail unprotected; our colonies in the Americas have received no orders to prepare their defences, and their garrisons are barely on a peacetime footing; India has been abandoned; the coasts of Africa are exposed to all kinds of provocation.'[62] Already the merchants of France's Atlantic ports viewed the future with alarm. War and abolition were twin threats to which they demanded an effective response.

In many of their addresses we can detect a level of sympathy for the *colons'* cause that went beyond shared economic interest. Among the merchants of La Rochelle and Nantes were men who had sent their sons to Le Cap or Basse-Terre, who owned plantations or shipping businesses in Saint-Domingue, who had spent a substantial part of their careers in the Caribbean. They did not consider themselves different people when they returned to France, or see their interests as conflicting with those of the *colons*, and they shared many of the same responses when it came to slavery and the slave trade. As the Revolution progressed, they were of course subject to continual pressure from associates and family members in the Antilles, a pressure that was political as well as personal, since the colonists were well aware of the influence they might have on the politics of the Atlantic ports. In La Rochelle, most famously, they established a pressure group in October 1789 to serve colonial interests, the *Société des Colons Franco-américains de la Rochelle*, a society which made no secret of its aims and methods, bringing to local politics the art of lobbying even as the institutions of these politics were being established and new political practices invented. It was to 'bring together all those owning property in the Antilles who were resident in the *généralité* of La Rochelle', to put pressure on the local authorities in the city and work closely with the newly established Club Massiac, which represented the interests of the *colons* in Paris. To join the society required payment of a subscription; the club's membership list contained twenty-seven names, though there may have been around thirty in all.[63]

Almost all, it appears, owned land or had business interests in the Caribbean, and these served to mould them into a single constituency. For in other respects they might seem to have had little in common: they included members of noble

---

[62] AD Loire-Atlantique, 1 ET A 27, 'Adresse à l'Assemblée Nationale' from the merchants of Nantes, delivered by Mosneron Dupin and dated 15 September 1790.

[63] Marcel Dorigny, 'Les colons de La Rochelle se mobilisent contre les *Amis* des Noirs: procès-verbaux de la Société des colons franco-américains de La Rochelle, 14 octobre 1789 – 27 août 1790', in Augeron and Caudron, *La Rochelle, l'Aunis et la Saintonge face à l'esclavage*, 223–30.

families from the Aunis and Saintonge; long-established merchants, some of them ennobled, who counted slaving voyages among their commercial activities; and young, thrusting merchants, *arrivistes* who had only recently set up business in the port. What they shared was a common focus on colonial trade and especially on Saint-Domingue, and a gnawing insecurity over the future. During the months of the society's existence they lobbied intensively in La Rochelle, and most especially among its merchant community, warning of the threats to their well-being and the dangers the port faced should ideas about the rights of man be extended to people of colour. In particular, they warned of the corrosive propaganda of those they regarded as trouble-makers, 'to thwart the execution of the plans hatched by ill-intentioned individuals [*des gens mal-intentionnés*] aimed against our peace of mind and our properties'.[64] There was no doubting whom they had in mind. They shared a distrust of 'philosophy' which was a commonplace of conservative thought, and they identified as their enemies all those who sided with the *Amis des Noirs* or who campaigned against the slave trade. Over the months that were to follow, as the Revolution became more radical, they would become much more persistent in their demands and would pose a greater and more immediate threat to their vested interests. For many in the merchant community, 1789 heralded a period of massive disruption which would destroy their businesses and transform their relationship with the colonies forever. For some, indeed, it spelt a new beginning, involving them in new waves of migration and tortuous journeys around the Atlantic world, journeys that in some cases would stretch from the French Atlantic ports to the Caribbean, to Port-au-Prince or Le Cap, then on to Havana or Santiago-de-Cuba, before moving on again to the United States, to New Orleans or Baton Rouge, Baltimore or Charleston, Norfolk or Philadelphia. By the end of the 1790s, a generation of Frenchmen—whether they had come directly from France or indirectly via the colonies—had spread themselves far across the eastern seaboard of the Americas.

---

[64] Claudy Valin, 'La filiale rochelaise de la Société des colons franco-américains', in Augeron and Caudron (eds), *La Rochelle, l'Aunis et la Saintonge face à l'esclavage*, 231–2.

7

The French Revolution in the Atlantic Ports

When the Revolution came, the merchants' interests were of course not the nation's foremost concerns, and the political arena was soon dominated by demands for rights and representation, for the granting of citizenship and the ending of privilege in all its forms: political and social as well as economic. In this regard, debate in the Atlantic ports was little different from that in the rest of the country: the collapse of the old order was primarily a story of political failure, a loss of faith in a system of government, a country-wide challenge to royal autocracy. Trading privileges were among those under attack, most notably the company monopolies that had been practised in commerce with the East and West Indies, but the main thrust of revolutionary rhetoric was political, focusing on abuses of power, noble privilege, and feudal exactions. There was a general sense of institutional crisis, a fear that local interests were harmed by creeping centralization, expressed in the pretensions of royal administration and the spreading tentacles of royal justice. The main issues of the immediate pre-Revolution were those of sovereignty and political legitimacy, institutional reform, and access to administration and justice. In many ways, they reflected the demands of the American colonists in 1776, which had become enshrined in the constitution of the United States. Across France the political debate echoed that in Paris, and, as Timothy Tackett has justly remarked, 'both participants and outside observers were intensely self-conscious of the historical significance of the times in which they were living'.[1]

Political demands had been most forcibly expressed in the *cahiers de doléances* that were drawn up during the winter months of 1788 and the spring of 1789 in preparation for the meeting of the Estates-General at Versailles in May. From Guienne, for instance, the region around Bordeaux, there were demands for a new constitution for France; for regular, statutory meetings of the Estates-General; for a system of justice that guaranteed speedy hearings and entitled everyone to trial by jury; and for root-and-branch fiscal reforms that would bring an end to feudal dues and guarantee a fairer system of national taxation.[2] There was nothing unusual in this: the drafting of provincial *cahiers* was left to lawyers and royal officials who adjudged what they thought to be important, and here as in most

---

[1] Timothy Tackett, *Becoming a Revolutionary: The Deputies of the French National Assembly and the Emergence of a Revolutionary Culture, 1789–90* (Princeton, NJ: Princeton University Press, 1996), 4.
[2] Charles Higounet (ed.), *Histoire de l'Aquitaine* (Toulouse: Privat, 1971), 392.

regions of France, these constitutional issues were retained for the final *cahier* sent to the King, whereas seemingly less important social and economic grievances that may have been peculiar to the area or limited to a particular sectional interest were often edited out. Demands for representation were widely shared across France's population, and came from every province of the country. It is significant, too, that many political grievances were shared by all three estates, especially those which sought to limit royal power and involve local people in the political process. The need for some degree of political reform was something on which all three orders could unite, both in town and in the countryside. It was a moment when the transition from traditional local politics to modern national politics was given new impetus and a new kind of consciousness seemed to be developing. For, even in matters of taxation and forced payments, distinctions were drawn. It was, as Gilbert Shapiro and John Markoff note, 'those burdens most often held to be essentially local – the payments to lord and Church – that were to be abolished', whereas 'the burdens that bound the village to the state were to be set right'.[3]

The initial response to the Revolution from the mercantile communities of the Atlantic ports might suggest a quiet satisfaction rather than alarm or apprehension about the future. Their views were largely in accord with the demands of the Third Estate for greater political rights and civil equality, they favoured moves away from company privilege in favour of economic liberalism, and many among them, like the Protestants of La Rochelle or the Jews of Bordeaux and Bayonne, benefited personally from the steps taken in the first months of the Revolution to guarantee their religious freedom. Moreover, if they had expressed some unease in the last years of the Ancien Régime about the potential impact of enlightened ideas and the future of the colonies, nothing had yet happened to threaten their commercial interests, as merchant vessels continued to leave from the Garonne and the Loire estuaries for West Africa and the Caribbean. They remained largely immersed in their business and family affairs, and their correspondence was generally devoid of politics. This should not surprise us, since the culture of merchant communities in the eighteenth century had been largely individualistic and strongly family-orientated, their values defined by family, commerce, and religion.[4] In so far as they spoke with a collective voice their interests were represented by their chambers of commerce, and it would not be until the first municipal elections, in 1790, that they established a broader political presence, on the newly created municipal authorities. Or they might respond as religious communities. The Protestants of La Rochelle provide an interesting case study here. Following the decree on 24 December 1789 that granted them civil equality

---

[3] Gilbert Shapiro and John Markoff, *Revolutionary Demands: A Content Analysis of the Cahiers de Doléances of 1789* (Stanford, CA: Stanford University Press, 1998), 409.

[4] Daniel Roche, 'Introduction', in Franco Angiolini and Daniel Roche (eds), *Cultures et formations négociantes dans l'Europe moderne* (Paris: Editions de l'Ecole des Hautes Études en Sciences Sociales, 1995), 11–24.

and access to all public offices—this after 160 years of exclusion—they quickly responded by standing in the municipal elections of the following month, providing one-third of the *officiers municipaux* (four out of twelve) and almost as high a proportion of the town's *notables* (seven out of twenty-five).[5] In 1791 a Protestant was elected as mayor; in 1792 another would command the city's National Guard.[6] In Bordeaux, where there had been far less of a history of religious persecution, Protestants were more inclined to concentrate on their commercial affairs, with the consequence that they were often less well prepared to respond to the political upheavals that followed.[7]

Though merchants did not always throw themselves into politics to the same degree as lawyers and members of the liberal professions, some of their number welcomed the Revolution as an opportunity for advancement. But the chance to do so was not equally available to all. In those cities, like Bordeaux, where there was a powerful legal fraternity, or where there were existing political institutions like an *intendance* or a *parlement*, it was perhaps inevitable that there was a ready-made political elite, men with legal minds who were naturally drawn to questions of civil rights and political representation, and to the defence of individual liberties through resort to the law. The *parlements*, in particular, had played a critical part in a region's political life under the Ancien Régime, when they had stood up for local rights and traditions in defiance of the King, remonstrating with ministers in defence of provincial liberties and risking closure and exile for their pains. As a result, they had established themselves as the defenders of provincial interests, including, at times, those of commerce. During the 1780s, for instance, when the American Revolution posed a threat to Bordeaux's colonial trade, the *Parlement* of Bordeaux had called on the government to take action in defence of the city's privileges in the Antilles; and through such interventions it had harnessed a degree of popular support among the shopkeepers and artisans as well. As a consequence, when the *parlementaires* returned home from periods of internal exile, they were often greeted with joy and acclaim by the people, who celebrated by bedecking their houses and setting off fireworks.[8] Over the century the provincial *parlements* attracted the services of the leading constitutional and commercial lawyers of the day, and they would figure among the foremost spokesmen for the Third Estate when, in 1789, their cities were called on to select deputies to send to Versailles.[9]

But among the Atlantic commercial cities Bordeaux was something of an exception, in that it was a centre not only of trade but also of the law, of royal

    [5] Olga de Saint-Affrique, 'Les protestants rochelais pendant la Révolution', in *La Rochelle, ville frontière: actes du colloque des 28 et 29 avril 1989* (La Rochelle: Rumeur des Âges, 1989), 140.
    [6] Jean-Noel Luc (ed.), *La Charente Maritime: l'Aunis et la Saintonge des origines à nos jours* (Saint-Jean d'Angély: Bordessoules, 1981), 295.
    [7] Séverine Pacteau de Luze, *Les Protestants et Bordeaux* (Bordeaux: Mollat, 1999), 117–19.
    [8] John Rylands Library, Manchester, *Récit de ce qui s'est passé à Pau en Béarn les 19, 20 et 21 juin 1788*.
    [9] Doyle, *The Parlement of Bordeaux and the End of the Old Regime*, 203–14.

administration, and of the Catholic hierarchy. In La Rochelle, Le Havre, Saint-Malo, or Nantes the merchants faced no such competition and in these cities commerce dominated public life to an extent that would have been impossible in Bordeaux. In La Rochelle, for example, the cultural life of the town was dominated by the greater merchants, the 'seigneurs du comptoir' like Daniel Garesché, who succeeded one another at the head of the Chamber of commerce and who collectively constituted the grande bourgeoisie rochelaise. Among them Protestants formed a tight and proudly defensive group, eager to stake their claim to social pre-eminence.[10] In Nantes, too, the wealth of the merchant community and the place they occupied in the economic life of the nation gave the Île Feydeau an undisputed place among the city's elite, and when it became known in 1788 that the King intended to call an Estates-General, the merchants of Nantes showed an immediate desire to be represented, asking that they be allowed to send two deputies to represent the commercial interests of the city and trying to rally other ports to support their cause. The campaign achieved some success, the King granting that there should be at least one merchant among the deputies elected for the Nantes region; and on 18 April they were duly rewarded when a merchant and former consul, Jacques-Nicolas Guinebaud, was duly elected to represent the trading interest at Versailles. The merchants also composed a list of forty-three grievances, the majority of which were incorporated in the cahier de doléances that was sent to Versailles. These covered four broad areas that were deemed to be of prime importance to the prosperity of the area: commercial administration, foreign and colonial trade, trade with the interior, and the financing of commerce. The merchants looked to the King to encourage commercial enterprise through a mixture of liberalization and protection.[11]

During the early months of the Revolution, it was still difficult for most merchants to see it as a major threat, as their commercial activities remained relatively secure and there was little in their personal experience to suggest the upheavals to come. They were well aware, of course, of events elsewhere in France, some of which could not but arouse fears: they heard the uncompromising language that was used against the rich, and observed the signs of hatred that were being shown towards the noble and privileged. They could not condone these outbursts; some of their number had spent a large part of their lives buying exactly that kind of privilege to gain access to the select society of what Paul Butel has termed 'the patricians of commerce'.[12] They could not regard everything they witnessed with equanimity. But revolution had not yet been translated into violence or disruption, and these were the things that the merchant community

[10] Claudy Valin, 'La bourgeoisie rochelaise dans la Révolution', in La Rochelle, ville frontière, 55–64.
[11] Michel Le Mené and Marie-Hélène Santrot (eds), Cahiers des plaintes et doléances de Loire-Atlantique (4 vols, Nantes: Conseil Général de la Loire-Atlantique, 1989), vol. 1, 157–62.
[12] Paul Butel, Les dynasties bordelaises de Colbert à Chaban (Paris: Perrin, 1991), 111.

most feared. The La Rochelle merchant Pierre-Jean van Hoogwerff, who was originally from Holland, was speaking for many when he wrote to his brother in St Petersburg in 1789 with the reassuring news that if the Revolution had unleashed troubles and disorder in other parts of the country, 'thank God, our province remains utterly tranquil'.[13] He needed to offer reassurance, since for many the very concept of revolution spelt violence and disorder, and early reports of lynching and mob violence in Paris did little to calm fears. The absence of social disorder at home and the maintenance of peace abroad were their two principal objectives, and the preconditions on which they were dependent if their trade was to continue to flourish.

Talk of the Rights of Man did not arouse great anxiety, at least initially. The issue was seen in terms of native-born Frenchmen, the equality of all, whatever their social status, to enjoy the same fundamental human rights, the same rights in law. And if the Declaration of the Rights of Man made all legally equal, it did not detract from property rights; property, indeed, was specifically guaranteed as one of the basic human rights that should be enjoyed by all, the final clause of the Declaration establishing, seemingly unequivocally, that 'since property is a sacred and inviolable right, no one may be deprived thereof unless a legally established public necessity obviously requires it, and upon condition of a just and previous indemnity'.[14] Of course, with hindsight, these two guarantees—of the civil rights of all men on the one hand, and of the inviolability of property on the other— could not fail to raise awkward questions about the legitimacy of slavery. In 1789 some local *cahiers de doléances* did insist that slavery was morally wrong, arguing that there could be no slaves on French soil or in France's colonies in the Americas.[15] It is true that Condorcet, Brissot, and like-minded political leaders published pamphlets urging the total abolition of slavery and the slave trade; and the *Amis des Noirs* had become an active pressure group for abolition. But, when compared to England, expressions of public outrage remained muted. There were no anti-slavery petitions in France of the kind that assailed the British parliament at this time, and the evidence of the *cahiers* suggests that the level of public concern about France's role in the African slave trade was strictly limited.[16] Abolitionism was a cause for the liberal elite.

The Declaration did not talk of equality in purely abstract terms. It recognized a truth that was unprecedented in European history, that every citizen, even the poorest and the least educated, was entitled to enjoy the same basic human rights

---

[13]   Brice Martinetti, 'Les résistances du négoce rochelais et la première abolition de l'esclavage', *Revue du Philanthrope*, 4 (2013), 156–7.

[14]   John Hall Stewart, *A Documentary Survey of the French Revolution* (New York: Macmillan, 1950), 115.

[15]   Le Mené and Santrot, *Cahiers des plaintes et doléances*, vol. 1, 159.

[16]   Seymour Drescher, *Capitalism and Antislavery: British Mobilization in Comparative Perspective* (Oxford: Oxford University Press, 1987), 54.

as those who were well-born and believed they had entitlements. But this raised as many questions as it answered. Who should be considered a citizen? What constituted property? And how could the rights of black slaves be sustained without undermining the property rights—rights that were equally sacrosanct, it seemed—of the slave-owners? If in 1789 the constitutional monarchy was prepared to live with this apparent contradiction, by 1794, following slave insurrections in Saint-Domingue, the Republic would conclude that men had natural rights of which they could not be deprived, and that distinctions of race and ethnicity could no longer be allowed to prejudice the fundamental rights of all.[17] In 1793 France's commissioner in Saint-Domingue, Léger-Félicité Sonthonax, outlawed slavery in the northern part of the colony, and some months later his colleague Étienne Polverel extended the abolition to cover the rest of the island. The Convention then took the momentous step of formally abolishing slavery in all its colonial possessions, and that at a time when its European trading rivals were still free to engage in slaving. For the slaves it was a moment for rejoicing, but for the planters in the islands and the merchants of France's Atlantic ports, it meant the enactment of their worst nightmare.[18]

But that was for the future. The year 1789 was characterized by a general enthusiasm among the revolutionaries for reform, with all, administrators and lawyers, merchants and liberal nobles, seemingly content to place their faith in the Estates-General. But what the majority favoured was moderate change, not radical action involving crowd violence, like the attack, in response to news of the assault on the Bastille, on the Château des Ducs de Bretagne in Nantes. They had no wish to overthrow the social order; rather they wanted to make it more flexible, and distinctions more porous, so that they could be allowed to play the role and to enjoy the prestige that they felt their talent merited. In a pamphlet on reforms to the social order, the Nantes merchant Mosneron *aîné* explained the extent of the changes he sought. He wished not to destroy the existing order, but rather to adapt it by removing the 'distinction between a nobility that was able to receive all the honours, without needing to display any merit, and commoners seen as unworthy of consideration in spite of their value to society'. He urged the creation of a new order that would lie between the nobility and the common people, and would be defined by talent and usefulness, to be composed of 'merchants, lawyers, doctors' and 'men of talent'. In other words, he wanted a social structure that reflected men's functionality and rewarded education and ability instead of being obsessed with their birthright.[19] He was effectively arguing for the existence of the bourgeoisie as a separate social entity, and for their recognition in law. He had no

[17] Pierre Serna, *Comme des bêtes: Histoire politique de l'animal en Révolution, 1750–1840* (Paris: Fayard, 2017), 306.

[18] Frédéric Régent, *La France et ses esclaves, de la colonisation aux abolitions, 1620–1848* (Paris: Grasset, 2007), 247.

[19] Pétré-Grenouilleau, *Nantes, histoire et géographie contemporaine*, 106–8.

interest in sharing power with the unskilled, the crowd, or the mass of the population.

Yet within weeks of the elections that sent deputies to the Estates-General, word arrived from Paris of a very different kind of revolution, one dominated by crowd demands and popular violence, culminating in the fall of the Bastille and the march of the women from the Paris markets to pressurize the King at Versailles. In Bordeaux, news of the Bastille was brought by special courier, taking only forty-six hours to reach the city, and taking the form of a letter from Paul Nairac, one of their deputies whom they had mandated to report on developments.[20] Nairac and his brother were members of a notable merchant family with vested commercial interests in both Bordeaux and La Rochelle; they had no reason to welcome radicalism or popular insurgency. His tone was sombre as he outlined the violence that had followed the King's threat to curb popular representation, and listed the deaths that had followed. But the city's reaction is interesting. Nairac's report was taken as a form of reassurance, proof that the crisis was over and that stability had been restored in Paris. As a consequence, normal trading could resume. Bordeaux's elite, it would appear, were less afraid of political radicalism in 1789—or even of Paris—than they were of a conservative reaction that might stifle or abort the entire revolutionary process.[21] And, in the many elections during 1790 to fill the new local authorities—for the department, the district, the municipal council, to say nothing of elections to the various local offices which the Revolution created—they demonstrated time and again their willingness to participate and to assume responsibility in the public life of their city. They staffed the new clubs and popular societies, were elected to offices in the popular sections, and provided officers for the National Guard. Nor were they swept aside after the declaration of the Republic, as the same groups continued to provide political leadership in the years from 1789 to 1793.

A similar pattern can be observed in all the major Atlantic cities, as members of their bourgeois elite profited from the ending of noble privilege and took the reins of municipal governance. Freed from the social and legal constraints of the Ancien Régime, they sought to control politics locally and to steer the Revolution on a moderate course. The figures speak for themselves. In Bordeaux, the elections of 1790 produced a municipality drawn from a relatively narrow social base. Of the twenty *officiers municipaux*, ten were merchants and four lawyers, with the others drawn from professional or business circles. The forty-two *notables* repeated the pattern, with fourteen (or a third) coming from the legal profession, and sixteen from the merchant community (a figure that rises to nineteen if we include a sugar-refiner, a shipbuilder, and the commercial agent of a shipping

---

[20] Michel Lhéritier, *Liberté: les Girondins, Bordeaux et la Révolution Française* (Paris: La Renaissance du Livre, 1947), 13–14.

[21] Forrest, *The Revolution in Provincial France: Aquitaine, 1789–99*, 62.

company).[22] In La Rochelle, the results were not dissimilar. The newly elected mayor was Goguet de la Sauzet, a *négociant-armateur*, and the *officiers municipaux* included fourteen other merchants, both Protestant and Catholic, who would ensure that the city's commercial interests were not ignored.[23] Similarly in Nantes, the merchant community played a significant role in the first months of the Revolution, dominating the permanent committee elected to run the city in 1789; but from 1790 the merchants had to share power with lawyers, doctors, and other members of the liberal professions, with merchants providing two-thirds of the *officiers municipaux* (twelve out of eighteen) and half of the notables (eighteen out of thirty-six). Significantly, however, it was not only members of the old merchant families who stood for political office. The revolutionary years were ones of social mobility, when new men joined the ranks of the mercantile elite and younger merchants, driven by personal ambition, arrived on the waterfront. The mayors who led Nantes in this period, Baco and Kervegan, typified this broader social group, men born into commercial families but not personally involved in Atlantic trade.[24]

But the urban elites did not have things all their own way. The new division of the territory in 1790, with its redistribution of administrative and judicial responsibility, set town against town in a competition for status and resource which generated inter-urban feuds and exaggerated longstanding rivalries. Such rivalries were exploited to challenge the concentration of too much power in a small number of large commercial cities, and the argument was made that a more equal distribution of administrative authority would be more egalitarian and hence more revolutionary. Many of the smaller towns emphasized their central position in their department and their close ties to the land, and they drew attention to their value as markets for the surrounding countryside.[25] Across the west and south-west of the country, petitions revealed the extent of anti-commercial feeling in many rural areas, and a resentment of the Atlantic port cities that emphasized their irrelevance to peasants and to the rural economy of their hinterland. Towns that were centrally positioned in the interior, or to which country people were in the habit of going on business or to market, could amass greater support because they were perceived as being useful to the population at large, a point that was repeatedly made in appeals to the constitutional committee in Paris. Legal centres claimed precedence over Atlantic ports on the grounds that

---

[22] AM Bordeaux, K16, Maires et officiers municipaux de Bordeaux, 1790; Alan Forrest, *Society and Politics in Revolutionary Bordeaux* (Oxford: Oxford University Press, 1975), 37–8.

[23] Claude Laveau, *Le monde rochelais des Bourbons à Bonaparte* (La Rochelle: Rumeur des Âges, 1988), 199–200.

[24] Pétré-Grenouilleau, *Nantes, histoire et géographie contemporaine*, 112–13.

[25] Ted W. Margadant, *Urban Rivalries in the French Revolution* (Princeton, NJ: Princeton University Press 1992), 442.

country dwellers went there to settle matters like land ownership and inheritance, custom commanding greater loyalty than commerce.[26]

So, while Nantes and Bordeaux were sufficiently dominant in their new departments to ensure their choice as *chef-lieu*, other ports faced more of a struggle. And even Bordeaux had to shrug off a plausible challenge from the market town of Libourne, which argued that it needed to retain its independence if it was not to be smothered by its larger neighbour. Bordeaux, the petition alleged, 'completely stifles Libourne, eclipsing it with its shadow and devouring it to the extent that, if Libourne were to remain part of this department, it would never be able to emerge from its obscurity'.[27] In this case, the petition was rejected, but a number of Atlantic ports experienced difficulty in staking their claims. The choice of Pau and Tarbes as centres for departments in the Pyrenees meant that there was nothing for Bayonne; even its claim for a district was dismissed in favour of Ustaritz. In the Charente-Inférieure, a department built out of the Ancien Régime provinces of Aunis and Saintonge, Saintes won out over La Rochelle, though Napoleon finally reversed the decision in 1810. To the people of the Charente, Saintes had all the hallmarks of a regional capital, while La Rochelle was a mere commercial appendage, irrelevant to local farmers, its attention transfixed by the colonies and the sea.[28] Similarly, Marseille had to give way to the historical precedence and inland position of Aix-en-Provence in its bid to be chef-lieu of the Bouches-du-Rhône; again, this would later be reversed in Marseille's favour.[29] And in Normandy, where Rouen was given the *chef-lieu* of the new department of the Seine-Inférieure, Le Havre struggled to gain any administrative function, being passed over for a district in favour of the small market town of Montivilliers. Once again, the arguments centred on its irrelevance to the local economy and its perceived failure to redistribute its commercial wealth to local people. As the villages of the surrounding area explained in a petition to the Assembly, Le Havre 'is properly speaking nothing more than an entrepôt for goods brought in from abroad to be sent on to all parts of the kingdom'. Its merchants were uninterested in agriculture and set only on maximizing their own profits; it was a city of 'rich capitalists well versed in speculation'.[30] Commercial ports that looked out to the ocean were regarded with suspicion and often with hostility by the inhabitants of the surrounding countryside, who saw their much-flaunted prosperity as irrefutable proof of their ingrained egotism.

---

[26] A wide range of municipal petitions can be found in AN, series D IV bis, papers of the Committee of Division, 1789–90; Alan Forrest, 'Le découpage administratif de la France révolutionnaire', in Centre Méridional d'Histoire, *L'espace et le temps reconstruits: la Révolution Française, une révolution des mentalités et des cultures?* (Aix-en-Provence: Publications de l'Université de Provence, 1990), 3–12.

[27] AN, D IV bis 8, petition from the town of Libourne, 1790.

[28] AN, D IV bis 5, petitions of La Rochelle and Saintes, 1790.

[29] AN, D IV bis 5, petition from the deputies of Provence in favour of Aix-en-Provence, 1790.

[30] AN, D IV bis 17, petition from the towns of the District in favour of Montivilliers, 1790.

But it is too easy to equate commerce with mercantile self-interest. The Atlantic ports were also centres of activism and of the political sociability on which the spread of revolutionary ideas was dependent. Cities like Nantes and Bordeaux produced their own newspapers and had a flourishing print culture, publishing political pamphlets that reported on national politics and increasingly challenged Paris in their news coverage. From the rather bland advertising sheets of the late 1780s, the local press evolved to offer a range of political opinion, from the clerical and monarchist to the radical and Jacobin. They had their own bookshops, printing presses, and a tradition of debate fostered in cafés, salons, and masonic lodges. After 1789, these were joined by a range of clubs and political societies where the local elite could meet with like-minded people to discuss revolutionary politics and plan political campaigns. Politics also infiltrated the theatre, with new plays staged on themes of current political or patriotic concern: the Bordeaux stage hosted productions with titles like *L'Heureux décret, ou la suppression des titres*, which openly gloried in the abolition of feudal titles, though they formed a small minority of the plays on offer: only in 1791 did plays with an overtly political theme exceed 10 per cent of the productions on offer.[31] The audiences, it appeared, preferred more classical productions.

More important than the stage, however, were the clubs and popular societies which sprouted in every town in provincial France, and in many villages as well, and which, along with the sections that were established to take charge of local politics in the larger cities, provided an outlet for political ambition and popular outrage. There is little doubt that they represented significant sections of public opinion, or that they sprang spontaneously from genuine partisanship. Many of them started as simple *salles de lecture* where people could catch up with the Paris newspapers; some clubs in smaller towns, indeed, devoted entire sessions to reading the latest news.[32] Or they began life as meetings in cafés, part of an urban sociability that had developed in the eighteenth century, where friends and people of similar views would read the papers and discuss politics. Others evolved, apparently seamlessly, from masonic lodges: some even held their meetings in the premises vacated by the freemasons, with the same men who had run the lodges installed as the society's office-holders. Though freemasonry was very unequally distributed across the country in the eighteenth century, two of the five regions where it was most popular were close to the Atlantic coast: the area around Nantes and Angers in the Loire valley and in the Aunis and Saintonge between La Rochelle and Bordeaux.[33] Here lodges were to be found in small country towns as well as in the major cities.

---

[31] Henri Lagrave, Charles Mazouer, and Marc Regaldo, *La vie théâtrale à Bordeaux des origines à nos jours* (Paris: Éditions du CNRS, 1985), vol. 1, 376–9.

[32] Michael L. Kennedy, *The Jacobin Clubs in the French Revolution: The First Years* (Princeton, NJ; Princeton University Press, 1982), 55.

[33] Gérard Gayot (ed.), *La franc-maçonnerie française, textes et pratiques, 18e–19e siècles* (Paris: Gallimard, 1980), 45.

It is perhaps no accident that these were areas where revolutionary clubs were also particularly numerous, especially across the south-west and the hinterland of Bordeaux, or where the Protestant religion was widely practised.[34] Protestants figured among those most attracted to freemasonry, with its tradition of free-thinking, and some of the Bordeaux lodges, particularly those of L'Amitié and L'Étoile, recruited massively from the Protestant merchant houses of the Chartrons, among both Bordeaux residents and merchants from Northern Europe.[35] After 1789, many of these same men would take their places in local clubs and popular societies, concerned to exercise an influence on public affairs that had been denied them in earlier periods because of their religion, and fearful that they might be seen as standing aloof from the Revolution in their community. Indeed, many Protestants became activists in the club movement, or gave proof of revolutionary patriotism in other ways. A former pastor, Jean-Paul Bétrine, was one of the founders of the Société des *Amis* de la Constitution in La Rochelle, and its president in 1791.[36] Two members of Bordeaux's Protestant merchant community, Laffon de Ladebat and Jean-Pierre Sers, were among the ten deputies the city returned to the Legislative Assembly.[37] And Protestant merchants—even among those who were politically conservative—gave generously to the national cause in response to a series of patriotic appeals. Garesché and Van Hoogwerff were among those who made notable contributions to the cost of defence in La Rochelle, with Demissy making a loan of 150,000 *livres* to the city authorities without any guarantee that it would ever be reimbursed.[38]

By the end of 1789, club life was an established part of political sociability, and there was a sufficient range of clubs to accommodate revolutionaries of every stripe. In Nantes, for instance, there were already nine societies or reading circles where the literate and politically aware could meet and discuss the affairs of the day. They were scattered across the city and appealed to men of the legal and mercantile professions, those with the interest to join and the money to pay the annual dues. They generally took their names from the streets where they stood or the buildings where they met: like the club du Port-au-Vin, de la rue Dauphine, de la rue Goyon, the club du Café, or the club des Cours Unis. Or else they advertised themselves as reading rooms where newspapers were made available and debate staged: such were the Chambre de lecture du Soleil, the Chambre du Port-au-Vin, the Chambre Nouvelle, or the Chambre de la Ville.[39] As the months passed they became increasingly political, subscribing to the Paris newspapers that best

---

[34] See, for instance, Ran Halévi, *Les loges maçonniques dans la France d'Ancien Régime aux origines de la sociabilité démocratique* (Paris: Armand Colin, 1984).

[35] Séverine Pacteau de Luze, *Les protestants de Bordeaux*), 112.

[36] Laveau, *Le monde rochelais*, 207.   [37] Pacteau de Luze, *Les protestants*, 122.

[38] Olga de Saint-Affrique, 'Les protestants rochelais', 142.

[39] Dominique Costa, *La Révolution à Nantes et la Vendée Militaire: Catalogue des collections départementales* (Nantes: Musée Dobrée, 1967), 11.

accommodated their views and attracting a clientele that was exclusively radical, or moderate, or, in rare cases, monarchist. But if they could enthuse at the views coming from Paris, they could be quickly disillusioned when they felt that their interests were undermined. In March 1790, the 130 members of the Chambre du Soleil wrote to Brissot to complain of the 'pernicious morality' that had come to dominate the columns of his newspaper, the *Patriote Français*, with its regular advocacy of the cause of abolition. Scathingly, they urged him to change the title of his paper, since there was nothing patriotic about it. In their eyes, Brissot, '*Monsieur l'Ami des Noirs*', was really no one's friend, 'condemning thousands of men, your brothers, to misery and despair'. He preached abolition with no regard for the 'inevitable' consequences for the people of Nantes, and they angrily cancelled their subscription. 'Keep your paper for your friends the Africans, but don't take the trouble to send it to us in future.'[40] Though slavery was not the principal focus of revolutionary politics, Nantes's merchants found it difficult to divorce politics from commerce and from their dependence on the slave trade.

New clubs and popular societies were created in all the Atlantic ports during the early months of the Revolution, with the aim of piling pressure on the authorities. Typical of these were the *Amis* de la Constitution in Nantes, set up in May 1790 in the buildings of the former Capuchin monastery in the merchant quarter of the city. Its initial aim was to promote the cause of moderate revolution, but, very quickly, the society faced an internal crisis, splitting into conservative and radical factions, with the radicals going on to win overall control. The new office-holders were less beholden to the city's merchant elite; they actively sought out a more popular membership and opened the club's doors to a wider cross-section of the citizenry, who could attend meetings as spectators in the public gallery. A somewhat disillusioned member left a clear, if rather jaundiced, account of what he had witnessed when, on a single day, the Club decided to admit more than 150 new members, at a stroke transforming the character of the meetings and creating what he regarded as a noisy, chaotic atmosphere, with members shouting each other down and constant interruptions from the public gallery. He was dismayed to hear one of the orators addressing the people in the tribunes, telling them that they were the new masters and that they must at all times hold the officers to account. He himself, unsurprisingly, did not return.[41]

By 1791, Bordeaux was home to a variety of popular societies representing a wide range of opinion and frequented by large numbers of those who went on to engage in a political career in the city. Some remained small, proved short-lived,

---

[40] Letter from the Chambre de lecture du Soleil, Nantes, 13 March 1790, in Léon Brunschvicg, *Souvenirs de la révolution à Nantes, ou la mémoire d'un Bleu,* ed. Jean-Clément Martin (Nantes: Reflets du Passé, 1982), 52.

[41] Alfred Lallié, *Les sociétés populaires à Nantes pendant la Révolution* (Nantes: L. Durance, 1914), 15–16.

or merged with bigger societies as revolutionary politics evolved. The Surveillants de la Constitution, for instance, were known for their moderation and commitment to legal process: their minute-books indicate support for the rights of man and for measures against those it regarded as the republic's enemies, especially royalists and refractory priests. And the Société Patriotique de la Merci, another of the more conservative clubs in the city, started as a reading circle for artisans, shopkeepers, and lesser merchants. By 1792, both had closed or had been forced to merge. The more durable Bordeaux clubs, and the ones that went on to dominate the city's political landscape, were the *Amis* de la Constitution (later renamed the *Amis de la Liberté* et de l'Égalité), which, despite being affiliated to the Paris Jacobins, took a more moderate political course and supported the city's deputies in national politics, while the rival Club National took up the cause of the more radical leaders in Paris. The Club—or the Club du Café National, as it had begun life—had, like so many others, been set up as a gathering-place for men of a republican persuasion, including some of the lesser merchants, traders, lawyers, doctors, and members of the liberal professions.[42] But by 1793 it had extended its social base to the more popular classes and had forged alliances with the radical sections of the city, those of a more egalitarian persuasion and less attuned to the needs of commerce. It was castigated by its opponents as a mouthpiece for the radical Jacobin Club in Paris and for deputies sent on mission from the new republican assembly, the National Convention.

But Bordeaux was not a radical city. Its elites remained intensely suspicious of the Paris Jacobins, and, even more, of the popular radicalism of the Paris streets. Of the city's twenty-eight sections, only half a dozen identified with the Jacobin radicals, the group now known as the Montagne in the Convention. The others took the side of the more moderate republicans in the chamber, those who supported Roland's administration in the early months of the Republic and were known as 'Brissotins' or 'Girondins', this last because of the strength of their representation in Bordeaux and its immediate hinterland in the Gironde. For them, as for Bordeaux's legal and mercantile establishment, the political coup of June 1793 which brought the Jacobins to power in the Convention was more than a minor irritant. They had no interest in provoking social turmoil and advocated a degree of social conservatism. They would continue to control the principal administrative bodies, the department and district authorities, the municipal council, and the majority of the sectional assemblies, throughout most of the revolutionary decade.

They were also active in the debates at the *Amis de la Liberté* et de l'Egalité, a society that was also known as the Club des Récollets after the former Franciscan monastery where they held their meetings. The politics of the *Amis* were resolutely

---

[42] Jeanne Melchior, 'Histoire du Club National' (thèse de doctorat, Université de Bordeaux, 1951), 16–18.

republican, and they provided a forum for deputies and municipal officials as well as for members of the city's elite and revolutionaries of a liberal persuasion.[43] Pierre Sers, the future president of the department, was one of their founder members, as were six of the men who went on to form the core of the Girondin group that represented the department in the Convention: Vergniaud, Gensonné, Guadet, Grangeneuve, Ducos, and Boyer-Fonfrède. Three of them, indeed, had assumed the presidency of the Society in the summer of 1790. The club continued to exert considerable influence both with the city authorities and across the wider department. The popular societies that were set up in the smaller towns of the Gironde, such as Libourne, Blaye, or La Réole, sought close ties with the Bordeaux society and looked to it for a lead, and so, through assiduous correspondence, the *Amis* were able to build a powerful network of support across the department. That support would prove valuable to them in moments of crisis. In June of 1793, when the Girondins became entangled in the so-called 'federalist revolt' against the Jacobin majority in the Convention, twenty-nine of those most implicated were men who had served their apprenticeship in the Society.[44]

The years of constitutional monarchy represented the high point for diversity and freedom of expression. With the declaration of the republic in 1792, the range of opinion that was tolerated was reduced as first royalists and then constitutional monarchists found that their views had become unacceptable. In some cases their printing presses were seized and their editors arrested. Royalism became equated with counter-revolution, and those holding royalist meetings or publishing monarchist tracts risked charges of sedition. But most of the trading communities were not royalist. The principal division was between conflicting versions of republicanism, between moderates and radicals, Girondins and Jacobins. Clubs and popular societies found themselves forced to take sides, especially once the Paris Jacobin Club set out to build a network of like-minded societies up and down the country. Affiliation to the Paris Jacobins brought material advantages: local societies would be showered with favours in the form of pamphlets and speeches from leading Jacobins in the Legislative Assembly or the Convention. Rules of affiliation remained unchanged until the end of 1792, and the Paris society would not allow more than one affiliate in any town or city. Yet by the summer of 1791, before the mass secession of moderates in July, 439 clubs across France and beyond had received certificates of affiliation from Paris.[45] That secession changed the character of the Jacobins, and though initially members could join several clubs at any one time and debate with a range of republican opinions, this abruptly ceased when the Jacobins forbade dual affiliation. In cities with several clubs, like

---

[43] AD Gironde, 12L 19, list (undated) of 419 members of the Amis de la Constitution.
[44] Alan Forrest, *Society and Politics in Revolutionary Bordeaux*, 65–6.
[45] Michael L. Kennedy, *The Jacobin Clubs in the French Revolution: The Middle Years* (Princeton, NJ: Princeton University Press, 1988), 5.

Bordeaux, members had now to choose where their loyalties lay, and to choose in a very public way at a time when such choices could have fateful consequences. Nor did the Jacobins tolerate deviation from the agreed political agenda. When the *Amis'* language was adjudged too provocative, in February 1793, the Paris Jacobins had no compunction about returning their address and cancelling their affiliation.[46] Between Paris and the Girondin-led councils of many provincial cities there was little mutual trust. Tensions often seemed on the point of boiling over.

Matters came to a head in the summer of 1793, when a Jacobin coup, supported by the Paris sections, overthrew the Girondin administration and took control of government at the very moment when relations between the centre and many of the commercial cities were degenerating into open conflict. A number of departments moved to challenge the government's authority, a few declaring that they no longer recognized the Convention's legitimacy and setting up their own sovereign bodies, often called Commissions of Public Safety, to rule their part of the Hexagon. But they had no coherent ideology. Theirs was an act of defiance, sometimes backed up by armed force, which the Jacobins condemned as seditious; and it helps explain why, in the summer of 1793, participation in such movements—what the Jacobins termed 'federalism'—was seen as the most serious of political crimes.[47] A number of the ports were implicated, not least Bordeaux and Marseille, both of which had sent Girondins to the Convention and which counted their deputies among the twenty-nine Girondin leaders arrested and put on trial for their lives. They voted to take back their part of national sovereignty, and even to send their national guards to Paris to liberate the Convention from anarchist control. But they did not wish to break up the republic. That there was, in the strict sense of the term, no such ideology as federalism, that the deputies had no desire to destroy national unity, or that their quarrel was more often with the Paris popular movement and those who defended the September Massacres, was seen as immaterial. Provincial politicians had dared to defy Paris and the Convention in which all sovereignty had been concentrated. Bordeaux had not just responded to the desperate appeal of its deputies when it set up its popular Commission and disowned Paris. Its defiance, as Paul Hanson has emphasized, was born out of the crucible of local politics: it was, he insists, 'an integral part of the debate over sovereignty that had been waged over the past three years at both national and local levels'.[48] But that would not save the city from savage repression during the Terror that followed. A Commission Militaire was established to dispense military justice and to purge the authorities that had

---

[46] AD Gironde, Amis de la Constitution, minute of 25 February 1793.

[47] Alan Forrest, 'Federalism', in Colin Lucas (ed.), *The Political Culture of the French Revolution* (Oxford: Pergamon, 1988), 309–27.

[48] Paul Hanson, *The Jacobin Republic under Fire: The Federalist Revolt in the French Revolution* (University Park, PA: Penn State University Press, 2003), 244.

led the department into rebellion. In all, 302 death sentences were passed, and though the Commission was especially brutal in its treatment of those adjudged to be *aristocrates* (a charge that resulted in 160 executions), fifty-three of the death sentences were passed on those convicted of 'federalism'.[49]

The other Atlantic ports were less tempted by the siren voices of federalism. In Nantes, as in many other provincial towns, the municipality reacted with alarm when they heard news of the Jacobin coup, and for a moment seemed inclined to offer support to Breton departments like the Finistère and the Morbihan in their opposition to Paris. But wiser counsels soon prevailed, and their backing was almost immediately retracted.[50] The picture was very similar in La Rochelle. Here the departmental authorities first expressed support for the federalist demand that a rival assembly to the Convention be set up in Bourges, but then quickly rescinded their motion, while the clubs in La Rochelle, Rochefort, and Saintes were united in their support for the Paris Jacobins and their condemnation of Bordeaux's initiative.[51] In truth, by the summer of 1793 neither Nantes nor La Rochelle could afford to focus its attention on federalism when there was a source of danger, and of counter-revolution, much closer at hand. The previous March had seen the beginning of the rising in the Vendée that would engulf five or six departments of the west of France —and much of the territory separating the two cities—in a civil war between republicans and royalists, supporters and opponents of the Revolution. The rebels were led by local nobles and enjoyed strong support from the Catholic clergy; for many, indeed, the uprising had some of the ideological intensity of a Christian crusade. Towns hesitated to join the insurrection, and both Nantes and La Rochelle would remain republican strongholds in a bitterly divided region, urban centres that stayed loyal to Paris and strove to restore order amid the confusion and violence of their rural hinterland. When military levies were imposed in the spring of 1793 to increase the strength of the armies, both cities filled, and even exceeded, their quotas without difficulty. Their focus during the summer months was necessarily on the Vendée, their anger reserved for the royalist nobles and refractory priests who, in their view, were the principal fomenters of the revolt.

News of the insurrection spread fast. The first the cities knew of the uprising was in early March, when troops under General Marcé advanced on the affected areas with orders to quell the rebellion. The force included regular units from Rochefort, along with National Guards from the immediate region, among them around 400 men from La Rochelle. At first there seemed little reason to panic, as it was assumed that the troops would have no difficulty in defeating poorly armed

[49] Pierre Bécamps, *Les suspects à Bordeaux et dans le Département de la Gironde, 1789–99* (Paris: Imprimerie Nationale, 1954), 176.

[50] Pétré-Grenouilleau, *Nantes, histoire et géographie contemporaine*, 116.

[51] Jean-Marie Augustin, *La Révolution Française en Haut-Poitou et pays charentais* (Toulouse: Privat, 1989), 193.

peasants, but when news came on 20 March that the army had been routed near Pont-Charrault, with the losses including some twenty of the town's National Guards, La Rochelle was left fearful and traumatized. As retreating soldiers found their way to the city, panic spread, and the popular mood turned ugly. Danger lurked at every corner. The rebels, it was claimed, had descended on the little town of Marans and were closing in on the gates of the city itself. They were 'within a day's march', said one report, another that they were about to be invaded by 'brigands'.[52] Then paranoia took over. The counter-revolutionaries were commanded, it was rumoured, by priests, the customary villains in the republican narrative. La Rochelle became tense and vengeful, and, following the example of the Paris Jacobins, the authorities looked for scapegoats for an 'inexplicable' defeat. The unfortunate Marcé was accused of treason and, put on trial for his life, taken to Paris to appear before the Revolutionary Tribunal. On 21 and 22 March the anger of the crowd focused on six priests who were passing through the port on their way to being deported. On the quayside insults were hurled and stones rained down on them, and as the National Guard withdrew, the authorities stood by while they were stripped and disembowelled, and had their heads impaled on sticks and borne aloft through the town. And if four people were put on trial out of the hundreds who had been present at the massacres, three were acquitted; the fourth, a twenty-eight-year-old wigmaker, was sent to prison but later freed on appeal. He was adjudged to have become involved only because of the events of the Revolution, which meant that his violent excesses were excusable.[53]

It was no accident that the crowd should have vented their anger on priests, whom many saw an undercover agents for royalism and counter-revolution. Anticlerical feeling was strong from the very beginning of the Revolution, with the monastic orders attacked for their greed and wastefulness, the tithes which ordinary people paid to support their upkeep a major source of anger. Here, as in other areas of the country, anticlericalism was fuelled by the refusal of large numbers of clergy to take the constitutional oath imposed by the Civil Constitution of the Clergy in 1791. In La Rochelle, for instance, the best indication we have is that around 40 per cent of the clergy (thirty-seven out of ninety-three) took the oath; in Nantes 23 per cent (twenty-one out of ninety-two); and in Bordeaux 37 per cent (seventy-three out of 197); while in the smaller port towns to the north, such as Vannes, Rochefort, or Ploërmel, the proportion taking the oath seldom reached double figures.[54] Many of the refractories refused to leave, taking shelter with former nuns in Catholic safe-houses and continuing to hold services in

[52] Jacques Péret, 'La Rochelle et la Vendée', in La Rochelle, ville frontière, 226–9.

[53] Pierre Lemonnier, 'Les journées des 21 et 21 mars 1793 à la Rochelle', Bulletin de la Société des Archives Historiques: Revue de la Saintonge et de l'Aunis, 32 (1912), 203–10.

[54] Timothy Tackett, La Révolution, l'Eglise, la France: le serment de 1791 (Paris: Le Cerf, 1986), 359, 375, 385, and 397.

isolated hamlets or outdoors on hillsides. As the war in the Vendée dragged on, they were accused—often with good reason—of spreading subversion and offering succour to the 'royal and Catholic army' against the Republic. Jean-Baptiste Carrier, writing to the Convention from his mission to the West, was unapologetic in his condemnation of priests. 'Reason raises men to the level of the Revolution,' he wrote, 'prejudices, superstition, fanaticism fade before Philosophy's torch.' He noted how Minée, who had once been a bishop and was now president of the Department, had spoken out against the errors of the priesthood, and found comfort in the fact that five priests in the diocese had followed his example and 'paid the same homage to Reason'. In the same letter, he informed the deputies that ninety refractory priests had been herded on to a ship and drowned in the Loire.[55] He reported the news without any comment or suggestion of regret. Refractory priests were enemies of the Revolution; in Carrier's view they deserved no better.

Revolutionary propaganda was insistent that the Vendée was backward, with a peasantry who were both fanatical and barbaric.[56] And the clergy themselves did little to deny their influence in the struggle. Many of the bishops had gone into exile following the Civil Constitution, communicating with their clergy from the safety of Italy or Spain, the majority unrepentant in their rejection of both revolutionary politics and Enlightenment philosophy. They greeted the Vendée as a symptom of moral regeneration and hoped that it signalled the end of the revolution in France. The Bishop of La Rochelle, de Coucy, showed a typical intransigence in his condemnation of everything the Revolution stood for. He had left France for Spain in June 1791, where he settled in the diocese of Toledo. From there he had fulminated against the Revolution, condemning any measure of compromise, from the oath of liberty and equality in August 1792 to submission to the laws of the Republic in May 1795. From Guadalajara in August 1795, he wrote to the former priests of this diocese, condemning the Revolution for its attacks on Catholicism and for its indifference to religion, for which he blamed the baneful influence of Luther, Calvin, and Jansen, before lambasting it for 'the absurdities of paganism' and 'pure atheism or the god of Spinoza'. He urged them to make no compromise with revolutionary law, since no law can exist in a society that does not recognize God; to recognize the laws of the Republic could only be an act of 'folly'.[57] Like many of the upper clergy, de Coucy identified wholly with the Counter-revolution, the local nobility, and the monarchy.

---

[55] Letter to the Convention, 17 November 1793, in E.H. Carrier (ed.), *Correspondence of Jean-Baptiste Carrier during his Mission in Brittany, 1793–94* (London: Bodley Head, 1920), 120.

[56] Anne Rolland-Boulestreau, *Les colonnes infernales: Violences et guerre civile en Vendée Militaire, 1794–95* (Paris: Fayard, 2015), 49–71.

[57] François Uzureau, 'L'évêque de La Rochelle en 1795', *Bulletin de la Société des Archives Historiques de la Saintonge et d'Aunis*, 41 (1926), 109.

For him, the Republic was anti-Christ, especially after the closure of Catholic churches and the criminalization of the clergy.

Nantes' proximity to the Vendée meant that here the Terror was principally turned against those who had taken up arms against the Republic, been captured, and been brought to the city for trial before the criminal tribunal and a series of military commissions. The majority of those accused were country-dwellers from the villages and small towns of the *bocage*; while some may have had friends and relatives among the accused, the people of Nantes were seldom directly implicated in the insurrection. Yet the scale of the repression could not fail to make an enduring impression on them, as those who had fought in the Vendean army were convicted on simple identification and thousands of death sentences were handed down. In his classic study of the Terror, Donald Greer claims that 3,548 death sentences were passed in the Loire-inférieure, the highest number of any French department, including the Seine.[58] But that is an official figure that greatly underestimates the numbers killed, many without recourse to the law. As prisoners were brought to Nantes after Vendean defeats, the judicial process proved too slow, and the guillotine, installed on the traditional place of execution on the Place du Bouffay, too cumbersome for the task before it. As a consequence, the guillotine was soon supplemented by an unofficial Terror, with batches of suspects taken from the city's prisons—many from the old Entrepôt des Cafés which had been requisitioned and turned into a jail—to be mown down by gunfire in the Carrières de Gigant or bound together and drowned in the Loire. Few citizens could have remained unaware of what was going on, as tumbrils rolled through the streets, rotting bodies floated on the river, and the sound of the nightly firing squad reverberated through the city.[59] Many of the prisoners, piled in insanitary cells and denied any form of medication, died of their wounds, fevers, and disease. When these deaths and the mass executions are included in the figures, Jean-Clément Martin has concluded that the total number of deaths in the first six months of 1794 was around 12,000. As well as insurgents, many of whom were simple peasants, they included nobles and refractory priests, around ninety of whom were drowned in the waters of the Loire.[60]

The list of victims included relatively few merchants or ship-owners, since they were not deeply implicated in the revolt. In La Rochelle, for instance, the merchant community was relatively unaffected by an essentially political Terror. But in cities farther removed from the Vendee, merchants risked becoming a target for Jacobin

---

[58] Donald Greer, *The Incidence of the Terror during the French Revolution: A Statistical Interpretation* (Cambridge, MA: Harvard University Press, 1935), 147.

[59] Bruno Hervé, 'Noyades, fusillades, exécutions: les mises à mort des brigands entre justice et massacres en Loire-inférieure en l'an II', *La Révolution Française: Cahiers de l'Institut d'histoire de la Révolution française*, 3 (2011), 1–13.

[60] Jean-Clément Martin, *La Loire-Atlantique dans la tourmente révolutionnaire* (Nantes: Reflets du Passé, 1989), 88.

hatred as committees of surveillance investigated their business dealings and deputies on mission from Paris ordered their arrest. Their wealth invited resentment, while commerce was too easily confused with greed and speculation at a time when it was seen as a citizen's duty to put the public interest ahead of private profit. The pattern across the Atlantic ports was uneven, with the degree of persecution dependent on the priorities and personality of individual terrorists. In Nantes, though the authorities had a list of mercantile fortunes and could have used it to destroy the merchant elite, they showed little desire to do so. It is true that thirty-six merchants—of whom fifteen were engaged in fitting out ships for Atlantic trade—were included among the 132 citizens of Nantes whom Carrier despatched for trial to the Revolutionary Tribunal in Paris. But most were magistrates and nobles, and none was executed. Moreover, of the thousands condemned to death in Nantes itself, only four were merchants or the relatives of merchants, and they were condemned not for trading, but for supporting the insurrection in the Vendée.[61]

The picture in Bordeaux was very different, especially after the arrival on mission of Marc-Antoine Jullien, who had a passion for egalitarianism which he shared with the more extreme Parisian *sans-culottes*. Jullien arrived in Bordeaux with a mission to reverse what he saw as the lax administration of his predecessors, Ysabeau and Tallien, to punish those who had participated in the federalist revolt the previous summer, and to purge the elite of a city he believed to be corrupted by greed, a *foyer de négociantisme*. The two months he spent in Bordeaux marked the peak of the terror in the city: 198 people were executed on the Place Nationale, two-thirds of the total for the entire revolutionary era.[62] Jullien unleashed a campaign of systematic persecution against Bordeaux's merchants for economic as well as political crimes. Of course he had some excuse for this, in that so many merchants had been implicated in the federalist revolt and had given their support to the Girondin cause; they were politically compromised in a way that the majority of Nantes merchants were not. But that was not his sole motive. Even those merchants who had supported the Revolution were suspect as men whose goal was less to work for the cause of liberty and equality than to replace the nobility as the dominant social and political class in the city. 'There have been many mercantile cabals here,' he wrote to Robespierre, 'and liberty has become venal. I am on the trail of the guilty parties, and the Committee of Surveillance will help me in my search.'[63] It did a thorough job: of the 279 merchants who were arrested, 119 appeared before the Commission Militaire,

[61] Pétré-Grenouilleau, *Nantes, histoire et géographie contemporaine*, 118–19.

[62] Forrest, *Society and Politics*, 238.

[63] Pierre Bécamps, *La Révolution à Bordeaux, 1789–94: J.-M.-B. Lacombe, président de la Commission Militaire* (Bordeaux: Éditions Bière, 1953), 188.

and twelve received death sentences.[64] Some were charged with no political crimes; the only charges against them were of speculation and profiteering.

Though the judges were particularly interested in their political affiliations and their reaction to the federalist revolt, their economic dealings were also scrutinized, and those who could not demonstrate that they had made sacrifices for the Revolution were treated as suspect. Merchants who could point to service in the National Guard or contributions to the war effort could expect to be acquitted, and those who had just continued trading for their personal profit generally escaped with a fine or a short period of imprisonment. But these were years when commercial ventures could easily assume a political connotation, and there trouble lay. A merchant on the rue Sainte-Cathérine, Jacques Henri, was seemingly careless in the goods he handled; convicted of selling woollen products bearing royalist insignia and jewellery engraved with monarchist symbols, he was sentenced to death.[65] Maurice Albert, a thirty-year-old *commis-négociant*, was unwise enough to speculate in currency on behalf of his firm, buying specie at an excessive price and thus undermining the value of the *assignat*. For that, too, he went to the guillotine.[66] Passing money abroad, refusing to use paper currency, corresponding with sons or agents in foreign ports—these were areas where commercial and political crime merged, and where economic transactions could have counter-revolutionary connotations.

Commercial activity alone seldom incurred a death sentence, but merchants had to tread carefully. They were routinely subject to arrest and imprisonment, seals were placed on their registers, and their correspondence was scoured for evidence of wrongdoing. Merchants passed across frontiers, even into war zones. They traded in many different currencies, and the temptation to speculate—in *assignats*, in hard currency, even in national lands—was something that came naturally to them. And the colonies offered particular temptations. As one Bordeaux merchant, François Bonnaffé, explained in a letter to his agent at Le Cap, the colonies provided opportunities for rich pickings, which many could not resist. He talked of a rush of speculation in the Caribbean, as merchants sought to trade paper for hard currency before the paper lost all its value. But, he added, it should not be undertaken lightly. 'In the present circumstances, it is a dangerous operation for anyone engaging in it. One would be seen as a currency speculator, which is a bad reputation to have at this time.' A few months later, writing to an associate in Port-au-Prince, he again warned that trade should only be conducted in *assignats*, despite the huge losses incurred when 170 francs of paper bought

[64] Victor Daline, 'Marc-Antoine Jullien, après le 9 thermidor', *Annales historiques de la Révolution française*, 36 (1964), 161.

[65] AD Gironde, 14L41, Commission Militaire, dossier Jacques Henri.

[66] AD Gironde, 14L4, Commission Militaire, dossier Maurice Albert.

only 100 francs in coin.[67] Commerce, too, had to be conducted with politics in mind.

For the merchant community, surviving the revolutionary years took a degree of guile, as trade could easily be confused with speculation and the accumulation of profit was seen by the more extreme revolutionaries as an act of selfishness that rendered merchants instantly suspect. The president of the Commission Militaire in Bordeaux, Jean-Baptiste Lacombe, had little doubt that rich merchants were a privileged elite who did nothing for the public good and concentrated single-mindedly on their business interests. Those who appeared before his court were frequently accused of an 'égoïsme' that was demonstrated by their success in making money. They had, it was inferred, neglected their duty towards others, to the state, and the defence of the public weal, and all for personal profit. In his judgement of one merchant, Jean-Louis Baux, Lacombe was explicit in his condemnation not just of Baux, but of the entire 'caste' he represented. Lacombe insisted that the tribunal could only applaud the arrest of Baux, 'for he belongs to a caste which, like that of priests and nobles, has made every effort to overthrow the Republic, has grown fat on the pure substance of the people, and has seemed to support Liberty only to impose its despotism more clinically on the debris of the aristocracy'.[68] In his eyes, merchants' greed and cupidity condemned them, for they went hand-in-hand with contempt for others and a lack of concern for the welfare of the mass of the citizenry. The degree of their guilt might differ, but it was well-nigh impossible to be a good merchant and a good citizen.

Foreign merchants in the Atlantic ports had additional reasons to exercise caution, especially in their correspondence with relatives abroad. Many, of course, had welcomed the Revolution, whether as bourgeois opposed to noble privilege, as traders eager to end company monopolies, or as Protestants grateful for their new-found liberties. And some, despite the threat which the Revolution presented, continued to identify with the Republic even through the months of Terror, fulfilling their civic duties and expressing quiet support for the revolutionary authorities. Jacob Lambertz, a German merchant long established in La Rochelle, was scrupulous in this regard, and his journal, which he wrote up practically every day from 1784 until 1801, is an enduring testimony to his loyalty and good sense.[69] He was careful to remain uncritical of government policy, and where he discussed the war in the Vendée, it was as a patriot, supporting the revolutionary cause, taking pleasure in reporting rebel defeats, and participating in public celebrations of victory. In his professional life, he avoided the most obvious

---

[67] AD Gironde, 13L18, Comité de Surveillance de Bordeaux, dossier François Bonnaffé.

[68] Philippe Gardey, *Négociants et marchands de Bordeaux. De la guerre d'Amérique à la Restauration, 1780–1830* (Paris: Presses Universitaires de Paris-Sorbonne, 2009), 199.

[69] AD Charente-Maritime, 4J 1808, *Journal de Jacob Lambertz* (MS, 4 vols, 1784–1801); Emmanuel Garnier and Frédéric Surville (eds), *Climat et révolutions: Autour du Journal du négociant rochelais Jacob Lambertz, 1733–1813* (Saintes: Le Croît vif, 2010), 269–526.

pitfalls. He did not trade in currency on European markets and took no part in colonial traffic or the slave trade, concentrating on the brandy trade and sales to the Baltic. He therefore saw no reason to get involved in the squabbles between the *Amis des Noirs* and the Club Massiac that so disrupted the merchant community. He was careful to contribute to successive *dons patriotiques*, modestly and unostentatiously; he handed over his silverware and his wife's jewellery as a gift to the Nation; and he duly joined the city's Garde Nationale.[70] He attended all the festivals held in La Rochelle during the Revolution, joining in the celebrations and public balls to show his support. He rejoiced when the republic was declared in 1792, and fraternized with 'good sans-culottes' at a civic banquet in the Year II. He fully understood that he must be seen to be integrated into the social and political fabric of the city, and was eager to conform. But there were times when it was wise to stand back, to remain an outsider on the fringes of the Revolution. He refused to stand for the municipal council, for instance, even though the council was led by his close friend and fellow-merchant Samuel Demissy. Lambertz insisted that this was the right thing to do, citing his belief that 'a man born outside the territory of the Republic should abstain from taking any position of public office'.[71] It was also a matter of self-preservation in a political climate he did not fully understand.

Like many others, Lambertz made the judgement that it was prudent to concentrate on his business affairs. It was his way of negotiating a revolution that repeatedly questioned the values and the commercial ethic of the merchant community, and which, on so many occasions, tempted men into political choices that they might live to regret. But the Age of Revolution brought other challenges, too, challenges emanating from overseas and from the wider Atlantic world. For many merchants in the west-coast ports, as for the planters and agents in the West Indies, political demands at home would soon be dwarfed by an even greater threat, as the country was plunged into a war that cut the trade routes on which their business depended, and as revolution spread from France to the Caribbean, leading to slave insurrections, plantation-burning, massacres, and expulsions on an unimagined scale. Slavery would be abandoned, and the slave trade decimated. Saint-Domingue would be lost, first to the Spanish and British navies, then to Toussaint Louverture and the world's first black revolution. Within a few years, the merchants' comfortable world would be shaken to its foundations, and their companies and their ports condemned to decades of decline.

---

[70] Garnier and Surville, *Climat et révolutions*, 32.   [71] Ibid., 35.

8

Merchants, Planters, and Revolutionary Politics

The merchant response to reform in 1789 had initially been largely positive, with many joining with other leading members of the Third Estate to demand political rights and the abolition of privilege. But already there were clouds on the horizon, not least the future of the slave trade itself. The Declaration of the Rights of Man was seized upon by abolitionists, bolstered by the presence in the Assembly of prominent members of the *Amis des Noirs*, as the weapon they needed to attack the very institution of slavery, and their demands served to spread anxiety in merchant circles. Among their concerns was the close link that had been established between several of the leaders of the anti-slavery movement with abolition-ist circles in the United States; for Brissot, Clavière, Bergasse, and others, the struggle to abolish the slave trade was part of something broader, a move to introduce 'American liberty' into France.[1] As a result of their activity, the issue of slavery, which had been of pressing concern only to a small minority, an elite of philosophical thinkers, risked becoming a central plank of the Revolution itself. Slavery, and more crucially the slave trade, became the topic of animated and often acrimonious debates, with merchant opinion divided, and battle lines drawn between what they saw as two unpalatable extremes—the abolitionist claims of the *Amis des Noirs* on the one hand, and the demands of the planters on the other, concerned above all to maintain the profits of slavery and to exercise as much freedom as they could over their commercial transactions, liberating themselves from what they increasingly saw as the tyranny of France. In Saint-Domingue there were reports of rioting by elements within the Creole community. The future of the colony was causing friction among whites, too.

The merchant communities of the leading Atlantic ports sent deputations to lobby in Paris for what they identified as their political and economic interests, often setting up correspondence committees to advise their deputies and to establish common policies with other ports. The central importance of the various chambers of commerce in representing their merchant communities (or of com-mittees of merchants where, as in Le Havre, no chamber had yet been constituted) soon became apparent. Organization was all-important if the merchants were to

---

[1] Marcel Dorigny and Bernard Gainot (eds), *La Société des Amis des Noirs, 1788–99. Contribution à l'histoire de l'abolition de l'esclavage* (Paris: Editions UNESCO, 1998), 26.

succeed in gathering support for their cause. They circulated documents between ports in the first instance. They then extended their campaign to neighbouring towns and cities to gather support from industrialists and shopkeepers. And they developed a third sphere of mobilization in the National Assembly.[2] In Bordeaux, as early as August 1789 the city's Chamber of commerce formed a committee of its members to instruct their deputies in Paris.[3] Interestingly, some of the larger merchants in the port chose to serve on the committee, a sure sign of the significance which commercial houses attached to the Chamber's work. And Bordeaux's deputies would in turn figure among the most prominent speakers on colonial questions in the Assembly's debates.

But what was their purpose, and against whom were they campaigning? Few of their members were radical in a political sense, putting the defence of their commercial interests above more ideological considerations. But they felt isolated from events over which they had no control. They were, first and foremost, anxious for news of developments in other ports and in the Caribbean at a moment when the *colons* were agitating to end the *Exclusif,* or what remained of it after the Peace of Paris in 1763, and claiming the right to trade directly with countries other than France. This was, perhaps, the most important change: in a few short months it had become clear that there were real differences between their objectives and those of French merchants, and it could no longer be assumed that they were pursuing the same economic goals. But there was one goal that they did continue to share, and that was a commitment to the institution of slavery, from which both, in their different ways, profited.[4] They feared losing out to the abolitionists, to what the Bordeaux chamber called the 'incendiary doctrine of the *Amis des Noirs*' as it pleaded with other chambers of commerce to 'unite their efforts to prevent the bitter blow with which our national commerce is threatened'. And they sought financial backing from the government to prevent economic stagnation, asking that bonuses be paid for every ship leaving on a slave voyage.[5] In the short term, at least, their fears seemed exaggerated. Slaving was not immediately banned, the first months of the Revolution counting among the boom years as slave ships continued to leave from the Gironde and the Loire estuaries until 1793. Slavery and human rights could, it seemed, co-exist in relative harmony, and on 8 March 1790, following a major debate on the colonies, the Assembly decreed that the revolutionary principles of Liberty and Equality should not be applied to slaves in France's overseas possessions. The Assembly would leave the planters to their own devices.[6]

---

[2] Lucie Maquerlot, 'Les résistances au Havre de la Constituante à la Convention', *Cahiers de l'histoire et des mémoires de la traite négrière, de l'esclavage et de leurs abolitions en Normandie,* 2 (2009), 23.

[3] AD Gironde, 8J 703, Adresses, pamphlets sur le commerce et les colonies, 1790-3.

[4] Maquerlot, 'Les résistances au Havre', 16.

[5] Éric Saugéra, *Bordeaux port négrier, 17ᵉ-19ᵉ siècles* (Paris: Karthala, 1995), 115.

[6] *Le Moniteur,* debate of 8 March 1790.

News of the vote was eagerly awaited in the Atlantic port cities ,and was all the more welcome when it was transmitted to them by a man they trusted, Jean-Baptiste Nairac, who had sent slave voyages out from La Rochelle and was, in every sense, one of their own. Nairac had been sent by the Chamber of commerce of La Rochelle to act as an observer at the meetings of the Estates-General, and subsequently at the National Assembly; from there he reported back regularly on the deputies' comments on the slave trade and on the dangers which the Revolution posed to its continued prosperity. The speeches of those opposed to the trade—not least the crusading tones of Mirabeau in favour of abolition—were read with anxiety by the merchants of the Atlantic ports. On 6 March, two days before the decree was passed, Nairac had already sensed a change in the deputies' mood, and could report from Paris that the majority had finally moved towards the maintenance of the trade and were of a mind to legislate on the subject. So, he wrote, 'I can today announce to you with certainty or something close to certainty that these major interests will be treated, as I have never ceased to hope that they would, in a reasonable manner and one that conforms to the interests of commerce.'[7] Three days later, by way of a courier to Nantes, he wrote to them again, this time little short of exultant. He expressed the hope that mercantile interests would be satisfied by the decree, which, in his view, maintained all their rights. His only regret concerned the tone of the decree, as he noted that its language was affected by the new political correctness of the day. The issue of the slave trade was not properly contextualized, he said, adding that 'we must pardon those enthusiasts for liberty, who, after establishing its general principles, did not wish to attack them openly'.[8] Perhaps so; but the substantive issue seemed resolved. The French Atlantic remained open for business.

But still the planters were not satisfied, and they repeatedly tried to recruit the merchant communities of the French Atlantic ports to offer more forthright support, with the chambers of commerce their key points of contact. From the earliest months of the Revolution they flooded the chambers with pamphlets, printed speeches, and other forms of propaganda, insisting on their commonality of interest and calling on them to offer moral, economic, and (in extreme instances) military support. They understood the threat which the ideals of the Revolution posed to the colonies and their slave economy; and they lambasted the *Amis des Noirs* for what they saw as a false and dangerous philanthropy that would destroy their way of life and, with it, France's position in the world. When France extended civil rights to free men of colour in 1791, the planters argued that their entire social system was under threat. And when slaves did revolt, burning plantations and forcing thousands of *colons* to flee, they regarded this as proof that

[7] Jean-Michel Deveau, *Le commerce rochelais face à la Révolution: correspondance de Jean-Baptiste Nairac, 1789–90* (La Rochelle: Rumeur des âges, 1989), 202.
[8] Ibid., 203.

they had been right from the start, attacking what they saw as misplaced and craven liberal morality for the damage inflicted on the colonies. In Saint-Domingue they suspected that the slaves were helped by sympathizers in the white and mulatto communities, expressing surprise at the degree of organization and suggesting that the plotters' aim had been to capture and burn Le Cap itself.[9] In France and in French communities in the United States and across the Caribbean, they placed blame for the violence squarely on the shoulders of the *Amis*, arguing that it was they, through their support for free people of colour, who had encouraged and enflamed the slave rebellion.

One forceful exponent of this view was Bernard-Barnabé O'Shiell, who owned a plantation in southern Saint-Domingue and whose family had become rich through the slave trade. From exile in Philadelphia, he wrote about the injustices that had been thrust upon the *colons*, insisting that the *gens de couleur* were the 'direct and immediate force of the slave revolt'.[10] Another refugee from Saint-Domingue, the Marquis de Rouvray, agreed, and he had no doubt where the blame should lie. Some years later, writing to his daughter from exile in Philadelphia, he pointed the finger at the *Amis des Noirs* and reminded her of the pamphlets which he had penned back in the first months of the Revolution. 'It was in the month of June 1789 that I wrote that the sect of the *Amis des Noirs* contemplated the destruction of all thrones, all forms of government, all religions, of the globe.' Their warped ideas of philanthropy, he believed, were, more than any other element, responsible for the ills that had overtaken the colony in the intervening years.[11]

That, of course, was a planter's view of events, a view forged in a world dominated by slavery and the plantation economy and exacerbated by what he and his fellow-*colons* had endured. In their eyes, the liberalism of the French Revolution was a false god that threatened both their economic prosperity and their position of racial superiority in Saint-Domingue. They saw it as the delusion of Parisian intellectuals who had no experience of colonial life, and they looked to the Atlantic ports of France for allies in their struggle.

But the merchants of France's west coast ports would be difficult to convince, and in 1790 and 1791 Bordeaux's Chamber of commerce pointedly sought other opinions, often from ships' captains returning home from the islands, that could provide an independent view of the violence in Guadeloupe and Saint-Domingue. They took such reports seriously, and when fresh news arrived of troubles in the

[9] Carolyn E. Fick, *The Making of Haiti: The Saint- Domingue Revolution from below* (Knoxville: University of Tennessee Press, 1990), 102.

[10] Ashli White, *Encountering Revolution: Haiti and the Making of the Early Republic* (Baltimore: Johns Hopkins University Press, 2010), 81.

[11] Malcolm McIntosh and Bernard Weber (eds), *Une correspondance familiale au temps des troubles de Saint-Domingue: lettres du marquis et de la marquise de Rouvray à leur fille, Saint-Domingue—Etats-Unis, 1791–96* (Paris: Société de l'histoire des colonies françaises, 1959), 109; White, *Encountering Revolution*, 81.

islands, a call would go out to the principal merchants in the port to assemble in the Chamber to assimilate its significance.[12] They feared that the Creoles were seeking to exploit their proximity to the United States and to maximize their own profits by selling their produce on the open market; and they knew of the reputation of the Caribbean for smuggling and contraband. In this regard, they saw a clear conflict of interest between the freebooting islanders on the one hand and the merchants, importers and shipping agents of France's Atlantic ports on the other.

But how did the chambers of commerce of the Atlantic ports interpret their interests in the early months of the Revolution? The discussions of the Bordeaux Chamber in 1789 and 1790 suggest that the two issues that dominated their agenda were a persistent unease that the government might abolish the slave trade and a shortage of hard currency that was harming liquidity and making trading conditions more difficult.[13] These were not uniquely commercial issues: as they explained in an address to their deputies in the Assembly, any damage inflicted on commerce would have social ramifications, too, since it would both affect public finances and spread misery and unemployment among the population at large. The suspension of shipping in the port would, they insisted, 'have knock-on effects on all classes of citizens', and this would in turn present a risk of tumult and disorder.[14] They feared such disorder not only because they had witnessed in Paris the violence that could result, but also because they felt the anger of the city's workers turning against themselves, an anger that was fuelled by unemployment and by allegations of grain-hoarding and price-fixing.[15] These allegations were, they protested, unfounded, but they were creating class conflict in the city that would lead to insurrection. The merchants liked to see themselves as the guardians of the social well-being of their fellow-citizens, and they staked their claim to speak in the name of the community at large. Trade, they believed, lay at the heart of the city's economic and cultural life, and if trade were to decline these risked withering and dying. They felt a responsibility to the wider community which they had no intention of betraying.

Defending Bordeaux's interests could mean rejecting pleas for assistance from elsewhere. And so, when in 1791 the Chamber debated a plea from the planters of Martinique to intervene following violence on the island, the merchants held back from making any statement that could enflame opinion. In an address on trade and the colonies, the Chamber eschewed any language that might be seen as political or partisan, any hint of favouring one side against the other, instead observing what they termed 'the most impartial neutrality'. Even if it was clear to

[12] AD Gironde, C 4438, Chambre de Commerce de Guienne, registre de délibérations, 1791, folio 6.
[13] AD Gironde, C 4259, Chambre de Commerce de Guienne, registre de délibérations, 1789, folio 51.
[14] AD Gironde, C4266, 'A MM les Députés de Bordeaux à l'Assemblée Nationale', 28 August 1791, folio 212.
[15] AD Gironde, C4438, Chambre de Commerce de Guienne, registre de délibérations, 1791, folio 4.

many of those present that one side was more to blame, they realized that it was not in Bordeaux's interest to get involved in what was a matter for Martinique. 'Commerce could not act as an interested party,' noted the Chamber, 'far less should it presume to pass judgement.'[16] Its role should be limited to maintaining prosperity and, through prosperity, to contributing to social harmony at home. For this reason they refused to support the planters' plea to be recognized as a province of France or to establish a degree of autonomy from the metropole. Provinces enjoyed rights and traditions, and for this reason alone, in the merchants' view, any such claim must be resisted. The fact that some colonists had been born there, or that they had emigrated there to make a new life freed from the constraints of French laws and privileges, should make no difference, and the different chambers all insisted that Saint-Domingue and the other Caribbean islands were, and could only be, colonies whose role and duty were to serve the interests of France and contribute to its prosperity. The public exchange with the planters' lobby could often be bitter. In the Year III, for instance, a French merchant in Philadelphia expressed his disdain for the planters and for what he saw as their overblown political pretensions. Their claims to autonomy, he believed, had little basis in fact or in law, and he declared, somewhat dismissively, that 'the colonies are possessions, inalienable possessions, if you like, but they are nothing other than that. Their relations with the metropole are founded quite simply on trade.'[17]

The relations between the planters and the revolutionaries had never been easy. From the very beginning of the Revolution, the concerns of the *colons* had been clear, with many fearful of reform and some prepared to align themselves openly with the cause of monarchy and political counter-revolution to defend their interests. Others seemed ready to engage with the new revolutionary state. Some of their representatives, who were in Paris in 1788, offered to help draw up a new constitution for the islands; but the white planters in Saint-Domingue were not consulted directly, and there was resentment that it would be France, and not Saint-Domingue, that would take the final decision on matters that uniquely concerned them. Elections to the Estates-General were hastily called on the initiative of a Committee of the *Colons*, but with no legitimation as they had not been called by the King. In all, thirty-one deputies were chosen, sixteen of them planters living on their *habitations*, the other fifteen plantation owners resident in France. But the elections were greeted with hostility and widespread indifference. The *colons* understood, as Gabriel Debien explains, that even if the deputies loyally represented their grievances in Paris, their very participation in the system meant

---

[16] AD Gironde, C 4438, Chambre de Commerce de Guienne, 'Réponse aux nouvelles de troubles à Martinique', 10 September 1791.

[17] Manuel Covo, 'Commerce, empire et révolutions dans le monde atlantique: la colonie française de Saint-Domingue entre métropole et Etats-Unis, ca. 1778 – ca. 1804' (thèse de doctorat, EHESS, 2013), 657.

that all initiative relating to Saint-Domingue would henceforth lie with the French government, and that their space for independent action would be severely curtailed. They would be treated as a colony, without the powers of a province. More seriously, amid the calls for political reform and for the cause of human rights, their slave-holding lifestyle was directly threatened. Within two months they reacted by setting up a club to press for their interests, the interests of the white *colons*, in opposition, should it prove necessary, to the claims of the French merchant community. Battle lines were being drawn, and the Club Massiac, which would champion the interests of the West Indian planters in France and would spearhead reaction to colonial reforms, was born.[18]

Central to these interests, of course, was the maintenance of slave labour on the plantations and of the slave trade that provided it. The language of human rights which the Revolution promoted did not promise well, and the planter lobby was soon persuaded that abolitionists in France would stop at nothing—even the loss of France's colonial possessions—to salve their liberal conscience on the question. A pamphlet published in Paris in June 1789 took the attack to the abolitionists, branding them as ideologues of the most harmful kind, the 'defenders of the blacks' who could justly have labelled themselves 'persecutors of the whites'. The anonymous author scoffs at their belief that slavery was 'a revolting form of usurpation', or that it was 'the greatest evil that could exist on earth'.[19] It was, he argued, the wrong starting point for debate. The deputies should consider what was being put at risk by their ideas: not only their prosperity but France's entire colonial project, a project which Britain was keen to destroy. The pamphlet concluded that, while no one would claim that the slave economy was perfect, its abolition would destroy many livelihoods and that, if any other labour system could be found to produce the same results, then, and only then, could slavery be safely abolished. The French should not be expected to solve the world's problems alone. 'Slavery is an evil', it conceded, but an evil that was born in Africa; 'it exists, and it is not the *colons* who are responsible for it'. In time-honoured style, it down-played the cruelty of slavery as it was practised in the Americas and painted an idealized picture of simple but healthy living on plantations overseen by kindly and paternalistic planters. While conceding that slavery might be vicious in principle, it insisted that it need not be vicious in practice.[20]

Besides, by 1791 they were facing a new crisis with reports of slave violence and a rejection of governmental authority that both jeopardized French control of the island and spread panic among merchants in France. Addressing the National Assembly, a delegation from Le Havre insisted that it was not just their own losses

---

[18] Gabriel Debien, *Les colons de Saint-Domingue et la Révolution: essai sur le Club Massiac* (Paris: Armand Colin, 1953), 64–6.

[19] Anon, *Réclamations et observations des colons sur l'idée de l'abolition de la traite et de l'affranchissement des nègres* (Paris, 1789), 6.

[20] Ibid., *passim*.

that concerned them; it was the future of France itself. 'They are afraid when they see the sources of national prosperity wither,' they explained, 'when they see the prosperity of the State, the raw materials that fuel manufacturing, the foodstuffs needed to sustain the poor all vanishing along with their fortune.'[21] The majority firmly believed that, in some form, the institution of slavery must be maintained. In another address to the National Assembly, the merchants of Bordeaux made what had become the customary defence of the slave trade, declaring themselves fearful of the misery that abolition would mean for France. Slavery was, of course, to be abhorred, yet there were compelling social reasons to maintain it, 'considerations of public and general interest' that must overrule 'ideas formed by the heart'. The merchants, too, insisted that slavery was the key to the whole colonial system that lay at the heart of France's economic growth. And they went on to question, in the customary language of the anti-abolition lobby, claims that slavery had brought misery to millions of Africans. Those people had been enslaved in Africa, where they had been rescued from death in war; if they were condemned to hard work in America, their fate was not so different from that of the paid labourer in Europe; and if some slaves were abused by cruel masters, they were surely a minority. Besides, slavery was the basis of a whole social system, and humanitarian arguments could be advanced in its defence. There was no natural state to which the slaves could be returned. 'It would be a mistake,' the merchants insisted, 'to see Africa as a part of the world where men enjoyed the plenitude of their rights.' By bringing Africans to the New World, French slavers might even have saved them from certain misery and early death.[22]

But the merchants had little wish to identify too strongly with the interests of the *colons*, for their principal concerns lay elsewhere. Alongside their expressed fear of popular insurrection went that, traditional in merchant communities, of involvement in yet another war. Their commerce and their profits had suffered badly in the wars of the eighteenth century, and merchants were only too keenly aware of the danger which another naval war with England represented. Did revolution make war more likely? From the outset this question was being asked, and, despite the insistence of the revolutionaries that they would never initiate war against other peoples, there was reason for circumspection. In July 1790, in response to demands for an enhanced armaments programme, they expressed alarm lest the move be misinterpreted and actually cause a new war. They saw such a programme as menacing, as a hostile or belligerent act. They were, they said, as patriotic as any other group, but they admitted to having concerns about the increased tension between states. 'We fear,' they said, 'that a first hostile act,

---

[21] Address from citizens of Le Havre, 8 December 1791, *Archives Parlementaires de 1787 à 1860: recueil complet des débats législatifs et politiques des chambres françaises*, vol. 35, 660.

[22] AD Gironde, Fonds Bigot, 8J 703, 'Adresse des négociants de Bordeaux à l'Assemblée Nationale relative à la proposition d'abolir la traite des Nègres' (n.d.).

even if it were to be disavowed by the Nation and its representatives, might compromise our possessions, our peace of mind, and our fortunes.'[23] Memories of losses incurred in the Seven Years' War and the War of American Independence were too raw, and for many too painful, to forget, and it was not in the interests of the merchant community to put their hard-fought prosperity at jeopardy.

In short, the merchant communities were apprehensive from the outset, fearing that in implementing its ideals, the Revolution might unleash forces that it could not control and upset the racial balance on which the colonial economy depended. They listened to the arguments on both sides, to the *Amis des Noirs* as well as the Club Massiac; and they received address after address from the owners of *habitations* in Saint-Domingue soliciting their support and asking them to intervene with the government in Paris. But too often the intervention they sought meant sending troops to the Caribbean and the use of military force to defend the plantations, especially after violence broke out and the *colons* and their families faced physical dangers. The chambers of commerce were faced with a dilemma. Did they urge military intervention to reinstate a social and ethnic order on which their trade seemed to depend? Did they make sacrifices in support of planters who had expressed the desire to distance themselves from the mother country and end all trading monopolies with France? Or did they take a very different risk, that by alienating the colonists they would further drive a wedge between them and Paris?

It was clear to many in the French port cities that their interests and those of the colonists did not always coincide, and that, despite their French origins and the strong links that many of them maintained with France, the Creoles had become a people apart, driven by quite different priorities from their continental cousins.[24] Their loyalty to France and its government could not be taken for granted. In an address of August 1791, a group calling themselves the 'merchants and ships' captains of Le Havre' informed the government of the new depths of anger that they had witnessed in Le Cap. Some colonists were even talking of welcoming the British into Saint-Domingue as they held Paris responsible for the social and political degradation they had suffered. They insisted that the revolutionary ideals espoused by the National Assembly constituted 'a perfidious and bloodthirsty doctrine' that would snuff out the last embers of colonial prosperity and would result in economic ruin.[25] Such was their outrage that the two communities, French and Creole, could no longer be seen as sharing common interests, and

---

[23] AD Gironde, 8J 703, Fonds Bigot, Chambre de Commerce de Guienne, address by merchants of Bordeaux to National Assembly, 13 July 1790.

[24] Pierre de Vaissière, *Saint-Domingue: La société et la vie créoles sous l'ancien régime, 1629–1789* (Paris: Perrin, 1909), *passim*.

[25] AD Loire-Atlantique, 1 ET A 28, 'Adresse à l'Assemblée Nationale, jointe à une lettre du Havre du 30 août 1791.

that calls for independence from France were becoming more insistent. A political crisis, warned the merchants, was looming.

The primary source of conflict between the revolutionaries and the white population of the Antilles in the summer of 1791 was no longer the vague threat of what the National Assembly might do at some unspecified date in the future. It was a specific measure, the decree of 15 May granting full civil rights to free men of colour, including the right to stand for election to the colonial assemblies, a measure which, as we have seen, resulted in a much sharper division between free and enslaved, between whites and mulattoes on the one hand and black Africans on the other. It resulted in something of a social revolution in the Antilles, with mulattoes rushing to take advantage of their new freedoms, buying property, investing in plantations, and becoming slave-owners in their turn. For the white *colons*, this had another effect: in a society where rights largely coincided with ethnicity, the reform resulted in a perceived loss of status, depriving them of a privilege that had been theirs alone. Most hated the change, and warned of the danger that it would incite further demands and violence, even that it would prove to be a staging-post towards the liberation of the Caribbean's black slaves. In response, petitions from Nantes, Dunkirk, Saint-Malo, and Bordeaux warned of the disaster that threatened, bringing the end of the colonial system as well as of the slave economy. But merchant opinion in the port cities was not unanimous on this point; indeed, for some, granting civil rights to free men of colour was a question of simple justice and a safety-valve against future violence. In Bordeaux, merchants spoke out for as well as against the decree, earning the congratulations of the *Amis des Noirs* for their selflessness. On 10 July the *Amis* congratulated the city for its magnanimity, and for putting the rights of man above base self-interest. The mayor had written to other cities and to the committees that had been formed in the colonies in support of the decree, in defiance of what the *Amis* called 'the notorious calculations of the traders in human flesh and the *colons*'. Nothing, they insisted, could be 'more touching' or 'better reasoned' than the case that had been set out.[26] But it won few friends in the colonies.

What angered many of the planters most was the attack on their authority which the decree of 15 May implied. They had not been consulted on the wording of the decree, and they felt bitter that their knowledge of the situation on the ground, on the plantations and in the sugar fields, should have counted for nothing. The letters sent by the Marquise de Rouvray to her daughter express something of the bitterness felt by leading members of the planter community at the indifference shown towards them by the radicals in the Assembly. Like her husband a royalist with counter-revolutionary instincts, she resented being left out of the discussion almost as much as she feared the implications of the measure

---

[26] Saugera, *Bordeaux port négrier*, 113.

itself. 'It is not the decree itself that is most shocking', she insisted, so much as 'the violation of our right to pronounce on that class of men who will now engage the Assembly in terrible consequences'. Unfortunately, she observed, there were currently very few proprietors on their estates; most were in France, leaving agents and factors in charge. And they were the people whose interest and experience made them the best judges.[27] Their silence merely left the way open for the demagogues of the *Amis des Noirs* who had, she believed, the deliberate aim of causing trouble, 'because it is in periods of popular violence that these people commit their crimes'.[28]

There was, however, from the planters' perspective, one saving grace. The National Assembly had already decided, as an article of the constitution, 'that no law would be passed on matters concerning the inhabitants of the colonies except when they had asked for it in due form and in precisely-worded terms'. And therein lay their salvation. On this the mercantile communities of the Atlantic ports were largely agreed. The merchants of Nantes, for instance, warned that the decree of 15 May, though 'sublime in the eyes of philosophy, and dictated by the love of humanity', would have had fateful consequences 'but for the fact that it would be impossible to carry it into law in the colonies'.[29] This clearly was the cause of great relief, since it indicated that the powers of the government in colonial matters were not unlimited. In Bordeaux the merchants noted approvingly that the Assembly's decree had specifically recognized that no law could be passed in Paris on the legal status of slaves except where it was requested to do so by the colonial assemblies themselves.[30] For many in the French merchant community, this was a crucial safety-valve, since the *colons'* conservatism on questions of slavery could surely be assumed. They found it quite natural that the colonists should demand protection from some of the government's more radical measures, and they accepted that the law of France could not adequately provide for their needs. When a conflict of interests arose, as in this case, the merchants of the Atlantic ports seemed to assume that it was their duty to speak up on the colonists' behalf, often adopting a paternalistic tone that reflected their one-sided vision of metropolitan-colonial relations, and implying that, as a result of their regular commercial exchanges with the islands, they were uniquely placed to represent them in the affairs of the nation.[31]

It was a bold claim, and one that came under concentrated attack from supporters of abolition. They, too, recognized the importance of the Assembly's

[27] McIntosh and Weber, *Une correspondance familiale au temps des troubles de Saint-Domingue*, 16.
[28] Ibid., 20.
[29] AD Loire-Atlantique, 1 ET A 28, 'Pétition à l'Assemblée Nationale par les citoyens commerçants de Nantes', 20 May 1791.
[30] AD Loire-Atlantique, 1 ET A 28, 'Adresse du Département de la Gironde à l'Assemblée Coloniale', 24 May 1791.
[31] AD Loire-Atlantique, 1 ET A 28, 'Pétition du commerce de Nantes à l'Assemblée Nationale', 26 February 1791.

concession and feared that it would dilute the reforming purpose of the legislation by maintaining the ethnic and juridical superiority of the white planters. In a strongly worded pamphlet, Brissot turned his fire on Antoine Barnave, one of the early revolutionary leaders and an outspoken opponent of extending citizenship to non-whites. In granting decision-making powers to the colonial assemblies, argued Brissot, he had violated the principles of the Declaration of the Rights of Man, to which he had been so deeply committed back in 1789. For what it meant was that the Assembly would never try to impose a measure that had not the approval of the white population. 'Colonies' here meant 'whites'. 'And what do the whites want?' he demanded rhetorically, before going on to tease out his own meaning: 'That the men of colour should not be active citizens; as a consequence, you are stripping the men of colour of their rights, whether you do so formally or by the uncertainty into which you cast them.' Either way, it meant an inversion of the liberal progress which the early Revolution had so consistently championed.[32] And it left those of mixed blood defenceless against the despotism of the white colonists. What future was there for them other than through violence? For 'they are victims handed over to their oppressors, unless, taking advantage of their right to resist oppression, they take up arms against the whites and force them to give them justice'.[33] The *abbé* Grégoire pressed home the point. 'Would you dare to imply that only whites are born and live free and equal in rights?' he challenged Barnave. 'Would you seek to relativize this morality, which applies equally to all regions of the world and to all historical periods?'[34]

What followed would be a crisis every bit as serious as the *colons* had predicted, with a succession of riots and insurrections, arson attacks on plantations, and murders of plantation managers.[35] Saint-Domingue in the summer months of 1791 staged the first successful slave rising in the French Caribbean, though there had been earlier attempts at insurrection in Martinique, Guadeloupe, St Lucia, and French Guyana as well as in various parts of Saint-Domingue itself.[36] Trade plummeted, and commercial anxiety was soon reflected in a new burst of addresses and pamphlets from the merchant cities of the Atlantic and Channel coasts. Some tried to be emollient, appealing to the moderation and reasonableness of the deputies and praising the new constitution that had been drawn up for the islands. It was, declared the Chamber of commerce in Dunkirk, right that civil liberties should be granted to *gens de couleur*, though the hostility with which the decree had been received in the islands, and the extreme violence that had greeted

[32] *Lettre de J.-P. Brissot à M. Barnave, sur ses rapports concernant les colonies, les décrets qui les ont suivis, leurs conséquences fatales* (Paris, 1790), 4–5.

[33] Ibid., 6.

[34] Abbé Grégoire, *Lettre aux Philanthropes, sur les malheurs, les droits et les réclamations des gens de couleur de Saint-Domingue et des autres îles françaises de l'Amérique* (Paris, 1790), 7.

[35] For details of the violence that broke out in France's colonies, see Chapter 9.

[36] Yves Bénot, 'The chain of slave insurrections in the Caribbean, 1789–91', in Dorigny (ed), *The Abolitions of Slavery*, 147–8.

it, gave them cause for thought. 'All the news that we are getting from Saint-Domingue confirm that the colony is in a state of great ferment,' it declared: 'minds are embittered, troubles at their peak, trade with France exposed to the most extreme reverses, and public finances threatened at their very source.' These were, added the merchants emphatically, 'the sad consequences that result from those prejudices which reason and sane philosophy no doubt reprove, but which have established a line of demarcation that cannot be suddenly rescinded without risking the gravest dangers'.[37] Their colleagues in Saint-Malo were less diplomatic. The only possible beneficiaries of the decree, they insisted, would be Great Britain and her empire, with France necessarily the loser.[38] It was a note of despair which would be repeated at every juncture in the crisis, the allegation that Britain not only was benefiting from French misfortunes but also was manipulating the situation for her own ends. In his *Traité d'économie politique et de commerce des colonies*, published in 1801, Pierre-François Page noted that Britain made no attempt to hide her imperialist aspirations or her hunger to seize France's colonies. With Britain, he claims, it is 'what she calls her prosperity'—he defines this as 'the capacity to appropriate all the riches of the world'—that allows her to 'demoralize men, corrupt governments and overthrow nations'.[39]

Suspicions of British motives extended to every aspect of colonial policy, with some concluding that the British had deliberately sought to undermine order In France's colonies by encouraging slave unrest. By the autumn of 1791, reports of violence on the plantations were legion, some involving arson, the wanton destruction of property and the killing of plantation owners and their families. In most instances, news of slave insurrections came to the west-coast ports not by way of the Assembly but directly, from ships' captains and their crews on their return from the islands, some of whom brought alarming tales of massacres and orgies of violence. In Nantes in 1791, for instance, some of the first reports of the slave insurrection came from the captain of a slave ship, the *Trois Frères*, which had left Saint-Louis on 29 September and arrived into Nantes on 12 November; his account was lurid and horrifying, but he was not an eye-witness and was merely passing on—possibly in an exaggerated form—rumours that he had picked up while in the Antilles. On another occasion, the captain of *Le Courier du Cap* changed course and diverted to Nantes so that he could inform his fellow-townsmen of the terrible things he had heard. On both occasions the reports spread panic, though the accounts were, of course, unverified.[40] Merchants were

---

[37] AD Loire-Atlantique, 1 ET A 28, 'Adresse du commerce de Dunkerque à l'Assemblée Nationale', 12 September 1791.

[38] AD Loire-Atlantique, 1 ET A 28, 'Pétition des citoyens commerçants de Saint-Malo, à l'Assemblée Nationale, attachée à une lettre du 20 septembre 1791, en réponse au décret du 15 mai'.

[39] Pierre-François Page, *Traité d'économie politique et de commerce des colonies* (Paris, an IX), ix.

[40] AD Loire-Atlantique, 1 ET A 28, 'Lettre du commerce de Nantes aux commissaires envoyés à Paris', 15 November 1791.

prudent by nature, seeking verification where they could, and they expressed relief when the initial reports were denied. But the slave revolts were more than local incidents; taken together they posed a threat to the entire colonial system, and the chambers of commerce shared in the general sense of crisis.

As the weeks passed and the scale of the disaster became clear, reports of murder, kidnapping, and plantation-burning alarmed the entire merchant community, especially those whose relatives had settled in Saint-Domingue or whose companies had employees and agents in the islands. The communities on the two sides of the Atlantic were too entangled, and family interests were too entrenched, for the slave insurrection to pass unheeded. As the violence escalated, moreover, the *colons* appealed directly to the outside world for assistance, to their nearest neighbours in Cuba, Jamaica, and the eastern seaboard of the United States, but also to their relatives and their commercial contacts in France. They felt outraged at being abandoned to their fate, insisting that the insurrection must be quelled and asking for food, weapons, and troops to be sent from the metropole. Some appealed directly to the merchants of the Atlantic ports. One *colon*, Delaville, explained that the island economy now lay in ruins, so that 'all we now think of is defending ourselves; the choice is between victory and death'. Another, Guillaud, addressed his woes directly to the people of Nantes, those he claimed as his fellow-citizens. 'Will you, brave and generous Nantais, whose courage is the equal of your worth, leave your brothers to be massacred, to have their throats slit, your brothers who have suffered for so long?' Rather plaintively, he reminded them of the *colons'* deep-seated loyalty to France. 'They are entirely devoted to you and are fighting as much for you as they are for themselves.'[41]

In response, the slave ports sent a further deputation to Paris to lobby the Assembly. There they also met deputies sent from Saint-Domingue, who, understandably, presented a highly alarmist picture of the misery that had befallen their colony and its inhabitants, the picture of 'horrors of a kind of which history knows no example'. On the plain of Le Cap, they reported that all buildings 'without exception' had been razed to the ground; that no trace remained of the 224 sugar factories that had stood there, and that some 1,600–1,800 coffee plantations had been ravaged. If the violence had temporarily calmed, no one dared to hope that it was over, and few believed that the ambitions of the men of colour were now sated. Here the *colons* gave vent to the full range of their racial prejudices and nightmares, claiming that their woes all stemmed from the moment when rights and racial distinctions on the island became blurred. 'The conduct of many of them has always been suspect', they declared; 'their plan was to have all the whites murdered in a single night so that they could become the masters of the colony'; and they were convinced that the mulattoes had only offered protection to their

---

[41] Armel de Wismes, *Nantes et le temps des négriers* (Paris: Éditions France-Empire, 1992), 165.

masters because they assumed the revolt was over and hoped to save their own skins. The white population still feared the mulattoes, believing that many were traitors to France who were waiting for their moment to rise again, spreading sedition in a bid to subvert the rest of the population. By diffusing such alarmist images, the deputies hoped both to raise money for the colonists and to persuade the assembly to take the exceptional steps that they believed were necessary to defend the colonial interest.[42]

These exceptional measures almost always involved the use of military force, calls for which became more frequent and sustained after the slave revolts in 1791 and 1792. With opinion in the Atlantic ports radicalized by news of these insurrections, some of their deputies, like Jean-Baptiste Mosneron from Nantes, pressed for French troops to be sent to the islands to defend the planters, but the motion was lost as a majority in the National Assembly now favoured the cause of abolition.[43] Besides, which army should they send, and for what purpose? In the Assembly, as in municipal councils, clubs, and popular societies across the West, there was increasing distrust of the aristocratic army officers inherited from the Ancien Régime, many of whom had aligned with the monarchy and who might, it was widely assumed, sympathize with the slave-owners. Their preference was to send out units of the National Guard, which would be more alert to questions of liberty and human rights and less liable than regular units to be contaminated by what Bordeaux's Club National referred to as 'aristocratic gangrene'.[44] This was not a view restricted to the republican left, and the more moderate club in the city, the Amis de la Constitution, agreed. Bordeaux was the first port to offer to send troops to Saint-Domingue, opening a register where those willing to 'go to America to support the decree of 15 May on the men of colour' could volunteer for the voyage.[45] Soon other ports followed, citing Bordeaux's initiative as a sign of patriotism and self-sacrifice. For sending troops to Saint-Domingue was no longer seen as a way of helping the colons; rather they were lending support to the French authorities on the island in a measure that enjoyed the full support of the mulattoes, anxious to secure the benefits of the legislation passed in their favour. On 19 June, indeed, it was the spokesman of the mulatto population, Julien Raimond, who demanded that France despatch 6,000 volunteers to Saint-Domingue to reinforce their position.[46] His plea did not go unheeded. It was one of Bordeaux's deputies, Guadet, who in October urged the Assembly to send troops to the island, adding that the people of Bordeaux would gladly contribute a

---

[42] AD Loire-Atlantique, 1 ET A 28, letter from deputies from the delegation sent to Paris to the Chamber of commerce of Nantes, 23 November 1791.

[43] Steve Chaigneau, 'Un exemple de mobilité sociale dans le monde de l'armement nantais du dix-huitième siècle' (D.E.S., Université de Nantes, 1967), 116.

[44] AD Gironde, 8J 703, response of the Club National of Bordeaux to the decree on slavery, 21 May 1791.

[45] Maquerlot, 'Les résistances au Havre', 47.   [46] Ibid., 47.

battalion of National Guards to aid the cause, even though it meant sending them 1,800 miles from home.[47] Opinion in the slaving ports had shifted significantly. It was no longer united in opposing reform, but had evolved since 1789 in line with the Revolution's policy towards the colonies. By this time it enjoyed the full support of the politicians—most frequently linked to the Girondins—who led the municipal councils, clubs, and sections of the West.

In April 1792, the new Legislative Assembly took incisive action, sending 6,000 troops to Saint-Domingue to support the work of the civil commissioners it had sent to the island, Étienne Polverel and Léger-Félicité Sonthonax. Both were committed revolutionaries who had denounced the institution of slavery; and though their official instructions were to restore peace and put down the slave insurrection, they had little sympathy with the *colons* and adopted a different agenda, advancing the cause of the mulattoes, offering concessions to the black slaves, and antagonizing many of the white settlers, not least among the *petits blancs*. In Saint-Domingue they found themselves facing two very different challenges: a domestic challenge from the new French governor, General François [can you avoid dividing and hyphenating 'François'?]-Thomas Galbaud, himself a slave-owner, who was supported by the crews of naval ships in the harbour at Le Cap; and a foreign challenge when France declared war on Spain and the Spanish appealed for the support of the black insurgents in Saint-Domingue. Faced with this double danger, the commissioners responded by outbidding the Spaniards, calling on the thousands of adult males among the slave population of Le Cap to take up arms, in return for which they would be granted their freedom. Though this fell well short of full emancipation, it was a turning-point in French colonial policy. But it proved insufficient to win the loyalty of the wider black population. On 29 August 1793, the commissioners finally took the momentous step of ending slavery on Saint-Domingue, effectively ruling that the Declaration of the Rights of Man now applied to the colonies.[48] To enslaved populations across the Americas this sent an empowering message, and an exhilarating one. Not only had a European power abandoned the institution of slavery, but slaves, Africans like themselves, had the capability to liberate themselves from bondage.

For many of the white *colons*, however, already shocked and demoralized, this was the final betrayal. They had seen plantations burned, families killed, and livelihoods destroyed by the slave insurrections in Saint-Domingue. They felt that they had no choice but to leave, a few returning to France, but many seeking refuge in other slave societies across the Americas, some fleeing to neighbouring Caribbean islands, others to the United States. The exodus which had begun as a

---

[47] Guadet, speech to the Legislative Assembly, 30 October 1791, *Archives Parlementaires*, 34, 528.

[48] Jeremy D. Popkin, *A Concise History of the Haitian Revolution* (Oxford: Wiley-Blackwell, 2012), 48–59.

trickle of desperate planters and merchants in the early months of the Revolution rapidly turned into a flood.

Some returned to France, but reluctantly and apprehensively, to a France convulsed by revolutionary forces they distrusted and did not properly understand. The first returnees came in the autumn of 1791 as they fled from their plantations and burned-out homes, the women and children often crowding on to the first ships to sail from the islands to Nantes or Bordeaux. All the ports that had engaged in colonial trade received their quota of refugees: Bordeaux, Marseille, La Rochelle, Le Havre, and especially Nantes, the city that had seen so many emigrants leave France to make their fortune. Most came on French merchant ships on their return voyage from the Caribbean, others, especially those who had initially fled to the United States, on American or British ships, in some cases after long and tortuous voyages through foreign ports. Or else they were caught up in the war, some spending long months in captivity. Bailly, for instance, who came originally from the Loir-et-Cher, fled the flames of Le Cap to Philadelphia, where many of his fellow *colons* took ship for France. But he preferred to return to Saint-Domingue, and in Port-au-Prince he was imprisoned by the British.[49] It was only after his escape that he finally found a ship to take him to Nantes. The vacillating fortunes of the war in the Caribbean only made his fate more uncertain and his escape more confused and entangled.

Those who returned to France were often penniless, having lost everything that they possessed in the rioting; they had no credit with merchants and bankers in France, and they were being repatriated to stave off disaster. Not all were refugees. Some were planters who had set up home in France before the Revolution and were now returning from their colonial possessions; others returned to join parents, children, or extended families. But many had nowhere to go, an indiscriminate mixture of victims of the insurrection, planters and *petits blancs*, clerks and soldiers, artisans and shopkeepers, mulattoes and whites, many lost and bewildered, seeking shelter with strangers and working out how to make a living now that they had no land and no slaves. Those with families in France might pass quickly through the port cities on their journey home. Those without often stayed, in or near the Atlantic ports, making little attempt to integrate into the local community, their eyes still firmly turned towards the ocean and the world they had lost. During the revolutionary years these 'Americans' would become a familiar sight on the streets and around the docks of all France's Atlantic ports. In Nantes alone, the *bureau de secours* set up to distribute aid to the destitute processed applications for some 1,500 refugees during the revolutionary decade.[50]

---

[49] Marcel Grandière, 'Les réfugiés et les déportés des Antilles à Nantes sous la Révolution', *Bulletin de la Société d'Histoire de la Guadeloupe*, 33–4 (1977), 13.
[50] Grandière, 'Les réfugiés et les déportés des Antilles à Nantes', 4–7.

This did not guarantee them a warm reception from the population of the host cities.

The number of letters and petitions from Le Cap and Port-au-Prince diminished as their white residents left and official communication with the islands declined. Besides, there was soon no agency in the French ports through which planters could communicate with the merchant community. After 1790, when the French chambers of commerce were abolished, such news as was received often came through individual trading houses and families. And their tone varied enormously. Some of the letters were cries for help from planters as they saw their lands and their livelihoods destroyed. Others tried to reassure relatives in France or to emphasize such positives as remained. The correspondence of Pierre Letestu with his son-in-law, Elie Lefebvre, provides a good example of a calm, gently optimistic commentary on the events around them. Letestu had worked in many different aspects of the Atlantic trade: he is variously described as an *armateur, capitaine de navire,* and *planteur,* as well as a *négociant* in Honfleur. He now lived in France, corresponding actively with those of his friends who were still resident in the Caribbean. He clearly wanted to believe that plantation life could be resumed following the violence of the previous year. In September 1792, for instance, in response to news of the troubles on Saint-Domingue, he tried to be reassuring, suggesting that they were fortunate, and that the plantation they owned in the south of the island had been spared the worst of the ravages in the north. If supplies of coffee had been looted on the plantation, he remarked, the slaves had not revolted and they were now preparing to bring in the new harvest. 'You can still console yourself that amidst this general misery you are among the least badly treated.' His correspondent recognized that the troubles might not be over, and that there could be further disturbances as the full fallout from revolutionary ideas of liberty and equality was understood. But his tone remained positive, the words those of a man who was still thinking to a future in Saint-Domingue and expressing a deeply held patriotism, a determination that the war in Europe was there to be won, and that France must now concentrate on beating the Prussians.[51] The years that followed might be difficult, but they did not quench his optimism. By January 1796, indeed, it is clear that he felt sufficiently safe to go back himself to see the extent of the damage; it was, of course, a journey fraught with dangers after the massacres that had swept his and surrounding plantations.[52] But, again, it emphasized the degree of commitment that many Frenchmen still felt to the island and their belief that France could still play a significant role in the Caribbean.

---

[51] AD Calvados, F 5545, Fonds Letestu, letter from Pierre Letestu to Élie Lefebvre, 29 September 1792.
[52] AD Calvados, F 5545, Fonds Letestu, letter from Élie Lefebvre to Madame Letestu, 19 nivôse 4 (9 January 1796).

For many, their flight in the face of slave insurrections was intended as a temporary displacement, not a permanent dislocation. They were frightened and angered by the losses they had suffered and by the savagery of the attacks on their families and those of others. They declared themselves shocked by the extent of the racial hatred they had encountered, and by the legacy of bitterness it had left behind. Some, indeed, admitted to new levels of fear, fear of being attacked and targeted, their families massacred. And they talked of the spectre of uncontrolled slave violence which was such a persistent theme in race relations in the United States, and especially in the antebellum South.[53] But they were not deterred from life in the colonies, nor disabused of the need for a slave economy. Besides, those who had spent a lifetime in Guadeloupe or Saint-Domingue found it difficult to forget the world they had left behind, and—as paintings and sketches of the period show only too clearly—they were haunted by the rich colours and texture of island life.[54] The tropical landscape of the Caribbean islands, the luxuriant vegetation, and the gentle pace of life in the plantation houses, all left indelible memories and aroused feelings of affection and nostalgia. If they sought shelter along the eastern seaboard of the United States, or in Cuba or Jamaica, it was often with the intention of making a rapid return once the political climate improved. That optimism would only dissolve with time, and for many of those forced to flee their homes in Le Cap or Jérémie in the aftermath of the murders and arson attacks, there would be no return. They would make their lives in the Americas, in a world dominated by trade and shipping, coffee and sugar cane, a world that identified them as American and where ties with France became increasingly tenuous. For some, indeed, the leaving of Saint-Domingue was only the start of a series of migrations back and forth across the Atlantic world, whether as planters, merchants, shipping agents or crewmen, soldiers or adventurers. In the best of cases they transferred their enterprise and acumen elsewhere, building up huge fortunes and investing in the expansion of America. In the worst, they might find themselves reduced to penury, stripped of all resource and thrown on the mercy of church charities and French communities in the lands where they sought refuge. For them the Saint-Domingue revolution marked the beginning of new challenges, and of a new life of uncertainty.

[53] François Furstenberg, *In the Name of the Father: Washington's Legacy, Slavery and the Making of a Nation* (London: Penguin, 2006), 169–70.
[54] Musée d'Aquitaine, *Regards sur les Antilles: Collection Marcel Chatillon* (Bordeaux: Musée d'Aquitaine, 1999).

9

War and Revolution in the Caribbean

For thirteen years, from 1791 to 1804, France's Caribbean islands were in an almost constant state of turmoil and revolutionary insurrection, instigated in part by the political upheavals in France. But the revolution here took a very different course from that in Paris or the French provinces. Of course, people in the Caribbean followed events in France with interest and concern as ships from Nantes and Bordeaux arrived with letters, newspapers, and pamphlets carrying the latest information. People read them avidly, and they passed on what they read, whether through snatches of conversation among French sailors in quayside bars or by whispered messages passed between slaves as they worked the sugar cane.[1] But the root causes of revolt were much more deep-seated, owing far more to the harsh reality of life on the plantations and the everyday indignities of enslavement. As Haitian historians emphasized at a conference in 1989 to mark the bicentenary of the French Revolution, the contrasts between France and Haiti were too important to be overlooked.[2] Haitians were well aware that 'it was not Paris that rewarded us by abolishing slavery, it was the rising of Haitians against servitude that led to it being renounced over there by the Convention. Just as it was not the Consul – Napoleon – who dictated an original political solution to Toussaint; rather it was Toussaint, the black man, who forced Bonaparte to follow that line.'[3] In short, this was Haiti's moment, not that of the colonial motherland. Haitians, not Frenchmen, were the principal actors in the revolution that engulfed Saint-Domingue, though they learned from the French and their revolutionary ideas, just as they in turn by their actions affected the course of France's revolution at home.

Haiti, after all, lay far from Paris's hemisphere. And though many of its inhabitants were immigrants to the Caribbean—Frenchmen crossing the Atlantic in quest of riches or adventure, or Africans condemned to the hell of the Middle Passage and a life in slavery—their experiences were transformed by the conditions they found there. The Caribbean was a different world, more closely drawn

---

[1] For a discussion of the spread of revolutionary ideas across the Atlantic world, see Janet Polasky, *Revolutions without Borders: the Call to Liberty in the Atlantic World* (New Haven: Yale University Press, 2015).

[2] Colloque 'Haïti et la Révolution Française: filiations, ruptures, nouvelles dimensions', Port-au-Prince, 5–8 December 1989.

[3] Michel Hector, 'Colloque de Port-au-Prince, 5–8 décembre 1989', *Revue de la Société haïtienne d'histoire et de géographie*, 46/166 (1990), 16.

towards the eastern seaboard of the United States than it could ever be to Europe. Here there were other sorts of conflicts from those that coloured French, or, indeed, European life. Two predominated. One was the colonial rivalry between Britain, France, and Spain that was such a major part of life in the eighteenth-century Americas. The other was the perennial struggle within Saint-Domingue and each of the Caribbean colonies between three main social groups, 'the slaves seeking freedom, free coloureds fighting racial discrimination, and colonial elites seeking greater autonomy or independence'.[4] And since 1783 they had before them the example of the United States, whose revolution had brought a colonial people their independence. These were the issues, more than anything that happened in France, which defined the revolution in the French Caribbean.

In 1789, the white colonists had seemed in total control, the only group to enjoy privileges and political rights. But they were not united among themselves, with something of a class division forming between the great landowners on the one hand and the small-scale plantation farmers on the other. Each group pursued its own narrow self-interest. The *grands blancs* wanted greater political autonomy, but also looked to maintain their position as a social elite, whereas the *petits blancs* were more concerned to strengthen the privileges that fell to them through the colour of their skin. Some argued for greater independence from France while hoping for a social revolution within the white population of the island. They opposed any concessions to the free people of colour, favouring the creation of what Robert Stein has characterized as a 'popular, racist state'. He cites one *petit blanc* as saying that Saint-Domingue had three enemies: 'the philanthropists who supported the free men of colour and the slaves, the ministers who ruled the colony from Paris, and the aristocrats who dominated colonial society'.[5] With so much accumulated bitterness, it is little wonder that the *petits blancs* were among the most committed opponents of the revolutionary ideas that emanated from France. Here the issue of race could not be ignored, as it so often was in the National Assembly.

Identity in the Caribbean was largely defined by race. The French Revolution here was largely about race, the rejection by its non-white inhabitants of the limits on their freedom resulting from discrimination, combined with the demand that the freedoms guaranteed by the French Declaration of the Rights of Man should apply to them, too. Discrimination was not new in France's colonies, of course, but was now more politicized and aroused greater resentment. Curiously, perhaps, it was not the slaves who were the principal victims of colonial policy in the last years of the Ancien Régime. Indeed, their condition may even have seen some

[4] David Geggus, 'Slavery, War and Revolution in the Greater Caribbean, 1789–1815', in David Barry Gaspar and David Patrick Geggus (eds), *A Turbulent Time: The French Revolution and the Greater Caribbean* (Bloomington: Indiana University Press, 1997), 5.

[5] Robert Louis Stein, *Léger Félicité Sonthonax: The Lost Sentinel of the Republic* (London and Toronto: Associated University Presses, 1985), 33.

improvement as a result of reforms to the Code noir in the 1780s, which forbade slave masters from killing or mutilating their slaves and from striking them with a rod.[6] Rather, it was free blacks and men of mixed race who complained that they were the targets of a new, repressive policy which denied their rights in law and defended the privileged position of the whites. Having established their free status and enjoyed the liberties that this gave, they found themselves increasingly the victims of prejudice, both legal and social, with qualities that gave them a disturbingly feminized identity. White writers attributed vices to those of African descent—they were supposedly effeminate, narcissistic, and emotional—which cut them off from white society, excluded them from elite positions, and restricted their opportunities of advancement.[7]

Those born to mixed-race families posed a particular problem for the authorities because of their role in colonial society. In Guadeloupe a census taken in 1789 listed 3,044 free people of colour along with 13,466 whites and more than 85,000 slaves: here their role was relatively modest.[8] But in Saint-Domingue they were almost as numerous as the white population, with around 28,000 people listed as *gens de couleur libres* compared to 30,000 white colonists. Earlier in the century they had enjoyed legal equality with whites under the terms of France's Code noir, but this equality had been progressively chipped away since the mid-1760s, with laws restricting the numbers of manumissions and forbidding entry into certain professions.[9] To add to the sense of confusion, as Frédéric Régent has shown, not all mulattoes were free, and not all slaves were black. While all those arriving from Africa were, of course, enslaved, they were not the majority of the slave population. By the eve of the Revolution, three out of four slaves had been born in the Caribbean and one in eight was of mixed race. The rules of categorization were complex, and a man's status was ultimately defined by colour, by his birthplace (whether he was a creole born in Guadeloupe or a black man from West Africa), and by the degree of *métissage* in the case of those born to white masters. As a result, the term *gens de couleur* had no single meaning that was accepted by all. Some, indeed, used it indiscriminately to describe all those who did not belong to the white race.[10]

Legal restrictions were imposed for one reason only: to ensure the maintenance of a white dominance that was based on skin colour. As a result, in 1789 the issue

---

[6] Carolyn E. Fick, 'The French Revolution in Saint-Domingue: a Triumph or a Failure?', in Gaspar and Geggus (eds), *A Turbulent Time*, 61.

[7] John D. Garrigus, '"Sons of the Same Father": Gender, Race and Citizenship in French Saint-Domingue, 1760–92', in Christine Adams, Jack R. Censer and Lisa Jane Graham (eds), *Visions and Revisions of Eighteenth-century France* (University Park, PA: Penn State University Press, 1997), 137–8.

[8] Françoise Koest, *La Révolution à la Guadeloupe, 1789–96: dossier des Archives Départementales* (Basse-Terre, 1982), 1ère partie, 'La Guadeloupe en 1789', document 8.

[9] Jeremy Popkin, *A Concise History of the Haitian Revolution*, 24.

[10] Frédéric Régent, *Esclavage, métissage, liberté: la Révolution Française en Guadeloupe, 1789–1802* (Paris: Grasset, 2004), 15.

of race was openly discussed; it could no longer be concealed or hidden from public gaze. Race had been turned into a key political issue in the colonies, and free people of colour were no longer prepared to suffer in silence. They were determined to be engaged in the political process, or, in John Garrigus' words, 'to enter the colonial public'.[11] For the more aspirational of them that meant achieving complete equality with whites, equality in law, in access to the professions, in property-ownership, and in political representation. It did not necessarily turn them into radicals, however, since in other respects they might have quite conservative aspirations. An early pamphlet, the first to be written by a man of colour, spoke of a society where whites and mulattoes would be grouped together as a single class of free men, where mulatto slaves were to be freed at birth, but where those born black were destined for slavery. It was a specious argument, based on the claim that those of mixed race belonged to America, a continent where slavery was unknown, whereas 'the colour of the blacks indicates their origin in Africa' and condemns them to be slaves.[12] In short, they were less concerned to abolish privilege than to acquire it, to join the white colonists as Saint-Domingue's ruling class.[13] They had no interest in other forms of equality and strongly opposed extending civic rights to slaves.

Race was a three-sided issue in the French Caribbean, where whites, blacks, and mulattoes had different identities, and different demands. The slaves were not widely thought of as having the potential to be citizens; indeed, the language used to describe them was demeaning and disparaging, comparing them to animals rather than human beings. In contrast, those of mixed race were vociferous in demanding rights for themselves, and they had representatives in Paris who pressed their interests in the National Assembly. They were often wealthy men whose lifestyle differed little from that of the whites, and a substantial number of them owned slaves in their own right. In the new political context of 1789, they tended to take a maximalist view of what was due to them. Hence, when the Assembly passed its decrees on colonial governance in 1790 they interpreted these, far more widely than the texts actually suggested, as a mandate for greater freedom. And when the white colonists, quite predictably, chose to ignore the new law and continued to exclude the mulattoes from any form of political participation, conflict became inevitable between the men of colour and the colonial authorities, a conflict that was pursued in the name of the Revolution's own core values. As the wife of one of the colony's deputies in Paris wrote, all the

---

[11] John D. Garrigus, *Before Haiti: Race and Citizenship in French Saint-Domingue* (Basingstoke: Palgrave Macmillan, 2006), 234.

[12] *Précis des gémissements des sang-mêlés dans les colonies françaises, par J.M.C. Américain, Sang-mêlé* (Paris, 1789), 7.

[13] David Geggus, *Haitian Revolutionary Studies* (Bloomington: Indiana University Press, 2002), 162.

mulattoes 'are determined to give their last drop of blood to uphold the decrees and defend their rights'.[14]

The aspirations of the mulatto leaders had implications that extended far beyond their own community. How, in particular, would the black population react? Many felt that the very sight of free men of colour winning full civil rights would constitute a provocation and encourage the huge slave population of the island to rise in order to seize rights for themselves, which in turn undermined what the planters saw as their property rights. Relations between whites and mulattoes deteriorated during the first months of the Revolution, with a series of violent attacks on plantations owned by mulattoes and with free men of colour volunteering to join citizen militias to protect their lives and properties from white lynch mobs. Then, in October 1790, the French National Assembly supported the claims of the free coloured population, spreading further alarm among the white colonists. So when Vincent Ogé, one of the coloured representatives in Paris, landed back in Saint-Domingue after stopping off in London to receive the blessing and funding of Thomas Clarkson and in Charleston to buy arms for a future conflict, the colonists were in no mood for concessions.[15] Ogé demanded that news of the Assembly's decrees be disseminated and that the people of colour be informed of their newly gained rights. And he held out the threat that, if his demands went unheeded, the coloured population would ally with black leaders to overthrow the white elites and destroy their privileges.

An armed clash was not long delayed. But Ogé was a better political agitator than a soldier: he managed to raise only a small force of a few hundred militiamen, which the whites had little difficulty in defeating. Many of the rebels were taken prisoner, and Ogé and his principal collaborator, a mulatto coffee-planter called Jean-Baptiste Chavannes, were extradited, on the instructions of the governor-general, Philippe-François Rouxel de Blanchelande, from the Spanish part of the island to face trial in Le Cap. The retribution that followed was ferocious and exemplary. Ogé and Chavannes were condemned to death and horribly tortured before being broken on the wheel in the public square at Le Cap, and nineteen of their followers were sentenced to hang.[16] As news of the executions spread across the colony, the mulattoes responded with anger, an anger that was combined with the realization that they now had nothing to gain from cooperating with the whites. Any thought of compromise seemed pointless, and they increasingly turned to violence in defence of their cause. In the South Province, an armed band of more than 600 men of colour beat off the white force that was sent

---

[14] Letter from Mme Larchevesque-Thibaud to her husband, 5 November 1790, in Jeremy Popkin, *Facing Racial Revolution: Eyewitness Accounts of the Haitian Insurrection* (Chicago, IL: University of Chicago Press, 2007), 45.

[15] Robert Debs Heinl and Nancy Gordon Heinl, *Written in Blood: The Story of the Haitian People, 1492–1995* (Lanham, MD: University Press of America, 2005), 37.

[16] Popkin, *Concise History*, 32.

against them. Racial violence had been unleashed as political positions hardened on all sides.

If the violence was temporarily contained by military action, its root causes had not been resolved and continued to divide the population. Julien Raimond, who represented the people of colour in Paris and put their views to the Assembly, warned in early 1792 of the new dangers the colony faced, not least the danger that extreme revolutionaries, driven by idealism, would spread dissension among the slaves. The men of colour were now free to enjoy their liberties, he argued, but what did that signify when their lives were endangered by slave violence? The problem, he believed, lay in the Assembly itself, in the enthusiasm of so many of its members, in allowing the heart to rule the head. Deputies, he claimed, were wilfully seeking to cause a slave revolt. 'We see it happening, but we are forced to keep our mouths shut...men are drunk with liberty!'[17] Raimond was convinced that there could be no comparison between the claims of the free coloureds and those of the black population. Their case, he insisted, was based not in abstract ideology but on the sterling contribution they make to the colony's welfare. 'The free men of colour are land owners in the colonies, they pay their taxes; these qualities give them the right to be heard at a moment when troubles are tearing apart the colony and threatening it with imminent ruin.' To deny them representation was to deny them natural justice. For, said Raimond, 'the citizens of colour form more than half the free population of the colony; they own half the land and a third of the men who cultivate it; and they do not share in the huge debts incurred by the white colonists'.[18] Their claim for full citizenship was based on merit. And if the National Assembly did not understand this, it was because 'it was too occupied with the interior of the kingdom to be able to think of us'.[19]

In the following year, in a submission to the Convention, Raimond went further, accusing the white colonists of having twisted the revolutionary message for their own ends. 'The white colonists have stolen for themselves the benefits of the Revolution, when at most they formed one-twelfth of the population of the colonies: so it was evident that the revolution would be frustrated by the eleven-twelfths to whom it brought no benefit.' Here he was thinking, as others were beginning to think, beyond the mulatto community. He was talking of the black majority, who formed nine-tenths of the population, and urged that they, too, must benefit from the revolution. 'We should let them participate in this revolution,' he wrote, 'by bringing about a considerable improvement to their lot.' By doing so, he argued, the slaves could be won over to the revolutionary side, and they would not be susceptible to the lure of counter-revolution.[20] It was

---

[17] Julien Raimond, *Véritable origine des troubles de Saint-Domingue* (Paris, 1792), 3.
[18] Ibid., 4.   [19] Ibid., 7.
[20] Julien Raimond, *Réflexions sur les véritables causes des troubles et des désastres de nos colonies, notamment sur ceux de Saint-Domingue* (Paris, 1793), 5–6.

a significant change of direction which presaged future alliances in the struggle for Haiti.

The Assembly's decree granting rights to people of colour did nothing to reduce racial tensions on the island; rather it embittered relations between the whites and the revolutionary leaders in Paris and hastened the resort to armed force. In 1791, the French government sent its first troops to quell revolts on Saint-Domingue, but the numbers they despatched were never sufficient to maintain order on the island. Later in the year, they sent the second battalions of fourteen line infantry regiments and seven battalions of National Guards, together with a small number of dragoons, though these were soon withdrawn to France. In 1792 a further 6,000 men followed, but again these soon proved inadequate to the task of separating the different ethnic groups, with the consequence that successive governors turned to troops drawn from the non-white communities on the island, from the mulattoes in the first instance, then from freed slaves, incorporated into units known as *Légions de l'Égalité*. With war declared in Europe, troops could no longer be spared in France, and necessity dictated that they mobilize a mass army on the island. By the time Spanish and British forces invaded in 1793, the French army in Saint-Domingue consisted primarily of native soldiers, an army of 50,000 men led by a small number of officers drawn from Europe.[21] It was a situation that was unique in the French Republic.

The colonists had enjoyed an uncertain relationship with the Revolution during its early stages. They looked to win greater commercial autonomy from France and urged Paris to pursue a policy of economic liberalism that would free them to trade with their American neighbours. At the same time, they remained over-whelmingly opposed to any idea of human rights that would give equality to other racial groups, and particularly to slaves. It was in this spirit that the Colonial Assembly on the island, dominated by white planters, forbade the publication in Saint-Domingue of the Declaration of the Rights of Man in 1789, in defiance of the law and of the government in Paris. It is difficult to blame them for being afraid, as they knew they would be hopelessly outnumbered in any conflict. There were nearly half a million black slaves on the island compared to only 30,000 white planters; plantation discipline was notoriously harsh; and during the century of Saint-Domingue's existence as a French colony there had been a long history of slave risings and attacks on plantations. Runaway slaves roamed the island or hid in the luxuriant undergrowth of upland areas. Some fled for a few days to escape punishment or register discontent at their working conditions, with the majority returning to life on their plantation. But there was also a long-established tradition in the Caribbean of *marronnage*—there is really no equivalent term in English— that was deeply engrained in Saint-Domingue and which alarmed the plantation

[21] Marcel Auguste, 'L'armée française de Saint-Domingue: dernière armée de la Révolution', *Jahrbuch für Geschichte von Staat, Wirtschaft une Gesellschaft Lateinamerikas*, 28 (1991), 87–92.

owners. Slaves would defy their masters by running away for good, with no intention of returning to slavery; they took refuge in the farthest corners of the island; and they lived an independent life in armed bands of self-liberated slaves which troubled the colonial administration and threatened violence against any slave-owner who tried to recapture them. Maroons were seen as desperadoes prepared to rob and kill to maintain their liberty, and maroon bands were associated in the *colons'* minds with voodoo ceremonies and blood sacrifices.[22] During the Revolution they assumed a political dimension, too, as *marronnage* became a form of protest among the Africans and an expression of their hatred for slavery and the plantation system.

In the febrile atmosphere of the 1790s, many *colons* feared the worst. Instances of nocturnal banditry were blown out of proportion, and implausible claims made about the number of maroons roaming the island. Indeed, there is evidence that the number of runaways may have been declining during the last decade of the Ancien Régime. But that did not prevent the spread of panic when news of slave attacks and plantation burnings reached the cities. The young patriot Albert Simon, now earning his living as a musician in Port-au-Prince, wrote in 1791 that the city had been reduced to a state of alarm. Rumours flew around uncontrollably, especially about events in France; violence lurked on all sides; and there were repeated reports of slave risings. In these circumstances, business could not flourish; for eight months, Simon claimed, he had been unable to make any money as the city emptied, and people fled to the mountains or bought a berth on a ship to France or to New England. Debts were left unpaid as creditors abandoned their homes in panic.[23]

Whereas in 1789 the white colonists' reactions to the Revolution were divided, in the years that followed the race issue served to unite them against any radical change. It also hardened attitudes among the non-white population, and not least those of mixed race. So, when the French government voted free men of colour the privileges of citizenship in 1791, the mulattoes responded with dismay, condemning the measure as falling woefully short of the ideals of liberty and equality that had been promised by the Revolutionary leaders. The decree applied not to all free people of colour, but only to those whose parents had also been free. It left many disappointed. Even those who were free experienced little material improvement as a result of the decree. Racial prejudice did not disappear overnight; nor did the workplace segregation of the pre-revolutionary years, when certain posts had been, de facto, reserved for whites. They still felt materially and socially disadvantaged. There were few men of mixed race among the great plantation owners or

---

[22] David Geggus, 'Marronage, Vodou and the Slave Revolt of 1791', in Geggus (ed.), *Haitian Revolutionary Studies*, 69–80.

[23] Jacques de Cauna and Richard Beckerich, 'La Révolution à Saint-Domingue vue par un Patriote', *Revue de la Société haïtienne d'histoire et de géographie*, 46/161 (1988), 31–2.

the wholesale merchants who worked for the export market. Colonial administrators were still white, often men who had come directly from France. Judges were white; indeed, the law was overwhelmingly a white preserve; and here the Revolution changed nothing. Those professions which were truly mixed, or where the men of colour dominated the labour market, remained largely the same, and it was principally in agriculture, in local commerce and textile manufacturing, in the building trades, and in shipping that they could seriously compete.[24] It was this lack of opportunity which the mulattoes sought to combat when, once they were granted civil rights, they bought *habitations* and challenged the white planters on their home ground, leaving them feeling increasingly threatened. A conflict of interest had been opened up which served to exacerbate racial tensions on the island throughout the 1790s.

The worst fears that had been voiced in Nantes and Bordeaux in the early months of the Revolution were soon realized on the plantations of Saint-Domingue as the colony was rapidly engulfed in riot and violence. That violence took several different forms as the different groups rebelled against the grant of civil rights to the free coloured population. The white *colons* were the first to revolt. When news of the decree of 15 May 1791 reached the colony, virtually the entire white population of the island declared their opposition to the measure and refused to countenance its implementation. Most provocatively, they refused to allow free men of colour to exercise their civic rights by participating in their assemblies, with some white slave-owners even arming their black slaves in a bid to repress the free coloureds' protests. The French governor, Blanchelande, prevaricated, and felt that he had no choice but to inform the government in Paris that, should they instruct him to enforce the law, humiliation would ensue. Reluctantly, the deputies reversed their order, leaving the civil rights of people of colour to the discretion of the whites. Confusion was only made worse by the arrival from Paris of France's first civil commissioners, Sonthonax and Polverel, to oversee the implementation of the new law, and they were horrified to find how much real power had slipped from French control. The unfortunate Blanchelande was accused of treachery and royalist sympathies, recalled to Paris in 1792, sent before the revolutionary tribunal, and guillotined. Though there is little doubt that he did sympathize with the royalist cause, the problems he faced were not all of his own making. In the hateful atmosphere of Saint-Domingue the colonial administration was powerless; indeed, in Carolyn Fick's estimation, 'power belonged to any group or party strong enough to seize it, or, more pertinently, to obtain it through political deceit and manipulation'.[25]

[24] Frédéric Régent, *La France et ses esclaves, de la colonisation aux abolitions, 1620–1848* (Paris: Grasset, 2007), 204–6.

[25] Fick, *The Making of Haiti*, 122.

It was at this time, too, that the third of the island's racial groups, the black slaves, entered the fray, when, on 22 August 1792, a huge slave insurrection broke out, directed against both individual slave-owners and the whole system of slavery in the North Province. It would spread rapidly across the country and would mark the start of an insurgency that would last until well into 1793, setting plantations ablaze and destroying much of the wealth and infrastructure of the island. The insurrection was clearly planned. We know that on 14 August, a meeting of slaves drawn from the best-educated and most trusted slaves on more than 100 plantations took place on the Lenormand de Mézy estate, where they took the decision to rebel. We also know of a secret meeting of the rebels eight days later at Bois Caïman, some five miles from Cap Français, to agree their tactics. This meeting undoubtedly took the form of a war council where the insurgents strengthened their resolve. They would, they agreed, first attack their own plantations, then burn others round about. In a ritualistic ceremony that may have had its roots in voodoo or West African religious ceremonies, the rebels administered a blood oath and sacrificed a pig in preparation for war. We have few reliable details of what happened, and accounts became exaggerated in the telling. But they sent shock-waves through the white community, for whom the insurgents were primitive and barbaric, an image they repeated over and over again in reports and petitions to Paris and to commercial associates back in France.[26] The first histories of the insurrection, which were written from a strongly anti-revolutionary standpoint, often repeated these claims, blaming the black insurgents and the Jacobin legislators in equal measure. An anonymous work of 1795, for instance, published in Paris under the title *Histoire des désastres de Saint-Domingue*, compared the atrocities committed on the island to the massacres of supposed counter-revolutionaries in mainland France, in the Vendée, Lyon, or the Vaucluse, as a result of which, it claimed, people could no longer be expected to react with the same emotion, or show the same feeling and empathy, to the 'long series of misfortunes' suffered by France's colonists.[27]

The violence the planters suffered was often extreme, both in Saint-Domingue and in Guadeloupe, where a series of slave revolts in 1793—at Bailiff and Trois-Rivières in April and at Sainte-Anne in August[28]—drove many French settlers off their *habitations* and into exile on other islands of the Petites Antilles. Charles-Gabriel Gondrecourt was one who suffered mightily at rebel hands. The owner of a sugar plantation in Trois-Rivières, on the south coast of Basse-Terre, he fled in April when the rebels attacked, returning only to find his property devastated and his family massacred.[29] Gondrecourt believed he had been deliberately targeted:

[26] David Geggus, 'The Bois Caïman Ceremony', in Geggus (ed.), *Haitian Revolutionary Studies*, 81–92.

[27] Anon., *Histoire des désastres de Saint-Domingue* (Paris: chez Garnery, 1795), 27.

[28] Françoise Koest, *La Révolution à la Guadeloupe, 1789–96*, introduction.

[29] AD Guadeloupe, 2E 3–7, Etude Jaille, minute from the *procureur-syndic* of Trois-Rivières, 14 June 1793.

his wife and children had been murdered, his farm animals butchered, and thirty-eight of his slaves either killed or led away by the assailants.[30] He returned to a sickening sight. But he would have been wrong to dismiss the slaves as primitive or ill-informed. They knew far more of the political situation on the island than most of their masters acknowledged. They understood that their enemies were deeply disunited: they knew of the tensions among the whites; they had observed the struggle between them and people of colour; and, of course, they were hugely aware—and often deeply resentful—of their lowly position at the bottom of Haitian society. They had their own culture, and increasingly their own leaders, and it is significant that these leaders were able to take full advantage of the weaknesses of the plantation owners to attract support as they passed from village to village, burning, destroying, and killing as they went. There was a strong element of revenge in these killings. Planters and estate managers who had earned their hatred during years of whippings and humiliations now risked being specially targeted. But there was also evidence of wanton cruelty, involving indiscriminate violence and affecting men who had considered themselves good masters. Often it was absentee owners who had had little contact with their slaves or involvement in the management of their estates who were targeted, learning at home in France that their Caribbean properties had been laid waste and burned.

A rare (and somewhat literary) personal testimony was left by a young, unnamed Creole who had been in France to complete his education and who, fortuitously, returned to his family's plantation on the day before the insurrection broke out. Identifying totally with the white planters, he joined the forces that were sent out against the rebels, and within days was aghast to learn that his own plantation was one of those that had been torched. When he arrived on the scene, he found everything reduced to ashes, the water mill, the aqueduct, even the homes of the plantation slaves. The sheer violence of the destruction he has witnessed leads him to reflect and to question. 'Why', he asks, was there 'such fury in the devastation?'. And he adds: 'It could not be out of hatred for us personally—we were complete strangers. We had been in France from our earliest years, and then the revolt broke out the day after our return, and so we were never allowed to live among them.'[31]

Support for the insurgents varied widely from place to place, with some slaves killing with an almost joyous abandon, while others stayed back to protect their masters and their families. One planter, François Carteaux, acknowledging his

---

[30] AD Guadeloupe, 2E, Fonds de notaires, dossier 41, Elizabeth-Jeanne-Guillaume Desvergers, épouse Charles-Gabriel Gondrecourt.

[31] Althea de Puech Parham (ed.), 'Mon Odyssée' (anonymous manuscript memoir, Puech Parham Papers, Historic New Orleans Collection); for an abridged version see Althea de Puech Parham (ed.), *My Odyssey: Experiences of a Young Refugee from Two Revolutions* (Baton Rouge: Louisiana State University Press, 1959). For an excellent discussion of the text, see Jeremy Popkin, *Facing Racial Revolution*, 59–92.

good fortune that his slaves offered him protection, was nevertheless puzzled. 'I no longer had the whip to command them,' he wrote after his return to France; 'my rights over them had almost no further basis. With a word they could have refused to work and left me. Why is it that neither my work team, nor many others in the area, ever took this decision?'[32] While Carteaux does not attempt to answer his own question, he implies that there might be some emotional bond, a sense of underlying loyalty that explained the slaves' conduct. He would also like to imply—and this was a favoured theme in *colons'* accounts—that it showed slavery to have been a less exploitative system than the abolitionists pretended, and to justify his own conduct as a planter. He does not stop to consider whether the slaves had perhaps just acted out of self-interest, assessing the risks of rebellion and the terrible retribution that might follow.

The insurrection spread with alarming speed, taking many of the plantation owners by surprise and finding their managers unprepared. From an original core of 1,000 or 1,500 men, the insurgents gained support as they passed from plantation to plantation, and by the end of November they may have been 80,000 strong. Frantic pleas for help were sent to other sugar islands, to Jamaica, Cuba, and Santo Domingo, as well as to the southern United States, but to little avail, and, with the city of Le Cap in flames, the colonial authorities were forced to turn to free blacks and mulattoes to help fight the insurgents and salvage something of the local economy. The level of destruction throughout the Northern Province was quite devastating, with sugar and coffee plantations consigned to fire, and slave-owners taken prisoner, shot, or forced to flee. An early estimate put the loss in the productive value of sugar at nearly 40 million *livres*, as all the plantations within fifty miles of Le Cap were reduced to ashes. The countryside, and with it the island's economy, lay in ruins.[33] The extent of the destruction, coupled with the viciousness of many of the attacks, showed the extent of the underlying hatred of the oppressed, and the *colons* were no more restrained in their treatment of non-whites when they fell into their clutches. Nor were French sailors on naval vessels in dock at Le Cap, who, taking their lead from the new, hard-line French governor, François-Thomas Galbaud, would prove themselves willing accomplices. Any blacks who were captured faced summary execution; some were tortured before being thrown into the sea to drown. Across the island, atrocity was met with atrocity. At Jérémie, for instance, white *colons* seized free men of colour and imprisoned them in the hold of a ship, where they callously infected them with smallpox, with the consequence that around two-thirds of them died.[34] It was a war in which no mercy was shown on either side, a dirty war that left a bitter legacy of hatred and intolerance.

---

[32] François Carteaux, quoted in Jeremy Popkin, *Facing Racial Revolution*, 177.
[33] Fick, *The Making of Haiti*, 105.
[34] Popkin, *Concise History*, 46.

If race defined the revolution in the Caribbean, war brought it to a head, a war that had its roots in the dynastic wars of the eighteenth century, fought by the European colonial powers of Britain, France, and Spain in pursuit of economic and political advantage. The war in the Caribbean was not just about the balance of power between European states; it was about resources, autonomy, and the claims and counterclaims of different sections of the population. In February 1793, France declared war on Britain, and then on Spain, which had immediate consequences for France's colonies in the Caribbean. By the end of that year, British troops had invaded the western part of the island, while Spain, now in an alliance with the slaves in their revolt against the *colons*, threatened the eastern part. In the months that followed, the leaders of the slave revolt showed that they were skilled at playing off the various European armies, while the *colons* remained resistant to any thought of compromise with the mutineers and further alienated the revolutionary government in Paris. Matters came to a head in the summer of 1793, when France's civil commissioners, Sonthonax and Polverel, freed the black population from slavery, and the *colons* realized that they could hope for little from France, instead pinning their hopes on Spain and Britain to defend their lives and property. In this spirit, some among them signed an accord with the British Governor of Jamaica, which offered them the protection of Britain and its military garrison. The news of their initiative was received by the French authorities, both in Paris and in Philadelphia, with unconcealed disgust; they saw it as a deliberate act of defiance and an act of treason.[35]

Figures are sparse and often unreliable, but it has been estimated that between September 1793 and May 1794, around 4,500 whites chose to return to their homes in the occupied zone.[36] Under attack from the black population of the island, they were prepared to swear loyalty to George III and to entrust their future to Britain, which occupied the northern part of the island for four years from 1794 to 1798, in return for a promise of security. This, of course, further alienated the revolutionary government back in France, which vilified them as counter-revolutionaries and royalists, and as enemies of the French people. But for those whose plantations had escaped the ravages of the insurrection, Britain offered more than military protection. Thanks to the occupier, the plantation owners again had an outlet for their crop, with access to British and American commercial networks and to Hamburg as a centre for redistribution across Europe.[37] They could continue to make profits in these years by turning to merchants and shippers

---

[35] Laurent Letertre, 'Le consulat de Philadelphie et la question de Saint-Domingue, 1793–1803' (mémoire de maîtrise, Université de Nantes, 2000), 13–14.

[36] David Geggus, *Slavery, War and Revolution: The British Occupation of Saint-Domingue, 1793–98* (Oxford: Oxford University Press, 1982), 228.

[37] Guy Saupin, 'La gestion des plantations antillaises durant les guerres révolutionnaires: l'alternative des États-Unis et de l'Europe du Nord', in Anne de Mathan, Pierrick Pourchasse, and Philippe Jarnoux (eds), *La mer, la guerre et les affaires: Enjeux et réalités maritimes de la Révolution Française* (Rennes: Presses Universitaires de Rennes, 2017), 271.

from outside France, and by breaking long-established contracts with French merchants and French ports. But the extent of Britain's aid was not unlimited, and the occupation did nothing to resolve the underlying racial tensions that beset the colonists.[38]

In the rest of the island, where French rule was maintained, a social and political revolution had taken place, and the French found themselves increasingly reliant on their allies in the free-coloured community as they struggled to maintain control. They faced opposition from two sides: from the white colonists on the one hand, who sought greater autonomy, and the black insurgents on the other, insurgents who by 1794 had their own political leaders and had learned to play off the various European powers when they saw advantage in doing so. Foremost among them was François-Dominique Toussaint, a former slave who had been granted his freedom back in 1776. Toussaint, who had been educated in Saint-Domingue by the Jesuits, was a man of great political and diplomatic skill as well as military talent, and, though he had not played a major part in the earlier violence, he now emerged as a military and political leader of the first rank.[39] In 1793 he took the name by which he is known to history, Toussaint Louverture.[40]

One of his first actions, amidst the chaos of that year, was to take up arms against the French on the side of Spain. He did so not out of any love for Spain or for the slave societies that Spain maintained in Santo Domingo and Cuba. Rather, like the other rebel leaders Jean-François and Biassou, he hoped that a Spanish alliance would further the cause of his own people. The Spaniards had offered freedom, land, and various civil privileges to slaves who fought for them and to their families, and this some months before the French commissioners made any offer of freedom of their own. Toussaint would appear to have waited for France's response before choosing sides, but when that response came he judged it insufficient. First, the French commissioners freed slaves who agreed to fight for the republic in French units. Only later did they extend the promise of freedom to others in the black population. Besides, these were emergency measures applicable only to Saint-Domingue or to particular provinces of the island; they did not represent a change in national policy towards slavery. Only in the spring of 1794 did the government in Paris adopt a decisive stance, when it found itself forced to choose between the interests of the *colons* and the rights of black slaves. On 4 February the National Convention voted to abolish slavery—not the slave

---

[38] Manuel Covo, 'Commerce, empire et révolutions dans le monde atlantique: la colonie française de Saint-Domingue entre métropole et États-Unis, 1778–1804' (thèse de doctorat, EHESS, 2013), 58.

[39] Toussaint has inspired many biographers and disciples. They include Caribbean radicals like C.L.R. James, *The Black Jacobins* (London: Penguin, 2001). For an overview, see Charles Forsdick and Christian Høgsbjerg (eds), *The Black Jacobins Reader* (Durham, NC: Duke University Press, 2017).

[40] There is no agreed explanation for this choice of name, though it has been suggested, by the *Encyclopedia Britannica* among others, that it may be linked to his mastery of guerrilla tactics in war.

trade, not the status of a minority of the black population, but slavery as a legal condition. France was the first slave-owning country in the world to take such a momentous step. The world would now take notice.

Toussaint could feel with some satisfaction that he and his black supporters had forced the deputies' hand. Whether it was this precise moment that won him to the French cause is a matter of conjecture: he did not explain his apparent alienation from Spain, and there are hints that he may also have resented his treatment at Spanish hands. But, for whatever reason, in the spring of 1794 Toussaint abandoned Spain and pegged his colours to the cause of France, changing the face of the war in the Caribbean. France, which had seemed on the point of losing Saint-Domingue to English and Spanish attacks, was back in charge of her colony. David Geggus assesses the multiple effects of Toussaint's volte-face. 'In a brief campaign,' he argues, 'Spain's hopes of conquest were smashed and French rule in Saint-Domingue was saved. England's chances of seizing the richest prize in the Caribbean practically vanished, and the cause of black emancipation gained a champion whose talents were to ensure its eventual triumph against all attempts to restore slavery in *la perle des Antilles*.'[41] Toussaint placed himself and his 4,000 troops under the command of the French general Laveaux and accepted French rule in the colony. And though this did not guarantee a French victory in the war—the Royal Navy was still in a position to enforce a blockade of the colony—Toussaint was now able to keep both British and Spanish forces at bay.

Abolishing slavery and winning black support had become key tactics in the war, as France's allies in the black and free-coloured communities, Toussaint and André Rigaud, freed slaves on the territories they controlled and fought with units of black troops. This both boosted recruitment and won support from civil society at a time when slavery still operated in British-held areas of Saint-Domingue. It undoubtedly helped the French cause. By 1795, Spain had withdrawn from the war, and by the Treaty of Basle ceded the eastern part of the island to France. In turn, the British were pushed back and contained, though the British occupation, which was maintained at great cost in human life, lasted until the withdrawal of the last troops in 1798.[42] The British maintained the institution of slavery in the zones they controlled; but with their departure slavery was abolished across the whole of Saint-Domingue. Elsewhere in the Caribbean, the war had also swung in France's favour: the French had retaken Guadeloupe, leaving the British with only one of France's former sugar islands, Martinique.

But relations between Toussaint and Paris were not always easy, and under the Directory he acted increasingly as an independent ruler in Saint-Domingue and

---

[41] David Geggus, 'The "volte-face" of Toussaint Louverture', in Geggus (ed.), *Haitian Revolutionary Studies*, 119.

[42] Geggus, *Slavery, War and Revolution*, 388–9.

less as the representative of France. In his negotiations with the French Republic, he was prepared to recognize the overall authority of France as long as the limits of that authority were clearly defined. He conceived of it not as direct rule, but as a form of administrative supervision, leaving him in control of the internal and external affairs of the island and guaranteeing the liberty of the black population. This was a pragmatic compromise, what Pierre Pluchon has termed 'a disguised independence', and it largely suited both sides: French ownership of the island may have been something of a fiction; but by maintaining this fiction, peace could be preserved and military intervention averted, at least in the short term.[43] Toussaint demonstrated his diplomatic skills during this period in his negotiations with Paris and his dealings with the British authorities. But already his policies contained the shoots of future conflict. His increasingly authoritarian treatment of his rivals and opponents drew criticism from republicans, not least his decision to expel the French commissioner, Sonthonax, from the island. In the meantime, inter-community relations rapidly worsened. The *colons* who had once seen him as the saviour of France's interests on the island increasingly denounced him as vainglorious, temperamental, and unpredictable in his dealings with others. In 1800 he installed his court in Le Cap and, on his own authority and in defiance of instructions from Paris, sent an army to annex the former Spanish territory of Santo Domingo.[44] His soldiers spread havoc and consternation among the inhabitants as they advanced, and panicked protests flooded in to the offices of government in Paris.

Any chance of securing a long-term settlement in Saint-Domingue was shattered when, after the coup d'état of 18 Brumaire, it became clear that the new First Consul had no interest in sustaining abolition and no principled objection to the institution of slavery. His concern was maintaining France's colonial empire, and securing the wealth that might once again flow from it. So, in 1800, while promising to maintain liberty in those colonies where slaves had been freed, he also vowed to resist abolition elsewhere, including in Santo Domingo and in France's colonies in the Indian Ocean. But black leaders in territories where slavery had been abolished—like Saint-Domingue and Guadeloupe—wanted further reassurance. From Le Cap Julien Raimond wrote to Bonaparte in August 1800, asking for confirmation that their freedom would be guaranteed and also that measures would be taken to abolish slavery in France's other colonies. He got no reply.[45] Indeed, there is evidence that in both the East and West Indies, Napoleon's policy was geared to gaining the support of the white planters by overturning some of the reforms of the republican years. The reputation

---

[43] Pierre Pluchon, *Toussaint Louverture: un révolutionnaire noir d'Ancien Régime* (Paris: Fayard, 1989), 199, 374.

[44] Pierre Branda and Thierry Lentz, *Napoléon, l'esclavage et les colonies* (Paris: Fayard, 2006), 80.

[45] Yves Benot, *La démence coloniale sous Napoléon* (Paris: La Découverte, 1992), 35.

which he built in other policy areas as a modernizer building on the reforms of the revolutionary era had little resonance in the colonies, where he dreamt of restoring the colonial glory of the eighteenth century. Unsurprisingly, perhaps, the restoration of French control over Saint-Domingue would be the central plank of that policy.

Events moved quickly to a head after Toussaint in 1801 proclaimed a constitution for the colony, a document which acknowledged Saint-Domingue as a part of France's overseas empire and which largely mirrored the current French constitution, but which he issued on his own authority, without referring it to Paris. Crucially, the document forbade all forms of racial discrimination and ruled that slavery was abolished forever. The only distinctions that were permitted were those based on 'virtues' and 'talents'. The administration of the colony was passed to a governor, who would rule on behalf of France, and it fixed the governor's term as five years. But there was one exception. For the present, to avoid any ambiguity, 'the Constitution appoints as governor citizen Toussaint Louverture, general in chief of the army of Saint-Domingue, and, in recognition of the important services he has rendered to the colony, in the most critical circumstances of the revolution, and at the express will of the grateful inhabitants, the reins of power should be given to him for the rest of his glorious life'. To guarantee continuity, he was also given the right, in secret, to name his successor, a privilege which further underlined his autonomy from metropolitan control.[46] Toussaint was laying down his own terms and conditions, creating a personal fiefdom in Haiti. For France, and for Napoleon in particular, it was a challenge that was surely a step too far.

The French response was military confrontation. The government had come under growing pressure from both white and free coloured leaders to contain Toussaint, whom they denounced for his high-handedness and his resort to violence. Planters, in particular, some of whom had returned to Saint-Domingue and had witnessed the state of their former estates, expressed anguish at the scale of destruction and the loss of fertile lands that had been carefully amassed and ploughed over generations. One such planter, Michel-Étienne Descourtilz, recorded his observations on Leclerc's expedition and on the state of his former plantation, in his *Voyages d'un naturaliste*, published in Paris in 1809. Here he tells of the bloodshed he encountered and relates his captivity at the hands of Toussaint's soldiers, though, like many such narratives, his account is surely embellished. More interesting are his thoughts on the working of the plantations under Toussaint's regime and the destruction of rich cotton fields and banana groves by those he condemns as 'Negro anarchists'. Where his family estate had once produced 400,000 pounds of cotton every year, it was now reduced to barely

---

[46] Constitution of the French colony of Saint-Domingue, proclaimed on 8 July 1801, reprinted in Pluchon, *Toussaint Louverture*, 573–87.

50,000, and lands that previously sustained 980 field workers—then slaves—now had only 120 free labourers. Despite the prohibitions issued by Toussaint's government, many of them had subdivided the land into tiny garden plots on which they spent all their time. 'I saw a few cultivators,' he recounts, 'and a couple of animals scattered around in the immense field called the garden, the men working with hoes, the animals grazing on weeds that the lack of ploughing had allowed to grow in what had once been such well-tended land.'[47]

Napoleon, of course, aimed at more than mere containment, and in 1801 the moment seemed ripe to rebuild French colonial strength in the Atlantic. In the previous year, France had regained Louisiana from Spain, and Napoleon dreamt of reconquering some of the colonies Britain had seized in the Caribbean, with the aim of re-establishing France as the major force in the Gulf of Mexico it had once been. He planned not just to re-establish political control in Saint-Domingue, but to turn it once again into an economic powerhouse for the French economy, and that meant recreating the prosperous plantation system of the Ancien Régime. Sugar and coffee could only be farmed, he believed, with black slave labour. Hence he had no desire to abolish slavery in Martinique or other territories that had been ruled by the British, and he soon determined that Saint-Domingue, too, could not flourish without slavery. This meant ending the independence of action to which Toussaint had become accustomed—a dangerous political step. Napoleon, however, was in no mood for compromise: he wanted a prosperous colony, farmed to modern European standards, and using African field labour. Friction seemed unavoidable.

Almost as soon as peace was signed with Britain at Amiens, Napoleon despatched an expeditionary force to Saint-Domingue to restore French colonial rule. It was placed under the command of Victor-Emmanuel Leclerc, a young general in whom he had faith: Leclerc had served with him in Italy and was his brother-in-law, having married his sister Pauline. Leclerc had left France in 1801 with around 20,000 troops, many of them seasoned soldiers from earlier campaigns; and at around the same time Napoleon sent a much smaller force to Guadeloupe under General Antoine Richepanse. Both had the dual mission of retaking control and restoring the slave economy in territories where blacks had enjoyed a new breath of freedom, and he knew that news of the troops' arrival would have an incendiary effect.[48] The generals were warned that they must preserve the greatest secrecy about their intentions, lest they enflame opinion. For this reason it was left to them to choose the most propitious moment to publish the decree restoring slavery.[49] But if Napoleon really believed that the missions could be conducted in secrecy, he was deluding himself. Toussaint was alerted to Napoleon's intentions by

---

[47] Michel-Étienne Descourtilz, 'Voyages d'un naturaliste' (3 vols., Paris, 1809), here vol. 2, 94–7, in Popkin, *Facing Racial Revolution*, 275–6.
[48] Popkin, *Concise History*, 120–2.
[49] Branda and Lentz, *Napoléon, l'esclavage et les colonies*, 128.

newspaper reports, and he hastened to strengthen his defences. Meanwhile, rumours that the slave system was about to be re-imposed spread like wildfire among the blacks of Saint-Domingue, leading to fierce armed resistance. In vain did Leclerc point to the military cost and appeal to the Minister for the Navy, Decrès, not to re-impose slavery if he wanted to advance the military campaign. For he now had to fight popular fears as well as military force. 'All the blacks are persuaded,' he wrote in August 1802, 'by the letters that have come from France, by the law re-establishing the slave trade, and by the decrees of General Riche-panse restoring slavery in Guadeloupe, that we want to enslave them again, and I can only get them to disarm by long and stubborn fighting. These men simply do not want to surrender.'[50] He knew he could not win. Paris had given him neither the men nor the material resources that he would require to destroy their resolve.

Though the expedition was to end in disaster, the first signs were not unprom-ising for the French as a number of Toussaint's units in the remoter areas surrendered or agreed to join Leclerc's army. In the cities, however, rebel resist-ance was more determined, and bands of insurgents defied the French by burning houses, businesses, and surrounding plantations before retreating to the hills and conducting a bitter guerrilla campaign against the invader. The two principal cities, Le Cap and Port-au-Prince, were reduced to ashes. In the countryside beyond, both sides fought with savage ferocity in a war characterized by tit-for-tat killing and intermittent racial massacres. Everywhere that white planters had stayed or returned to their plantations, they risked being slaughtered by the insurgents, killings carried out, very often, by the very men who had been their former slaves. The wrongs of lifetimes spent in slavery, the whippings and systematic humiliations suffered at the hands of their masters, injected bitterness and hatred into relations between the various ethnic groups.

Of course, contemporary accounts tend to associate barbarism and atrocity with the black population. 'The negroes or brigands show no mercy to the whites who fall into their hands,' wrote an army doctor from Le Cap in mid-insurrec-tion: 'they gouge out their eyes…and sometimes, in their more humane moments, they bleed them as we bleed pigs.'[51] These accounts were always written by white observers or by planters who had escaped to the towns. But it is important to recognize that atrocities were not limited to one side, and that the French were also guilty of crimes of brutality and inhumanity, especially in the final months of the conflict when the French commander, Rochambeau, realized that the war was lost and unleashed a policy of terror on the island. There were tales of captured black soldiers being herded on to ships in the harbour and

---

[50] Letter from Leclerc to Decrès, 6 August 1802, in Paul Roussier (ed.), *Lettres du général Leclerc, commandant-en-chef de l'Armée de Saint-Domingue en 1802* (Paris: Société de l'histoire des colonies françaises, 1937), 199–201.

[51] *Officier de santé* Guilmot and *adjudant-commandant* Dembowski, *Journal et voyage à Saint-Domingue, 1802* (Paris: Librairie historique F. Teissèdre, 1997), 66.

gassed in their holds; of summary executions of prisoners which the generals did nothing to disavow; of men being tossed overboard and drowned; of others having bloodhounds set upon them to tear their flesh from their bodies.[52] Atrocity begat atrocity as the war grew more bloody, the thirst for vengeance more unquenchable. Toussaint himself was taken as a prisoner to France and left to die in a prison in the Jura. His successor, Jean-Jacques Dessalines, who had led resistance in Port-au-Prince and inflicted a major defeat on the French in the battle of Vertières, near Le Cap, took violence to its logical extreme, ordering the extermination of all whites on the island. For them, survival was the most they could hope for. The defeat of Napoleon's ill-fated expedition also marked the end of any substantial French presence on Haiti.

Dessalines' victory on the battlefield came as a bitter blow to French pride at a time when Napoleon's armies were establishing a reputation for their invincibility in Europe. At the same time, the tactics of the rebels in the mountains sapped their spirit after months of guerrilla fighting. But, as Toussaint himself realized, a war against Europeans in the climate of the Caribbean would not be won by arms and tactics alone, and the French defeat in this campaign owed as much to fevers and disease as it did to military science. Yellow fever had been feared by colonists and ships' crews throughout the century, and it now hit the French as it had afflicted the British and Spaniards before them. The Haitians knew the vagaries of their climate and they fully understood the damage that the arrival of the hot season could do to Europeans' health. Indeed, Toussaint saw the climate as a legitimate weapon in the war, slowing his march and delaying his engagement with the French in the knowledge that the fever season would not be long delayed. Within three months of Leclerc's arrival in Saint-Domingue, he reported to Paris that he had fewer than 12,000 fit soldiers of the 20,000 who had accompanied him from France. By 6 June that number had fallen to only 10,000 still in arms: in the previous three months, he wrote, he had lost 1,200, 1,800, and 2,000 men, with the ravages of the war adding to the impact of the hot season. Each month, he reported that the crisis became more desperate. The men's symptoms varied— light headaches, followed by stomach pains and shivering for some; a sudden debilitating attack for others: but of those who went down with the fever, no more than a fifth survived. Le Cap, which had once been the source of such prosperity for Europeans, was now little more than a graveyard. Three generals or brigadier-generals were among the victims; in one case, all his secretaries had died with him. Nor was the hecatomb restricted to the military. Leclerc draws attention to the fate of seven merchants who had come out from Bordeaux to settle in Le Cap, all of

---

[52] Bernard Gainot, '«Sur le fond de cruelle inhumanité: les politiques du massacre dans la Révolution de Haïti', *La Révolution française. Cahiers de l'Institut de la Révolution française*, 3 (2011), «Les massacres aux temps des Révolutions», 1–16.

whom had died within a single week.[53] As for Leclerc himself, he would not see France again; within weeks he had joined the long list of victims of yellow fever.

For Haitians and people of African descent across the Americas, the events of these fifteen years provided a beacon of hope, and Toussaint went on to become a Caribbean icon. But for the white *colons,* and for the merchants of France's west-coast ports who supplied them, his legacy was rather different, as they came to terms, often slowly and reluctantly, with the fact that Saint-Domingue was now lost and that France's Caribbean empire could never be recreated. Napoleon's sale of Louisiana to the United States in 1803—the price was 50 million francs and a cancellation of debts worth a further 18 million francs—acknowledged a change in his priorities and signalled a withdrawal from the American hemisphere. Any further military intervention in Saint-Domingue now seemed fruitless, and though some former colonists did devise plans to invade the island, they could not escape the difficulties that any invading force would face when it landed. In a plan to reconquer Haiti penned in 1806, one former colonist, Cuizeau, warned that the French must be careful to respect the social distinctions that existed in Haitian society and take care not to cause offence, since misunderstandings and imagined slights would lose them public support. They must also be prepared to fight a special kind of war. It was not just a question of numbers, he insisted— though, as Dessalines had called up the entire male population between the ages of sixteen and fifty, the numerical odds would be overwhelming. It was also about the approach they should adopt. The enemy might not be great tacticians, he argued, but they were familiar with the topography of Haiti and would adjust their tactics to reflect the landscape. The French must be prepared to face guerrilla fighters who would take full advantage of natural hiding places to ambush the invader. No force that came unprepared for such conditions could hope to defeat them.[54]

For good reason, it may be thought, no such invasion was mounted, and the former *colons,* now scattered across the Atlantic world, were left to dream of what might have been. The defeat of Leclerc's expedition was to be a turning-point for the white population of the island, as the failure to restore French rule and the slaughter that followed signalled the end of the French colonial presence on Saint-Domingue. In November 1803, Dessalines and Rochambeau signed a treaty coordinating the evacuation of the French army from Le Cap and purporting to guarantee the safety of the troops and of any civilians who wished to leave. The Haitian leaders followed up ten days later by proclaiming Haitian independence under the authority of 'the Black People and Men of Colour of St. Domingo', a phrase that calmly evaded the question of where any remaining white colonists would stand under the new regime. Slavery was abolished, they declared, and its

[53] Letter from Leclerc to Decrès, 6 June 1802, in Roussier (ed.), *Lettres du général Leclerc,* 154–5.
[54] National Library of Jamaica, MST 161, Cuizeau, 'Plan pour la conquête de Saint-Domingue, 1806', 6–9.

abolition would be upheld by any means, by violence where necessary.[55] And while it is true that a few *colons* did struggle on in post-independence Haiti—indeed, one of the signatories of the act of independence was a white Creole, Nicolas Pierre Mallet, a planter from the south coast of the island who had led his former slaves against the French army[56]—they constituted only a tiny proportion of the thousands of Frenchmen who had left France before 1791 to start a new life on the plantations or in the mercantile district of Le Cap. The vast majority fled, some taking their slaves with them into exile and few believing that they would ever return. Most of their material possessions were abandoned, and their homes and plantations left untilled and unprotected. For many it was a choice between life and death as they scrambled on to small boats in coastal creeks or bought themselves passages on the few merchant vessels still plying a passage to Europe or to other Caribbean islands. Those who had not already been driven out by fires and slave uprisings during the revolutionary decade felt that their time in Saint-Domingue was now over and that, if they valued their lives and considered the future of their families, they had no choice but to leave. In the new republic of Haiti, they were no longer welcome.

In Guadeloupe, Napoleonic policy was no less reactionary, his determination to re-impose French rule no less stringent. The revolutionary years had seen slavery abolished and French revolutionary ideas proclaimed, but the island had also been ruled by royalists and had endured invasion by the British in a decade marked by continued violence and periodic insurrection as rival factions and racial groups fought one another for power. The arrival from France of Victor Hugues in 1794 marked the high point of republicanism in Guadeloupe, as he celebrated republican festivals, imposed a policy of dechristianization, and announced the abolition of slavery in the colony. But his was a regime of a highly authoritarian and personal kind, and he soon fell out with the Directory in Paris, refusing to impose the Constitution of the Year III and maintaining a kind of neo-Jacobinism on the island.[57] The consequence was yet another victory for political conservatism, as the Directory sent a new representative to Guadeloupe in 1798—Desfourneaux—to replace Victor Hugues and impose its own orthodoxy. The French provided troops to repress insurrections against him, most notably by *métis* who were distrustful of France's intentions towards them. Then, in 1802, a French force under Richepanse disembarked on the island, disarming the rebel soldiers and putting down the insurrection. Order was rapidly restored, and the leader of the revolt, Louis Delgrès, was killed along with up to 1,000 of the rebels. In the aftermath of the insurrection a conservative polity was restored, republicans

---

[55] David Armitage and Julia Gaffield, 'Introduction: The Haitian Declaration of Independence in an Atlantic Context', in Julia Gaffield (ed.), *The Haitian Declaration of Independence: Creation, Context and Legacy* (Charlottesville: University of Virginia Press, 2016), 5.

[56] David Geggus, 'Haiti's Declaration of Independence', ibid., 26–7.

[57] Régent, *Esclavage, métissage, liberté: la Révolution Française en Guadeloupe*, 368–9.

were sent into exile, and royalists were allowed to return to the plantations they had abandoned. In 1803, slavery was instituted, in accordance with Napoleon's wishes. Those blacks who had gained their freedom since 1789 lost it again, and free status was reserved for those who could prove that they or their families had already been free before the Revolution. People of colour arguable suffered the greatest loss of status. The elite who had taken part in the rebellion were exiled or decimated, while the others found themselves stripped of their rights and their citizenship.[58] The freedoms which they had won back in the heady days of the Revolution were now but a distant memory. To make matters worse, in 1810, British forces once again took possession of the island.[59] Guadeloupe's future, like that of France's other colonial possessions, would be decided by war and by the peace negotiations that followed at Vienna.

[58] Ibid, 436–8.
[59] Anne Pérotin-Dumon, *Être patriote sous les tropiques* (Basse-Terre: Société d'histoire de la Guadeloupe, 1985), 330.

10

The Saint-Domingue Diaspora

The revolutionary crisis not only brought Saint-Domingue's prosperity to an end. It halted the migration from Europe which had built up the colony's white population across the previous decades, and made many of those who had settled on the island fearful for their future. A huge exodus of *colons* followed—of planters and commercial agents, soldiers and administrators, artisans and tradesmen of all kinds, along with their wives and children—effectively ending France's presence on an island that had accounted for more than three-quarters of the country's colonial trade just a few years previously.[1] Just when they left and where they chose to go depended on individual circumstance, but they left because of fear, fear of racial attacks and murders, of property-burning, or slave insurrection. From 1790 and the initial campaign for civil rights by men of colour, the white *colons* had felt reason to fear, since from the outset the insurrections in Saint-Domingue always had a racial character and were directed principally against them. As revolutionary tracts arrived from France urging the enslaved population to seize their civil rights, their anxieties grew more pressing. Crisis point was reached in August 1791, when, following a nocturnal oath-taking at Bois-Caïman, a strike was called on the plantations that unleashed a wave of slave violence. The brutality of the attacks that followed shocked and terrified the *colons*; it demonstrated as never before the collective power of the black community; and it was murderous. By the end of the year, more than 1,000 sugar and coffee plantations had been destroyed, and around 400 white colonists had been slaughtered.[2] The French government had been unable to save their lives or their properties, and many colonists, among them some of the very richest, were driven to seek shelter elsewhere.

This would prove to be the first of a number of key moments in the revolutionary decade which persuaded the *colons* that the time was right to leave. It was not only those who lived on rural plantations who felt vulnerable to attack. The insurgents turned against the white population in the towns and cities, too, and there was widespread panic, notably in 1793, when the torching of Port-au-Prince

---

[1] François Crouzet, 'Wars, blockade and economic change in Europe, 1792–1815', *Journal of Economic History*, 24 (1964), 569.

[2] Ada Ferrer, *Freedom's Mirror: Cuba and Haiti in the Age of Revolution* (Cambridge: Cambridge University Press, 2014), 2.

led to the evacuation of 10,000 people to Norfolk, Virginia.[3] Outside events could also drive settlers to abandon their properties and flee: for some it was the arrival of a French expeditionary force on the island, for others the threat of invasion by Britain or Spain. A succession of panics spread among the white population during the 1790s, leading to the flight and migration of large numbers of people. Not all of those who left intended leaving for good. Some hedged their bets, entrusting their estates to managers in their absence, still dreaming of a time when revolution and insurrection would be a thing of the past. But with the passage of the years these hopes faded, and the *colons* were forced to accept that they would not and could not return.

There were a number of turning-points, when Saint-Domingue seemed to slip ever further from their grasp. The proclamation of abolition was one, the ending of the slave economy without which many thought colonial culture impossible. The British invasion was another, though some viewed the British as the least bad of the options available, offering the possibility of working again with slave labour. For that reason, too, the return of the French in 1798 was not seen as reason for rejoicing. They did not trust the government to look after their interests, or the army to help restore their privileged position in society, as they saw increasing numbers of black troops deployed, both in the colonies and in mainline regiments. Their distrust was especially reserved for the National Guard which dealt with policing on the island. At one time it had been the preserve of white colonists, but as the political and military crisis evolved, it was opened up to all ethnic groups, including the former slaves, while the demands of the war led to the withdrawal of regular units of the army for service in Europe.[4] But it would be the failure of Leclerc's expedition to retake Haiti in 1802 and the subsequent racial purge that Dessalines unleashed which convinced even the most resolute that they had no choice but to leave. The carnage was not restricted to the white settlers: between 1791 and 1804 some 60,000 French soldiers had been killed on Saint-Domingue, along with up to a third of the black population of the island.[5] The *colons* may have left with feelings of relief, but few did so joyously. Especially for those Creoles who had lived all their lives on Saint-Domingue, leaving was seen as a personal loss, as a defeat that for many meant abandoning the only lifestyle they had known.

But if they were to seek refuge elsewhere, where could they go? The decision was often forced on them by the emergency they faced and the possibilities for escape. But in general terms, they had three alternatives, as Madeleine Dupouy

[3] Natalie Dessens, 'Napoleon and Louisiana: new Atlantic perspectives', in Christophe Belaubre, Jordana Dym, and John Savage (eds), *Napoleon's Atlantic: The Impact of Napoleonic Empire in the Atlantic World* (Leiden: Brill, 2010), 66.

[4] Bernard Gainot, *Les officiers de couleur dans les armées de la République et de l'Empire, 1792–1815* (Paris: Karthala, 2007), 73–4.

[5] Annie Jourdan, *Nouvelle histoire de la Révolution* (Paris: Flammarion, 2018), 492.

explains when discussing the papers of three families who faced exactly this dilemma. They might head for the United States and make their way in the dynamic economy of the eastern seaboard; they might seek out another Caribbean island with a plantation economy and climate similar to those of Saint-Domingue; or they might return to France, a nation in the midst of revolution and now ravaged by war, a country very different from the one they had known. It was not an easy choice, as any course of action involved change and adaptation.[6]

For those who had families back in France and who accepted that their colonial adventure was behind them, there might seem to be only one answer: they would buy a passage on a ship from Nantes or Bordeaux and return home to France. And many did. But it was not always as simple as that. Some of the planters were men of strongly royalist views, who regarded the Revolution with unabated horror, or scions of noble families for whom a return to France in the years of the republic would constitute a threat, perhaps to life itself. Others, the many artisans and craftsmen who had sought their fortune in the Islands, might have grounds of their own to make them hesitate. Some had left home through poverty, or were orphaned and without a close family to return to; or they might have signed on as indentured workers in the service of others to get the price of their passage to the colonies.[7] Besides, not all had grown prosperous during their years in the Caribbean, and many had emerged burdened with debts which they could not easily repay. In Bordeaux the merchant Lorenz Meyer describes the lot of 600 refugees who had arrived in the city piled one on top of another in the hold of a ship, and who were now kept at government expense in the buildings of a bare, unfurnished convent. He draws an unsparing picture of their misery—of men, women, and children who had lost everything and were cooped up in sordid cells, black and white alike, living, as he puts it, 'like animals'. They were given only the minimum food rations needed if they were to avoid dying of starvation, and they complained of being left without bread for several days. 'I shall never forget,' he writes, 'the distressing sight of these miserable people covered in filthy rags, nor the awful feeling I had when I realised my powerlessness to relieve their suffering.'[8] For many refugees from the islands, if they had no families to return to, this was the welcome that awaited them when they docked in a French port.

Not all were reduced to such conditions, of course, but for those who came to France as refugees from Saint-Domingue there might be little choice. The lucky ones were those who planned in advance, or the women and children sent home to

---

[6] Madeleine Dupouy, 'La diaspora transatlantique des familles dominguoises Droüillard, D'Espinose et Lamaignère', in Éric Dubesset and Jacques de Cauna (eds), *Dynamiques caribéennes: Pour une histoire des circulations dans l'espace atlantique, 18ᵉ–19ᵉ siècles* (Pessac: Presses Universitaires de Bordeaux, 2014), 116.

[7] Corinne Janin, 'Les engagés pour les Antilles à partir des rôles d'armement nantais, 1722–1772' (mémoire de maîtrise, Université de Nantes, 1971), 2.

[8] Louis Desgraves, *Voyageurs à Bordeaux du dix-septième siècle à 1914* (Bordeaux: Mollat, 1991), 100.

France before violence broke out and they were forced to flee. The early arrivals included unaccompanied children whom merchant firms in Nantes or Bordeaux had agreed to evacuate at their own expense.[9] Less fortunate were those who remained behind on the island, only to be driven out by massacres or by disasters like the burning of Port-au-Prince in June 1793 or Dessalines's purge of the white population ten years later. They were forced to evacuate their homes and leave all their valuables behind as they boarded ships to the nearest safe haven, often to the ports of the eastern seaboard of the United States. For the first time in their lives they found themselves reduced to penury and dependent on public charity, and they often discovered that they were not welcome in the United States. White *colons* were condemned for their failure to hold and protect the colony, which Americans were liable to ascribe to moral failings and depravity.[10] Indeed, the American authorities, unsettled by the incursion of French planters and their families in 1793 and fearful lest they spread revolutionary contagion, hastened to put them on ships and to send them in convoys, under escort, to Europe. They arrived, in Brest or Nantes or Bordeaux, in the midst of a war, having escaped the dangers of the Atlantic crossing and the attentions of British warships, fugitives from slave violence.[11] Smaller numbers arrived from France's other Caribbean islands, Guadeloupe and Martinique, after the British invaded.[12] Some were bewildered by what they found: for many it was the first time they had set foot on French soil; and while others may have been born in France, often in the west and south-west to which they now returned, they had left for the New World several decades previously and had few real contacts to which to turn. They had little conception of the changes which the Revolution had wrought, and they found the country they returned to very different from the one they had left behind.

At first the French responded by offering public assistance to those arriving from the Caribbean and supplying them with basic necessities, food and simple accommodation, but as the numbers arriving continued to rise, especially with the defeat of Leclerc's mission to Saint-Domingue, the authorities imposed restrictions in a bid to limit their own exposure to the crisis. It was recognized that immigration was a regional problem, largely limited to the west-coast ports. In July 1802, the government decreed that state assistance to refugees from the colonies should cease except in the five cities where they were most concentrated— Bordeaux, Marseille, Nantes, Lorient, and La Rochelle. Others would have to

[9] Marcel Grandière, 'Les réfugiés et les déportés des Antilles à Nantes sous la Révolution', *Bulletin de la Société d'Histoire de la Guadeloupe*, 33–4 (1977), 25–44.

[10] Ashli White, 'The Saint-Dominguan Refugees and American Distinctiveness in the Early Years of the Haitian Revolution', in David Geggus and Norman Fiering (eds), *The World of the Haitian Revolution* (Bloomington, IN: Indiana University Press, 2009), 249.

[11] A list of the colonists who arrived in Nantes from Saint-Domingue across the decade can be found in Grandière, 'Les réfugiés et les déportés des Antilles', 75–159.

[12] Shorter lists of deportees from Guadeloupe and Martinique can be found in ibid., 161–4, 165–8.

make their way to these cities if they hoped to receive money from the state, which, of course, exacerbated the problem for the cities concerned. In the case of Bordeaux, the mayors of the three municipal authorities were allocated funds to relieve hardship among former *colons*, both those who had fled slave insurgency in the Caribbean and those who had been captured by the British and had been returned as prisoners-of-war from British gaols or from prison hulks moored in naval ports like Portsmouth and Chatham. Among the refugees were mothers with small children, who were given priority. But funds were limited. Those without lodging were interned in institutions, often in buildings that had previously been used by the army; and they were provided with a soup kitchen, with a budget to cover 4,000 rations of soup. Distinctions began to be drawn between claimants: only white settlers would be helped, and those who could demonstrate that they had been proprietors in Saint-Domingue.[13] For black refugees and men of colour, the conditions imposed were much harsher. They were not allowed to re-embark for the colonies; they were kept out of Paris; and the government proposed to incorporate the able-bodied males among them in military units whom they would send under white commanders to islands off the French coast, the Îles d'Hyères, the Île d'Oléron, and the Île d'Aix.[14]

Petitions flowed in from former colonists who now found themselves destitute and unemployed, their lives seemingly without purpose, abandoned by a government to which they claimed to have remained loyal. They had been men of substance, landowners and merchants, before misfortune struck; and they now suffered from boredom, a sense of uselessness and waste. Though they petitioned for alms, what many really wanted was to get out of France, to return home to the Antilles, the place they still thought of as home. And indeed, when names were removed from the list of *colons* in receipt of assistance, the reason most commonly given was not death or sickness, but the decision, once they were able to believe that peace had been restored, to leave France to resume the life they had left behind in the Caribbean. Entry after entry tells the same story: 'left for Saint-Domingue with his wife and three children', 'left for the colonies', 'embarked for the Antilles'. Some, at least, prepared to pursue their dream until the bitter end.[15] They did not stay in France long enough to benefit from the 150-million franc indemnity which the French sought from Haiti in 1825 to reimburse them and their descendants. Those eligible for compensation included not only white colonists but also planters and slave-owners of colour who had remained loyal to France and has passed into exile. In all, around 12,000 people benefited, at great

[13] AD Gironde, 4M 908, letter from Minister of the Interior to Prefect of the Gironde, 5 ventôse 12.
[14] AD Gironde, 4M 908, letter from Minister of the Marine and Colonies to the Préfet Maritime in Rochefort, 3 messidor 10.
[15] AD Gironde, 4M 908, Third arrondissement of Bordeaux, lists of *colons* in receipt of assistance, 21 vendémiaire 10 and 15 pluviôse 10.

cost to the Haitian economy.[16] Payments to individuals were still being made in Bordeaux well into the Third Republic. A list drawn up by the Prefect in 1876 of those entitled to such payments contained thirty-eight names, thirty of them women, most often widows living on modest investments and trying to maintain a degree of demure respectability in their old age.[17]

Not all of those who arrived from the colonies in metropolitan France were white; among them were mulattoes threatened by insurrection, and black servants who had either fled aboard ship or had come to France with their masters or as servants to ships' captains. There was nothing new, of course, in seeing Africans in the Atlantic port cities; they had been a familiar sight for much of the previous century. And though many then moved on to Paris, it was through the ports of the Atlantic coast that more than nine-tenths of them had come to France.[18] But attitudes changed dramatically after the violence in Saint-Domingue, and those fleeing from the island were often met with suspicion by the French authorities, who saw them as a possible source of further trouble. Black immigrants were supervised; some found themselves the victims of false denunciations. From the moment they landed they were under surveillance, with Napoleon's government insistent that steps be taken to prevent their illegal entry into France. In 1807, the Prefect of the Gironde was ordered to find secure accommodation for any new arrivals from French colonies landing without express permission from the colonial governor, and to intern any blacks arriving in the city other than by sea.[19] To do this, he required accurate information about the numbers who had arrived in Bordeaux from the Caribbean since the first risings on Guadeloupe and Saint-Domingue, information that was meticulously collated by the administration in October 1807. In all there were 164 names on the list, ninety of them black, the others mulattoes. They had come to Bordeaux at different moments in the Revolution in response to different crises across the Antilles, from Saint-Domingue and Martinique, Guadeloupe, St Lucia, and Marie-Galante. They included widows, men of working age, and mothers with small children: the oldest was sixty-eight, the youngest no more than one year old. They worked in the professions open to people of colour in the French colonies: carpenters, painters, stonemasons, manservants, farm workers, and day labourers among the men, seamstresses, laundresses, and domestic servants for the women. They posed no threat to the people of Bordeaux, but events in the Caribbean had aroused suspicions and anxieties, making the city a far less welcoming place.[20]

---

[16] Ana Lucia Araujo, *Reparations for Slavery and the Slave Trade* (London: Bloomsbury, 2017), 87.

[17] AD Gironde, 8M 18, Secours accordés aux descendants des colons de Saint-Domingue, 1870–1899.

[18] Erick Noël, *Être noir en France au 18e siècle* (Paris: Tallandier, 2006), 106.

[19] AD Gironde, 1M 332, letter from the Minister of Interior to the Prefect of the Gironde, 4 August 1807.

[20] AD Gironde, 1M 332, 'État des Noirs, Mulâtres et autres Gens de Couleur existant à Bordeaux', 5 October 1807.

Some *colons*, of course, had no wish to move to Europe in the first place, or to make peace with a France which they held responsible for so many of their woes. They preferred to remain in the Americas, hoping to maintain the colonial lifestyle they had become used to. To this end, they tended to avoid other French islands like Guadeloupe or Guyane, where they imagined themselves threatened by the same social threats as in Saint-Domingue and the same loss of privilege that they had already suffered. They preferred to seek a new life on other islands, where slave societies still flourished, uncontaminated, as they saw it, by the germ of anti-colonial revolt. Some went straight to the new United States, to the coastal towns of Virginia, South Carolina, Georgia, or Louisiana, in the last of which they could also hope to mingle with local people who spoke French. But French culture was not everything. These years also saw colonies of exiles from Saint-Domingue springing up on English and Dutch sugar islands in the Caribbean like Trinidad, Jamaica, Saint-Martin, and Curaçao, as well as in the Spanish colonies of Santo Domingo and Cuba. These were territories that had not previously had a signifi-cant French presence, but which now held out a double promise. They were defended by foreign navies, which offered protection against any French attack, a quality that was especially valued by those planters looking for a temporary shelter before returning—as many still imagined they would—to Saint-Domingue. And for those who were contemplating a more permanent exile, these territories offered many of the benefits they had once enjoyed: they had plantation econ-omies, they grew sugar and coffee, and, most important of all, they tolerated slavery. They were places where a *colon* could hope to live out his life in peace, unencumbered by French egalitarian doctrines or by the threat of slave revolts, and hope to enrich himself as he had previously done in Haiti.[21]

Jamaica was Britain's most significant rival to Saint-Domingue, a prosperous colony with a long-established settler community and two important, yet con-trasting, urban centres in Kingston and Spanish Town. Kingston was a thriving seaport, a commercial city which was at once a major entrepôt for the African and British trades, a destination for slavers from West Africa, and a staging point for European merchants trading with South America.[22] Among the urban centres in the British American colonial world, it ranked behind only Philadelphia and New York for most of the eighteenth century, and ahead of Boston: the figures produced by Jacob Price give its population in 1790 as 26,000, at a time when Philadelphia, the largest city in the United States, had around 42,000 inhabitants, New York a little more than 33,000, Boston around 18,000, and Charleston some 16,000. As a measure of comparison, Le Cap had around 15,000 inhabitants on the

---

[21] Gabriel Debien, 'Les colons de Saint-Domingue réfugiés à Cuba, 1793–1815', *Revista de Indias*, 14 (1954), 560.

[22] Jack P. Greene, *Settler Jamaica in the 1750s: a Social Portrait* (Charlottesville: University of Virginia Press, 2016), 153–4.

eve of the Revolution, and Havana, the capital of plantation-rich Cuba, more than 40,000.[23] But in terms of commercial wealth Kingston surpassed all its rivals, and it was the dream of sharing in this wealth that continued to lure merchants, including some of the refugees from Haiti, to settle there.

Jamaica's capital and second city, Spanish Town, had a very different appeal. It was the centre of colonial administration, the place to which ships arriving and leaving the island had to report, though it was sited back from the coast and had little commerce of its own. But its best days were behind it, and by the 1790s it was a city visibly in decline, with few new public buildings under construction, little private investment, and no military presence once the island's garrison was redeployed to Kingston in response to the needs of war.[24] It had the air of a cultured administrative centre, home to Jamaica's government and law courts, a place to which the richer planters came to take the air and mix with high society.[25] In his *Account of Jamaica and its Inhabitants*, published in 1808, John Stewart pointed to the dignity of its public buildings, describing Spanish Town as 'the genteelest and handsomest town in the island'.[26] But it was a fading glory, one that appealed mainly to army officers and royalist planters looking for a refuge abroad, and it was in Kingston that the majority of the French *émigrés* congregated, a city that had welcomed Frenchmen fleeing from religious persecution in the past and where Creole refugees mingled easily with French royalists and revolutionaries and with immigrants and seamen of many nations.[27] Being French did not result in social exclusion. They received a warm welcome in Jamaica, with their families and their households, and were not impeded in any way. When, for instance, Madame Fourche, a rich plantation owner from the southern part of Saint-Domingue, crossed to Jamaica in late 1791 'for fear of brigands', as she put it, she was admitted to Kingston with around twenty of her slaves.[28] It was not seen as a problem.

That warmth quickly dissipated, however, once Britain and France were at war, and after news arrived of slave insurrections and the torching of plantation houses on Saint-Domingue. At a stroke the presence of French Creoles became a source

[23] Jacob M. Price, 'Economic function and the growth of American port towns in the eighteenth century', *Perspectives in American History*, 8 (1974), 126; Price, 'Summation: The American Panorama of Atlantic Port Cities', in Franklin W. Knight and Peggy K. Liss (eds), *Atlantic Port Cities: Economy, Culture and Society in the Atlantic World, 1650–1850* (Knoxville, TN; University of Tennessee Press, 1991), 263.

[24] James Robertson, *Gone is the Ancient Glory: Spanish Town, Jamaica, 1534–2000* (Kingston: Ian Randle, 2005), 137–42.

[25] B.W. Higman, 'Jamaican Port Towns in the Early Nineteenth Century', in Knight and Liss, *Atlantic Port Cities*, 117–18.

[26] John Stewart, *An Account of Jamaica and its Inhabitants, by a Gentleman, Long Resident in the West Indies* (London: Longman, 1808), 12–13; Robertson, *Gone is the Ancient Glory*, 143.

[27] Higman, 'Jamaican Port Towns', 141.

[28] Philip Wright and Gabriel Debien, 'Les colons de Saint-Domingue passes à la Jamaïque, 1792–1835', *Bulletin de la Société d'Histoire de la Guadeloupe*, 26 (1975), 21.

of panic, as they were associated in Jamaican minds with what they feared most, dangerous revolutionary ideas from France and a cruel and vengeful black population that risked spreading anarchy among Jamaica's slaves. The free access that had previously been accorded to them was quickly removed, and the island's borders were more closely policed. From April 1793 new arrivals were treated with suspicion: those intending to stay in Jamaica were questioned by magistrates and they had to produce certificates of previous good conduct, with the sole exception of those who had already sought and been granted British citizenship.[29]

Despite these precautions, there were moments when the authorities risked being overwhelmed: in 1796 following the evacuation of the population of Port-au-Prince; or in 1798, when, following the departure of French troops, waves of refugees arrived from Saint-Domingue, doubling overnight the numbers living in Jamaica. The governor's report on 29 October 1798 put the influx at 900 white settlers, 317 people of colour, and around 1,600 slaves.[30] The situation would soon be further complicated, as the return of French refugees to Haiti was discussed during trade negotiations with Toussaint Louverture, and then the failure of Leclerc's expedition led to the evacuation of French troops to Jamaica and the presence of many French prisoners-of-war on the island. Moreover, the refugees included free people of colour and slaves, whose presence was seen by the Jamaican authorities as a major security problem. Increasingly tight regulations were imposed on the French as the planter assembly in Jamaica barely concealed its feelings of hysteria.

Sir George Nugent, the governor from 1801 to 1806, expressed particular alarm. A number of French prisoners-of-war, officers in the army sent to Saint-Domingue, were living freely on parole in Kingston and Spanish Town, and Jamaican planters worried that French revolutionary agents might be at work among their slaves. Nugent wanted French prisoners to be returned to Europe and free people of colour and black slaves without masters to be sent back to Haiti, while he encouraged white planters among the refugees to migrate to New Orleans or to Cuba. Like many of those he administered, he believed that Jamaica would be better rid of them.[31] From a purely policing point of view, he may have been right, though there is very little evidence that such ideas ever entered their minds. Almost as soon as they had escaped Saint-Domingue, indeed, many of the planters were already scoping the territory to see where they might hope to buy land or establish new plantations. If they looked with favour on Jamaica, it was as a colony where slave-holding was still legal and where they could hope to maintain their accustomed lifestyle. Some had chosen to settle there only because it had seemed

[29] Ibid., 85.   [30] Ibid., 89.

[31] Sir George Nugent, correspondence with Admiral Sir John Duckworth, summarized in Kenneth Ingram, *Sources of Jamaican History, 1655–1838: a bibliographical survey with particular reference to manuscript sources* (2 vols, Zug: Inter Documentation Company, 1976), vol. 1, 385.

to offer safety from slave insurrection at home; large numbers of them believed that, in the dire circumstances they faced, the English fleet provided the best protection. After the wars were over, that protection was no longer a priority, and when, in 1833, slavery was abandoned in Britain's colonies, their interest in Jamaica largely ceased. Many of them left for good, generally for Louisiana, where they started afresh on new plantations which they could resettle with their slaves.[32]

Jamaica was always a minority choice for refugees from Saint-Domingue, however, and it benefited from relatively little long-term settlement. Rather it was seen as a place to which to retreat in periods of violence, from which a judicious return might be made when conditions allowed. In the early years of the Revolution, that was generally true of Cuba, too, a nearby island which could offer a short-term refuge before returning to the place they still thought of as home. Indeed, it could be argued that for many French planters, Cuba might seem a more intimidating environment: unlike the islands of the British Caribbean, Cuba was a place where little French was spoken, where there was no tradition of Huguenot migration or of cooperation between the two colonial powers. The small groups of *colons* from Saint-Domingue who crossed to Cuba in 1791 almost certainly thought of it as a safe haven where they would stay until they could return home, but as the war dragged on and the Revolution in Saint-Domingue became more intolerant, they came to see Cuba as a place for permanent settlement, where they would establish a thriving French planter community, growing coffee and bringing more productive farming methods and increased levels of mechanization to Cuba's plantations. They were welcomed as innovators who would boost coffee production and contribute to the island's prosperity.

They came in large numbers, some directly from the plantations of Saint-Domingue, others by way of Jamaica and Santo-Domingo, to Havana in the first instance, though many then headed for the relatively undeveloped east of the island around Santiago de Cuba. The French migration formed distinct waves, especially in the years from 1799 to 1804 when, encouraged by the ambitions of the enlightened Spanish governor of Cuba's eastern province, Sebastian Kindelán, more than 19,000 *colons* were admitted.[33] In 1799, after the English evacuated Saint-Domingue, few Frenchmen followed them to England, most preferring to try their luck in Cuba while they waited to see what settlement Toussaint would offer. They came as temporary migrants, many intending to return, and though they built new fortunes in Cuba, many held on to their property, in both land and people, in the territory they still refused to call Haiti.[34] But with the years their

---

[32] Wright and Debien, 'Les colons de Saint-Domingue passés à la Jamaïque', 198.

[33] Maria Elena Orozco Lamore and Maria Teresa Fleitas Monnar, *Formation d'une ville caraïbe: Urbanisme et architecture à Santiago de Cuba* (Pessac: Presses Universitaires de Bordeaux, 2011), 51.

[34] Ferrer, *Freedom's Mirror*, 182.

optimism faded, and following the failure of Leclerc's expedition any hopes of a return were dashed, with the consequence that most elected to stay. They were by then well established on the island, in contrast to those who, in 1803, after the defeat of the French and the evacuation of Port-au-Prince, followed the refugee route to Cuba. Many of these people were desperate, leaving the bulk of their possessions behind when they fled. They stepped on shore in total disarray: seamen and soldiers, white *colons* and men of colour, merchants and colonial administrators, coffee planters and slave-owners, tradesmen, clerks, seamstresses and bartenders all disembarked in Havana, bringing the myriad problems of people stripped of their livelihoods and of everything they owned.[35] But a number of them came with money, and were able to prosper, buying land for a fraction of its cost in Saint-Domingue and working it with slave labour, turning the empty lands around Santiago into flourishing coffee plantations like the ones they had left behind. It was a remarkable transformation: if in the months before the French influx eastern Cuba had a total of eight coffee farms, in 1804 alone fifty-six new ones were established.[36]

Of course, not everything was simple. The planters faced new challenges, not least a shortage of labour in a country which had relatively few slaves, a fraction of the number available in Saint-Domingue. Cuba did not seem like an island paradise. Pierre Collette, a coffee grower who arrived in 1803, described some years later what he had to cope with in the hinterland of Santiago. 'Thrown upon Cuba with only a few domestics as my only resource,' he wrote, 'uncertain that I would keep them, seeing how easily negroes here leave their masters, the cost of living, as miserable as it seems, is very expensive. Rent is sky-high due to the number of refugees.'[37] Moreover, while the Cuban authorities were eager to welcome more white colonists, they categorically refused to admit slaves from Saint-Domingue, because they, like the Governor in Jamaica, had deeply held suspicions that slaves who had lived through the turbulence of the Haitian revolution would go on to import seditious views into Cuba. Keeping them out altogether proved impossible, however, and what Rebecca Scott has called 'a delicate game of cat-and-mouse' developed between the authorities and ships' captains intent on disembarking their cargoes of black fugitives for sale into slavery.[38] Many were sent ashore secretly along the shoreline, often under cover of darkness. Wherever they went in the Americas, it seemed, a reputation for being uniquely disruptive preceded them.

---

[35] Gabriel Debien, 'The Saint-Domingue Refugees in Cuba, 1793–1815', in Carl A. Brasseaux and Glenn R. Conrad (eds), *The Road to Louisiana: The Saint-Domingue Refugees, 1792–1809* (Lafayette, LA: Center for Louisiana Studies, University of Southwestern Louisiana, 1992), 38–9.

[36] Ferrer, *Freedom's Mirror*, 181.

[37] Debien, 'The Saint-Domingue Refugees in Cuba', 85–6.

[38] Rebecca J. Scott and Jean M. Hébrard, *Freedom Papers: An Atlantic Odyssey in the Age of Emancipation* (Cambridge, MA: Harvard University Press, 2012), 52.

In official documents in Cuba, the *colons* were generally listed as *émigrés* or refugees from Saint-Domingue, and their occupation was commonly given as planter or landowner on the coffee plantations. Not all were rich. On the list of men taking the oath of loyalty to the Spanish crown in Santiago de Cuba in 1808, a wide variety of trades and professions was represented: carpenters and stonemasons, schoolmasters and shoemakers, sailmakers and shopkeepers. Whole communities had been forced to flee, and in Cuba they tried to carry on their lives. Less frequent are specific indications of their birthplace in France, though it is clear that a high percentage of them had been born in Europe before coming out to the Caribbean. And where we do know their place of origin, it is often in the west or south-west of France, either the port cities from which they had sailed or the provinces that lay behind them. Le Havre, Saint-Malo, Nantes, and Bordeaux all figure, unsurprisingly; but they also came from small towns and villages from Brittany to Poitou and Saintonge to Languedoc.[39] Frenchmen who had already migrated to the French colonies in the Caribbean had been forced to move on, an itinerant population in search of stability across the Atlantic world. Their movements are reflected in Santiago's population statistics for these years. At the end of the 1790s, the city's population stood at just more than 20,000, including 6,100 white settlers; by 1803 these figures had risen to 29,596 and 13,865, with the number of slaves also increasing. Five years later, in 1808, when many of the French *colons* were expelled, the white population fell to 10,797. But the number of black slaves continued to rise, doubling from 1792 to stand at 10,459 in 1808, and changing the ethnic balance of the city for all time.[40]

Among those whose odyssey had started in the west of France were men whose fortunes placed them among the elite, the *grands blancs* of the plantations or of merchant capitalism who often acted as intermediaries with the island authorities. The most famous is probably Prudencio Casamayor, who rapidly became one of the wealthiest and best-known figures in Santiago society. He had been born in the Béarn, had come to Saint-Domingue in 1785 at the age of twenty-two to work as registrar to one of the big estates, and, like many others, he sought refuge in Cuba in 1798. In Santiago he set up in business, investing in coffee estates and making loans and money advances to French settlers when they experienced cash-flow difficulties. He carried out official business, too, negotiating over the rights of neutral shipping and acting as an official translator for the Spanish authorities.[41] Of the early arrivals in Cuba, some were army officers and administrators, often royalists, who had deserted from the republican cause as they lost faith with the

---

[39] List of those taking the oath of loyalty in the Eastern Province of Cuba (Santiago de Cuba), 1808, reproduced in Alain Yacou, 'L'émigration à Cuba des colons français de Saint-Domingue au cours de la Révolution' (thèse de 3e cycle, Université de Bordeaux-3, 1975), 624–44.

[40] Agnès Renault, *D'une île rebelle à une île fidèle: les Français de Santiago de Cuba, 1791–1825* (Rouen: Publications des Universités de Rouen et du Havre, 2012), 475.

[41] Ibid., 105.

Revolution. They were easy to integrate, as were the richer planters, anxious for their future, who had left Saint-Domingue at the first sign of trouble. Typical of this wave of refugees was Jean Delaunay, originally from Bordeaux, who fled Saint-Domingue in 1791 to establish a coffee plantation at Callajabos.[42] A later arrival was Jacques-Philippe-Guillaume Tornézy from La Rochelle, who as a young man had settled with his family in Saint-Domingue, where they lived through the horrors of the 1790s. Using his correspondence, Gabriel Debien has followed his wanderings through the Atlantic world. In 1802 he reported that his life's work in Cul-de-Sac was at risk because of the wanton violence of maroons on the plain around his property. In the following year he was forced to flee with his wife and young family to start afresh in Cuba, determined 'to get back to work in this country until the fate of the colony in Saint-Domingue is settled, one way or another'. He found the land he required without much trouble; more difficult was the search for men to work it. Interestingly, he did not look to newly arrived slave ships from Africa, but to his own community, other French plantation owners who, like himself, had fled from Saint-Domingue. And by 1808 he was beginning to exude confidence as he noted the beginnings of something approaching prosperity.[43]

The French had been well received in Cuba, not least in their destination of choice, Santiago de Cuba, which had shown itself appreciative of the economic benefits which their presence bestowed. For Santiago owed a lot to French settlers, a debt that exceeded the injection of wealth from the new coffee plantations and that reflected its transformation from a rural city into a sizable colonial capital. The arrival of the French coincided with two major building projects that reflected the city's new status: the construction of a colonial governor's residence and of a new cathedral to replace the one destroyed in the earthquake of 1766. The French played their professional part, too, with men from Bordeaux and the south-west, like Lestapis, Chaigneau, and Casamayor, prominent in every aspect of the city's life, commercial and cultural, as well as contributing to its architecture and town planning.[44] Their arrival coincided with a renaissance of taste and refinement and a new consciousness of their heritage and their eastern Cuban identity. They ensured that their children were taught by tutors from Caen and Bordeaux; they decorated their houses with doors and windows of neo-classical design and with iron balconies reminiscent of those in Bordeaux; they even founded a theatre and a café-concert like those to be found in French cities. The civilization they brought

[42] Alain Yacou, 'Francophobie et francophilie au temps des révolutions française et haïtienne', in *Cuba et la France: Actes du Colloque de Bordeaux* (Pessac: Presses Universitaires de Bordeaux, 1983), 64.

[43] Gabriel Debien, 'De Saint-Domingue à Cuba avec une famille de réfugiés, 1800–1809', *Revue de la Faculté d'Ethnologie de Port-au-Prince*, 8 (1964), 18–20.

[44] Lamore and Monnar, *Formation d'une ville caraïbe*, 12.

was nostalgically French in style and symbolism.[45] Their presence was seen as a benefit by the Spanish-speaking majority, especially by the richer Cuban planters, but there were political motives for receiving them, too. Some among the Cuban leadership had not abandoned the hope that by weakening Saint-Domingue they could make Cuba the richest plantation state in the Caribbean. A few may still have dreamt of recovering Haiti for the Spanish crown.[46] When the Haitian republic was declared, Cuba made no move to give it official recognition.

In 1808, however, politics intervened incisively when Napoleon declared war on Spain and invaded the Iberian Peninsula, forcing the Bourbon king from the throne and replacing him with his brother Joseph, and forging a new alliance between the Spanish Bourbons and Great Britain. When news of Napoleon's invasion reached Havana, and of the reprisals that had followed the massacre of French soldiers in Madrid on the Dos Maios, the warm welcome that had been extended to the French suddenly dissipated, as the presence of 10,000 enemy nationals in Cuba's second city became seen as a threat and anti-French rhetoric and patriotic sentiment quickly surfaced. The French, it seemed, were incapable of good, and the same authorities who had welcomed them as slave-owners on the plantations now attacked them for the mistreatment of their slaves. They were attacked for their lack of Christian piety, their atheism, and their contempt for marriage. They represented a threat to moral values, men who, in the words of the Havana governor, 'make slaves work on festival days, do not baptise them, or instruct them in our holy religion'.[47] And though many were induced to take loyalty oaths to the Spanish Crown, they were suspected of undermining Spain's authority on the island. In March the Captain-General informed people in Havana of the French invasion of Spain, and warned of its consequences for Cuba. Some French immigrants, he claimed, had assumed 'the arms of seduction and corruption...to facilitate their infernal plans for the island'; and three days later, in response to popular anger, he ordered the expulsion of the French from Cuba. Rioting and looting followed, as excited mobs in Havana and across Cuba gathered to taunt and abuse French settlers at their homes and in bars and workshops. Families to whom they had offered protection were now, because of events across the Atlantic world, threatened and intimidated, and Cubans of Spanish origin raised funds to help fight Napoleon back home. The French were obvious and accessible targets. By the end of 1809, the French émigrés in Cuba's eastern province had largely left the island, leaving those who remained to blend in as best they could with Cuban society and culture.[48]

[45] Ibid., 60–2.   [46] Yacou, 'Francophobie et francophilie', 60.

[47] Matt D. Childs, '"The Revolution against the French": Race and Patriotism in the 1809 Riot in Havana', in Christophe Belaubre et al., Napoleon's Atlantic, 127.

[48] Ibid., 136.

If they were to stay, they had to pass various tests imposed by the authorities and answer to the surveillance committees (*juntes de vigilance*) that were set up in all towns with sizable French populations. Those who had become naturalized, or who had married Cuban women and had children by them, had little trouble in establishing their right to stay. Frenchmen who had been in Cuba since before the Revolution were favourably treated. They were deemed to have residency rights, as were soldiers who had fought with the British against revolutionary France. The others—and they were the great majority of the *colons*—were ordered to leave, even if not all were thrown out immediately. Some looked for ways of changing their status by seeking last-minute naturalization or taking an oath of loyalty to the Spanish monarchy in the hope of being granted a stay of execution. But for the majority, as the papers of the vigilance committee in Havana make clear, there was to be no reprieve: of 482 French applicants, only 106 were given permission to stay. Some 90 per cent of those whose cases were reviewed had come from Saint-Domingue during the years of troubles, mostly from the north of the island, but of their place of origin in France we know much less. If they mentioned a birthplace it was at their own discretion, and only sixty-three in this sample did so. Many were just marked as being from 'France'; but we know a more precise place of origin in a few cases (five were from Nantes, four each from Paris and Bordeaux, two from Marseille). To the Cuban authorities it was a more recent identity—their link with Haiti and its turbulent past—that mattered most.[49]

Forced to move on yet again, the wandering French population had to decide where to move next. Some, once again, were tempted back to France, disillusioned by the vagrant lifestyle that had been forced upon them. But most preferred to stay in the Americas, and for them the most obvious destination was the United States, and especially Louisiana, the former French colony which Napoleon had sold to the US government six years earlier. As a French and Spanish possession in the later eighteenth century, Louisiana had attracted relatively few settlers, and the territory was eager for economic development, welcoming the idea of an influx of French planters who could help grow its population and open up the lands along the Lower Mississippi valley. In the 1780s it had rarely been the first choice of French refugees fleeing Saint-Domingue. They had preferred to move to other destinations; Santiago de Cuba, Kingston, Santo Domingo in the Caribbean, or to cities along the eastern seaboard of the United States.[50] But after 1803 Louisiana's moment appeared to have come, generally as a second destination for French families who had already spent several years of exile elsewhere. In 1809 especially,

---

[49] Gabriel Debien, 'Réfugiés de Saint-Domingue expulsés de La Havane en 1809', *Anuario de Estudios Americanos*, 35 (1978), 571.

[50] Nathalie Dessens, *From Saint-Domingue to New Orleans: Migration and Influences* (Gainesville: University Press of Florida, 2007), 21.

migrants flocked in to New Orleans, many from Santiago de Cuba, and they made the city the pivotal point of a Saint-Domingue diaspora across the Atlantic world.

In this spirit the governor, William Claiborne, welcomed the refugees from Cuba who flocked to Louisiana in 1809, chartering ships to bring them from Havana to New Orleans and agreeing with the US President that they be viewed as a special case in view of the miseries they had suffered.[51] But he was soon overwhelmed by numbers, with at least 6,000 Creoles descending on the city within a few weeks, and in August 1809 he wrote to the Mayor of New Orleans, James Mather, to express his alarm. Though French refugees had been warmly received, he noted, 'their number is becoming so considerable as to embarrass our own citizens', adding that he would 'render a service to such of the French as may not yet have departed from Cuba by advising them to seek an asylum in some other district of the United States'. There was another problem, too, and one that would be replicated in all the states to which migrants came. The migrants they were happy to receive were white, and preferably affluent, with money to invest. 'As regards the people of colour who have arrived hence from Cuba,' wrote Claiborne, 'the Women and Children have been received. But the males above the age of fifteen have ... been ordered to depart. I must request you, Sir, to make know this circumstance, and also to discourage free people of Colour of every description from migrating to the Territory of Orleans. We have already a much greater proportion of that population than comports with the general Interest.'[52] Just as in Cuba, the reputation of 'men of colour' for violence and insubordination made them unwelcome in Louisiana, as it did throughout the states of the eastern seaboard.

The sheer scale of the migration and the suddenness with which refugees arrived in New Orleans posed problems for the authorities. In the course of 1809, fifty-five vessels arrived from Cuba loaded with refugees: forty-eight of them were from Santiago, six from Baracoa, the other from Havana. Between them they brought at least 6,060 French refugees, all expelled at short notice from Cuba and many of them destitute.[53] In June the Secretary of State, Robert Smith, reported that on a single day a fleet of vessels had arrived from Santiago with nearly 2,000 refugees on board, who, after escaping from Saint-Domingue, now found themselves forced to seek sanctuary once more. In all, there were 1,975 people, 666 of them white settlers and their wives and children, 626 free people of colour, and 683 slaves. It was an enormous number to assimilate at one time, especially since many would be dependent on local charities for weeks, sometimes

[51] Ibid., 582.

[52] William Claiborne, letter to James Mather, mayor of New Orleans, 9 August 1809, in Dunbar Rowland (ed.), *The Official Letterbook of W.C.C. Claiborne, 1801–1816* (6 vols., Jackson MS, 1917), vol. 4, 401–2.

[53] Winston C. Babb, 'French refugees from Saint-Domingue to the southern United States, 1791–1810' (PhD, University of Virginia, 1954), 76.

months, after reaching the United States.[54] The arrival of so many slaves from another colony created legal dilemmas, too.

The United States had abolished the slave trade, but not the institution of slavery, in 1807, which caused some consternation among the Louisiana officials. In the states of the eastern seaboard it was left to the state authorities to decide their fate, but Louisiana was still a 'territory' and had not yet been incorporated as a state, and the territorial legislature had not yet made any provisions for implementing the law.[55] It was therefore left to the federal government to decide what the law meant for the migrants from Cuba. The legal situation here was further complicated by Spanish legislation in the 1790s, when the New Orleans *Cabildo* had expressly forbidden the import of slaves from the French sugar islands. But the law had been widely ignored, and had been revised in 1800; but now that Louisiana was American, did this have any relevance?[56]

Black slaves arrived with their masters in large numbers in 1809, and some among them were alone and without resource. Should they be admitted? How should they be looked after? And whose responsibility should they be? Smith pointed to a decision by Congress that seemed to allow for them to be returned to their masters, but where masters were unable to prove their ownership of the slaves, their future was uncertain, and many were held captive in the holds of the ships until decisions could be taken on their future. Even where the masters could legitimately prove ownership, uncertainties remained, and the relative silence about the attempts of white exiles to bring their slaves to the colony is striking.[57] The slaves themselves were often aware of the tenuous legal position, and some petitioned for their freedom, arguing that since their servitude had been legalized under French or Spanish law, nothing had been determined about the terms of enslavement that should apply in Louisiana. A simple transfer was not a foregone conclusion. And where the exiles appeared to be benefiting from advantageous conditions, this caused anger among the American population. As Claiborne noted in a letter to Smith, 'if you should give yourself the trouble to read the newspapers of this place, you will perceive that the asylum afforded here to the unfortunate exiles from Cuba continues a cause of great complaint against me.'[58] Whatever it did, it seemed, the legislature risked unleashing a hostile reaction.

There was, of course, a settled Francophone population in Louisiana, many of them of long standing, having arrived around 1755 from Acadia and the St Lawrence estuary to escape persecution. Frenchmen had also arrived during the

[54] AD Gironde, 73J 44, letter to Claiborne from Robert Smith, Secretary of State, 20 June 1809.
[55] Ashli White, 'A flood of impure lava: Saint-Dominguan refugees in the United States, 1791–1820' (PhD thesis, Columbia University, 2003), 255.
[56] Babb, 'French refugees from Saint-Domingue', 73.
[57] White, 'A flood of impure lava', 253.
[58] William Claiborne, letter to Robert Smith, 5 August 1809, in Rowland (ed.), *The Official Letter-book of W.C.C. Claiborne*, vol. 4, 400.

Revolution, both directly from France and from Saint-Domingue, although their motives and political persuasions—ranging from extreme radicalism to visceral royalism—had made them a problem for the authorities and for the French consular service in Philadelphia and across the nation.[59] Some did not hide their disappointment on seeing New Orleans for the first time: the city's population in 1803 was no more than 8,000, education and cultural provision were underdeveloped, and there was little of the urbanity that characterized life in Le Cap. The new wave of migrants had to adjust to a city undergoing rapid expansion and plagued with disease and crime; as the twenty-year correspondence of Jean Boze and his fellow-refugee Henri de Sainte-Gême makes clear, they faced constant dangers and threats to health and life: 'extreme climatic conditions, disease and mortality, fires, criminality, violence, and the many accidents the city endured'.[60] Or else they moved out of New Orleans to the rural hinterland, where many established plantations and bought slaves, and settled into a distinctly French style of living. They remained intensely conscious of their French identity, but also of shared roots in Saint-Domingue, corresponding with friends across the Caribbean and with refugees elsewhere in the United States, and holding regular meetings in bars and cafés, like the fittingly named Café des Réfugiés in New Orleans, which they made their own.[61]

In official registers, a number made specific reference to their place of origin, a place where they still had family and may still have thought of as home. A few examples will suffice to illustrate the wide range of trajectories they had followed. Jean Langouran was from Bordeaux and for some years traded with Saint-Domingue, where he acquired a plantation employing forty slaves; in 1785 he had moved with his wife and family to New Orleans in the hope of greater commercial success, but had been forced on again, this time to Honduras.[62] Another Bordelais, Pierre-Louis Berquin-Duvallon, had come to the Americas to claim the family plantations in southern Saint-Domingue, where he became royal prosecutor in the seneschal court at Le Cap. He moved subsequently to Louisiana to escape the violence on the island, but immediately hit problems when he tried to bring his slaves. They were promptly arrested, as it was against the law to bring slaves from Haiti into America, and Berquin-Duvallon found himself facing financial ruin and unwanted judicial entanglements.[63] The transfer to the mainland United States was not always problem-free.

---

[59] Laurent Letertre, 'Le consulat de Philadelphie et la question de Saint-Domingue, 1793–1803' (mémoire de maîtrise, Université de Nantes, 2000), 16.

[60] Historic New Orleans Collection, MSS 100, Sainte-Gême Family Papers; Nathalie Dessens, *Creole City: A Chronicle of Early American New Orleans* (Gainesville: University Press of Florida, 2015), 30–1.

[61] Dessens, *From Saint-Domingue to New Orleans*, 49.

[62] Gabriel Debien and René Le Gardeur, 'The Saint-Domingue refugees in Louisiana, 1792–1804', in Brasseaux and Conrad, *The Road to Louisiana*, 140.

[63] Ibid., 167.

If New Orleans was the most popular destination for French migrants in the early nineteenth century, it was far from alone in welcoming French refugees during the years of turbulence in Saint-Domingue. From the early 1790s, the United States was seen as a land of refuge for Frenchmen, both those fleeing the Revolution at home and those under attack in the French Caribbean. Colonies of French exiles formed in a number of east-coast ports, some setting up in commerce or shipping, but the majority forced to seek employment in manual trades or throwing themselves on the charity of local people. Charleston, Savannah, Baltimore, and Norfolk Virginia all had important French-speaking communities, as did the capital, Philadelphia, cities that became natural choices for those fleeing murder and civil strife in Saint-Domingue. Many knew little English and craved conversation in French; in Charleston we know that there were five separate attempts in these years to set up French-language newspapers, though two of them seem never to have appeared, and ultimately they all failed. Those editors about whom something is known were themselves former *colons* in Saint-Domingue who sought support from fellow refugees; but they failed to find enough subscribers, itself a symptom of the transient nature of their stay in Charleston.[64]

For many the voyage to America, whether directly from Saint-Domingue or after an interlude in Cuba, was the final segment of a tortured journey that had begun on a ship on the Loire or the Garonne. Those who settled in Charleston may be taken as typical in this regard: among the merchants, ships' captains, administrators and their wives who formed the majority of their number, recent research has identified twenty-six whose place of birth is given as one of the port cities of France's west coast. Twelve had been born in Bordeaux, seven in Nantes, and a further seven in La Rochelle. The oldest had been born in 1726, the youngest in 1786, sixty years later. A few had arrived as prisoners from Saint-Domingue, victims of the state of war in the Caribbean. And they had entered the United States by very different routes, through New Orleans, Philadelphia—at the time the country's temporary capital—or in one case, Providence, as well as directly into Charleston itself.[65] For the majority of those who had begun their odyssey in Nantes or Bordeaux, the United States was the end of a long, often turbulent passage.

Their challenge, of course, was now to make their way in America, and to provide financial independence for themselves and their families in a new environment to which they had not intended to come. Many found it difficult, and they were often seen by those already resident in the ports where they landed as a target

---

[64] James W. Hagy and Bertrand Van Ruymbeke, 'The French refugee newspapers of Charleston', *South Carolina Historical Magazine*, 97/2 (1996), 139–44.

[65] I wish to express my gratitude to Syrine Farhat, who kindly allowed me to cite these conclusions from her research on French immigration into Charleston.

for charity rather than a source of commerce. Like any refugees, they were distressed people in need of help, with harrowing tales to tell. Marie Sauton, for instance, had suffered at every stage of a traumatic journey that had started in Lyon. With another Lyonnais, Jean-Baptiste Audin, she had come to Port-au-Prince to go into business, setting up a shop selling perfumes, ladies' dresses, and other luxury articles before disaster struck. Audin had gone on ahead to Havana with the most valuable articles from the shop as a precaution against attack, and she had intended to follow. But on his return journey the ship on which he was a passenger had been captured by 'the black brigands of Saint-Domingue', and all the passengers, Audin among them, had been massacred. She had then left Saint-Domingue in panic, taking the rest of her stock with her, on a Spanish schooner bound for Cuba, but it had been captured by an English frigate, and, she claimed, 'we were all inhumanly despoiled and robbed of all we possessed'.[66] In Santiago she had met and married another French exile, Jean Augustin, a coffee planter originally from Chinon, near Tours. Now in the United States, she sought, for a second time, to make a fresh start.[67]

The first response of American cities to the arrival of French refugee families was often the offer of alms. As early as February 1794 Congress allocated 10,000 dollars 'for the relief of certain inhabitants of Santo Domingo', suggesting that each state should set up a committee of 'humane persons' and others of a philanthropic disposition to allocate the money to 'such of the inhabitants of St. Domingo resident within the United States as shall be found in want of support'.[68] But it did not take Congress to get the process started; the sight of suffering had already moved local people to charitable activity. In Charleston Daniel DeSaussure assured Edmund Randolph in Philadelphia that they had already established a local committee, and had collected 12,500 dollars for charitable giving (the allocation from Congress added a further 1750 dollars for the state of South Carolina). This, he told Randolph, 'has been nearly distributed amongst about 430 people, in supplying them with clothing, blankets and firewood during the winter and in a regular distribution of a certain weekly allowance in money according to the number in families and circumstances'. The people currently in receipt of charity, he added, were around a hundred women and children, as well as 'a few old and sick men' who had first call on funds.[69] Their problems would not be resolved overnight, and the challenge of providing relief for French refugees who arrived penniless in the Carolinas would last well into the nineteenth century.

[66] Tulane University, MS 223, Augustin, Wogan and Labranche Family Papers, extract from the records of the Secretariat of the French Government in Santiago de Cuba, 15 ventôse 12.

[67] Tulane University, MS 223, contracts of sale for Augustin's coffee plantations in Santiago de Cuba, 9 July 1809.

[68] South Carolina Historical Society, MS 1022/11/121/5, DeSaussure Family Papers, letter from Edmund Randolph to Daniel DeSaussure, 27 February 1794.

[69] South Carolina Historical Society, MS 1022/11/121/5, letter from Daniel DeSaussure to Edmund Randolph, 9 April 1794.

In 1816, a Société Française de Bienfaisance was founded by concerned citizens, men who were themselves in many cases refugees from Saint-Domingue or whose families had come as Huguenots at the end of the seventeenth century. The record books of the society continue until 1994, by which time it had evolved into a friendly society for the French community in Charleston.[70]

Some did more than give money, especially during the 1790s when alarmist tales reached America about the slave insurrection in Saint-Domingue. A Baltimore merchant, Duncan McIntosh, who had become rich trading with the French army in the Caribbean, was honoured by the *émigré* community in the city for his success in bribing black officials in Le Cap to enable Creole planters to escape.[71] Various land schemes were devised that sought French refugees to open up territory in the interior, some of them of a charitable nature. But not all went as planned. The ill-fated village of Azilum in the Susquehanna valley in Pennsylvania, for example, was the brainchild of General Louis de Noailles, the brother-in-law of Lafayette, who saw it as a refuge for royalists and liberals fleeing the vengeance of French Revolutionary justice. But over time its focus changed, as many of the royalists returned to France to serve Napoleon and Azilum became a refuge for planters' families from Saint-Domingue.[72] In 1794 it had become an incorporated company, the Azilum Company, backed by two of Pennsylvania's foremost politicians, John Nicholson and Robert Morris; as the articles of agreement make clear, the parties had 'entered into an association or company with the purpose of settling or improving one or more tracts of country within the state of Pennsylvania'.[73] The project, not untypically, ended in failure when it emerged that the company that was selling the shares had not established its rights to the land in law, and the scheme became mired in allegations of corruption.[74]

The most famous champion of refugees from Saint-Domingue was the Philadelphia banker and philanthropist, Stephen Girard, who maintained an assiduous correspondence with other families from the colony, offering them assistance, advising them on trading conditions, helping them find work, and offering loans from his bank so that they could set up in business. Girard was himself from Bordeaux, a ship's captain who had served his apprenticeship on merchantmen between Bordeaux and Le Cap and who—as Etienne Girard—had become American almost by chance when his ship was forced aground at the mouth of the

---

[70] South Carolina Historical Society, MS 0294.00, Records of the Société Française de Bienfaisance, Charleston, 1816–1994.

[71] Ashli White, *Encountering Revolution: Haiti and the Making of the Early Republic*, 83.

[72] Elsie Murray, *Azilum: French Refugee Village on the Susquehanna* (Athens, PA: Tioga Point Museum, 1956), 20.

[73] Historical Society of Pennsylvania, AM 820, Asylum Company minute book, 1794, share certificate dated 9 June 1794.

[74] Historical Society of Pennsylvania, MSS 21, Asylum Company, 1794, correspondence.

Delaware River by a British cruiser in 1776.[75] By the time of the Napoleonic Wars, he was a successful merchant and ship-owner in Philadelphia and had taken American citizenship, had established a huge fortune in trade with the West Indies and Northern Europe, and would go on to be heavily involved in America's lucrative far eastern trade.[76] For French exiles in Philadelphia, he was more than a source of information about the state of Saint-Domingue and of advice on when it might be safe for them to return.[77] He was, more generally, a friend and benefactor to the exile community in America, and a founder member of the Philadelphia branch of the Société Française de Bienfaisance.[78] By the time of his death in 1831, he had become one of the richest men in America, but he remained staunchly loyal to his roots and to his friends. Acquaintances from Bordeaux would seek his assistance when they first arrived in America, and he gave what help he could, employing his ships' captains, plying to and from ports across Europe and the Caribbean, as a rich source of news.[79] And so, when Saint-Domingue went up in flames, Girard sent ships to the island to bring the survivors to the United States, contributing to the flotilla of more than forty vessels that cleared Philadelphia alone in May and June 1794.[80] Though fully immersed in the world of American commerce, he remained well integrated in a wider Francophone community. Even in 1805 he still noted, approvingly, and with just a suggestion of nostalgia, that in Philadelphia 'one would find, daily, opportunities to speak French'.[81]

[75] Max Dorian, *Un Bordelais: Stephen Girard, premier millionnaire américain* (Paris: Éditions Albatros, 1977).

[76] Donald R. Adams Jr, *Finance and Enterprise in Early America: A Study of Stephen Girard's Bank, 1812–31* (Philadelphia: University of Pennsylvania Press, 1978), 6.

[77] American Philosophical Society, Philadelphia, Stephen Girard Papers, letters 1793: 305, 311, 349.

[78] Stephen Girard Papers, letters 1805: 295; 1807: 299.

[79] Stephen Girard Papers, letters 1801: 164; 1804: 383.

[80] James Alexander Dun, *Dangerous Neighbours: Making the Haitian Revolution in Early America* (Philadelphia: University of Pennsylvania Press, 2016), 7.

[81] White, *Encountering Revolution*, 38.

11
Economic Stagnation and Decay

The early years of the Revolution were years of lobbying and petitioning for the merchant communities of the French Atlantic as they tried to persuade the assemblies in Paris of the importance of Atlantic commerce and France's continued presence in colonial markets. Much of their anxiety was focused on the slave trade and on the implications of revolutionary ideology for commercial prosperity. Many among them, as we have seen, were deeply pessimistic about what the future would hold, especially should revolutionary France become embroiled in another colonial war with England and the sea routes to the Americas be threatened. But these were worries for the future, and in the first years of the Revolution there seemed little reason for their doom-laden prognoses. Most merchants welcomed the abolition of company monopolies and the opening up of the Atlantic to free trade. Between 1789 and 1793, the port of Marseille handled around 3,000 merchant ships each year; before Saint-Domingue was lost, Bordeaux sent some 200 ships each year to the colonies; and in Nantes the number of vessels leaving for the Caribbean continued to rise, year on year.[1] Indeed, in 1792 the port of Nantes recorded its highest levels of commercial activity and shipping movements, with some 230 vessels fitted out for the high seas.[2] As yet, there was little to suggest that the revolutionary years would condemn the city to years of stagnation and decline.

Slaving ports continued to fit out voyages to West Africa during the first years of the Revolution, before slave violence and plantation burning destroyed the market for slaves. Captives continued to be taken from West Africa to the Caribbean, and the vast majority of them, around 90 per cent, were delivered for sale in Basse-Terre or Le Cap, where they were sold at a profit.[3] We have very few accounts of individual voyages in these years, but the few ships' logs that do survive give little hint of an impending crisis. Most voyages continued to follow the traditional route between the French coast, West Africa and Saint-Domingue, but some were more complex, with vessels remaining at sea for many months

---

[1] Philippe Haudrère, 'La Révolution de 1789 et la flotte de commerce française', *Académie de Marine, communications et mémoires*, 1989/3, 47; Karine Audran, 'Les armements de Nantes et Saint-Malo sous la Révolution, le Consulat et l'Empire', in Silvia Marzagalli and Bruno Marnot (eds), *Guerre et économie dans l'espace atlantique du 16ᵉ au 20ᵉ siècle* (Bordeaux: Presses Universitaires de Bordeaux, 2006), 256.

[2] Olivier Pétré-Grenouilleau, *Nantes: histoire et géographie contemporaine*, 128.

[3] Nathalie Touzeau, 'Étude des expéditions négrières nantaises sous la Révolution Française au temps des Droits de l'Homme' (2 vols, *mémoire de maîtrise*, Université de Nantes, 1993), vol. 2, 10.

without regard for the changed political situation at home. A good instance is the *Patriote*, a slave ship fitted out by the Bordeaux firm of Journu *frères*, which left Bordeaux in 1788 on what turned out to be a long and gruelling voyage, under three different captains over a period of twenty-seven months. The voyage, as recorded in the ship's *journal de bord*, was a sort of tour of France's eighteenth-century empire. From France it sailed east into the Indian Ocean, calling at Pondichéry and the delta of the Ganges, apparently in defiance of the East India Company monopoly, before continuing to the Île Bourbon (Réunion) to load a cargo of slaves, whom it transported on a horribly long passage to the Caribbean, first calling at the Cape of Good Hope to take on food and water before continuing across the Atlantic to land at Martinique and finally at Saint-Domingue. The ship was battered by heavy seas that flooded the cargo deck, and the captives were afflicted by extreme cold in the southern African winter, factors which, when taken along with the number of weeks spent at sea, contributed to an unusually high death rate among the 216 Africans on board—28.5 per cent, which compared with an average of around 8 per cent for the 1790s, or 13.25 per cent for the entire period of the Atlantic slave trade. Scurvy was the major scourge on board, accounting for the deaths of forty-one of the sixty-one slaves who died on board. In contrast, and rather untypically for slaving voyages in the eighteenth century, the ship's crew survived the voyage without loss, to return to Bordeaux in 1791.[4]

The early Revolution may even have helped expand Atlantic trade by opening up opportunities for independent merchants. But some were already expressing unease at the speed of growth and fears that the economic bubble would burst. One such was the young merchant Benoît Lacombe, who had moved to Bordeaux from his native Gaillac during the last years of the monarchy. Though, like others from the interior regions of the country, he had been attracted to the Atlantic coast by the promise of huge profits, Bordeaux's very affluence aroused his anxiety that the city might have expanded too fast and that its wealth was built on fragile foundations. 'Fragile' was the word that came immediately to his mind when he talked of the merchant economy, a fragility that distinguished it from the towns and cities of the interior. Bordeaux, he believed, was 'a proud colonial city' that had grown too rapidly on the promise of future profits that might never materialize, and he contrasted this with what he took to be the substance of inland cities with a strong agricultural base. 'The upland areas of the interior,' he mused, 'the Quercy, the Rouergue, the "mountains" all descend on the merchant city in search of the precious sacks of grain which their misery has made unobtainable.' And he concluded with a strong and powerful image of Bordeaux when a food crisis

---

[4] Joël Gosnave, 'Une expédition négrière bordelaise à la fin du 18e siècle, étude du journal de bord du *Patriote* (1788–1791)', *Revue historique de Bordeaux et du département de la Gironde*, 3ᵉ série, 17 (2011), 67–91.

struck home, of 'the Atlantic city besieged by the men and women of the lands it had patiently controlled; what a strange world this is in times of crisis, as if the city had grown too big and had to answer for the state of dependency it had imposed on the entire region!'.[5] Disillusioned, he decided to return to Gaillac and the commercial world he knew.

Lacombe was unusual in predicting disaster so early in the Revolution, for the threat was not immediately apparent. For the period of constitutional monarchy was also a period of peace, and, as the merchants of the west-coast ports immediately recognized, it was the maintenance of that peace that determined their fortunes. The first hostilities, it is true, the land war launched against Austria and Prussia, had little immediate effect on the Atlantic ports. What threatened to destroy their fortunes was the declaration of war on Britain in the spring of 1793, and the resumption of the long-standing naval conflict between the North Atlantic's principal colonial powers, a war fought as much over colonies as it was over the balance of power in Europe. As with previous conflicts, it had the effect of disrupting established trade routes and reducing the profit margins on colonial commerce. And while there were particular threats to Atlantic merchant houses that stemmed from revolutionary or imperial policy—the impact of the General Maximum in 1794 and of the massive inflation of the *assignat* that followed, for example—these had only a temporary effect.[6] It was the war at sea that disrupted the Atlantic shipping lanes and blocked off France's traditional markets, cutting the Atlantic ports' links with its most productive colonies. Saint-Domingue, of course, was lost to revolution as we have seen. But the Lesser Antilles were lost to war, as the British occupied Guadeloupe and held Martinique for eight years from 1794 to 1802. To make matters worse, in an attempt to stave off food shortages and to prevent the flight of capital, the French government placed restrictions on exports. French merchant houses found themselves deprived of their traditional markets, and though the Atlantic ports registered some recovery after 1795 by using neutral shipping from Denmark, the Hanseatic ports, and the United States, this did not provide a lasting solution to their woes.[7] In so far as it is possible to separate the war from the regimes that waged it, we must conclude that it was the war with Britain that was principally responsible for their decline, ushering in a period of recession that lasted, with only short interruptions, until 1809.[8]

The war may have started in the name of revolutionary liberty, but its ideological character soon dimmed as a whole generation became embroiled in a conflict about power, colonies, and empire. The fighting continued through a

[5] Joël Cornette, *Un révolutionnaire ordinaire: Benoît Lacombe, négociant, 1759–1819* (Paris: Champ Vallon, 1986), 180.

[6] Florin Aftalion, *The French Revolution. An Economic Interpretation* (Cambridge: Cambridge University Press, 1987), 76–85.

[7] Gardey, *Négociants et marchands de Bordeaux*, 225–6.

[8] Pétré-Grenouilleau, *Nantes: histoire et géographie contemporaine*, 128.

succession of coalitions, first during the Directory, then under the Consulate and Empire, when the war dominated public policy and the economy, consuming ever-greater resources and concluding only with Napoleon's defeat in 1814. Much of the country's commercial and industrial production was diverted, yet again, to supporting the war economy, while the Atlantic coast was blockaded by the British in a counter-measure to Napoleon's Continental System, preventing the import of the very colonial goods that had formed such a substantial part of French trade. The length and scale of the war was unprecedented, and the numbers of men called upon to fight were much higher than in previous campaigns, with the draining effect of annual conscriptions more and more resented. France was increasingly wearied by war and weakened by the continued diversion of resources to feed the war economy. But the experience was troublingly familiar. Between 1689 and 1815, Britain and France had fought each other in no fewer than eight wars, and had been at war for a total of fifty-six years; and these conflicts had increasingly focused on questions of trade and colonies.[9] This was a sphere where Britain, with her strong naval tradition, was always at an advantage. It was an advantage that gave Britain the military and naval capacity to see off her rivals, and to expand her overseas empire at the expense of the French Crown.[10] It was an advantage she would exploit fully in the French revolutionary and Napoleonic Wars.

Britain had more warships than France, at times in the ratio of three to one; the Royal Navy kept a higher proportion of them at sea; and crucially, Britain had a much larger pool of skilled seamen that she could call upon in time of war.[11] During the eighteenth century Britain had won almost all her sea battles with France, largely through a wider tax base and a fiscal state which the French monarchy could not match, allowing the British government far more freedom in raising revenue to rearm or to recruit additional troops for war.[12] As a consequence, it was generally France's merchant marine that suffered more grievously from attack and arrest, and the ports that serviced it that were threatened with decline. Indeed, the only Atlantic ports that derived any material benefit from war were those where the navy was berthed, Brest and Rochefort, to which sailors from across Brittany and the west of France were drafted to defend the coasts and civilians were recruited to provide services for the navy. For Brest in

[9] François Crouzet, 'The Second Hundred Years War: some reflections', *French History*, 10 (1996), 432–50.

[10] François Crouzet, *De la supériorité de l'Angleterre sur la France: l'économie et l'imaginaire, 18e–20e siècle* (Paris: Perrin, 1985), *passim*.

[11] Jean Meyer and John Bromley, 'The Second Hundred Years War', in Douglas Johnson, François Bédarida, and François Crouzet (eds), *Britain and France: Ten Centuries* (Folkestone: Dawson, 1980), 164–9.

[12] Patrick O'Brien, 'The nature and historical evolution of an exceptional fiscal state and its possible significance for the precocious commercialization and industrialization of the British economy from Cromwell to Nelson', *Economic History Review*, 64 (2011), 408–46.

particular, the resumption of war was seen as a rare moment of economic opportunity, for its history across the long eighteenth century had been one of slow decline. In the words of the civil engineer reporting on the condition of Brest in 1784, 'The war is the only time when it is prosperous. Whereas the provinces groan under the weight of the burden on civilians, Brest is enriched and embellished through the arrival of those who flock there as crewmen on its many ships.'[13] Farther south, Rochefort would also benefit from an increase in naval investment during the Revolutionary and Napoleonic Wars, though to a lesser degree than either Brest or its Mediterranean counterpart, Toulon.

Trading ports enjoyed no such benefits. Across most of the Atlantic ports the impact of the war was both savage and immediate, as their trade lines with America were cut and bans were placed on goods imported from France. It was not only Atlantic trade that was affected: at certain moments trade within Europe was also interrupted, most notably between 1792 and 1795, when hostilities with Prussia prevented French vessels from trading with the Baltic. Similarly, when a peace was signed in 1795, there was an immediate resurgence of trade and growth in commercial profits, but this proved short-lived, as within a few years Britain would impose a continental blockade and shipping movements were again halted. The wine trade from Bordeaux and brandy exports from La Rochelle were among the businesses badly affected, with the consequence it was not only the coastline that suffered and much of the rural hinterland was condemned to recession, too. The effect on individual firms varied wildly. Some merchants ceased trading altogether, and did not resume their affairs when market conditions improved. In Bordeaux, we know of seventeen firms for whom closure was definitive, the merchants retiring to their country estates or investing in national lands to guarantee an income in their old age. Many others ceased trading in 1793, only to start up again when an opportunity presented itself.[14] In La Rochelle, for instance, as soon as the peace was signed with Prussia, trade with the Baltic resumed, and the merchants profited from it to amass capital with which to protect their investments against future calamities. In many cases, they used the money to buy new ships or to convert their existing vessels for use as privateers.[15] Bordeaux's merchants, too, rushed to renew commercial alliances with firms in northern Germany and Scandinavia, and the wine trade which had been savagely hit by the war in Europe was able to recover. In 1797, Bordeaux was once again exporting wine to the value of 14 million *livres*, and two years later exports

[13] Gérard Le Bouëdec, 'La Bretagne et la guerre: ruptures et modèles de développement économique maritime (15ᵉ – début 20ᵉ siècles)', in Marzagalli and Marnot, *Guerre et économie dans l'espace atlantique*, 218.

[14] Gardey, *Négociants et marchands de Bordeaux*, 232–4.

[15] Nicole Charbonnel, *Commerce et course sous la Révolution et le Consulat à La Rochelle: autour de deux armateurs, les frères Thomas et Pierre-Antoine Chegaray* (Paris: Presses Universitaires de France, 1977), 5.

reached more than 26 million *livres*, a figure close to the record established in 1773. Some of it even reached the British market, as neither country was inclined to end a trade which both saw as advantageous. Everyone, it seemed, was keen to resume their old, profitable ways when opportunity beckoned.[16]

The war at sea resulted in a hugely reduced volume of traffic to France's Caribbean colonies, and it was this, and the loss of the entrepôt trade that they had enjoyed for much of the century, that inflicted the most lasting damage on the west-coast ports. With the shipping lanes alive with enemy vessels and privateers, the transatlantic crossing had suddenly become much more perilous, the need to take shelter in less hospitable waters more frequent, and the risks of capture or loss correspondingly increased. These dangers deterred all but the most adventurous, including many who preferred to sail uninsured rather than pay the greatly inflated war rates for insurance cover. The insurance registers for the port of Bordeaux show the extent of the decline, showing 1086 entries in 1791, and a very similar number in 1792—here some pages of the register have been torn out— before declining during 1793 to relatively paltry figures. During the three months of the federalist crisis in the city, for instance, between July and September 1793, only twenty-three ship-owners paid to insure their vessels.[17] In part, this reflected a dramatic reduction in the number of ships setting sail for the Antilles, which was common to all the Atlantic ports following the declaration of war. But it also illustrates the exceptional costs that fell on those merchants who did continue to insure their ships and their cargoes, costs that were themselves a deterrent to investment in further cargoes. The years from 1793 to 1795 were years of despair for many in the merchant community.

Even the periods spent off-shore, in the roads off the Garonne estuary, incurred a charge, usually around 1.25 per cent of the cargo's value. But it was the rates charged to insure vessels on the high seas that fluctuated most wildly. Against the risk of damage through storms and currents—what the insurers termed 'risques de mer'—the premium by the summer of 1793 had risen to around 4.25 per cent of the sum insured, and by September merchants were being charged around 5.25 per cent to insure journeys to Cayenne or Port-au-Prince, or to Mauritius in the Indian Ocean. Voyages to the United States continued to command a rate of 4.25 per cent, though return trips, when ships were heavy with rich colonial produce, could cost more: François Bonnaffé paid 7.25 per cent for a journey from New Orleans to Bordeaux in early August. In these months, anyone venturing out to sea was seen as an insurance risk, and even the short trip down the coast from Nantes to Bordeaux was not cheap: 1.75 per cent in July, 2.75 per cent a month later. These sums did not cover the much greater risks of losses through war. A merchant seeking insurance against war loss only was charged a premium of

[16] François Crouzet, 'Bilan de faillite', in Pariset (ed.), *Bordeaux au 18ᵉ siècle*, 493–4.
[17] Bibl. Mun. Bordeaux, MSS 1570, 1582, insurance registers of the port of Bordeaux, 1791–3.

15.25 per cent; for a comprehensive 'tous risques' policy the cost was routinely around a fifth of the total sum insured, with 20.25 per cent quoted for both the Caribbean islands and the Indian Ocean. Even on the supposedly safer crossing from Philadelphia to Bordeaux, an all-risk policy could cost 15.25 per cent by late July.[18] For some these rates represented an unsustainable cost, a drain on their company's resources which they could not afford. They were a poignant reminder of the threats that all faced with every voyage they undertook.

The premiums charged were a faithful reflection of the levels of risk, as each voyage became a gamble against ever-worsening odds. Many merchants, including a number of the most prominent commercial houses in the port, deemed the risk too great, turning instead to safer forms of investment as they saw out the war years. Or else they sought to share the risk among themselves, small groups from within the business community banding together to fit out their ships collectively, or luring investors by offering shares in the venture on the financial markets of Paris or Bordeaux.[19] Merchants were increasingly forced to look for other expedients as they laid up or sold their Atlantic vessels, some turning from long-distance commerce to European trade, and from carrying colonial produce to trading in wine, timber, or textiles within Europe. Or they invested in other ventures entirely. These were years where some of the established merchant community preferred to sink their capital in property: in town houses, of course, but also in land, especially in the better vineyards and country estates. More commonly, they balanced their activity, as they had always done, investing alike in land, real estate, commerce, and privateering. They remained largely averse to risk, and were attracted by those investments that promised returns. In the context of war, land purchase was simply another form of investment.[20]

Most spectacularly, real estate sales to merchants in Bordeaux and its suburbs during 1798 and 1799 rose to three times their previous level in what can only be seen as a huge speculative bubble.[21] The profits of the slave trade were used to shore up family properties and to purchase land and buildings, which often came on to the market at attractive rates because of the government's policy on *biens nationaux*. The homes of *émigré* nobles and convicted counter-revolutionaries joined abbeys and religious houses on a suddenly inflated property market where superb properties could be acquired cheaply, and at a time when the very act of

---

[18] Bibl. Mun. Bordeaux, MS 1570, insurance register of the port of Bordeaux, entries for July–September 1793.

[19] Jean-Pierre Poussou, 'Les activités commerciales des villes françaises de 1789 à 1815', *Histoire, Économie et Société*, 1 (1993), 106.

[20] Paul Butel, 'Revolution and the Urban Economy', in Alan Forrest and Peter Jones (eds), *Reshaping France: Town, Country and Region during the French Revolution* (Manchester: Manchester University Press, 1991), 46.

[21] Paul Butel, 'Crise et mutation de l'activité économique à Bordeaux sous le Consulat et l'Empire', *Annales historiques de la Révolution française*, 199 (1970), 113.

purchasing such properties might be taken as a sign of patriotism.[22] It was not just the slaving ports, but much of the interior, regions like the Médoc, Poitou, and Anjou, where *biens nationaux* were bought up by merchants who had accumulated savings from the profits of trade. Not all, of course, were in a position to do so: mercantile fortunes differed hugely. Some of the oldest merchant houses sustained significant losses in these years, like Bouteiller, Chaurand, and Louis Drouin in Nantes, who between them lost nearly 24 million *livres*. But others made money during the Revolution and seized the opportunity to establish a presence on the Atlantic waterfront.[23]

They were the exceptions. Reports emanating from France's port cities during the revolutionary years were almost universally gloomy, portraying the war as an eternal evil from which there seemed to be no escape. No port was spared. As the *Journal du Commerce de Bordeaux* lamented in 1799, the misery of their merchants was widely shared, and the correspondence they received from other ports only confirmed their own experience. They were afflicted by losses and economic threats on all sides—'the general shortage of currency, the bankruptcy of many commercial houses, among them some of the most distinguished, the trouble caused by the British navy in all our dealings with foreign parts'.[24] The municipal authorities in La Rochelle concurred, and claimed that in 1799, after six years of war, their town 'now offers the frightening spectacle of human misery'.[25] In 1802, the commerce commission in La Rochelle added some explanation and, while expressing relief that the spectre of war had been removed, it reflected on the damage that had been done to its commercial capacity during the previous ten years. Tariffs were hindering growth, it claimed, while French merchants faced 'usurious' rates of interest at a time when their foreign competitors, in Britain and the Netherlands, did not. France's banking system was, the report insisted, uncompetitive and too inflexible to promote trade. Markets had been lost that would be difficult to recover. Most damaging, however, was the loss of Saint-Domingue, which had skewed colonial trade with the Caribbean in Britain's favour and deprived the French Atlantic of its principal resource. The merchant community wanted an end to what they condemned as the 'demagogy' of the republic on human rights and slavery, and pressed for government intervention to salvage something from the 'disaster' of Haitian independence.[26] As traders, they believed that they faced possible

---

[22] Silvia Marzagalli, *Les boulevards de la fraude: le négoce maritime et le Blocus Continental, 1806–13* (Lille: Presses Universitaires du Septentrion, 1999), 260–2.

[23] Olivier Pétré-Grenouilleau, *L'argent de la traite. Milieu négrier, capitalisme et développement: un modèle* (Paris: Aubier, 1996), 177.

[24] Gardey, *Négociants et marchands de Bordeaux*, 228.

[25] Philippe David, *Un port de l'océan sous le Directoire: La Rochelle, 1796–1799* (La Rochelle: Pijollet, 1955), 166.

[26] BM La Rochelle, 2662B, 'Mémoire de la Commission de Commerce de La Rochelle, en réponse aux Questions du Ministre de l'Intérieur, par sa lettre du 1er frimaire X'.

obliteration, a fear that would prove unduly alarmist. But their losses were real enough. And if Bordeaux, Le Havre, and Marseille managed to retain at least a proportion of their pre-war commerce through a quarter of a century of war, some of the smaller ports lost more. La Rochelle, in particular, ceased to play a major part in the national economy.[27]

Just as they had in previous wars, merchants turned to a variety of expedients to survive. Perhaps the most common of these was the use of neutral flags, since French commercial shipping was more exposed to arrest and seizure, and trading in the name of a neutral nation in wartime had a long-established and respected pedigree. During the War of American Independence, when the thirteen colonies had severed their ties with Britain, American ships had started trading with French ports to find a market for tobacco and to import the arms and manufactured goods they required for the war effort. Although the Americans returned to Britain when the war was over—they were deterred by France's policy on state monopolies and by the poor credit facilities on offer compared to London—commercial networks had been established that could be called upon again after 1793.[28] The declaration of war resulted in a revolution in the terms of trade, with first Britain, then France, abandoning their monopoly of colonial trade—in France's case, the long-contested *Exclusif*—and opening colonial ports to neutral shipping, in particular to American vessels which were best placed to profit from these markets and were eager to develop trade links with Europe's colonies.

France also encouraged direct trade by neutral shipping, and by this means kept the Atlantic open and Europe supplied with colonial goods even in the darkest years of the British blockade. Between 1795 and 1815, the pilots' register in Philadelphia lists 226 ships arriving from Bordeaux alone.[29] Whereas the Royal Navy would routinely intercept French ships on the high seas, neutrals bringing goods into French ports were seldom troubled. British warships were more interested in seizing rich cargoes from the Indies than they were in the strict implementation of a Continental blockade; starving France into surrender was not a top priority.[30] Similarly, the Revolution's expedient of creating *agences commerciales* in the west-coast ports did little to expand French trade, concentrating

---

[27] John G. Clark, *La Rochelle and the Atlantic Economy during the Eighteenth Century* (Baltimore: Johns Hopkins University Press, 1981), 225.

[28] Silvia Marzagalli, 'La mise en place d'un réseau commercial et marchand: Bordeaux et les États-Unis à la fin du 18ᵉ siècle', in Damien Coulon (ed.), *Réseaux marchands et réseaux de commerce: concepts récents, réalités historiques du Moyen Âge au 19ᵉ siècle* (Strasbourg: Presses Universitaires de Strasbourg, 2010), 92–5.

[29] Silvia Marzagalli, *Bordeaux et les États-Unis. Politique et stratégies négociantes dans la genèse d'un réseau commercial* (Geneva: Droz, 2015), 171.

[30] Pierrick Pourchasse, 'Speculations and Embargoes on the Grain Trade at the Time of the Revolutionary Wars, 1792–95', in Katherine B. Aaslestad and Johan Joor (eds), *Revisiting Napoleon's Continental System. Local, Regional and European Experiences* (Basingstoke: Palgrave Macmillan, 2015), 75–9.

instead on keeping the sea lanes open and maintaining a supply of foodstuffs to the population through the use of neutral vessels.[31]

The opening of the Atlantic to neutrals provided an enormous boost to the eastern seaboard of the United States; and for some French merchants, those willing to take risks in wartime conditions or able to produce false papers and sail under a neutral flag, the profit on a transatlantic voyage could be tempting. But the regulations on neutral status raised other problems for the trading community. How much should it cost French merchants to acquire neutral status? Which ports had they the right to enter as neutrals? What forms of trade were available to them? And, most important of all, how far would their neutrality be recognized and respected by third parties? These were among the questions that exercised French merchants during the war years, and when peace was temporarily restored in 1801 by the treaty of Amiens, and the commercial ports were asked to advise the government on the measures that would be necessary to revive the economy, these were among the issues they most frequently raised. The answers they provided were often deeply conservative as they sought to reassert rights which the Revolution had swept away. So, alongside proposals to re-establish tariffs on foreign imports and foreign shipping entering France, the newly re-established Chamber of commerce in Nantes sought advice on the future status of French ships which had been sailing as neutrals during the war years and whose captains had been obliged to pay a substantial sum for the privilege. The merchants were not pressing for innovation. They wanted to reintegrate their vessels into the French merchant fleet, and they asked for the return of the money they had paid. After the forced internationalization of the market that had come with war, they were eager to re-establish control and to reclaim exclusive access to colonial markets.[32]

Another expedient, to which reference has already been made, was privateering. With the conditions for legitimate trading so difficult, a possible route to profit, as in previous wars, lay in fitting out vessels as corsairs and mounting attacks on English merchantmen returning from the Caribbean. The French government explicitly encouraged privateering, reminding merchants on the eve of war in 1793 that it was not forbidden by any law, adding that, if hostilities broke out with any other European power, then 'every French citizen is free to do whatever his patriotism suggests is appropriate'.[33] In 1795 the Committee of Public Safety went further, specifically informing merchant firms that, given British naval superiority and the inability of the French navy to provide protection, they should think positively about arming corsairs. And so, in time-honoured fashion, many

[31] Gérard Le Bouëdec, 'Les négociants lorientais, 1740–1900', in Silvia Marzagalli and Hubert Bonin (eds), *Négoce, ports et océans, 16ᵉ–20ᵉ siècles* (Bordeaux: Presses Universitaires de Bordeaux, 2000), 105.
[32] AD Loire-Atlantique, 1 ET C3*, Chambre de Commerce de Nantes, minutes of meetings of 30 ventôse XI and 7 ventôse XII.
[33] Charbonnel, *Commerce et course*, 57.

responded by applying for the *lettres de marque* that would give them legal protection for activities that otherwise risked being classed as piracy.[34] But engaging in *la course* was not cheap, whether the captain simply armed his ship for a hazardous voyage to the Americas or, as was more usual, lurked in waters closer to home in the hope of surprising some English merchantman returning laden from the colonies. The ship-owner had to provide a caution in case of illegal captures that he would have to make good. There were extra costs involved in arming and fitting out the ship, and in employing additional crewmen to man the cannon and confront boarding parties.

There were more physical challenges, too. The vessel itself might easily be lost; indeed, a high percentage of corsairs were lost on their maiden voyage from port. The crew were risking their lives when they signed on, and they had a right to their reward, which in La Rochelle was customarily the equivalent of one-third of the overall profit from the voyage. These profits could be high, as privateers were often at sea for only a few months, lying in wait for English ships laden with cotton, spices, or indigo as they returned from Jamaica or India. But of course there was no guarantee of a financial return; the Royal Navy was vigilant, and they might face patrols along the French coastline. Skills of seamanship were required to avert danger, as ships were lost on offshore rocks as much as they were captured in the Atlantic sea lanes. A merchant had to be reasonably confident, and have adequate reserves, before he would risk everything on privateering. Patriotism was never going to supply sufficient motivation; for the merchant, as for the ship's crew, a privateering voyage was primarily an act of speculation, a game of poker in a very uncertain market.[35]

That so many merchants were tempted by privateering shows how desperate they had become, how the sort of gamble to which most of them were temperamentally averse had turned into a necessity if they were to stay in business. But the various ports reacted very differently, embracing privateering with more or less enthusiasm. In some, like La Rochelle, merchants shied away from risk, while in others, notably Saint-Malo, history and maritime tradition were tightly linked to privateering. Saint-Malo played little part in slaving or in colonial trade; its main strength was in fishing, its seamen skilled in manoeuvring small craft at speed, which made them well suited to the rigours of *la course*. With the Channel increasingly under British control, many Malouins saw privateering as the only way open to them to earn a livelihood at sea, and between 1793 and 1800 they are reckoned to have earned a profit of several million francs.[36] Out of 722 French corsairs registered between 1796 and 1801, La Rochelle fitted out only twelve,

[34] Forrest, *The Revolution in Provincial France: Aquitaine*, 256–8.

[35] Charbonnel, *Commerce et course*, 68–70.

[36] Karine Audran, 'Les armements de Nantes et Saint-Malo sous la Révolution, le Consulat et l'Empire: crise ou transition?', in Marzagalli and Marnot, *Guerre et économie dans l'espace atlantique*, 256–9.

which did little to enhance the performance of the port. In contrast, privateers clustered in ports close to international borders, like Dunkirk in the north or Bayonne, close to the Spanish frontier, which sent out thirty-five vessels in 1798 and a further twenty-four the following year. Bordeaux, too, had merchants prepared to take the risk of fitting out their ships for war—a total of 163 of them between 1796 and the return of peace after Amiens in 1801.[37] And in Nantes, where the collapse of the slave trade gave privateering a short-term boost, 132 ships were fitted out for *la course* in these years, though this did little to restore the port's fortunes. Nantes remained largely becalmed, with the consequence that by 1802 its international profile had been largely lost. From being a flourishing entrepôt for colonial produce, Nantes was reduced to exporting regional goods from Brittany and the Pays de Loire, textiles and leather hides, wine, butter, and honey.[38] Bordeaux, too, was increasingly engaged in regional rather than global trading.

The accounts of foreign merchants, diplomats, and visitors to the Atlantic ports leave little to the imagination. When the Hamburg merchant Philippe-André Nemnich landed at Bordeaux in 1809, he was aghast at the scene of desolation that confronted him, a vista of deserted quays and silent streets, in a city where nothing moved.[39] But he provided few details. The American consul in Bordeaux, also writing in 1809, was more forthcoming about the state of decay. There was, he said 'nothing but despair and misery' in trading circles, before continuing: 'Grass is growing in the streets of this city. Its beautiful port is deserted except for two Marblehead fishing schooners and three or four empty vessels which swing on the tide.'[40] One traveller who did leave a substantial record of his stay was the German pastor Lorenz Meyer, who undertook the overland journey from Paris to Bordeaux in the summer of 1801. The buildings still stood, proud and solid, along the quays from the Chapeau-Rouge to the Chartrons. The port continued to be busy with shipping, he noted, but with foreign ships importing their produce, not the Bordeaux fleet that had once dominated the commerce of the city. His impressions were necessarily clouded by the rapid decline of trade, the number of merchant houses that had been ruined or forced out of business, the smell of decline on every side. Meyer does not hide his sense of loss. 'The antique splendour of Bordeaux is no more,' he lamented; 'It is clear wherever you look. The Stock Exchange is still thronged with merchants but most of them are just there out of habit. Business is rare. The internal trade in wine is the only one not to

---

[37] Paul Butel, 'L'armement en course à Bordeaux sous la Révolution et l'Empire', *Revue historique de Bordeaux et du département de la Gironde*, NS 15 (1966), 54.

[38] Pétré-Grenouilleau, *Nantes*, 129.

[39] Odette Viennet, *Une enquête économique dans la France impériale: le voyage du hambourgeois Philippe-André Nemnich, 1809* (Paris: Plon, 1947), 84–95; Patrick Crowhurst, *The French War on Trade: Privateering, 1793–1815* (Aldershot: Scolar Press, 1989), 20.

[40] Crouzet, 'Wars, blockade and economic change in Europe', 571n.

have disappeared.' This is largely, he suggests, because wine merchants can diversify their activities and sell other products to eke out their business. This war, he inferred, had not been like the earlier wars of the eighteenth century, from which the ports had rapidly recovered. Once-proud *négociants* and ships' captains now avoided ruin by seeking out cargoes of fruit to supplement their income. His voice is tinged with regret as he poses the question, rhetorically and with a touch of disdain, 'in former times, who would have gone out of their way to get commission on the sale of plums?'[41] Who, indeed? But now, he infers, the situation has changed. France's wealth and prosperity are under threat. The values that had sustained economic growth are no longer respected by the new political class. Who, he implies, has any choice but to survive as best he can in a world where trade and commercial well-being have been sacrificed to revolution and war?

There is little reason to doubt that the years from 1790 to 1815 spelt decline not only for many Atlantic merchants but also for the wider communities whose livelihoods they supported. As Jean-Pierre Poussou has pointed out, trade was essentially an urban activity, and it was the cities that suffered most critically during the Revolution and Empire. Cities that had acted as a magnet for the populations of surrounding regions for much of the eighteenth century saw migration cease as the Revolution ushered in an era of population decline and economic retrenchment: between 1790 and 1801 the population of Paris fell from 620,000 inhabitants to fewer than 550,000; of Lyon from 150,000 to around 102,000; of Bordeaux from 120,000 to 93,000.[42] And for those left in the cities, not least the Atlantic ports, unemployment soared as local industries contracted and closed. The 1811 industrial enquiry on Bordeaux shows the extent of the city's decline. Whereas in 1790 there had been thirty sugar refineries, by 1811 there were only nine, and they employed only fifty workers compared to 450 on the eve of the Revolution. It was the same story in the rope works, where the number of factories was halved and the workforce cut from 900 in 1790 to only forty. The story in Nantes was similar. The manufacture of highly coloured *indiennages*, the textiles so prized by African traders, which had employed 2,000 workers in 1792, provided work for only 270 in 1799. With the return of peace in 1801, prosperity briefly returned, with five works employing 1,300 people; but again the boom was cut short by the resumption of war. In 1806 the three factories that were still open provided employment for only 160 workers, and by 1812 only two mills and thirty workers remained. Cotton-printing, a trade that had been sustained by African markets during the boom years of slaving, had been almost completely wiped

---

[41] Maurice Meaudre de Lapouyade, 'Impressions d'un Allemand à Bordeaux en 1801', *Revue historique de Bordeaux*, 5 (1912), 169–70.

[42] Jean-Pierre Poussou, 'Révolution de 1789. Guerres et croissance économique', *Revue économique*, 40, 6 (1989), 176.

out.[43] In Bordeaux's hinterland, winegrowing was also hard hit by the blockade and the loss of luxury markets that resulted from Napoleon's Continental System. In November 1811, a Chamber of commerce report claimed that of the 10,000 workers receiving assistance at home, the majority were men who had formerly been employed in the vineyards and bottling plants.[44] So much of the local economy was dependent on the Atlantic that, after years of blockade, industrial activity was largely at a standstill and the entire city was affected. It was the port workers and industrial workers, not the merchants, who were the principal sufferers.[45]

The brief respite in the war that followed the Peace of Amiens allowed a few Atlantic merchants to retrace their steps and rediscover the world they had lost. Without fear of seizure and the loss of valuable cargoes, they could dream of resuming former practices and exploiting colonial markets again. It was perhaps the only moment since the first declaration of hostilities when traders could hope to recover some of the commerce they had lost to Britain, and when, conservative as ever, some tried to reopen the triangular trade with Africa and the Caribbean on which their profits had once depended. The spring of 1802 held out new hope: in March the peace treaty was signed that returned to France her former colony in Martinique, and, two months later, Napoleon authorized both slavery and French participation in the slave trade. Presented with the opportunity to resume slaving, some could not resist, and a new spirit of optimism swept the Atlantic cities. In the ten months following legalization, vessels sailed for Africa from almost all the Atlantic ports (Nantes, Bordeaux, Le Havre, and Honfleur, as well as Marseille, were all involved); twelve ships were despatched from Nantes alone.[46] But the most precious prize, Saint-Domingue, was not reconquered, and that loss overshadowed any other gains. French merchants fitting out slave voyages had to choose between selling their cargo in Martinique and heading for an international market they imperfectly understood in Havana or Buenos Aires.

They also had to trade in unpredictable market conditions, for though France was temporarily at peace, the owners, merchants and investors in a slave voyage were conscious of the fragility of that peace and of the preparations that were already being made on both sides of the Channel for war. There was, it is true, less competition in the Atlantic slave lanes, as the number of slavers plying the waters from Africa to the Caribbean had fallen in the war years. But profits were not assured, as the voyage of the Nantes slave ship *La Bonne Mère* in 1802–3 shows. At first glance, this may seem strange, since in many ways it could be seen as an

[43] Guicheteau, *La Révolution des ouvriers nantais*, 77.

[44] Butel, 'Crise et mutation de l'activité économique à Bordeaux sous le Consulat et l'Empire', 199 (1970), 122–5.

[45] Marzagalli, *Les boulevards de la fraude*, 14–16.

[46] Éric Saugera, 'Une expédition nantaise sous le Consulat: la *Bonne-Mère*, armement Trottier, 1802–03', *Enquêtes et documents*, CRHMA Université de Nantes, 13 (1987)<IBT>, 38.

exemplary voyage. The ship left the Loire estuary in good weather, reached Bonny on the African coast after only fifty-five days, completed its trade with local merchants in a further fifty days without falling prey to fever or disease, and set sail again before the West African climate took its toll on the crew. They embarked a cargo of around 300 Ibos, and again benefited from a short crossing time of no more than six weeks, the minimum for the Middle Passage. The slaves survived the voyage, and 298 captives were duly sold to planters in Martinique. The sums raised by the sales were then invested in colonial produce and the *Bonne Mère* was able to return unharmed to the French coast, the last ship to reach Nantes before the resumption of the war at sea.

On paper this might seem to have been excellent business, but the reality was rather different. At the planning stage the merchant fitting out the voyage, Mathurin Trottier, had had great difficulty in attracting investors, and had had to turn to Paris to raise the capital needed to buy and crew the ship. The price of the slaves in Martinique and the exchange rate for colonial currency both fell below their expectations, whereas the insurance rates quoted in the colonies for the return voyage were higher. But most damaging of all was the reception they found on their return, with long days spent in the roads waiting while their cargo was signed off by customs, and poor demand for colonial goods once they had entered port at Nantes. The mouth-watering profits they had predicted in their prospectus could not be realized. Indeed, Eric Saugera estimates that the voyage may just have broken even, or at best returned a very modest profit.[47] But these were the post-war trading conditions to which they had to acclimatize. The golden era of the pre-war years was no more than a distant memory.

With the resumption of war with Britain, the Atlantic ports were plunged once again into a new and more desperate phase of uncertainty. The economic prospects were again threatened by Napoleon's Continental System and by the British response, the Orders in Council, blockading the coast of Continental Europe and forbidding any neutral ships from moving between ports controlled by the Empire. The Milan and Berlin Decrees of 1806 and 1807 had the effect of distorting commerce, just as the combined effects of British, French, and American trade policies damaged the Atlantic economy by asphyxiating trading links and dislocating industrial activities linked to Atlantic trade.[48] This did not mean, of course, that all trade ceased; neither government required that, or considered it desirable, and the blockade was routinely breached. Indeed, from 1810 onwards Napoleon issued navigation licences that sanctioned trade in certain colonial goods, with the specific goal of reviving a flagging commerce. But customary trade patterns were disrupted, and even coastal shipping (*cabotage*) suffered. More of Bordeaux's wines were transported overland, while the trade in salt, extracted

[47] Ibid., 33–66.   [48] Crouzet, 'Bilan de faillite', 499–500.

from the marshes along the Atlantic coast and traditionally shipped through Nantes, was similarly disrupted. The salt, exported across Europe, especially to Belgium, Holland, the Hanseatic ports, and Italy, was customarily carried by sea, but with the war and the British blockade, sea routes were impeded, and the bulk of the salt was carried, at far greater expense, through the interior, on barges and river boats. For boatmen on the Loire it brought a rare explosion of activity, with the consequence that, long into the nineteenth century, the period between 1805 and 1814 was talked of as a golden age.[49] But for the merchants and seamen of Nantes, the collapse of *cabotage* represented yet another attack on their prosperity, another symptom of the port's decline.

For a brief period, Napoleon's loosening of trade restrictions appeared to bear fruit, and the years from 1810 to 1812 saw a temporary upturn in both colonial trade and the ancillary industries that depended on it. In Nantes, indeed, the tonnage of ships entering the port equalled and even briefly exceeded the levels that had been reached before the war. But it proved to be a short interlude in an otherwise depressing story of stagnation, before the final years of the Empire were once again marked by recession. The principal problem for European shipping now lay in the disruption to trade caused by the war in the Baltic and the Hanseatic ports. This was no longer a direct consequence of the Continental System, since after 1812 many of Napoleon's former allies ceased to ban trade with Britain, thus weakening Napoleon's hand in his trade war with London.[50] And at around the same time—in June 1812—Castlereagh, who had assumed control of Britain's foreign policy, revoked the Orders in Council which Canning had introduced in 1807.[51] But if the blockade and counter-blockade were over, the long years of war had taken their toll, with the consequence that economic activity remained sluggish. Maritime tonnage had fallen away, as had tax receipts, which affected the ports' prosperity in a different way. Nantes, for instance, which had handled 237,000 tons of cargo in 1790, registered only 147,000 tons in 1816.[52] And where Bordeaux had recorded tax revenues of 1,700,000 francs in 1809, this figure had fallen to 1,400,000 francs four years later.[53] Recovery would not occur quickly, and those observers who commented on the run-down appearance of their docks and harbours in the later years of the Empire were simply acknowledging the material impact of years of decline.

---

[49] Emmanuel Brouard, 'Le Premier Empire, âge d'or du commerce du sel à Nantes et sur la Loire', *Annales historiques de la Révolution Française*, 390 (2017), 25–50.

[50] Silvia Marzagalli, 'The Continental System: a view from the sea', in Aaslestad and Joor (eds), *Revisiting Napoleon's Continental System*, 86.

[51] Aleksandr Orlov, 'Russia and Britain in international relations in the period 1807–1812', in Janet M. Hartley, Paul Keenan, and Dominic Lieven (eds), *Russia and the Napoleonic Wars* (Basingstoke: Palgrave Macmillan, 2015), 85–7.

[52] Pétré-Grenouilleau, *Nantes*, 128.

[53] Laurent Coste, 'Bordeaux et la restauration des Bourbons', *Annales du Midi*, 105 (1993), 28–9.

With the advantage of hindsight, we can see that war and the Continental blockade wreaked real damage on the Atlantic economy, though at the time the French government promoted the policy as beneficial to trade and pointed to French commercial success. It was presented as a form of protectionism, keeping British and British colonial products out of Continental markets and preserving them for French merchants and French vessels. And for some at least in the west-coast ports, it restored something of the monopoly position they had enjoyed with the *Exclusif*, especially once the government began to issue licences and authorize trading voyages. But few were truly satisfied: the volume of trade was reduced, and the paperwork that was imposed on merchant houses was hugely resented. It would be difficult to guess this, however, from a cursory reading of the public addresses by mayors and chambers of commerce in the Napoleonic period. Public ceremonial was lavish, and expressions of approval for the Imperial regime beguilingly uncritical. In Nantes, the new festival of Saint-Napoleon—introduced in 1806—was celebrated with due *éclat*, with the official documents showing how the day was to be celebrated, with a religious ceremony in the churches, but also with a show of public adulation for the Emperor, along with a mixture of illuminations, wine, and dancing that ensured a decent level of popular partici-pation.[54] Expressions of gratitude and admiration were, of course, to be expected, and no city could afford to forget the debt it owed to the Emperor. Nantes was happy to oblige, the show of public enthusiasm reaching its apogee in 1808 when Napoleon visited the city. The city authorities organized a lavish reception, with a guard of honour provided from among the wealthiest merchants in the port. There was no public hint of dissent.

Expressing criticism of the government was discouraged, which makes it impossible to deduce with any certainty what the majority of merchants in France's west-coast ports really thought of the Continental System. Even the most guarded criticism had to be expressed cautiously and respectfully, and in carefully coded language. So when in 1808 the newly reconstituted Chamber of commerce of Bordeaux petitioned the Emperor to amend his commercial policy, it proceeded cautiously. First, it was careful to lavish praise on Napoleon and on the wisdom of his Continental System.[55] His policy had been just what France had needed to counter British pretensions, it declared, and the counter-measures adopted by Britain had attracted just reprisals. But—and here the chamber chose its words carefully—prolonging any further the measures outlined in the Berlin and Milan decrees might now be counter-productive, since neutrals, espe-cially the Americans, had been frightened by the British into staying away, and

---

[54] AD Loire-Atlantique, 1 M 194, dossier of addresses from local mayors and programmes for the fête, 1806-7.
[55] Alan Forrest, 'Experiencing the Continental System in the cities of the French Atlantic', in Aaslestad and Joor (eds), *Revisiting Napoleon's Continental System*, 215–16.

French trade was languishing. So now was perhaps the time to show a little flexibility. The chamber insisted that it was not criticizing the Emperor's policy, nor in any way working to Britain's benefit. But his goal had surely been achieved, and it could be useful to France if the measure were to be reversed, if only as a short-term measure. It asked Napoleon to consider giving neutral shipping permission to 'come to France either in ballast, or bringing goods and merchandise from the Americas', and to do so without fear of arrest. They could then take on French cargoes in the Atlantic ports and take 'our wines, our spirits, our manufactures of all kinds' across the oceans, where they could tell others of the prosperity of France and 'the justice which they have obtained from Your Majesty'. It was a carefully crafted document, half mission statement, half eulogy, and it made its point clearly. Any benefits that might have been derived from the Continental System belonged in the past, and it was time to get back to the business of attracting and maximizing France's overseas commerce.[56] Others concurred. In August of the same year, the city of Nantes urged the Emperor to cease maritime hostilities, since 'peace on the high seas is the greatest encouragement that the commerce of our city can be accorded'.[57]

In correspondence with the chambers of commerce of the maritime cities, Napoleon and his ministers were careful to hold out the hope of future prosperity and to emphasize the government's determination to see them restored to their former commercial glory. From 1807 onwards, measures were taken to encourage merchants to risk sending their vessels to the Americas, holding out the promise of a degree of government intervention and protection. Blame was repeatedly attributed to the British and their desire to destroy French shipping, to destroy the prosperity of other nations to ensure their own; and Napoleon was quick to condemn those French merchants who collaborated with Britain and 'sacrificed the independence of their nation by shamefully accepting British sovereignty and sailing under a British licence'.[58] He wanted to encourage privateering in the western ports of France, but he was careful to warn against abuse, insisting that crews must be carefully checked and fearful lest the port cities become havens for deserters from naval service.[59] In the Emperor's eyes, nothing could take precedence over the war effort, and when he did intervene in favour of the merchant interest, there was usually a strategic purpose behind that intervention. In April 1808, for instance, fifteen commercial voyages were authorized to sail from Bordeaux to France's colonies in Martinique, Guadeloupe, and Cayenne. Nothing

---

[56] AN, AF IV 1307, petition of the Chamber of commerce of Bordeaux to the Emperor, 21 April 1808.

[57] AN, AF IV 1307, petition of City of Nantes to the Emperor, 8 August 1808.

[58] AD Charente-Maritime, 41 ETP 1, letter from Minister of Interior to Chamber of commerce of La Rochelle, 24 December 1807.

[59] AD Charente-Maritime, 41 ETP 1, letter from Minister of the Marine to Chamber of commerce of La Rochelle, 10 July 1809.

was left to chance. Vessels required permission to trade, their size and destination were registered, their crews approved, and all had to sail armed. If a merchant requested a military presence on board to defend the ship in the event of attack, this, too, was granted. In return, the government offered an incentive by taking a share of the risk: each merchant was required to split his venture into a stipulated number of shares, and the state would use its sinking fund to invest directly, taking up to a third of the shares to a maximum value of 60,000 francs. The merchants may not have appreciated state direction of commerce, but in these difficult circumstances it was seen as a way of reviving colonial trade.[60] They were in no position to protest.

This is not to say that they liked the imperial regime, or that the west-coast cities had any deep political commitment to Napoleon or the Empire. When the Continental System was introduced, the decree was received in relative silence; there was certainly no concerted response from the Atlantic ports, nothing beyond the formulaic statements of loyalty which were well-nigh obligatory and which offered little proof of genuine commitment. Indeed, much of the support they lent to the Empire would appear to have been conditional, a sort of tolerance that reflected their relief after the turbulence of the revolutionary years and was predicated on their capacity to renew their commercial activities. For some, Napoleon's willingness to reintroduce slaving to France's remaining colonial possessions was cause for celebration. For others, the measures he took to fund strategic voyages and to expand wine-growing in the south-west were evidence of a welcome entrepreneurialism. But their effect was limited. These measures did little to restore merchants' commercial fortunes, and by 1808 the tightening of the blockade and the extension of the war into Spain persuaded many that once again their interests were being sacrificed in the cause of military glory.

For evidence of genuine merchant opinion, it is necessary to wait until after Napoleon fell in 1814 and the Bourbons were restored to the throne, when they felt they could speak more freely about the effects of the Empire on their trade. Of course, they might have been tempted to exaggerate in the hope of currying favour with the new regime. But the tone is unmistakable as, in a series of addresses, they expressed their relief and gratitude that the Bourbons had returned and peace been restored, appreciation, too, that the restrictions imposed on commercial activity under the Empire could finally be relaxed. For behind the various expressions of joy, whether addressed to Louis XVIII, to the provisional government in Paris, or to the Duc d'Angoulême in Bordeaux, there was a common thread of argument and a shared pleasure that the fighting was finally over and trade could be conducted under peacetime rules. It may indeed be the case that it was the return of peace that was most warmly welcomed, more even than the change of

---

[60] AD Charente-Maritime, 41 ETP 1, letters from Minister of the Interior to the Chamber of commerce of La Rochelle, 9 November, 29 November, and 27 December 1810.

dynasty; for the merchants repeatedly described Napoleon's commercial policies as a calamity for their cities, and one from which they were eager to recover. Trade, they said, had for too long been subject to 'a false policy' and tormented by 'bizarre and destructive systems' which had led to depression and a sense of helplessness. Even the licences which had been issued in the later years of the Empire had been a 'dismal present' offered by a tax regime for which 'trade was the instrument and the dupe'. The high duties had left merchants with large quantities of colonial produce that they had found to be unsellable and had therefore left them with still higher losses. They of course welcomed the reductions that were decreed after the return of the Bourbons; but for some they had come too late. 'Entire fortunes have been wiped out,' they complained, 'and others have been dangerously undermined.' Even after the fall of the Empire, some were still asking for compensation for the losses they had incurred.[61]

But the war was over, and Napoleon, with his repeated demands for further conflict and his abiding hatred of England and her colonial wealth, was, they believed, consigned to history. This more than anything explains their relief as they looked forward to the post-war era, however much their horizons were now limited by the losses of the war years. But at least many in the merchant community began to feel a degree of optimism. The 'ocean', as a joint address by the Chamber and Tribunal of Commerce of La Rochelle expressed it, 'was no longer closed off to them'. And that in itself was enough to make men who had had little reason to see themselves as fervent royalists before the Revolution feel no qualms about celebrating Napoleon's downfall or welcoming the new government with expressions of undisguised joy. They believed, they said, that the years of stagnation would now be over, and they therefore 'blessed Providence, thanked the Senate and Government, and voiced their admiration for the sovereign and their joy that the throne of the Bourbons had been restored to the legitimate King'.[62] But the spring of 1814 would prove to be a rare moment of hope, before realism and disillusion set in again.

---

[61] AD Charente-Maritime, 41 ETP 231, folios 153–7, addresses of the chamber of Commerce of La Rochelle, 14 April, 18 April, 5 May, and 10 May 1814.
[62] AD Charente-Maritime, 41 ETP 231, folio 153, joint address of the Chamber of commerce and the Tribunal of Commerce of La Rochelle, 14 April 1814.

PART THREE
EMERGING FROM CRISIS

12

The Congress of Vienna and the Politics of Slavery

The peace which the merchant community had for so long craved was sealed in the spring of 1814 when Napoleon's desperate last stand against the Allies failed and France fell to a pincer attack from the east and from across the Pyrenees. Napoleon did not cede his throne without a defiant struggle, but, despite a heroic final resistance as Austrian, Prussian, and Russian forces invaded eastern France, superior numbers prevailed, and by the end of March the Allies were at the gates of Paris. His attempts to negotiate terms were rejected, as the other European leaders had convinced themselves that peace was unsustainable as long as Napoleon remained in power, and it was his marshals who took the decision to surrender, convinced that the only alternative was to invite a siege that would bring about the destruction of their capital city. Marmont, in particular, was convinced that the army, defeated and exhausted, was incapable of fighting another campaign, and that further resistance was fruitless; it was he, not the Emperor, who ordered the surrender of Paris. Other close advisors agreed, with marshals Ney, Lefebvre, and Oudinot refusing to march on Paris and expressing themselves unprepared to fire on the people of the city. Napoleon's brother Joseph took charge of the Emperor's young son, ordering the Empress to escort him out of Paris to safety. Within days they were on their way to Austria, a move that effectively removed any chance that the Allies would accede to Napoleon's request and allow him to assume the imperial throne.[1] There was to be no compromise with the Empire. Napoleon was exiled to Elba and, the Allies hoped, was thus condemned to leave the European stage for good. Louis XVIII returned from exile in England to assume his throne, and a large part of Napoleon's army was paid off or placed on *demi-solde*. France accepted the consequences of military defeat; her future, and the terms of the peace settlement, now lay with the Allied powers meeting at Vienna.

Before Paris fell, however, Bordeaux, Bayonne and other towns along the Atlantic coast were already in Allied hands. Even before Napoleon fought his desperate rearguard action in the east, in the *Campagne de France*, the south-west had been invaded by British troops from the Iberian Peninsula, who had pushed a dispirited French army back across the Pyrenees and on to French soil. By the final

---

[1] Dominique de Villepin, *Les Cent Jours ou l'esprit de sacrifice* (Paris: Perrin, 2001), 10.

weeks of 1813, the war on the Spanish front was effectively over, when Wellington scattered the remaining French forces and crossed the Bidassoa into south-western France. The British faced little armed resistance, other than in the Basque country, where local people, in time-honoured fashion, came to the defence of their communities and their valleys. Elsewhere, war weariness combined with economic neglect to turn many against the regime, and nowhere more so than in Bordeaux itself, where public apathy towards Napoleon often gave way to open hostility, and where, as defeat and humiliation loomed, desertion rates among the troops reached record levels. The royalist Edmond Géraud noted in January 1814 that in Bordeaux alone, some 500–600 soldiers had deserted in the previous three days, as a trickle had turned into a flood and young men sought safety in the anonymity of the city. The population, he believed, was complicit. In his view, and that of many on the royalist right, Bordeaux was 'tormented by a sense of grievance as profound as it was legitimate'.[2] It was a grievance born, of course, of economic decline and a sense that it had been abandoned by the imperial regime. It was strengthened by the undoubted desire of large sectors of the population for the return of peace; but there was an ideological element, too. Critically, public opinion in the city was by 1814 hostile to Napoleon and there were substantial royalist cells among the commercial elite. In short, Bordeaux was already prepared to welcome a Bourbon restoration.

The Allied force that set out towards the city was modest in size: some 6,000 men, in part drawn from Portuguese units in the British army, under a British commander, William Beresford. It was clear that they expected little resistance, for initial discussions with the city authorities had been held, and that they had no intention of laying siege to Bordeaux or of taking it by storm.[3] Indeed, when the soldiers approached the city gates, they encountered no military resistance. Famously, or perhaps infamously, Bordeaux's mayor, Jean-Baptiste Lynch, seemed only too eager, on 12 March 1814, to hand over the keys of the city to Beresford, declaring his loyalty to the royal cause and ostentatiously ripping off his tricolour sash to replace it with a white, Bourbon one, before welcoming the King's nephew, the Duc d'Angoulême, and his monarchist supporters into Bordeaux.[4] Lynch, himself a wealthy merchant in the Chartrons, openly sympathized with the royalist cause, and had agreed to prepare the way for a Bourbon succession. For some in Bordeaux it seemed an extreme and politically unpalatable position, conjuring up as it did memories of noble privilege and the injustices of the Ancien Régime. But the years of decay and commercial decline had sapped support for the Empire, while Napoleonic exactions and requisitions for the army had drained the

[2] Laurent Coste, 'Bordeaux et la restauration des Bourbons', 27–9.

[3] J. Rambaud, 'L'esprit public dans le Sud-ouest et l'entrée des Anglais à Bordeaux, 1814', *Annales historiques de Bordeaux et du département de la Gironde*, 7 (1914).

[4] Pierre Bécamps, 'Despotisme et contre-révolution', in Pariset, *Bordeaux au 18ᵉ siècle*, 474.

municipal coffers. City budgets had been slashed and their resources seized for the Treasury; in the last eight years of the Empire, declared an anonymous pamphlet in 1816, 'communes had been forced to hold their inhabitants to ransom by requisitions of every kind, the final convulsion of a government expiring as a result of mortal wounds it had inflicted on itself'.[5] Though support from the city's workers for the Restoration was far from assured, the merchant elite, whether out of commitment or self-interest, largely rallied to the royalist cause. Lynch's betrayal—as those remaining loyal to Napoleon unfailingly saw it—did not come as a shock, and it did nothing to undermine his reputation in the merchant community.

Some in the city were committed royalists who had lived through the revolutionary and imperial era in the hope of seeing a king restored to the French throne, men who had never accepted the legitimacy of the Empire and who had nurtured contacts with royalist agents in London over many years.[6] For them 12 March was a glorious moment, one that justified their faith and their commitment to the cause of counterrevolution, a commitment which they traced back to the first royalist gatherings in Bordeaux in the early 1790s. A rapid succession of royalist clubs had followed, both before and immediately after the Terror, when counter-revolutionaries felt it was safe to meet in clandestine gatherings, with names like the *Société de Belleville*, the *Société du Gouvernement*, or the *Institut Philanthropique*, where those opposed to the republic and Empire could network and plot together. The last of these, the *Institut Philanthropique*, was by far the most effective and the most enduring. Established in 1796 at the behest of the Comte d'Artois to coordinate royalist political activity in the south-west, it survived the Directorial years and the intense policing of the Empire, though it was temporarily suspended and reformed in 1801, 1803, 1806, and 1809.[7] Merchants were prominent among its members, many embittered by the experience of revolutionary violence and eager to see prosperity return, as one of their number, J.-S. Rollac, would explain in a pamphlet he published in 1816.[8] The Institute was well organized, he claimed, and that organization was key to its success. It had a small inner council that remained secret, a larger general council, and branches in the three *arrondissements* of the city. It issued a prospectus; planned operations to undermine the Empire; and established workshops to make arms and cartridges. Rollac openly boasted that royalists in the city had recruited a small army, under the command of another merchant, Papin. He was also eager to emphasize

[5] Anon, *De l'administration financière des communes de France, avec quelques applications à la ville de Bordeaux* (Bordeaux, 1816), 42.

[6] Georges Caudrillier, *L'Association royaliste de l'Institut philanthropique à Bordeaux et la conspiration anglaise en France pendant la Deuxième Coalition* (Paris: Société française d'imprimerie et de librairie, 1908).

[7] Albert Mengeot, *Le Brassard de Bordeaux: 12 mars 1814* (Bordeaux: Bière, 1912), 10.

[8] J.-S. Rollac, *Exposé fidèle des faits authentiquement prouvés qui ont précédé et amené la journée de Bordeaux, au 12 mars 1814* (Paris, 1816).

his own part in the enterprise. He had bought gunpowder pretending that it was for export, and had stored it in his vast cellars, where the military units were reviewed; he had taken great personal risks; and it was in his house that receptions were held and oaths of loyalty taken to Louis XVIII. He considered it an honour, he said, to have been involved in every one of the royalist societies that had been established during these years, and was proud of the work he had done for the monarchy.[9]

Rollac's enthusiasm for monarchy was not, of course, shared by all. Indeed, among the Atlantic ports Bordeaux was alone in declaring openly for Louis XVIII in this manner, and even here Lynch's actions spread confusion and division in the days that followed. The city authorities were assailed by doubt, with a number of municipal officials tendering their resignations, among them some of the richest merchants in the port. For the approach of the municipal authorities was not universally admired in the city, and there were many who saw it as treasonable. Lynch had hailed as liberators the troops of a foreign power still at war with France's legitimate government, even if he claimed to do so in the name of Louis XVIII.[10] Among those who retained any loyalty to Napoleon and who saw themselves as patriotic Frenchmen, this would always be a step too far. What was universally welcomed, on the other hand, even by opponents of the Bourbons, was the return of peace for which many had craved for so long. Peace spelt commercial opportunity, and for many that meant a resumption of the trade they had previously conducted, be that in wine or flour, colonial produce or slaves. Suddenly merchant houses that had disappeared from the quayside were reformed and families that had seemingly stopped trading threw themselves once more into commercial ventures. 'This country,' said the Prefect of the Loire-Inférieure in Nantes, speaking of the west of France, 'needs only the assurance of peace and it will resume its commercial ties.'[11] This was clearly what many looked to the King to provide, with the consequence that most merchants rallied to Louis XVIII without demur. They were not alone. In 1814 Bordeaux indulged in a brief show of unity, as the law and the professions, Atlantic commerce and the wine trade all seemed united in their support of the Bourbon cause. If only for a brief moment, Bordeaux seemed to take a shared pride in the part it had played in Napoleon's downfall and in its reputation as 'the city of 12 March'.[12]

Of course, the Bourbon Restoration would not be achieved without setbacks, most notably when Napoleon returned from Elba in the spring of 1815, forcing out the Bourbons and reclaiming his imperial throne during the Hundred Days. The return of the Empire brought the return of war and commercial uncertainty,

[9] Ibid., 16–18.   [10] Coste, 'Bordeaux et la Restauration des Bourbons', 41.

[11] Pétré-Grenouilleau, *Nantes, histoire et géographie contemporaine*, 131.

[12] Robert Dupuch, 'Le parti libéral à Bordeaux et dans la Gironde sous la deuxième Restauration', *Revue Philomatique de Bordeaux*, 1902, 21.

neither of which was welcome to the merchant elites, and Napoleon's appointment of Bertrand Clausel, a Napoleonic marshal who had distinguished himself as a commander in the Peninsula, as governor in Bordeaux inspired little confidence. He was coldly received, the lack of passion shown by the populace in marked contrast to the fervour they exhibited in their reception of the Duc d'Angoulême, and particularly the Duchess, the daughter of Louis XVI. Clausel did not endear himself to the people by threatening the local authorities with conscription as a punishment for what he regarded as the 'malevolence' of the population, which served to unite all classes of society against him. He remained in post for a month after Napoleon's second abdication, refusing to compromise with royalists and stepping up measures against returning *émigrés*; and few expressed regret when he finally departed.[13] In July 1815, the new prefect, the count of Tournon, wrote to a friend that 'the execration of Bonaparte has been stronger here than elsewhere; it is shared by all social classes, and little girls dance in the streets singing anti-Napoleonic songs'.[14] The Hundred Days had been an unwelcome interlude in a world where commerce and economic recovery were always a higher priority than political loyalties, and where Napoleon's Empire was seen as incompatible with the future maintenance of peace.

There were political niceties to be observed, too, in a climate where any suspicion of loyalty to Napoleon might unleash a police investigation and possible prosecution. All the Atlantic ports were subject to close surveillance in 1815, as they were seen as a likely escape route for Bonapartists hoping to flee France and settle in the New World. Paintings, prints, and etchings suddenly acquired a new sensitivity as the authorities sought to purge any association with the Empire, any suggestion of loyalty to the revolutionary or Napoleonic regime. In Nantes, the Chamber of commerce demonstrated the extent of this sensitivity in early December when it had to decide whether to accept a present of a silver vase from the city's mayor. The vase had been given to the mayor by the commander of the British naval station that had had responsibility for naval vessels cruising off the Atlantic coast, as a mark of his personal appreciation when the British squadron was finally withdrawn. The Chamber was uncertain how to respond, some members insisting that the gift was personal to the mayor and should remain in his possession, others arguing that they should accept it as a reminder of 'one of the most glorious periods in the history of the city hall'. They were clearly embarrassed by the offer and uncertain how it would be most politic to respond.[15] On the following day, the special police commissioner sent to the city turned their attention to another source of suspicion, as he had heard

[13] Jean Cavignac, 'Les Cent Jours à Bordeaux à travers la correspondance de Clausel', *Revue historique de Bordeaux et du Département de la Gironde*, NS 14 (1965), 69–70.

[14] André Tudesq, 'La Restauration, renaissance et déceptions', in Desgraves and Dupeux, *Bordeaux au 19e siècle*, 35–6.

[15] AD Loire-Atlantique, 1 ET C5*, Chambre de Commerce de Nantes, minute of 1 December 1815.

that a number of paintings commemorating Napoleon's visit to Nantes were still held in the Bourse, and he demanded an explanation. The Chamber, perhaps fortunately, had an answer that was timely and politically correct. The paintings had been loaded into chests and sent on a cargo vessel, the *Tennessee*, to be sold at auction in Philadelphia; any money raised would be profit to the Chamber, which would put it towards the cost of the innumerable repairs to the building made necessary by the previous years of neglect. The Chamber could take pride in the fact that it had not only rid itself of any lingering association with the Empire, but had a keen sense of the paintings' monetary worth. It was not going to indulge in gesture politics by ripping or burning them, preferring to realize their financial value and turn them into a useful investment for the city.[16] Though this may seem a minor incident in the context of momentous political change, it is a reminder of the extreme sensitivity of all sides during the Bourbon Restoration.

The Hundred Days had also put in jeopardy the peace terms which the Allies were prepared to offer and the place the country would enjoy in the ensuing world order, and this had worrying implications for the Atlantic ports. France, it could be argued, had been treated generously in the original Treaty of Fontainebleau in April 1814 and the Peace of Paris which followed on 30 May. It left France with slightly more territory and 600,000 more inhabitants than she had had before the war; and, crucially, it returned to France most of the overseas colonies which she had lost to Britain, providing the basis for commerce in colonial produce. In the Caribbean, indeed, Britain kept only two small islands, Tobago and St Lucia, while France recovered her East Indian islands to add to her Caribbean possessions in Martinique, Guadeloupe, and Guyana.[17] After Waterloo the terms imposed at Vienna on France within Europe were more severe, but the colonial settlement was left largely intact. For the Atlantic port cities, that in itself represented a considerable diplomatic victory.

But what many merchants wanted more than anything else was a return to past trading conditions which they still looked back upon as a golden age. Having access to their colonies represented one element in resurrecting Atlantic commerce. More important for many of them, however, was the right to resume their old trading patterns, and especially the triangular trade with West Africa and the Caribbean. And here so much had changed since the Revolution, both in France itself and across the broader Atlantic world. France, as we have seen, had abolished both the slave trade and the institution if slavery in the 1790s, though their legality had been restored by Napoleon in 1802. Her richest colony, Saint-Domingue, was now an independent republic which had itself banned slavery and

[16]   AD Loire-Atlantique, 1 ET C5*, Chambre de Commerce de Nantes, minute of 5 December 1815.
[17]   Timothy Wilson-Smith, *Napoleon, Man of War, Man of Peace* (London: Constable, 2002), 98–9.

had cut most of its commercial links with France. And if Napoleon had previously raised hopes that he might champion a return to slaving when the war was over, those hopes were dashed during the Hundred Days when, in pursuit of liberal support, he committed himself and the Empire to abolition. Almost immediately on his return to Paris, indeed, on 29 March 1815, Napoleon issued a decree from the Tuileries abolishing the slave trade. From that date no expeditions would be authorized either from French ports or from those of France's colonies. And though those slavers who had already left port were authorized to complete their voyages and sell their cargoes, they would be the last. In future no blacks could be taken legally into France's colonies for sale, whether by French ships or by others.[18]

Just as significant was mounting international pressure in support of the abolitionist cause. For since the beginning of the Empire, the international climate on the subject had changed dramatically, with the calls for abolition becoming more strident. Britain, where the abolitionist voice had been strong in parliament for two decades, made the slave trade illegal in 1807, with the United States following a year later. And though neither abolished slavery as an institution— slaves still worked the plantations of Jamaica and Barbados until 1837, and it would take the Civil War to force the American South to abandon the slave economy—Britain's parliament was not prepared to watch French merchants make profits where their own were forbidden to venture, while the cause of anti-slavery captured the popular imagination in large swathes of the country.[19] Spain, Portugal and, to a much lesser extent, Holland and Denmark still outfitted vessels for slave voyages, and the trade was not totally stamped out in the Anglo-Saxon countries, either. But there had been a sea-change in the moral climate, especially in Protestant northern Europe, which ensured that slavery and abolition remained at the heart of Atlantic politics. Merchants in the French ports were not unaffected by the calls to abandon the slave trade, and a number of former *négriers* chose this moment to withdraw from slaving and concentrate on markets that they considered less reprehensible. Some were deterred by the increased risks they incurred, while others had been affected by the ideals of the French Revolution. The Nantes merchant Thomas Dobrée is a good example of a leading trader who abandoned the Antilles in these years. His family's fortune in the second half of the eighteenth century had been built on sugar, coffee, and slaves, but he was attracted to revolutionary politics and served in the Nantes National Guard. By the later years of the Empire, he had abandoned the Caribbean to focus on other regions and other commodities, on whaling and the fur trade, and especially on the East Indies and China; in turn his son, fascinated by the world he had

---

[18] Imperial decree abolishing the slave trade, 29 March 1815, in Branda and Lentz, *Napoléon, l'esclavage et les colonies*, 345.

[19] Kielstra, *The Politics of Slave Trade Suppression in Britain and France*, 46.

discovered through trade, would become a leading collector of Oriental art and notable benefactor of his native city.[20]

The defeat of Napoleon and the gathering of Allied leaders at the Congress of Vienna provided Britain with what many saw as a once-in-a-lifetime opportunity to impose its abolitionist agenda on France. Since 1807, reformers had campaigned to end slaving not just in the British Empire, but in its entirety; for many, like Thomas Clarkson and William Wilberforce, theirs was the supreme moral cause of the age which it was Britain's duty to press on other European leaders.[21] Abolition was presented as a potent symbol of Britain's protestant morality, and abolitionists clamoured for action, unwilling, as they said, to be 'answerable for the guilt' of doing nothing.[22] At Vienna British ministers tried, without great success, to impose their moral view of the world on all the signatory nations, and especially on France, traditionally their most bitter rival in the North Atlantic. In Parliament, members were relentless in their pursuit of the cause. For Wilberforce, Clarkson, and other leading abolitionists the issue was the touchstone by which the Foreign Secretary, Lord Castlereagh, and the entire ministry would be judged. Would they impose Christian values on the French, or would they allow themselves to be outmanoeuvred by Louis XVIII and Talleyrand? For the British government, it was a public relations exercise at home as much as it was a diplomatic issue abroad, a crusade that was pursued in the London press as vigorously as it was by Quakers and by others in Parliament.[23]

For the abolitionists there was no room for compromise, and after the Hundred Days, when Napoleon abdicated for the second time, they felt that their moment had come as Britain had played a primary role in his defeat. Their leaders in parliament were already planning for total abolition across Europe. In a private letter Wilberforce wrote that he was 'extremely occupied, both mind and thoughts, with considering about, and taking measure for, effecting a convention among the great powers for the abolition of the slave trade'.[24] Samuel Whitbread, speaking to the Commons on April 28, expressed the hope that 'in the pending congress a decisive declaration would be made by all the allies against the continuance of this nefarious traffic; and that this declaration would be followed up by efficient acts on the part of each of those allies; at least, that the utmost influence of this country

[20] AM Nantes, 8Z, Fonds Privés, Papiers Thomas Dobrée; Léon Rouzeau, *Inventaire des papiers Dobrée, 1771–1896* (Nantes: Bibliothèque Municipale, 1968).

[21] See Christopher Leslie Brown, *Moral Capital: Foundations of British Abolitionism* (Chapel Hill, NC: University of North Carolina Press, 2006).

[22] Wilson, *Thomas Clarkson: A Biography*, 125.

[23] For a fuller discussion of Britain's espousal of abolitionism in 1814–15, see Alan Forrest, 'The Hundred Days, the Congress of Vienna and the Atlantic Slave Trade', in Katherine Astbury and Mark Philp (eds), *Napoleon's Hundred Days and the Politics of Legitimacy* (Basingstoke: Palgrave Macmillan, 2018), 163–81.

[24] Betty Fladeland, 'Abolitionist pressures on the Concert of Europe, 1814–1822', *Journal of Modern History*, 38 (1966), 356.

would be used to promote this desirable and desired end'.[25] Wilberforce went further, arguing before the House on 2 May that 'there never was a period when the general circumstances of all nations were more favourable to such a motion than the present'. It was surely, he continued, an unrivalled opportunity 'when all the great powers of Europe were assembled in congress to consider and discuss the very elements, as it were, of their own political rights'. He then, not uncharacteristically, got carried away by the religious import of the moment, concluding that when he examined the 'extraordinary succession of providential events which had placed the world in its present state of hope and security, he could not but contemplate in them the hand of the Almighty stretched out for the deliverance of mankind'.[26] It was a rhetoric that found a ready echo among Dissenters, many of whom believed that anti-slavery was a specifically Christian cause, and slavery 'a system full of wickedness, hateful to God, and a curse and disgrace to Britain'.[27]

The anti-slavery lobby at Westminster aimed to force through abolitionist measures in France and other slaving nations, whether or not their rulers acquiesced. They believed that the colonies which Britain had captured during the war, from France and Spain in particular, provided London with excellent bargaining counters in the negotiations to follow. Britain, it was implied, had won its war with France, on land in the Peninsula as well as at sea and in the colonies, and the peace should be Britain's, too. They urged the government to press home its diplomatic advantage, first recruiting those countries which had no direct interest in the slave trade (Russia, Prussia, and Austria), then putting pressure on the Dutch to heed 'the wishes of the British nation', before trying to wrest concessions from Spain and France. Some wanted to link the return of captured colonies to commitments to abolish slaving. Others were intent on stopping France, Spain, and Portugal from trading in slaves with immediate effect. Clarkson, believing that Louis XVIII was broadly sympathetic to the cause, suggested that the cession of an additional West Indian island to France could be the price of immediate French abolition. Talleyrand, who resisted all demands for immediate legislation, remarked that for the English the slave question had become 'a passion carried to fanaticism and one which the ministry is no longer at liberty to check'.[28] This perception was widely shared, and it became a handicap for British diplomacy when it sought to press the abolitionist cause. Castlereagh remarked to Liverpool in October 1814 that the extent of domestic pressure that was being exerted on the anti-slavery issue restricted his freedom of diplomatic manoeuvre, and he complained of 'the display

[25] T.C. Hansard, *The Parliamentary Debates from the Year 1803 to the Present Time*, vol. 27, 576, House of Commons, 28 April 1814.

[26] Hansard, *Parliamentary Debates*, vol. 27, 637, 2 May 1814.

[27] Journal of the House of Lords, vol. 63, 31; James Walvin, 'British Popular Sentiment for Abolition', in Christine Bolt and Seymour Drescher (eds), *Anti-slavery, Religion and Reform: Essays in Memory of Roger Anstey* (Folkestone: Dawson, 1980), 155–6.

[28] Jerome Reich, 'The slave trade at the Congress of Vienna', *Journal of Negro History*, 53 (1968), 132–5.

of popular impatience which has been excited and is kept up in England upon this subject'.[29]

For the British—but not for the French—abolition was a populist issue that excited political passions and drew huge crowds to street rallies. The French position at Vienna was more cautious. Talleyrand was explicit in acknowledging Louis XVIII's sympathy for the abolitionist cause, but he insisted that it was France's sovereign right to legislate on the question, and, while he recognized the force of English public opinion on the slave trade, he also understood the strength of opposition to abolition in the French merchant community. He therefore felt obliged to negotiate cautiously, telling Castlereagh that it was the King's firm intention to abolish the slave trade but adding a significant qualification: 'as much as would be compatible with the needs of our colonies'. For, even as Talleyrand was appeasing the British delegation, he was made aware by his own minister for the navy that if he tried to impose too stringent limitations, the government would encounter fierce resistance. As the minister wrote on 30 September 1814, if France were to agree to end slaving within a fixed period, the French had to be allowed to take full advantage of that period of grace to build up their colonial economy, or risk disaster. 'The needs of our colonies', he said, 'demand all the more imperiously the greatest possible extension of slaving and the highest level of commercial activity' if the trade was to end after a few years.[30] It would be impossible to cede to British pressure without leaving an indelible impression of weakness, of having sacrificed the interests of the Atlantic ports for diplomatic advantage.

In the event, British pressure for abolition achieved relatively modest results. The Treaty of Paris in May 1814 addressed only the future of the French slave trade, excluding mention of any of the other slaving nations. Under the terms of the Treaty, France was given back her Caribbean colonies but was not forced to agree to an immediate suspension of slaving. Instead, she was to be allowed a five-year period of grace during which to run down the slave trade and realign her commerce, five years in which slaves from West Africa could continue to repopulate the plantations in the West Indies and restore a flourishing slave economy to the islands.[31] And though Castlereagh was careful to keep the issue on the Vienna agenda, others had more important diplomatic priorities, and the future of the slave trade remained somewhat peripheral in the negotiations. For Talleyrand was not alone in rejecting Britain's demands. The other European slaving nations, which included Holland and Denmark as well as Spain and Portugal, were equally resistant, observing that Britain's attempts to police her own slaving voyages had

[29] John Bew, *Castlereagh: A Life* (London: Quercus, 2012), 388.

[30] Pascal Even, 'Le Congrès et l'abolition de la traite des Noirs', in *Le Congrès de Vienne ou L'invention d'une nouvelle Europe: catalogue d'exposition* (Paris: Musée Carnavalet, 2015), 151.

[31] Brian E. Vick, *The Congress of Vienna: Power and Politics after Napoleon* (Cambridge, MA: Harvard University Press, 2014), 195.

been less than wholehearted. For in the years following the Act of Abolition, British interest in the slave trade had not entirely ceased, even if the last legal British slaver, *Kitty's Amelia*, sailed in July 1807 out of her home port of Liverpool with all her papers in order.[32] Thereafter, though reputable merchants were largely deterred from further involvement in slaving, the less scrupulous seized the moment to turn a quick profit, the majority sailing under the flags of other nations. Initially British captains tended to choose American ships since this made simulation easier, but when the Navy began carrying out arrests in Caribbean waters, they increasingly turned to Spanish or Portuguese vessels. Nor was British involvement restricted to captains and crews. As Peter Grindal has noted, several prominent companies in Liverpool and London invested in, or in some cases owned, slave ships sailing under Spanish or Portuguese colours.[33] British firms also continued to supply goods for trade in West Africa, and British bankers, insurers, and industrialists all connived in the trade to a greater or lesser degree.[34] Britain's record was not quite as morally pure as the triumphant abolitionists would like to have claimed and as the European slaving nations were well aware.

For Europeans were increasingly the victims of British anti-slavery politics and the target of the campaign launched by the Royal Navy to curb the slaving activities of others. In the years from 1807 the Navy, whose task had only recently been to escort British convoys of slavers and protect them from foreign attack, had been policing the waters off West Africa and claiming the right to board and arrest the vessels of other nations, including neutrals that might be of assistance to the enemy. These initiatives centred on the Court of Vice-Admiralty that was established in 1807 at Sierra Leone, whose Chief Judge, Robert Thorpe, a British barrister and a committed abolitionist, showed quite exceptional ardour in prosecuting ships' captains caught with slaves on board their vessels, regardless of where the ships were intercepted and with little regard to their nationality. Spanish and Portuguese, Dutch and Danish vessels were intercepted and arrested, their captains were prosecuted, and the ships and their cargoes seized and sold, leading to a predictable outcry in the foreign ports concerned and to judicial appeals, some of which were upheld. For those countries that held territory in West Africa did have a legal right to trade; in Portugal's case, and in some others, this had been confirmed in a bilateral treaty with Britain. Thorpe effectively took the law into his own hands, inventing norms based on a mixture of British law, treaty law and such rules as were laid down by humanity and natural justice. The result, hotly disputed in other countries, was to place British jurisdiction above the international law of the sea and to lay claim to a judicial oversight that was not

---

[32] Peter Grindal, *Opposing the Slavers: The Royal Navy's Campaign against the Atlantic Slave Trade* (London: I.B. Tauris, 2016), 101–2.

[33] Ibid., 107.

[34] Marika Sherwood, 'The British illegal slave trade, 1808–1830', *Journal for Eighteenth-Century Studies*, 31 (2008), 293–5.

theirs.[35] In the eyes of the other nations involved, this was a further instance of British bullying. It is therefore unremarkable that discussion at Vienna quickly swung from the immorality of the Atlantic slave trade to the legal rights of shipping in neutral waters and on the high seas and the role played by the Royal Navy and its West Africa Station.[36]

Castlereagh and the British delegation did not leave Vienna empty-handed: it was just that most of what they achieved consisted of promises for the future, of statements of intent rather than clear political commitments. In a recent study of the Congress settlement, David King tries to portray this achievement in as positive a light as possible, given that the diplomats and political leaders present had more pressing matters to settle with regard to the balance of power on the Continent. 'On February 8, 1815, just days before his expected departure', he writes, 'Castlereagh could finally point to some success', when the Great Powers issued a joint declaration condemning the slave trade in seemingly unequivocal terms, describing it as 'repugnant to the principles of humanity and universal morality'. They further agreed on the importance of ending a scourge which, they alleged, had for so long 'desolated Africa, degraded Europe and afflicted human-ity', though there was no clear commitment as to quite when that would happen. The slave trade should be abolished as soon as possible; but only the Dutch could be pressurized into immediate abolition. France promised to do so in five years; Spain and Portugal agreed on eight years. Yet it was a start, and Britain took some satisfaction from it. Louis XVIII's words support for abolition seemed incontro-vertible: 'The King has promised to combine his efforts with those of England to work for universal abolition of the slave trade. This promise must be upheld.'[37] Human rights, for the first time, had been made a subject of a peace conference, and it looked as if anti-slavery had become a moral force that was difficult to counter.[38] Indeed, Wilberforce admitted privately, after meeting Castlereagh on his return from Vienna, that he was not unhappy with the outcome: 'I believe all done that could be done.'[39]

But without the right to search suspect vessels, Britain's powers were limited, and balancing the conflicting expectations of foreign states and British public opinion would never be easy. The United States, which had already abandoned the slave trade, was perhaps the exception. Here it proved relatively simple to find a compromise position: in 1817 Castlereagh offered the American ambassador to London, Richard Rush, 'a reciprocal right of search for slaves, and a limited

---

[35] Tara Helfman, 'The Court of Vice Admiralty at Sierra Leone and the abolition of the West African slave trade', *The Yale Law Journal*, 115 (2006), p. 1138.

[36] For an overview of the Navy's role, see W. E. F. Ward, *The Royal Navy and the Slavers: The Suppression of the Atlantic Slave Trade* (London: Allen and Unwin, 1969).

[37] Even, 'Le Congrès et l'abolition de la traite des Noirs', 153.

[38] David King, *Vienna, 1814: How the Conquerors of Napoleon made Love, War and Peace at the Congress of Vienna* (New York: Harmony Books, 2008), 217.

[39] Kielstra, *Politics of Slave Trade Suppression*, 54.

number of the armed vessels of each of the maritime states to be empowered to search'.[40] France presented the British government with an altogether more difficult problem. Louis XVIII had domestic concerns to address, especially in the merchant ports of the Atlantic coast, and he could not be seen to be giving in to British pressure while an army of occupation remained on French territory. Castlereagh had to make do with statements of intent which he could present to the British Parliament as a more limited diplomatic triumph. A further conference called for 1816 in London also failed to produce binding agreements, though the assurances given by the French at least had the result of diverting the main thrust of abolitionist attack from France to Spain, which refused to take any action before 1823, and then only in the seas north of the Equator. A series of bilateral treaties with Holland, Spain, and Portugal placed limits on their liberty to trade (in the cases of Spain and Portugal, Britain paid out £700,000 each in compensation).[41] But Britain's right to stop ships that were suspected of slaving remained contested by other nations and had no basis in international law until 1831, when it was at last recognized in a bilateral agreement between Britain and Louis-Philippe's France. However, in the meantime the French had themselves moved the debate forward by taking their own action against slave-traders off the Atlantic coast. Louis XVIII kept his promise to criminalize the slave trade, and by a royal ordinance of 8 January 1817 and the subsequent law of 15 April 1818 the trade was outlawed in France. This marked a considerable change of heart, and it meant that, when it was fully implemented, vessels caught slaving faced confiscation and their captains could be stripped of their command.[42] But it would be the early 1820s before the French navy had the capacity to enforce that law, leaving merchants free to decide for themselves whether to cease their participation in the trade or take a calculated risk by continuing slaving.

It would be wrong to imply, however, that the French government stood idly by in 1815 while slave voyages were planned and ships sailed freely from the Loire estuary for West Africa. Louis XVIII's public condemnation of the slave trade was not disingenuous, though he had to be careful not to allow it to sound like a concession born of weakness. For if the trade could be legally engaged in for a five-year period, the government did not have to give it its blessing or make life easy for those profiting from it. Legal entitlement was one thing; getting the necessary papers to engage in the trade quite another. And the minister whose responsibility it was to regulate French shipping, the navy minister Jaucourt, was no champion of slaving. On 23 August, he instructed French port authorities that no vessel that declared an intention to engage in the slave trade should be given permission to depart, in effect forcing the trade underground. His successor, Dubouchage, went one step further by telling governors in French colonies not to receive ships

---

[40] Bew, *Castlereagh*, 446.   [41] Ibid., 447.
[42] Even, 'Le Congrès et l'abolition de la traite des Noirs', 153.

carrying slaves, thus making the slaver's task doubly difficult. None of this was done very publicly: the royalist government was keen to imply that any blame for these measures attached squarely to the British with their single-minded obsession with ending the Atlantic slave trade.[43] But it was a step in the direction of abolition. Of course these measures did not stop French slave voyages in their entirety, any more than Britain had managed to drive the last slave ships out of Liverpool or Glasgow. However, they did begin a process of prohibition which forced colonial merchants and ships' captains to seek anonymity, to trade in secret, to hide their true purpose behind a range of subterfuges. It was a crucial step towards denying them legitimacy, and with it respectability. Naval patrols added to the risks which those who continued to engage in the slave trade had to accept.

As the Restoration years would demonstrate, not everyone was dissuaded by these measures or by fear of social ostracism. There were many in Bordeaux, La Rochelle, and especially Nantes who deemed the risks worth taking, and since it was the slave trade, and not the system of colonial slavery, that was under attack, there was still a rich market in the Americas for slave labour. Among the merchant houses which had engaged in the slave trade in the eighteenth century were a number whose overwhelming concern, with the return of peace, was to revive their fortunes by once again sending vessels to the coast of Africa to trade in slaves. These merchants had generally maintained their commercial contacts in the New World, and they saw no reason to sacrifice them; their mentality was still very much that of the late eighteenth century, leaving them completely unmoved by the abolitionist cause.[44] If there was still profit to be made from slaving, they had few qualms about despatching a new generation of vessels to West Africa and the Caribbean.

More dissuasive than the call of conscience were the messages they received from the West Indies, from agents and commercial partners left increasingly anxious by the news that reached them from France. The correspondence between two merchants, Lesage in Cayenne and Meyer in La Rochelle, in 1815 shows the extent of their despondency. Lesage points out that their warehouse in Cayenne is already working at a fraction of capacity and that the tariffs on trade with Guadeloupe and Martinique promise to be prohibitive. But it is the news that the slave trade will be abolished in five years that he finds most alarming. For, he asks, what is the use of five years to the local economy? 'If slaving is abolished in five years, we will have to give up all commercial activity; eighteen months will already have passed before the first slave ships arrive, and we'll have to stop trading nine months before the period of grace expires. More than two years will have slipped past without being able to do anything.' And in the remaining

[43] Kielstra, *Politics of Slave Trade Suppression*, 58–9.
[44] Pétré-Grenouilleau, *Nantes, histoire et géographie contemporaine*, 132.

period there are severe limits to what the economy of Cayenne can ingest. 'In the position in which we are going to find ourselves,' he concludes, 'if French ships do appear, Cayenne cannot purchase and feed more than 1000 or 1500 slaves each year.'[45] Neither Cayenne nor the islands of the Petites Antilles had the capacity to replace the huge colonial market that had been lost in Saint-Domingue, and that did affect the viability of the French slave trade. In the years after 1815 it would be the lack of commercial opportunity as much as the pressure of legislation that caused the slaving activity of the west-coast ports to fall into a terminal decline.[46]

It remained an open question under the Restoration whether the monarchy had the political will to end slavery in its colonial possessions or to suppress what remained of the slave trade. For we must recognize that, though it had been the first country in Europe to abolish slavery in February 1794, and though the principle of abolition was confirmed by the Convention in 1795, France's relationship with slavery over the previous twenty-five years had been anything but consistent. In May 1802, Napoleon had re-established the slave trade in France and had restored slavery in those colonies returned by Britain under the terms of the Treaty of Amiens. During 1802 and 1803, he in turn reintroduced slavery in Réunion and Mauritius, Guyana and Guadeloupe. For Napoleon at this time, slavery was clearly not an issue of conscience, certainly not when it stood in the way of French economic interest, and if he went on to proclaim an end to slavery during the Hundred Days, this was little more than a political ploy to win liberals to his side. Reform after 1815 was similarly ambivalent. While Louis XVIII confirmed the illegality of the slave trade in 1817, France, like the other slaving nations, did nothing to abolish the institution of slavery itself, which would remain in force in all of France's colonies until the mid-nineteenth century. Progress towards reform was slow and intermittent, with equality in law between whites and free men of colour—a right first gained back in 1791—offered in 1833 and the conditions of servitude re-examined and liberalized in 1845. But it was not until March 1848, and the arrival of the Second Republic, that France again proclaimed the total abolition of slavery and finally confirmed one of the great liberal reforms of the First Republic. This was no coincidence, for abolition had been turned into a specifically republican cause, one closely identified with the rights of man. Slavery was seen as an outrage to the ideals of republicanism, what Victor Schœlcher denounced as 'a crime of *lèse-humanité*'.[47] Before the advent of the republic, France's approach to abolition was more a matter of international

---

[45] BM La Rochelle, Fonds Meschinet de Richemond MS 2272, letter from Lesage in Cayenne to Meyer in La Rochelle, 18 April 1815.

[46] Frédéric Régent, *La France et ses esclaves, de la colonisation aux abolitions, 1620–1848* (Paris: Grasset, 2007), 289.

[47] Victor Schœlcher, Rapport au ministre de la Marine et des colonies, in *Le Moniteur*, 3 May 1848.

bargaining than of ideological commitment. It is scarcely to be wondered at that men who had made their fortune from the slave trade were able to convince themselves that in sending vessels out to Africa they were doing nothing that was morally wrong.

For, whatever Clarkson, Wilberforce, and their fellow abolitionists had started, they certainly did not achieve their goal of abolishing slaving in the immediate post-war world. Nowhere was abolition total. Britain and the United States might have legislated against the Atlantic slave trade during the Napoleonic Wars, but they did nothing to outlaw slavery on their plantations, nor did they resolve the more fundamental problem that sugar, coffee, and cotton production was deemed by most contemporaries to be uneconomic without slavery. Where the slave trade was criminalized, moreover, governments, even British governments, were not especially rigorous in ensuring that the law was respected, and ships continued to be fitted out for the slave trade after the war was over, albeit on a smaller scale and often, though not always, under the cover of a foreign flag.[48] The abolitionists' work remained far from complete. Even in Britain's Caribbean islands, slavery remained legal until the passing of the Slavery Abolition Act of 1833, and even then colonies like Jamaica and Trinidad turned to an apprenticeship system which kept former slaves on the land, in the process retaining many aspects of the unequal relationship with their masters.

In the United States, too, reformers could claim only a partial success. In the cotton-fields of the South, nothing changed; while even in the northern states slavery lingered well into the nineteenth century before abolition was proclaimed in Rhode island in 1842, in Pennsylvania in 1847, or in Connecticut in 1848.[49] And of course slavery was at the heart of the dispute that rent the United States apart and plunged the country into the Civil War. Elsewhere the picture is very mixed. In Central and South America, slavery and the slave trade were sometimes ended during the struggle for independence from European empires; in particular, the slave trade between Spain and her former colonies was abolished by 1842. But elsewhere a slave economy was maintained, and often it was only the destinations of the slave ships that changed as old markets were shut off and new ones opened up. Slaving vessels continued plying between the African coast and the Americas well into the 1870s and 1880s, increasingly serving the major slave markets of Puerto Rico, Cuba, and Brazil. For those with slaves to sell, there were still eager purchasers, and profits to be made. But it was no longer a triangular trade between Europe, Africa and the Americas: nineteenth-century slave ships mostly passed directly between West Africa and Cuba or Latin America. And though the French

[48] Marika Sherwood, 'The British illegal slave trade, 1808–1830', 293.
[49] Ana Lucia Araujo, *Reparations for Slavery and the Slave Trade: a Transnational and Comparative History* (London: Bloomsbury, 2017), 60–1.

continued to be implicated in slaving in the years up to 1830, and in slave-owning on the plantations of Martinique and Guadeloupe until mid-century, theirs was a declining role in a trade that was increasingly dominated by Catholic Southern Europe and by slavers based in Central America and Brazil.[50]

---

[50] For statistics, see the Transatlantic Slave Trade Database; David Eltis and David Richardson (eds), *Extending the Frontiers: Essays on the New Transatlantic Slave Trade Database* (New Haven: Yale University Press, 2008), 40–1.

13

The Illegal Slave Trade

If the law of 1817 committed the Restoration monarchy to outlawing the slave trade within a few years, reports from both French and foreign naval vessels showed how it was openly, and at times shamelessly, flouted. Merchants continued to trade as their slave ships eluded arrest on the high seas and in the waters off West Africa. And, as the abolitionist lobby repeatedly complained, they did so with apparent impunity, defying the law in pursuit of the generous rewards which slaving continued to offer. An abolitionist tract circulating in Paris in 1824 made the case for considering the legislation a total failure, such was the enthusiasm in commercial circles for sending out yet more vessels to Africa to purchase slaves.[1] The anonymous author cites a number of recent publications, from African newspapers to pamphlets by the *Amis des Noirs*, claiming to prove high levels of activity by French slavers in African waters. From the *Royal Gazette* in Sierra Leone, for instance, he extracts a report of the recent voyage by the British cruiser *Maidstone* off the African coast between Sierra Leone and Cameroon, which had resulted in its crew boarding nineteen ships, ten of them French. Their verdict was uncompromising. Of the schooler *La Théonie* from Nantes, the *Maidstone*'s captain observed: 'General cargo for the slave trade. Boarded on the Bonny River where it was trying to stay in order to take on a cargo of slaves.' The case of *La Sabine*, from Bordeaux, was similar. It had been 'prepared for 200 women and 300 men when we visited her; there were already at least 300 slaves waiting to be taken on board'.[2] The ships boarded were all provided with French papers to give them a semblance of legality, and the pamphlet concludes, unsurprisingly, with the damning indictment that 'the facts here speak for themselves, and if the French government does not intervene in a more incisive way that it has done to date, the world will conclude what is, alas, only too true, that this great nation is showing some repugnance at abolishing this odious traffic'.[3]

This was a reasonable conclusion to draw, given the wealth of evidence that French slave ships continued to ply the Atlantic with apparent impunity, though France's part in it undeniably declined in comparison with Spain, Portugal, or Brazil. But it remained significant until the end of the Restoration monarchy and

---

[1] Anon, *Traite des Nègres—Renseignemens tendant à prouver la continuation de ce trafic illégal* (12pp., Paris: imprimerie de Crapelet, 1825).

[2] 'Liste des vaisseaux abordés par les embarcations du vaisseau de S.M. le Maidstone, Charles Bullen Esq., capitaine', annexe to the pamphlet.

[3] *Renseignemens tendant à prouver la continuation de ce trafic illégal*, 3.

the signing of the Anglo-French treaty on abolition in 1831.[4] These were the peak years of clandestine or illegal slaving, as it is often described by historians of the nineteenth-century Atlantic. But as Serge Daget, the leading specialist in this phase of the French slave trade, explains, the words can be deceptive. It was impossible for slave vessels to operate in total secrecy. In Nantes, indeed, no vessel could engage in the trade without the whole city knowing: the ships were well-known, as were those who owned and insured them, those who captained and manned them, those who fitted them out for the sea and invested in their voyages. Insuring a slave ship required the complicity of large numbers of Nantes merchants, among them some of the leading houses on the Quai de la Fosse: in 1825, thirty-eight merchants were investors, and in 1826 no fewer than forty-six.[5] Such complicity was not considered in any way shameful in a city where the slave trade still commanded respect and guaranteed social standing. The Chamber of commerce was in the hands of slavers throughout the 1820s, and of the eleven judges on the commercial tribunal in 1825, ten were well known as slavers, including the president.[6] This was hardly an environment where abolitionists could expect to find a sympathetic ear.

The arguments used by the pro-slaving lobby had not been silenced either by the Revolution in France or by propaganda emanating from the other side of the Channel. The stakes were too high, since for many, especially in Nantes, the only way to rebuild the fortunes of the port was to resume the commerce they had been forced to abandon in 1791. Merchants and *armateurs* rushed to invest again in voyages to Africa in the hope of exploiting a favourable commercial climate, as planters, deprived of the shiploads of black labour on which they once depended, provided an enthusiastic market for slaves, bringing the expectation of assured prices and high profits. In the first years, of course, there was nothing illegal in their trading, no reason for self-doubt or clandestine activity. The greatest challenge lay in opening up new markets after the loss of Saint-Domingue. Martinique and Guadeloupe were a major market for French slavers, but increasingly French slave ships now moved further afield, especially to Cuba and the Spanish sugar islands. An abolitionist tract published in the late 1820s observed how Nantes merchants had exploited trade links with Cuba which they had not admitted publicly, and claimed that it was only with increased policing from the mid-1820s that their interest in the slave trade finally declined. Until then, the anonymous pamphleteer could see only greed and a shameful expansion of slaving in the port: whereas in 1816 only one vessel had sailed from the Loire to Africa, he claimed,

[4] Serge Daget, 'British Repression of the Illegal French Slave Trade: some considerations', in Henry A. Gemery and Jan S. Hogendorn (eds), *The Uncommon Market: Essays in the Economic History of the Atlantic Slave Trade* (New York: Academic Press, 1979), 430.

[5] Serge Daget, 'Armateurs nantais et trafic négrier illégal: une histoire sans petite boîte verte', *Enquêtes et Documents*, 13 (1987), 69.

[6] Ibid., 79.

the figures had risen substantially (seven in 1817, four in 1818, twenty-one in 1819, ten in 1820, twenty-one in 1821, six in 1822, fifteen in 1823, thirty-seven in 1824, and in 1825 a further forty up until the end of August). Only then did the numbers start to decline, as merchants were deterred by the risk of seizures and vessels that had been built for slaving out of Nantes were diverted elsewhere— notably, he claims, to ports in Holland.[7]

Abolitionists had, of course, every reason to exaggerate the number of slave voyages and the fortunes that were to be made from them; the pamphlet in question quotes figures of 60 million *livres* as the profit which Nantes owed to the slave trade, to be shared among the owners, crews, suppliers, and insurers of around 100 slave ships working out of the port. But such figures can claim no real authority; they take no account of shipwrecks, losses to privateers in the Caribbean, or capture by the Royal Navy; they overlook insurance losses, the deaths of crewmen, or the epidemics that customarily decimated the slaves piled up in the hold. They are, in other words, primed to shock, serving to redouble the horror of the slave trade itself. In a pamphlet of 1826, the *Société de la Morale Chrétienne* expressed outrage at the level of slaving still practised in France, and particularly in Nantes, where, they claimed, what its members had observed 'makes the hair stand up on the back of our necks'. The French flag flew more and more frequently over the abuses of the traders, they alleged, and the French were corrupting the African peoples with whom they trade. 'Along the Sherbro river, to the south of Sierra Leone, the misery and devastation that result from the encouragement given by French slavers to violence and looting surpass all description. The native merchants have become so avid for victims that several colonists from Sierra Leone who had come to the Sherbro to trade were seized and sold into slavery.'[8]

The *Société de la Morale Chrétienne* was one of the most influential pressure groups for abolition in Restoration France, and much of its force came from the association it made between Christian ideals and the cause of anti-slavery. In this it was much closer to the English non-conformist tradition of abolitionism than the enlightened discourses which had predominated in eighteenth-century France, and much of the material it published was, indeed, drawn from British sources. An inventory of the titles in the Society's library in 1824 showed that no more than ten originated in France, a small number when compared with the thirty authored by English abolitionists like Clarkson, Forster, and Wilberforce, or the many anonymous tracts that had been sent as gifts from their British counterparts.[9] The Society published a regular newspaper in which, once again, great

---

[7] AD Loire-Atlantique, 1J 191, 'Mémoire sur le commerce de Nantes sous la Restauration avec nos vieilles colonies, l'Amérique du Sud, les États-Unis, etc'.

[8] Bibliothèque Historique de Nantes, Fonds du Musée des Salorges, FMS B 238, Société de la Morale Chrétienne, 'Faits relatifs à la traite des noirs' (Paris, 1826), 54–5.

[9] Marie-Laure Aurenche, *Le combat pour la liberté des Noirs dans le Journal de la Société de la Morale Chrétienne* (2 vols, Paris: L'Harmattan, 2011), vol. 1, xi.

emphasis was placed on the progress of the abolition movement across the Channel, and it is surely significant that the leaders of the English movement—notably Clarkson and Wilberforce—hastened to join the French Society, seeing it as a valued ally in the international campaign against the slave trade, and using its networks to press home the shame of France's continued exploitation of Africans in pursuit of profit. They also published tracts and treatises in French right up until the moment in 1848 when the Second Republic voted the total abolition of slavery, pointing to the increasing isolation of France in a world that was turning against involvement in the trade. Abolitionists had achieved successes in countries seldom associated with the Rights of Man, they noted, and for France to be an anomaly was a source of curiosity and humiliation. In a tract printed in Cambrai in the late 1840s, signed by Clarkson under the title *Quelques mots aux amis de l'humanité sur l'esclavage et la traite des nègres*, those countries that had abolished slavery were listed: they included, most recently, Hong Kong in 1844 and the Swedish colony of Saint-Barthélemy in 1845. The pamphlet noted that the Bey of Tunis had taken the initiative of ending slavery in the territories he controlled. These were no longer exceptional cases; so surely the time was long past when France should accept the moral arguments and fall into line?[10]

The Society's newspaper campaigned relentlessly against the slave trade and French involvement in the human degradation it caused. It repeatedly informed its readers of the progress that was being made across the world in their shared crusade against the slave-owners, bringing news of abolition movements in Surinam, providing accounts of policing activities off Sierra Leone, and citing petitions by abolitionists from provincial towns across England. It railed against French government obfuscation of the issue. Above all, the Society drew the attention of its readers to abuses committed by the French in pursuance of the slave trade and to the reassuringly long list of slave ships reported captured at sea. The paper quoted a report from a Welsh sea captain, Captain Pince, who had just returned from Bonny on the Senegal coast and had brought what he regarded as incontrovertible proof of French misconduct. Not only had he encountered a slave ship with around 500 Africans on board, bound, he believed, for the Caribbean; he had also sighted a French corvette with more than 600 captives on its way to Réunion. This was not a simple slaver. It was a warship with twenty-two guns on board, and was commanded by an officer of the French navy. What greater proof could be needed of French government connivance?[11]

In abolitionist eyes, no crime was too heinous for the slavers, whose sole motivation was greed. But what caused the greatest shock was less the fact that

---

[10] Bibliothèque Historique de Nantes, Fonds du Musée des Salorges, G326 AFF, Thomas Clarkson, *Quelques mots aux amis de l'humanité sur l'esclavage et la traite des nègres* (Cambrai, n.d.).

[11] Extract from the *Morning Herald*, 28 December 1824, in Aurenche, *Le combat pour la liberté des Noirs*, vol. 1, 173.

Frenchmen were still engaged in the slave trade—that they had always suspected—than the apparent impunity with which they continued slaving even after it was outlawed by royal decrees. They took no notice, for instance, of the words of the French governor in Senegal in 1817 when he read the royal ordinance abolishing the slave trade. Almost immediately slaving was resumed with even greater intensity, and within days a French ship on Gorée Island, off the coast of Senegal, embarked 150 Africans to be sold into slavery in the Caribbean. The law was simply being ignored, since it was in no one's interest to enforce it. A petition to the Chamber of Deputies outlined some of the indignities to which the African population was subjected. In October 1817, it alleged, a slave ship from Saint-Louis got the prince of a rival tribe to attack a local village, supplying him with everything he would require to launch the attack—a boat, arms, munitions, and a crew of black sailors. 'The village was burned down, and in a single night 47 Africans were taken into captivity while 65 perished defending their huts and their liberty.'[12] Most damningly, the petition added that it would be impossible for this trade to flourish along the valley of the Senegal River unless the administration was complicit and French government employees were deriving profit from it. Local opinion, adds the writer, was unanimous in its belief that everyone, from the governor down, had an interest in the slave trade.[13] As a consequence, everyone also had an interest in concealing it from the eyes of the world.

If there was indeed political connivance of this sort, it was a serious embarrassment to the French government, which had entered into binding commitments with Britain to support the Royal Navy in rooting out the slave trade. The law seemed quite unambiguous. Any part played in the slave trade by French subjects or French vessels, no matter where in the world, or by foreign nationals living in territory owned by France, would be punished 'by the confiscation of the ship and its cargo'; where the ship was French, it was to be banned from operating in French waters. These offences would be judged by French courts that specialized in contraventions of trade and customs. And, to show the sincerity of its commitment, the French administration sent a copy of the law to London so that its terms would be understood by the British authorities.[14] Throughout the years that followed, Britain maintained diplomatic exchanges with Paris on alleged breaches of the law, passing on reports of illegal slaving by French ships, often from a network of correspondents whom it maintained in Africa. They made repeated criticisms of French customs officers who had allegedly taken bribes to turn a blind eye; and provided Paris with lists of French vessels that supposedly carried slaves. And yet, despite harbouring doubts about the good will of French

---

[12] 'Pétition contre la traite des noirs qui se fait au Sénégal, présentée à la Chambre des Députés le 14 juin 1820', 4.

[13] Ibid., 13.

[14] Affaires Étrangères, Nantes, Ambassade de France en Grande-Bretagne, A 93, Law of 15 April 1818 and covering letter to the British government.

officials, they also accepted French assurances that the accusations were exaggerated.[15]

In such circumstances, it is impossible to know with any certainty how many French ships may have engaged in the slave trade in the years after 1815. Too much business was conducted in the shadows, too many vessels and destinations deliberately concealed from the official record. But such figures as we have, the product of Serge Daget's painstaking research on the years from 1814 to 1850, suggest that some 730 vessels were involved in the illegal trade, leaving from French ports or from France's colonies in the West indies, Réunion or Senegal, with a number of them making repeat voyages to West Africa and on to the Caribbean.[16] The information on some of the vessels is understandably patchy. For 143 of the voyages we do not know the port of origin, or, for a fifth of the vessels, the name of its home port. But it is incontestable that the dominant slaving port in these years remained Nantes, which (even after discounting the large number of voyages where a vessel's home port is unknown) accounted for 43.6 per cent of the illegal traffic. Nantes merchants saw little reason to abort what were for many the habits of a lifetime, and in 1824 the port sent forty-seven expeditions to the west coast of Africa—a number that was one of the highest in its history, including in the final years of the Ancien Régime before Saint-Domingue was lost.[17]

In the eyes of many merchants, the law was there to be flouted. They decried their government's efforts to criminalize slaving when it was still flourishing across so much of the Atlantic world, and when others were so clearly continuing to make huge profits from the trade. After the revolution in Haiti and the abolition of slavery on the island, the market in slaves simply moved elsewhere. Cuba, as we have seen, benefited from the crisis in Saint-Domingue to build up its own plantation economy, and it was hungry for new shiploads of African slave labour. But Cuba did not act alone. Farther south, the slave trade between West Africa and Brazil went on uninterrupted: during the first half of the nineteenth century, Portuguese and Brazilian slave ships transported more than 2 million captives, the vast majority of them to Brazil.[18] Nor did it pass unnoticed that, even in countries that had officially banned the slave trade, slaving continued and illicit profits were amassed. The United States was perhaps the clearest instance of

---

[15] Affaires Étrangères, Nantes, Ambassade de France en Grande-Bretagne, A 93, letter to the governor of Guadeloupe from the directeur-général des Douanes in Pointe-à-Pitre, 29 March 1821.

[16] Serge Daget, *Répertoire des expéditions négrières françaises à la traite illégale, 1814–1850* (Nantes: Centre de Recherche sur l'histoire du monde atlantique, 1988).

[17] Éric Saugera, 'De Sidoine à Sophie Raphel, ou les lettres d'un capitaine négrier à sa femme pendant la traite illégale, 1824–1831', in Hubert Gerbeau and Éric Saugera (eds), *La dernière traite: Fragments d'histoire en hommage à Serge Daget* (Paris: Société Française d'Histoire d'Outre-Mer, 1994), 126.

[18] João José Reis and Flávio dos Santos Gomes, 'Repercussions of the Haitian revolution in Brazil, 1791–1850', in David Patrick Geggus and Norman Fiering (eds), *The World of the Haitian Revolution* (Bloomington, IN, 2009), 285.

public hypocrisy on the issue. While the US government officially deplored the slave trade, it did not succeed in policing its own coastline, and smugglers continued to bring enslaved Africans into Southern ports long after 1808. More significantly, American ships played a critical role in importing slaves to Cuba and Brazil across much of the nineteenth century, thus maintaining the international market in slaves and fuelling the rapid economic growth of slave economies.[19]

There was little that governments could do when so many interests connived to keep the trade profitable. In 1826, for instance, Britain and Brazil signed a treaty outlawing the trade in slaves, but this had only a limited impact, in part due to events in Brazil itself. In 1825, Uruguay declared its independence from Brazil, before founding an independent Uruguayan state in 1830—a state, moreover, that was desperately in need of agricultural labour. The outcome was predictable, as large numbers of African slaves, mainly children, were shipped to Montevideo as 'colonists' in order to avoid both Brazil's constitutional ban on the slave trade and the British cruisers patrolling the Atlantic.[20]

Especially in the early years after the Vienna Settlement, the law remained porous while the potential profits to be extracted from slaving proved a constant temptation. No country was above suspicion, and even some British slavers returned to illegal trading in defiance of their own navy and of public opinion at home.[21] Besides, in the immediate aftermath of war there was what Peter Grindal calls a 'period of aimlessness' in the naval campaign against the slave trade. The fleet had been reduced to peacetime levels. Ships were retired or sent to the breaker's yard, officers and men were paid off, and Britain's naval presence along the African coast reduced to a mere token, while the Jamaica and Leeward Islands squadrons were preoccupied with suppressing piracy in the Caribbean.[22] During the period of their special dispensation, French traders eagerly returned to slaving, and they found a ready market in Guadeloupe, Martinique, and beyond, with planters keen to buy a new generation of African slaves after the disruption of the war years. And when France finally started suppressing the trade in its colonies, French merchants and planters in the Antilles looked to circumvent the law, and, despite diplomatic protests, there was nothing the French could do to prevent it. In 1819, for instance, when a plantation owner in Guadeloupe, a widow, felt threatened by France's more punitive approach to the slave trade, she responded by selling her land and part of her sugar mill and leaving Guadeloupe for the Spanish territory of Puerto Rico, taking with her the twenty-two

[19] Randy J. Sparks, 'Blind justice: the United States' failure to curb the illegal slave trade', *Law and History Review*, 35 (2017), 53–79.

[20] A. Borucki, 'The "African colonists" of Montevideo: new light on the illegal slave trade to Rio de Janeiro and the Rio de la Plata (1830–42)', *Slavery & Abolition*, 30 (2009), 427–44.

[21] M. Sherwood, 'The British illegal slave trade, 1808–1830', *Journal for Eighteenth Century Studies*, 31 (2008), 293–305.

[22] Grindal, *Opposing the Slavers*, 231.

slaves who constituted her household. The French government demanded that Spain send her and her slaves back to Guadeloupe, but they received no satisfaction, in this as in similar cases.[23] The Spanish authorities had no interest in acceding to France's request. This was a New World where Old World rules simply did not apply.

The illegal trade was concentrated in three main periods. The first began in 1814 and continued until 1818, the years when slaving was officially discouraged but still technically legal. At this time there was little need to hide a ship's identity, or to fit out vessels in the colonies, removed from metropolitan France. A second phase, between 1819 and around 1828, saw the bulk of the illegal trade of the Restoration years, with 386 slave ships leaving from metropolitan France and several hundred more from the colonies or from unknown ports. A major feature of these years was the greater reliance on colonial ports for fitting out and harbouring slave ships, and the increased number leaving for Africa from Martinique or Guadeloupe rather than from Bordeaux or Honfleur. This trend continued into the third period, the years of government repression that followed the 1830 revolution, when slavers increasingly brought female slaves to the Antilles to compensate for the lack of able-bodied males and stimulate the birth rate in the enslaved population.[24] To avoid detection, they spread their net more widely, purchasing slaves in ports in east Africa to ship round the Cape of Good Hope and into the Atlantic. In addition, they began importing indentured labour from the Indian Ocean and the Indian sub-continent in an attempt to compensate for the fall in slave numbers: what became known as the 'coolie trade'. This must be seen as a complement to the traditional Atlantic slave trade, since Africans had also been taken to French possessions in the East Indies. On the island of Réunion in the Indian Ocean, for instance, the number of African slaves rose from 50,000 in 1804 to 59,000 in 1825 and 71,000 in 1830.[25] These developments made the work of patrolling the slave routes all the more difficult. Preventing slaves from east Africa entering the Atlantic, and stopping others being trafficked around the Indian Ocean, would be crucial elements in the war against slaving.[26]

In ports other than Nantes, the psychological attachment of commercial circles to slaving was less persistent, and the merchants who had engaged in the triangular trade in the last decades of the eighteenth century were less likely to return to it in the Restoration era. Some ports, like Lorient and Honfleur, were forced out of

[23] AD Guadeloupe, 1 Mi 699, letter from the Comte de Lardenoy on the illegal transfer of slaves to Porto Rico, Basse-Terre, 13 September 1819.

[24] Serge Daget, *La répression de la traite des Noirs au 19e siècle: L'action des croisières françaises sur les côtes occidentales de l'Afrique, 1817–1850* (Paris: Karthala, 1997), 96–9.

[25] Jacques Weber, 'Entre traite et *coolie trade*: l'affaire de L'Auguste, 1854', in Gerbeau and Saugera (eds), *La dernière traite*, 151.

[26] Douglas Hamilton, 'Representing Slavery in British Museums: the Challenges of 2007', in Cora Kaplan and John Oldfield (eds), *Imagining Transatlantic Slavery* (Basingstoke: Palgrave Macmillan, 2010), 139.

the slave trade altogether by competition from elsewhere or else they never recovered from the loss of Saint-Domingue. Bordeaux enjoyed greater diversity, as it had other trading interests, in the Baltic and North America, and found new markets in the Levant and the Far East. Marseille, stimulated by the colonization of Algeria, turned more towards the Mediterranean and North Africa. Nantes, suffering perhaps from the lack of a rich wine-growing hinterland to rival Bordeaux, seemed less able, and certainly less willing, to seek new challenges and it remained more dependent on the traditional slave trade to the Americas. Its sea captains and ship-owners had agents in Africa; they knew the currents and the coastline; they understood African tastes and the workings of the African market. Throughout the 1820s, ships would continue to leave from the Loire estuary for the trading posts of the Slave Coast and the Bight of Benin, many of them resuming what they still assumed to be the most lucrative form of Atlantic commerce. But were these all slave voyages? From the information available to us—information on the port of departure, the destination, or the cargo taken on board at Nantes or down-river at Pornic—it is tempting to assume so. But Serge Daget is surely right to counsel caution, since, even where a captain and a vessel had previously been engaged in the slave trade, trading conditions changed rapidly, the increased threat of prosecution posed a deterrent, and there is no necessary link between commerce with West Africa and the buying and selling of slaves. He has examined the log book of a Nantes vessel, *L'Africain*, in 1827, a ship whose earlier voyages had certainly been for slaving. But, just as in the eighteenth century, the slave trade was not an exclusive occupation, and this voyage was very different, carrying wood and tobacco, not guns, and trading with African merchants along the Akan coast for gold and metal currency.[27] Surprising as this might seem from a captain who had been deeply engaged with the slave trade in the past, his was a legitimate voyage which the law had no reason to repress. He could not be condemned on his reputation alone.

But the majority of voyages in these years were not legitimate, and both the British and increasingly the French navies scoured the seas in search of vessels that flouted the law by trading in 'black ebony'. It was not always easy to prove, unless the slaves were actually uncovered on board or the ships' papers contained an explicit reference to slave purchases. Ships found off the African coast risked being stopped and searched by naval vessels, but in the majority of cases, captains and crews could still hope to escape without charge. Where no firm evidence was found, the navy hesitated to make arrests, and even in those cases where it did, it was unlikely that the courts would convict. Without being able to produce a human cargo, prosecutors faced insuperable legal difficulties, and the merchants

---

[27] Serge Daget, *Un document exceptionnel: Le 'livre de l'or' d'une troque légitime sur le rivage Akan, en 1827* (Bondoukou: Université d'Abidjan, 1974), *passim*.

back in the French ports were unlikely to be troubled. Such evidence as there was generally focused on the ship, and ships could be got rid of, or reinvented. Of the vessels that plied the waters from Africa to the Antilles in the Restoration years, indeed, few made more than a single voyage before being sold or transferred to other business. And while this could, of course, reflect the harsh conditions of the crossing or suggest that the risks were becoming too great to sustain, it was often a means of avoiding capture and the confiscation of the vessel that would follow. For a ship-owner faced with a criminal charge, selling his ship could seem a cheaper option, even at a reduced price. His captain would be assigned to another vessel; the crew would be disbanded and disperse. Once sold, the ship would be renamed and assume a new identity; it would have a new owner; and there was no provision to pass convictions or penalties from ship to ship, or from owner to owner. Vessels suspected of involvement in the *traite* often changed names before going to auction. In this way they conveniently disappeared both from the clutches of their naval prosecutors and from the historical record.[28]

The fact that so much of the slave trade was conducted in clandestine circumstances, with ships and cargoes under threat of seizure, inevitably resulted in fraud and obfuscation which make ships difficult to identify and slaving expeditions difficult to track down. French captains turned to flags of convenience to hide their true identity; they sailed from neutral ports or returned to Europe through Holland or Denmark; they worked for foreign owners abroad; they falsified papers or engaged in other forms of fraud, often using willing agents on other Caribbean islands like Sainte-Eustache or Saint-Thomas. The Caribbean islands had a long tradition of contraband and tariff evasion that was there to exploit. French vessels were reported docking in Saint-Barthélemy to sell their cargoes, or of landing Africans by night along the coast of Guadeloupe, while customs officials obligingly turned a blind eye.[29] Even the official records held by the French port authorities (the papers of the *Inscription maritime*) could be rendered more or less eloquent about the precise destinations of ships leaving the French Atlantic ports. The legally required declarations were duly made—to Brazil, the United States, Cuba, Guadeloupe, or wherever—for voyages out of Nantes. In the ten years from 1824 these tables record 1,140 voyages (though their accuracy is uncertain: for the same years, 1,327 were reported in the annual returns to the ministry). But what do they tell us? The largest numbers were for Caribbean destinations (239 to Guadeloupe, 205 to Martinique, 102 to Cayenne), or to France's colonies of Réunion and Mauritius in the Indian Ocean (219 departures). But a considerable number of others sailed—or admitted sailing—for Africa: 128 to West or South

---

[28] Daget, 'Armateurs nantais et trafic négrier illégal', 83.
[29] AD Guadeloupe, 1 MI 699, letter from the French governor in Basse-Terre on illegal slaving operations on the island, 6 July 1831.

Africa, thirty-eight to Senegal, and a further five to Madeira or the Cape Verde Islands.[30] These were almost certainly engaged in the slave trade.

What is most interesting here is less the admission of some Nantes merchants that they were embarking for Africa than the multiple ways in which others, faced by tougher policing by the French authorities after 1826, sought to conceal their activities and to obfuscate their true intentions. When a vessel left the Loire estuary on a transatlantic voyage, who really knew its purpose, or its final destination? Voyages to Martinique and Guadeloupe could easily be diverted by way of West Africa and a cargo ship converted for slaving at sea. Many of the vessels leaving port were of a size and build that perfectly suited the slave trade; some, indeed, had already an established history of slaving. Besides, it is clear that the vessels that openly declared their destination as Africa were not alone in going there. As Daget pertinently observes, 'A ship that declared for Havana, Santiago de Cuba, Rio or Surinam – to say nothing of Bourbon, Cayenne or the French West Indies – would probably dock at one of these destinations; but how many of them did so with their human cargo?'[31] Where vessels diverted to West Africa to pick up slaves, how much of this activity got into their log books or into the historical record?

Like any commercial venture, a slave voyage was an investment, an investment on which it could be hoped that the investor would make a substantial return, and as long as the prospects of profit remained high, there would be men tempted by the risks involved. But how real were these risks? Slave ships were rarely stopped on the high seas, or in mid-Atlantic. Rather, searches were concentrated around the African coast, at those points like the Bight of Benin or the Bight of Biafra that were the centres of trade with African kings and slavers; in the waters off the French Caribbean islands of Guadeloupe and Martinique; or on the approaches to Cuba, where so many French planters had settled.[32] Off West Africa, the British had the added advantage of a string of forts, whereas the French had only one, on Gorée.[33] Here a number of French slave ships were stopped and arrested, and the volume of French slaving declined as a consequence. But the trade was not eliminated; rather, the presence of British patrols off traditional slaving regions of West Africa, like Seregambia and the Gold Coast, forced the slave ships further south, to West Central Africa and the Bight of Biafra. From there vessels of all the European slaving nations—the French included—continued to ship their African captives to the Caribbean, with Cuba the favoured slave market. In the twenty

[30] Serge Daget, 'Long cours et négriers nantais du trafic illégal, 1814 – 1833', *Revue française d'histoire d'Outre-Mer*, 62 (1975), nos. 226–7, 100.

[31] Ibid., 103.

[32] Agnès Renault, *D'une île rebelle à une île fidèle: les Français de Santiago-de-Cuba, 1791–1825* (Rouen: Publications des Universités de Rouen et du Havre, 2012); Maria Elena Orozco Lamore et Maria Teresa Fleitas Monnar, *Formation d'une ville caraïbe: Urbanisme et architecture à Santiago de Cuba* (Pessac: Presses Universitaires de Bordeaux, 2011).

[33] Gaston-Martin, *Nantes au dix-huitième siècle: l'ère des négriers* (Paris: Karthala, 1993), 227.

years to 1835, nearly 40,000 captives were taken from the Bight of Biafra into slavery in the Americas.[34] In this context, Britain's supposed victory on the issue at Vienna and in the bilateral treaties that followed must have seemed insignificant.

In the years after 1815, the principal threat to the slavers continued to come, as it had throughout the war years, from Britain, which had no intention of renouncing its bid to force foreign slave ships from the seas. Britain had started to pursue this policy in 1807, as we have seen, when it abolished its own slave trade, and during the war years it had taken upon itself to police the Atlantic shipping routes and the waters off the west coast of Africa, claiming the right to board and arrest the vessels of other nations, including neutrals, which were engaged in slaving. Even in wartime, judicial opinion was divided on the right of arrest outside British waters.[35] And with the return of peace, it was widely perceived by other nations as a blatant assault on their sovereignty.[36] For what Britain was claiming was unprecedented: the right to police the seas and to arrest ships suspected of engaging in the slave trade, a right that was not intended to be reciprocal and which had never previously been exercised in peacetime when the normal conventions of maritime law pertained. The distinction is a critical one. In wartime, states might exercise the right to board the ships of belligerent powers or those suspected of working for the enemy: that was more or less acceptable under international law. But for other rulers to accept Britain's claims in a world at peace would imply an acceptance of their diminished sovereignty, which might easily be regarded—as it was by Louis XVIII—as something of a humiliation. If Britain got her way on this matter, it would present a political challenge to the French government as much as an economic challenge to the prosperity of Nantes or Bordeaux.

In the event both governments played their hand cautiously, fully aware that a major diplomatic incident was to no one's benefit. The British took pride, publicly, in the seeming willingness of Louis XVIII to cooperate in suppressing the slave trade, while privately putting pressure on the French to curb slaving by French vessels, especially in Senegal, which had been returned to France in 1815. In a memorandum of 1817, the British governor of Sierra Leone, on the basis of reports he had received from private individuals 'upon whom I can place great reliance', concluded, somewhat chauvinistically, that the resumption of trading in Senegal and Gorée dated from the return of the territories to France. 'The slave trade had not only been entirely abandoned by the whole of the native merchants at Senegal and Gorée,' he announced, 'but they had turned their industry to more honourable means of earning their living.' But now he had been informed of

---

[34] Oscar Grandío Moráguez, 'The African origins of slaves arriving in Cuba, 1789–1865', in David Eltis and David Richardson (eds), *Extending the Frontiers: Essays on the New Transatlantic Slave Database* (New Haven, CT: Yale University Press, 2008), 184.

[35] Kielstra, *Politics of Slave Trade Suppression*, 63.

[36] For an overview of the Navy's role, see Ward, *The Royal Navy and the Slavers*, *passim*.

large-scale abuse, with slaves being taken on board ships from all over France, from Le Havre and Honfleur, Marseille and Nantes.[37] It was, he felt, for France to take action, especially as Britain felt that her own hands were tied by maritime law and international agreements. She could not continue to board and arrest foreign vessels at will.

With the return of peace, Britain felt obliged to respect maritime law and to moderate the behaviour of its naval commanders, not only in West Africa but across the entire Atlantic world. Some, clearly, did so with the greatest reluctance. A circular letter marked 'confidential' and sent to the commanders of a number of foreign stations on 14 July 1816 prescribed the use of common sense and restraint. It instructed them to abandon their policy of arresting the ships of friendly nations suspected of carrying slaves on account of the serious damage to British interests which the vigorous enforcement of that policy would entail. The officers were reminded that the right of search was a belligerent right that existed only in time of war, and that using it in peacetime could have consequences. At no other time, the Admiralty insisted, should 'any foreign vessel on the high seas be brought to and examined, much less detained, captured or sent in for condemnation'. If they did so, the letter continued, the Admiralty could offer them no protection or privileged status, since 'besides the displeasure of their own government, they would incur by such proceedings the risk of legal prosecutions on the part of the persons whose ships or vessels they might detain'.[38] The letter concluded by asking that the contents be passed confidentially to the captains of the ships under their command, and was a timely reminder that war against the slave trade would in future have to be pursued within the law, by other means. With this, the Court of Vice-Admiralty was wound up, and Britain concentrated its efforts to end the slave trade on exerting diplomatic pressure on its allies.

Britain's policy of search and arrest had been of doubtful legality since the end of hostilities in Europe. The other slaving nations, especially Spain and Portugal, challenged the right of Royal Navy vessels to stop their ships on the high seas, and so, of course, did France, which had been very specifically granted a five-year breathing space before its merchants were required to abandon the trade. Off the West African coast, however, naval activity did not cease, and French slave ships continued to be arrested and escorted to Sierra Leone despite legal uncertainties. A good instance is that of a Nantes vessel, Le Cultivateur, which left the Loire estuary in April 1815 on a voyage to Bonny and Guadeloupe, laden with the guns, powder, and gifts that were customary for trade with African princes. The purpose of the voyage was not in doubt, but that did not mean that the ship or its owners

[37] Affaires Étrangères, Nantes, Ambassade de France en Grande-Bretagne, A 93, 'Memorandum on the increase of the contraband slave trade since the restoration of Senegal and Gorée to the French', 8 November 1817.

[38] Affaires Étrangères, Nantes, Ambassade de France en Grande-Bretagne, A 93, Circular letter from the Admiralty to British commanders on foreign stations, 24 July 1816.

were breaking any law. They had prepared the voyage carefully, sailing during the period that was specified at Vienna for legal slaving and respecting the territorial limits that had been placed on French slave ships. But the *Cultivateur* was still arrested by a British schooner and its cargo seized. It was taken first to Sierra Leone, then to Plymouth for trial, where the owners, by now sure of their rights, instructed lawyers for the defence. Although legal proceedings were expensive, they were exonerated by the High Court of Admiralty, which duly released the *Cultivateur* on 16 November and returned it to its owners.[39] It was a salutary reminder that the Navy did not always work within the law and that it could not assume that all its actions would be upheld by the justice system. The cavalier days of Robert Thorpe were over, and both the Navy and the British government recognized that they had to proceed with caution, and in accordance with treaty arrangements between the maritime nations.

That message was conveyed most succinctly in December 1817 by the High Court of Admiralty in London, to which the case of another French vessel arrested off the African coast, the *Louis*, had been sent on appeal. The *Louis* had sailed from Martinique in January 1816 bound for the coast of Africa, where it was captured off Cape Mesurado, in what is now Liberia, by a British naval cutter, the *Queen Charlotte*. The *Louis* was then taken to Freetown, where she was condemned by the Vice-Admiralty Court of Sierra Leone. The case was based on a number of premises: that the slave trade was illegal in her home country, France, and banned by a treaty with Britain, as well as being 'contrary to the law of nations'; that as such, the *Louis* could seek no protection from the French or any other flag; and that her crew, in resisting the naval vessel, had 'piratically' killed eight of her crew and wounded twelve others.[40] But again the Admiralty judges were unimpressed, and the judgement was overturned, undermining the Navy's right to stop and search neutral shipping. The Court threw out any suggestion that engagement in the slave trade could be equated with piracy; and if it was not piracy, then where were the grounds for 'the right of forcible inquiry and search'?[41] How could Britain be justified in interfering with the free navigation of the seas to which all nations had an equal right? And how—before the search had been carried out—could the Navy know that a vessel had slave cargoes on board? In the opinion of the Admiralty judge, William Scott, so long as Britain's own security was not jeopardized by the slave trade, 'you have no right to prevent a suspected injustice towards another by committing an actual injustice of your own'.[42] Even if the British government viewed the slave trade as abhorrent, that was no reason in

[39] Éric Saugera, 'Une expédition négrière nantaise sous la Restauration: les comptes du *Cultivateur*, 1814–1818', *Enquêtes et Documents*, 16 (1989), 28–9.

[40] John Dodson, *A Report of the Case of the Louis, appealed from the Vice-Admiralty Court at Sierra Leone and determined at the High court of Admiralty, on 15 December 1817* (London, 1817), 2.

[41] Ibid., 40.

[42] Helfman, 'The Court of Vice Admiralty at Sierra Leone', 1151.

law for imposing a unilateral ban on the trade when it was exercised by others. Imposing its will on the nationals of other states, as Robert Thorpe had done in Freetown, was illegal and would be deemed an abuse of power.

The adjudication on the *Louis* was a landmark decision that spelt the end for Britain's unilateral efforts to repress the slave trade in the Atlantic, and marked the beginning of a new, multilateral approach by the countries most involved in slaving. Through a series of bilateral treaties between Britain, Spain, Portugal, and the Netherlands, they established Mixed Prize Commissions, with judges drawn from the participating jurisdictions, in an attempt to suppress the slave trade across the Atlantic world. Commissions sat in New York, Havana, Surinam, Rio de Janeiro, and various African ports, most notably Freetown. These commissions had no legal jurisdiction over individuals: the captain and crew of slave ships were to be handed over to the states to which they belonged for trial and sentence. But they did, crucially, have jurisdiction over the ships and their cargoes, which could be seized, impounded, and confiscated on order of the court.[43] Their role across the nineteenth century would be significant. By increasing the likelihood of confiscation, they lessened the viability of the slave trade for the French and other slaving nations and discouraged merchants from taking what they saw as exaggerated risks. But this came at a cost. On board slave ships, tension and desperation tended to increase, as fear of arrest pressed crews to cut journey times and impose firmer discipline on board. Where abuses occurred, where fevers and diseases broke out on board, where slaves or crewmen died, or mutiny threatened, there was no legal authority to which they could with any confidence turn. The years of illegal slaving were not easy for anyone, whether the slaves and slave-traders in West Africa or the captains and crews from Nantes. Voyages were often perilous, and life on board both violent and brutalizing. In the West Indies, crewmen were often reported as missing, abandoning the voyage or looking for another ship on which to return to France. But precise figures are difficult to verify. Slave ships had a long history of keeping inaccurate records, in part to maintain a degree of discretion about their activities, in part to minimize their costs in a bid to win over investors.[44] The clandestine conditions in which they were forced to trade merely made obfuscation, not to say outright denial, seem more tempting.

Relatively few of these illicit slave voyages are fully documented through the ship's log book, the account books of the owners, or the registers of correspondence between the ship's captain and the merchant back in Bordeaux or Nantes. But one example may serve to illustrate the extent of deceit that was deemed necessary to turn a profit from slaving by the mid-1820s. In 1824, a prominent Bordeaux *armateur*, François Fernandes, fitted out one of his vessels, the *Jeune*

---

[43] Ibid., 1152–6.
[44] Saugera, 'Une expédition négrière nantaise sous la Restauration', 16.

Louis, for a slaving voyage to the coast of Africa and Havana in Cuba.[45] Unusually for this period, the voyage is copiously documented, with the ship's log, the crew roll, the accounts for the voyage, a list of cargo loaded on departure, the correspondence exchanged between the captain and the owner, and even the interrogation of the captain on his return in 1825, all carefully preserved in the Huntington Library in California.[46] What these documents expose is the general air of fear and insecurity that was shared by all the parties concerned, as they sought, even when the voyage hit serious problems, to hide their identity and shield their activities from the eyes of the authorities. Illegality left everyone on board, as well as the owners and investors back in the French Atlantic ports, feeling that they were financially exposed and legally insecure. A slave ship could founder, could be captured by privateers, or could suffer mutiny on board, and the crew were in no position to appeal to the authorities or claim compensation from the courts. As a consequence, they had difficulty finding insurance for the voyage: no company would accept the risk, and this resulted in higher premiums and policies shared by thirty-nine different partners.[47] They feared their own government as much as the Royal Navy, since slaving was now officially illegal in both countries. When they were faced with disaster, they had, quite simply, nowhere to turn.

And disasters they certainly faced during what proved to be an ill-fated voyage. Though registered in Bordeaux, the *Jeune Louis* sailed from the Loire in the spring of 1824 with a captain and crew recruited in Nantes and across southern Brittany. Even as they sailed, the captain broke his hand and was unable to write, while two members of the crew did not even come aboard the ship, deciding at the last moment that it would be more prudent to remain on shore in Paimboeuf.[48] Their instincts were sound, for once at sea the ship was overtaken by persistent misfortune. The first master of the vessel died during the outward voyage and had to be replaced by the second-in-command, François Demouy, whose brutal discipline almost drove the crew to mutiny.[49] The death of the captain meant more than a change of command: it risked spreading panic among the ship's company, who knew that they were engaged in illegal activity and who had looked to the master to provide them with legal cover. Then the ship's surgeon caught a fever and died in early May, leaving the crew without the medical knowledge to fight disease. They enjoyed little luck, as a succession of tropical fevers tracked the ship on its voyage, both off the coast of Africa and in the West Indies. The master carpenter,

---

[45] Alan Forrest, 'La traite négrière sous la Restauration: à bord du «Jeune Louis» de Nantes', in Reynal Abad et al. (eds), *Les passions d'un historien: Mélanges en l'honneur de Jean-Pierre Poussou* (Paris: Presses de l'Université Paris-Sorbonne, 2010), 493–503.

[46] Huntington Library, San Marino, CA, Huntington Manuscripts (HM), French Slave Trade Papers, 1824–25, 'Voyage du *Jeune Louis* à la côte d'Afrique'.

[47] HM 44026, police d'assurance du brick «Le Jeune Louis», 1824.

[48] HM 43993, rôle de l'équipage du «Jeune Louis».

[49] HM 43991, rôle de l'équipage du «Jeune Louis», le 17 avril 1825.

the cook, and four seamen died of fever on the Gold Coast in West Africa; others reached Havana so weakened by dysentery that they were unable to continue the voyage and sought refuge in port. Like many other ships at this time, the *Jeune Louis* arrived in the Caribbean with a crew ravaged by disease and lacking even the most basic medical competence. It had lost eight members of its crew, was barely able to crawl into port, and left the stand-in captain with no choice but to take on additional crewmen in Cuba for the return voyage.[50]

If crew losses mounted, they were as nothing compared to the havoc being wreaked in the ship's hull, where 106 slaves died during the voyage of the 376 who had been taken on board in Africa, a death rate sufficiently horrifying to require some justification to the Cuban authorities. The captain maintained that the slaves had died of 'dysentery and natural causes', adding by way of explanation that the crew had themselves been so weakened by fevers that they had been unable to care for the men and women in the hold and had barely been able to steer the ship to harbour.[51] But this was not the whole story, for elsewhere we learn that nine of the deaths were suicides: eight of the captives had thrown themselves overboard into the ocean, while the ninth had chosen death by hanging, driven to despair by the condition he found himself in on board ship. Weakly, the captain sought to excuse himself by saying that there was nothing the crew could have done to prevent it, given that the slaves had been determined to escape their fate and had chosen death over a life in the plantations. But it is clear that he was unmoved by the loss of human life: slaves to him were cargo, men and women whose deaths drew no emotional response. Their deaths meant simply a financial loss to himself and the crew at the end of the voyage, and as he turned for home he was already considering how much income he had lost and how he might seek compensation from the ship's insurers.[52] The success of a slave voyage was, like any other, assessed through the final balance sheet.

It is hard to deny, however, that the straitened circumstances in which they operated had contributed to their vulnerability and put the success of the voyage at risk. At sea they had to watch out for naval vessels as well as foreign privateers as they sought to steer a safe passage to the Caribbean. Other captains knew that they had no recourse to the law, just as slave-traders in West Africa understood that they had no real interest in dallying in African waters to haggle for a better deal. The *Jeune Louis* was typical in this regard: according to Demouy, relations with the African princes with whom they traded had soured as they and their agents sought to take advantage of the French crew's need to trade quickly and to achieve a rapid turn-around. He had, he wrote, been forced to accept poor-quality slaves who had been turned down by other ships, which he blamed as a factor in

[50] HM 43995, «État des paiements pour soldes et décomptes».
[51] HM 43996, death certificate for slaves on board, 5 June 1825.
[52] HM 43987, letter from François Demouy to the owner, François Fernandes.

the high number of deaths registered during the Atlantic crossing. The king with whom he had been trading, Jacquette, had, Demouy believed, held him and his crew to ransom, imposing 'mediocre' trading conditions on the French, knowing that Demouy had little choice but to accept. 'We could not stay on any longer,' he wrote in the ship's log, 'we had to trade at any price and leave in a deplorable condition.'[53] In Cuba, again, he would complain that he was paid under the market price for his cargo, with the merchants and planters again exploiting the weakness of his bargaining position. For the danger of attack and interception never left him. Already off the African coast Demouy's vessel had been visited by an English warship, though on that occasion he had managed to prevaricate and avoid arrest. Nothing could be openly admitted, and during the entire voyage, when writing to the owner back in France, he carefully avoided all reference to the nature of his cargo. The risk of arrest was just as great on his return journey, and as he approached European waters Demouy had an important choice to make. Rather than dock in a French port, where he might be recognized and questioned, he chose to enter Europe through Antwerp, hoping in this way to avoid detection and the lengthy period of quarantine that might follow. Fear and insecurity were his constant companions.

When he docked in Antwerp in October 1825, Demouy's problems were not over. Antwerp was well known for its discretion in matters of illegal slaving, but the sudden arrival of an Atlantic commercial vessel of the size of the *Jeune Louis* could not fail to arouse local suspicions. Why was it in Antwerp? Where had it been during the previous months at sea? It looked like a slave ship, and the captain could not produce the paperwork he needed to prove his innocence. The log book showed that it had spent nearly four months off the African coast without, seemingly, engaging in any commercial activity; and the captain was subjected to close interrogation as to his movements and activities.[54] His story may have sounded plausible, but it was unprovable. He claimed to have gone to West Africa with a cargo of cloth, gunpowder, and alcohol, which he had sold in exchange for palm oil to take to the Americas. There, he said, he had sold the palm oil and taken on his present cargo of sugar and coffee. Since he could produce no bills or receipts to prove his claims, however, the port authorities were unconvinced, accusing him directly of having traded in slaves. But they, too, lacked proof and were therefore forced to release the ship after a short period of quarantine. For the captain and owner, this came as a welcome release, and, along with the majority of the crewmen, they returned to France. But the voyage could scarcely be hailed as a triumph. The costs which it had incurred had exceeded budget by nearly 20,000 francs, although the voyage still returned a healthy profit. That was what counted,

---

[53] HM 43991, report by François Demouy on his trade with the African kings, 1825.
[54] HM 44000, interrogation of Demouy on his return to Antwerp, 4 October 1825.

as, despite the risks and the social stigma involved, the *armateur* Fernandes fitted out another slave ship for Africa.[55]

He was not, as we have seen, alone, though by 1825 the risks of illegal slaving were becoming greater and the profits less tempting than they had been in the early years of the Restoration. But for a minority these risks still seemed worth taking, and it was not until 1831, when France stepped up its repressive measures against the slavers, that opinion in the merchant communities finally turned. In the more liberal mood of the July Monarchy, the illegal slave trade came under serious attack, so that it no longer held much appeal for the merchants of France's port cities. The shipping companies that had supplied vessels for the triangular trade either turned their attention elsewhere or quietly accepted defeat as the end of the slave trade became an inevitability. Some, like Guillet de la Brosse in Nantes, bought plantations in Réunion or invested in the coolie trade, the closest legal form of human trafficking still available.[56] The Atlantic slave trade had ceased to be viable as, two decades before Victor Schœlcher introduced legislation abolishing both the slave trade and slavery in France's colonies in 1848, the economic foundations that had sustained slavery were pulled away.

Emancipation had brought few economic benefits to the people of Haiti, however, as Schœlcher himself noted in 1839, when he became the first abolitionist to visit and write about the independent republic it had become. He returned a thoroughly disillusioned man, finding not the civilization he dreamed of, but a dictatorship that kept its people in poverty and ignorance. Few had work; there were no freedoms to be enjoyed; and 'Cap Haïtien is nothing more than the skeleton of the former Cap Français'.[57] The black population were, he believed, no better off than they had been before the first emancipation decree in 1794. But still he looked forward in hope. With a second abolition, he believed, they and the people of Guadeloupe and Martinique would be given new opportunities and would soon emerge from their current state of 'degradation'.[58]

Slowly and reluctantly, France had accepted the fact of Haitian independence and had renounced its claim to its former colony. But bitterness lingered long after 1804, in particular the bitterness expressed by the former *colons* who had drifted back to France, and to whom the government finally offered financial compensation for what they had lost. Its treatment of the new Haitian republic was notably less generous. At first, in common with the other colonial nations and with the United States, France did nothing to recognize the independence of Haiti or to

---

[55] HM 44013, letter from Fernandes to Demouy, 24 January 1826.

[56] Jacques Fiéran, 'Continuités familiales et ruptures dans la construction navale nantaise', *Enquêtes et documents*, 17 (1990), 155.

[57] Nelly Schmidt, 'Un témoignage original sur Haïti au 19ᵉ siècle: celui de l'abolitionniste Victor Schœlcher', *Jahrbuch für Geschichte von Staat, Wirtschaft und Gesellschaft Lateinamerikas*, 8 (1991), 334.

[58] Germain Saint-Ruf, *L'épopée Delgrès. La Guadeloupe sous la Révolution française* (Paris: L'Harmattan, 1988), 54.

establish diplomatic relations with men they still viewed as rebels and murderers. They seemed reluctant to accept what was for many a humiliating truth: that their army had been defeated by a slave insurrection, and that they faced a revolution they were powerless to oppose. But in reality much had changed. The vision they once cherished of an American empire was now illusory, ended as much by the sale of Louisiana as by the loss of Saint-Domingue; and in 1825 the Restoration monarchy accepted the inevitable. France recognized Haiti as an independent state and thus allowed it to join the community of nations. Economic consider-ations played a part here, as they feared for their colonial commerce, anxious lest a combination of the Monroe Doctrine and Britain's colonial expansion shut French traders out of the Atlantic market.[59] But they showed little grace or generosity, imposing a huge indemnity of 150 million francs on the young Haitian republic as the price of recognition. It was a decision that condemned Haiti to a future of grinding poverty, and which, in Alyssa Sepinwall's words, 'turned Haiti's *de facto* political independence into a crippling financial dependency'.[60]

---

[59] Alyssa Goldstein Sepinwall, 'The Specter of Saint-Domingue: American and French Reactions to the Haitian revolution', in Geggus and Fiering (eds), *The World of the Haitian Revolution*, 327.
[60] Ibid., 318.

14

The Slave Trade in Collective Memory

Silences can impart as much as words, and in the memory of the former slaving ports of France's Atlantic coast, their role in the African slave trade was, throughout much of the nineteenth and twentieth centuries, a subject to be passed over in silence. The conditions on the plantations that had been a major cause of the Haitian Revolution were largely ignored, as were the profits the French merchants and their agents had extracted from slavery, racism and colonialism.[1] What seems most shocking to us today, indeed, is the apparent absence of any public memory of the slave trade, or any acknowledgement of the role that it had played in building the cities' prosperity. As recently as the 1970s and early 1980s, little interest was shown in the subject, whether among historians, political leaders or local authorities, little desire to disinter a past which was seen by many as distasteful and as damaging to the public image of their cities. Their commercial prosperity was explained in terms that were much more socially acceptable, deriving from a spirit of enterprise and a healthy preparedness to embrace risk. It was part of an imperial story in which Africans played no active part, where slaves were passive victims rather than political actors, and where abolition was attributed to liberal Europeans rather than to black leaders or slave activists. It followed that the merchants of Bordeaux, Nantes, and Le Havre were responsible for their own success; they needed to feel no shame about their past, nor to acknowledge their debt to the sufferings of others.

Similarly, those most lauded for their services to the abolitionist cause were liberal Europeans—all French and all white. Leading abolitionists like Condorcet and Raynal, the *abbé* Grégoire and Victor Schœlcher, were represented as all-French heroes in the humanist tradition of the Enlightenment and the French Republic. The black insurgents who had led the campaigns for slave rights, men like Toussaint Louverture in Saint-Domingue and Louis Delgrès in Guadeloupe, were quietly forgotten, or pushed to the margins of the narrative. So when, in 1949, the government wished to commemorate the abolition of slavery by transferring the remains of a Great Man to the hallowed ground of the Pantheon, it was Schœlcher who was honoured, not Toussaint.[2] France was not alone, of course, in

---

[1] This subject is treated at length in Michel-Rolph Trouillot, *Silencing the Past: Power and the Production of History* (Boston, MA, 1995).

[2] Charles Forsdick, 'The Pantheon's empty plinth: commemorating slavery in contemporary France', *Atlantic Studies*, 9 (2012), 279.

seeking to gain kudos and prestige from abolition, or in denying the slaves agency in their liberation. In Britain, too, the darker aspects of the Atlantic slave trade were persistently submerged in the more honourable story of British abolitionism, with its liberal heroes like Clarkson and Wilberforce, virtuous men in whom the British people could take patriotic pride. Until relatively recently, indeed, the history of the transatlantic slave trade was deliberately omitted from British collective remembrance, to be replaced, a recent study suggests, by something more socially and morally acceptable, 'a stylised image of the campaign for its abolition, in the interests of maintaining a consistent national identity built around notions of humanitarian and philanthropic concern'.[3] In the depiction of their slaving past, Le Havre and Nantes did little that Liverpool and Bristol had not done before them.[4]

If the extent of this collective amnesia seems shocking today, it is because so much has changed in public perceptions of race and slavery over the last quarter-century. Until the last decade of the twentieth century, the port cities that had profited so greatly from the slave trade had sought to conceal a past which, they felt, implied a stigma on their reputation and an assault on their very identity. And historians, as we have seen, showed little inclination to research in areas where there was little interest or chance of funding: they had access to excellent collections of merchant papers and most preferred to write in a more positive vein, about prosperity, wealth creation and enterprise, the embellishment of the Atlantic ports which ensued. Political leaders concurred, sharing in the nostalgia of the cities' elites for a golden age of wealth and elegance. This nostalgia was expressed in eloquent, and not wholly untypical, terms by the mayor of Nantes in 1936 in a speech at a dinner of the *Ligue Maritime* celebrating the city's seafaring past. 'How could I fail to evoke the marvellous blossoming of our city two centuries ago that resulted from its spirit of adventure and the power of its shipping? It is a magnificent past that is written on the grey stone of our houses and on these proud facades facing on to the Loire that glory in the opulence of their finely-worked balconies and their grimacing caryatids.'[5] The slave trade merited no more than a passing mention, here or in the other slaving cities, until many years later.

But in recent years, this has changed out of all recognition. The first major initiative in understanding the importance of slaving to the Atlantic economy came in the 1980s, and in the city most affected, Nantes. Serge Daget, who had attracted a team of researchers to the University of Nantes to work on slavery and the triangular trade, persuaded the municipal authorities that this was a subject of

---

[3] Lucy Ball, 'Memory, myth and forgetting: the British transatlantic slave trade' (PhD thesis, University of Portsmouth, 2013).

[4] Geoffrey Cubitt, 'Museums and Slavery in Britain: The Bicentenary of 1807', in Ana Lucia Araujo (ed.), *Politics of Memory: Making Slavery Visible in the Public Space* (London: Routledge, 2012), 162.

[5] Didier Guyvarc'h, 'Nantes, la traite en mémoire', *Place Publique Nantes-Saint-Nazaire*, 29 (2011), 17.

wider public interest. In 1982, he drew up a detailed plan to hold a major international conference, 'Nantes 85'—the first ever to be organized in France—on the subject of the slave trade.[6] The timing was pertinent, as 1985 marked the 300th anniversary of the introduction of the *Code noir* to France's colonies, the document that provided a legal framework for slavery and established protocols governing the conditions under which slaves were held.[7] But the viability of the conference, and of various public displays and exhibitions that were planned across the city, was reliant on funding from the municipal council, and almost immediately local politics intervened. Was this, it was asked, an appropriate way to fund local history? Were there not aspects of the city's past more worthy of celebration and public funding? Financial support became the subject of public debate and inter-party wrangling, with first the Right withdrawing the promise of a grant, then the Left using it as a major plank of their election campaign. In the event, the wider cultural events that had been proposed had to be scaled back, with the consequence that only the academic conference went ahead, with support not from sources in Nantes or its *département*, but from an international agency, UNESCO.[8] The memory of the slave trade had indeed been resurrected, but in the process it had become a partisan issue, the outward symbol of deep divisions over the city's acceptance of its past.

The question of acceptance was common to all the slaving ports, but was especially acute in Nantes, where much of its material past had been destroyed by wartime bombing. Much of the city's shared memory is of a twentieth century scarred by two world wars and of Nantes' literary associations, most especially with Jules Verne.[9] But, above all, Nantes was defined by its links with the sea, and by the great merchant families of the Quai de la Fosse and the Île Feydeau who had contributed to its greatness. For much of the nineteenth and twentieth centuries, the years of prosperity had seemed an age away, hidden from the eyes of future generations by decades of decline, and there was little desire to question the city's myths of its past glories. In particular, there was a reluctance to admit any responsibility, individual or collective, for Nantes' slaving past. But the public debate over 'Nantes 85' left deep scars, and since then both historians and politicians have been prepared to advocate a more open and honest appraisal of the city's role in the slave trade.[10] For a page had been turned: it was time, as the

---

[6] Serge Daget, *La Traite des Noirs. Opération «Nantes 85»* (Nantes, 1982).

[7] Robert Chesnais (ed.), *L'esclavage à la française: le Code noir, 1685 et 1724* (Paris: Nautilus, 2006); Adriana Chira, 'Le Code noir: Idées reçues sur un texte symbolique', *Comparative Legal History*, 4 (2016), 251–54.

[8] Serge Daget (ed.), *De la traite à l'esclavage: Actes du Colloque international sur la traite des noirs* (2 vols, Nantes, 1988).

[9] Didier Guyvarc'h, 'La construction de la mémoire d'une ville: Nantes, 1914–1992', 600–1.

[10] Marc Lastrucci, 'L'évocation publique à Nantes de la traite négrière et de l'esclavage de «Nantes 85» aux «Anneaux de la Mémoire», 1983–1994' (mémoire de maîtrise, Université de Nantes, 1996), *passim*.

city's mayor, Jean-Marc Ayrault, wrote in the preface to a major exhibition on the slave trade staged in 1992 to mark the 500th anniversary of Columbus' discovery of America, for Nantes to perform an 'autopsy' on its own history and that of all the European ports that had engaged in the Atlantic slave trade in the two centuries from 1650 to 1850.[11] By holding the conference in 1985 and inviting participants from around the world to discuss slavery in all its aspects, and then by promoting the exhibition seven years later, Nantes took two pioneering steps in breaking what had been a stifling taboo both in Nantes and across France.

For some, in their quest for respectability, the taboo remained, and talk of the slave trade was discouraged.[12] They preferred to cling to their cities' myths and to their nostalgic vision of the past, emphasizing growth and enterprise, concentrating on what gave them added lustre. Bordeaux was typical in this regard, at least until the 1990s. It was the city of Montaigne and Montesquieu, of art and architecture, wine and commerce. But its part in the slave trade was passed over in relative silence. So when, in 1997, the twinned cities of Bordeaux and Bristol celebrated fifty years of international cooperation, they did so by holding a joint conference on the theme of 'The Port and the Imaginary of the Port'.[13] It was a significant subject for both cities: both had played a leading role in the triangular trade with West Africa and the Caribbean, and in both there was some awareness of the moral climate of the times. Yet only one paper was brave—or impolite— enough to discuss their shared heritage in this regard. The 'imaginary' concerned the islands, exoticism, and colonial comforts, while more disturbing topics like slavery were glossed over or erased.[14]

Perhaps we should not be too critical: the occasion was one for celebration rather than self-analysis. And there was evidence, during the 1990s, that Bordeaux was becoming more aware of its slaving past, aided, no doubt, by a renewed interest among historians at the University of Bordeaux in the colonies and communication between the two shores of the Atlantic.[15] In 1992, the Archives of the Gironde took a first step in opening up public debate when it marked the 500th anniversary of Columbus's discovery of America with an exhibition on the eighteenth-century slave trade.[16] And in 1999, on receipt of an important legacy of

---

[11] Jean-Marc Ayrault, introduction to the catalogue for the exhibition, *Les Anneaux de la Mémoire: Nantes-Europe/Afrique/Amériques* (Nantes, 1992), 9.

[12] See, for instance, Hubert Bonin, *Les tabous de Bordeaux* (Bordeaux: Le Festin, 2010).

[13] Colloque 'Le port et l'imaginaire du port: Bordeaux et Bristol, colloque international à l'occasion du 50ᵉ anniversaire du jumelage Bordeaux-Bristol' (Bordeaux, 1997).

[14] Christine Chivallon, 'Construction d'une mémoire relative à l'esclavage et instrumentalisation politique: le cas des anciens ports négriers de Bordeaux et Bristol', *Cahiers des Anneaux de la Mémoire*, 4 (2002), 177–202.

[15] Paul Butel set up a *Centre d'histoire des Espaces Atlantiques* at the Université de Bordeaux-III as early as 1981 with the aim of pursuing comparative economic and social history of the two shores of the Atlantic. The first issue of the Centre's *Bulletin* appeared in 1983, and nine issues were produced between then and 1999, publishing the results of research on the wider Atlantic.

[16] Archives Départementales de la Gironde, Exposition «La traite négrière», 1992.

iconographical materials from Dr Marcel Chatillon, who had represented the Ministry of Culture in Guadeloupe, the Musée d'Aquitaine curated a major exhibition of paintings, maps, and sketches showing how the French viewed the Antilles and outlining the memories they held for them.[17] In his preface the mayor, Alain Juppé, acknowledged that the city's experience of the islands was not wholly innocent, that Bordeaux's story was both of commercial prosperity and enslavement. The 'regard sur les Antilles' had to be balanced, a multiple gaze that took in both the 'tropical Edens' of the colonists and the insurrection of Toussaint Louverture.[18] If the people of Bordeaux remained deeply attached to the memory of its colonial past and especially to the Caribbean, they were not yet ready to place the African experience of slavery at the heart of their narrative.[19]

The change in public consciousness was a gradual one. Before the last decades of the twentieth century, there had been little public demand that slave ports acknowledge their slaving past. This was true of other slaving countries, too, and not only in Europe. In the United States, there were few monuments or memorials commemorating slavery before the 1990s; the new National Museum of African American history on the National Mall in Washington, a part of the Smithsonian Institute, is a creation of the twenty-first century, with legislation coming in 2003 and its formal opening in 2016. Indeed, Congress was long resistant to the idea of ethnically specific museums as part of the Nation's public history.[20] In Britain, too, progress was slow. Until relatively recently, anti-slavery continued to be viewed through the lens of abolitionists like Wilberforce, and none of the ports which had profited from the slave trade wished to take the lead in claiming primacy. It was a subject where it seemed more decent to maintain a dignified silence. But here, too, pressure-groups, often drawn from local immigrant communities from Africa or the West Indies, began to militate for recognition, and in 1994, in what would prove a landmark moment, National Museums Liverpool opened a major gallery, the Transatlantic Slavery gallery, to explore Liverpool's part in the African slave trade. It was an acknowledgement of the part that Liverpool merchants had played in shipping millions of African to the New World, and it was the first of its kind in Western Europe. In 2007, to mark the bicentenary of Britain's abolition of the slave trade, Liverpool would go further, opening a new Museum devoted to the whole subject of modern slavery. Its aim, in the words of its director, David Fleming, was ambitious: 'to address ignorance and misunderstanding by looking at the deep and permanent impact of slavery and the slave trade on Africa, South

---

[17] Musée d'Aquitaine, *Regards sur les Antilles. Collection Marcel Chatillon* (Bordeaux: Musée d'Aquitaine, 1999).

[18] Alain Juppé, 'Préface', in *Regards sur les Antilles*, 9.

[19] Marguerite Figeac-Monthus, 'Bordeaux et la traite', *Revue historique de Bordeaux et du Département de la Gironde*, NS 17 (2011), 25–7.

[20] Ana Lucia Araujo, 'Introduction', in Araujo (ed.), *Politics of Memory: Making Slavery Visible in the Public Space*, 4.

America, the USA, the Caribbean and Western Europe.'[21] Today the Museum sees itself as a vehicle for social change, openly campaigning for social justice and for an end to all forms of modern slavery, and it engages with its local community, especially with ethnic minorities in Liverpool. It also participates actively in the Federation of International Human Rights Museums.[22] This reflects a new consciousness of the importance of the slave trade, and a feeling of guilt for the crimes of the past. By 2007, the bicentenary of Britain's abolition legislation, that feeling was being shared across much of the Atlantic world. Having been for so long ignored or downplayed in national narratives, the black experience has finally found its place in both historical accounts of the slave trade and public representations in galleries and museums.

Far from continuing to hide their slaving past, the main Atlantic ports have shown a willingness to discuss it more openly, in exhibitions for the general public as well as in seminars restricted to scholars and specialists. In part, this may be ascribed to the chance factor of two anniversaries: the two hundredth anniversary of the first abolition of slavery in 1994, followed rapidly by the 150th anniversary of the second, in 1998. Anniversaries are important in raising popular awareness and focusing discussion, and it is surely not without significance that the resurgence of a collective memory of the slave trade in France should have taken place during the 1990s, just as public memory of the slave trade in Britain was reawakened during the celebrations to mark the bicentenary of the abolitionists' victory in 1807. Until then, though there were constant reminders of the slave trade in the fabric of French slaving cities—in Bordeaux, for instance, the private hotels of leading slave-traders like Nairac, Saige, and Balguerie now housed official buildings like the Prefecture or the tax office—this had little resonance with the public. There was what one historian has recently called 'a lack of readability and visibility' in these buildings, and in the street names and facades that people passed every day.[23] They had to be explained and given meaning in a new moral climate, and in both France and Britain the anniversaries of the 1990s and 2000s produced an opportunity to take stock and to consider how best to present slavery and the slave trade to a wider public.

The initiative in this campaign was largely political, though French academics, like those of the United States and Britain, were increasingly looking at slavery in a different way, often through the lens of cultural and post-colonial studies. It was a campaign by a part of its citizenry, in particular those of African and Caribbean descent, who demanded some recognition of the sufferings of their ancestors and

---

[21] David Fleming, 'Our Vision for the Museum', International Slavery Museum, National Museums Liverpool; see the museum website: http://www.liverpoolmuseums.org.uk/ism/about.

[22] Richard Benjamin, 'Museums and Sensitive Histories: the International Slavery Museum', in Araujo (ed.), *Politics of Memory: Making Slavery Visible in the Public Space*, 187.

[23] Anne-Laure Coste, 'Étude sur les représentations du passé négrier de Bordeaux: entre oubli et mémorisation' (mémoire de maîtrise, Université de Bordeaux-2, 2001), 73–4.

asked that France come to terms with both its colonial past and its multicultural present. Often they looked to the political left for support and leadership, and they took to the streets in defence of their claims and their communities, linking France's slaving past with the criminalization of black communities today and with periodic police shootings of unarmed black teenagers. In particular, they wanted their role as black men and women to be recognized at a time when mayors and municipal authorities, even as they denounced the slave trade as morally reprehensible, went out of their way to avoid mentioning race. Indeed, French politicians were prone to take moral credit for abolition rather than point the finger at those responsible. Jacques Chirac's words in 2006 are symptomatic, looking on the commemoration of the slave trade as a sign that France now had the courage to face its past. His words, uttered to justify the public commemoration of slavery, incensed the black community by heaping credit on the purveyors of memory. 'Slavery and the slave trade,' he said, 'were an indelible stain for humanity. The Republic can be proud of the battle that she won against this ignominy. In commemorating this history, France is showing the way. This is her honour, her grandeur, and her strength.'[24] For an increasingly voluble part of the black population, deriving pride from France's slaving past caused outrage; the slave trade could only be seen as a scar on France's reputation and a source of national shame.

When organizing events to mark the 150th anniversary of the abolition of slavery in 1998, local associations linked up with political movements, including a number that were affiliated to the CGT and to the French Communist Party. *DiversCités* organized in several of the former slaving ports, and militated for greater exposure of the facts of the cities' slaving past. In Nantes, the collective that was established to organize the festivities drew on the expertise of eleven associations, including the *Ligue des Droits de l'Homme*, *SOS-Racisme*, and Amnesty International.[25] Often they started by consulting locally and involving people of African and Caribbean descent. Thus in Bordeaux they set up study sessions to explore the city's colonial history and the work of the French Revolution of 1789 in abolishing the slave trade; they asked how best abolition should be commemorated and celebrated; and they explored links between the eighteenth-century slave trade and current problems, like the relations between France and Africa and North–South relations today. Academics and activists worked together to assess the damage wreaked by the slave trade in Africa and across the world, while local associations sought out traces of the slave trade in the modern city. A group called the 'Friends of Toussaint Louverture' demanded that street names be changed and

---

[24] Crystal Marie Fleming, *Resurrecting Slavery: Racial Legacies and White Supremacy in France* (Philadelphia: Temple University Press, 2017), 54.

[25] Emmanuelle Chérel, 'Le Mémorial: enjeux, débats et controverses', *Place Publique Nantes-Saint-Nazaire*, 29 (2011), 42.

that all trace of those merchants who had profited from the slave trade should be expunged.[26] Again, black and Caribbean groups were active in the movement as a young generation of French men and women came of political age.

Their activism was important, as it helped to politicize the moment. In Nantes, the *Anneaux de la Mémoire* brought academics and citizens together in a common cause: again they had a strong membership among students at the university and the black communities from the Nantes suburbs. They held meetings and published an annual review on slaving issues, the *Cahiers des Anneaux de la Mémoire*, and organized the inaugural exhibition on the slave trade at the city's main museum in 1992-4. This exhibition made the point that the slave trade is a central part of Nantes' history; but it created new polemics through the subjects it omitted, such as the provenance of money for the slave trade, or the illegal trade in the nineteenth century, or the role played by African chiefs and princes.[27] Theirs was, they insisted, a fight to correct past injustices, and, crucially, they were given financial assistance by the municipal authorities.[28] Events were planned bringing together historians and museum professionals on the one hand, political activists and members of the general public on the other, and for the first time the issue of race was given prominence.[29] A new sensitivity was being shown to the descendants of slaves, and there was at least a nod in the direction of recognizing France's multi-cultural composition. The different racial communities that are present in France today, and who make up the populations of the cities that Bordeaux, Nantes, and Marseille have become, expect to be consulted, and increasingly they are. Their aim, in the words of the *Anneaux de la Mémoire*, is 'to favour dialogue between our diverse cultures and to contribute to the fight against all forms of apartheid'.[30]

Outside France, the timing was curiously similar, and again immigrant communities and the descendants of slaves were deeply involved in raising public awareness. In Bristol, for instance, a Slave Trade Action Group was formed in 1996, bringing together a panel of curators, city councillors, and academics with the express purpose of acknowledging this part of Bristol's history. Their work over three years culminated in a major exhibition at the City Museum and Art Gallery in 1999, bearing the title 'A Respectable Trade?: Bristol and Transatlantic Slavery', which highlighted the part which the city had played in the African slave trade. The exhibition made no effort to conceal the cruelty of plantation life or the degradation of the Middle Passage; and it exposed the wide range of Bristol

---

[26] Dominique Belougne, 'Un travail d'une année autour des commémorations de 1998 à Bordeaux du 150e anniversaire de l'abolition de l'esclavage', *Institut aquitain d'Études Sociales*, 75 (2000), 35-9.

[27] Krystel Gualdé, '*Musée* versus *mémorial* ?', *Revue du Philanthrope*, 7 (2018), 103.

[28] 'Avant-Propos', *Cahiers des Anneaux de la Mémoire*, 1 (1999), 5-8.

[29] Madge Dresser, 'Remembering slavery and abolition in Bristol', *Slavery and Abolition*, 30 (2009),229.

[30] These words appear on the title page of the *Cahiers des Anneaux de la Mémoire*, the first number of which appeared in 1999.

businesses, from sugar-refining to iron smelting, that had profited from slaving. Many of the business leaders involved had been honoured as benefactors to the city, or were commemorated in street names in the centre of Bristol, and many Bristolians, as the catalogue acknowledged, felt uneasy about opening up this chapter of their city's past. 'Some would prefer to avoid the issue and its problems, others feel that denial is equally likely to create tension.'[31] The responses that the exhibition elicited would seem to support this view: indeed, the reactions of Bristolians were not so different from those of their counterparts in Nantes or Bordeaux. But the moment heralded an important change, with increasing demands that the names of those who had engaged in slaving should be erased from the public sphere.

There was no shortage of candidates for erasure in any of the Atlantic port cities. In Bordeaux, where merchants were well respected and figured prominently among municipal officials and benefactors, streets and squares often commemorated their work. Several had been mayors or city councillors in the nineteenth century, or else they had enjoyed rich and varied careers in commerce, trading in wines and colonial produce as they built up their fortunes and bestowed largesse on the city. Their names were especially frequent in the nineteenth-century suburbs of the city, in the Chartrons, of course, but also in the newer areas stretching out towards the Barrières or towards Saint-Jean. Few of them were thought of as slave-traders, but it was not long before anti-slavery campaigners found evidence of their involvement or that of their fathers before them. Gradis, Laffon de Ladebat, Baour, Balguerie-Stuttenberg, Mendès, and Couturier had all made a substantial fortune from the triangular trade, and a number of them had invested in sugar plantations in the Caribbean. Increasingly intolerant of what they saw as Bordeaux's culpable silence over these fortunes and their provenance, lobbying groups and voluntary associations formed to raise public awareness, and some, like *DiversCités*, were increasingly political in their demands, insisting that those who had profited from the slave trade should no longer be honoured in the streets of France's ports.[32] When in 2009 they campaigned for streets like the Rue Saige to be renamed, however, they received short shrift from the city's mayor, Alain Juppé, who noted that the merchants had made many other contributions to civic life and dismissed their demands out of hand. To date no streets in Bordeaux have been renamed as a result of the campaign, and other slaving ports have also resisted the pressure to change. But the efforts of the campaigners continue, demanding the removal of all trace of some of the more racist or repressive figures in the French Caribbean, and a few have met with more success. Most famously,

---

[31] Madge Dresser and Sue Giles (eds), *Bristol and Transatlantic Slavery: Catalogue of the Exhibition 'A Respectable Trade?: Bristol and Transatlantic Slavery at the City Museum and Art Gallery, Bristol, 1999* (Bristol, 2000), 9.

[32] Danielle Pétrissans-Cavaillès, *Sur les traces de la traite des Noirs à Bordeaux* (Paris: L'Harmattan, 2004), 43–66.

Antoine Richepanse, a slave-owner and the general notorious for his role in the brutal suppression of the slave revolt in Guadeloupe, was expunged from the street maps of Paris at the insistence of the then mayor, Bertrand Delanoë: in 2002 the rue Richepanse was formally stripped of its slaving associations to bear a new name, the rue du Chevalier-de-Saint-Georges, that quite explicitly honoured the son of a Haitian slave.[33]

Campaigners, of course, want more, and routinely search out the names of local merchants, planters, or ships' captains who were tarred with accusations of slave-trading, and demand that local authorities follow Delanoë's example and purge them from public memory. School pupils have felt mobilized, where their *collèges* or *lycées* have taken the names of slave-owners or colonial figures, to protest and to demand change: in 2017, there was even a campaign across much of France calling for the renaming of all establishments called after Louis XIV's minister, Colbert, on the grounds that he had legalized the institution of slavery and was therefore complicit in a crime against humanity.[34] Antislavery has turned into a campaign issue for the left, and with it the destruction of all public memory of what they see as a horrific episode in France's colonial past. For some groups in France today there seems no reason for compromise, and no one connected to the slave trade should be accorded any public recognition. Or, if the slave trade is to be memorialized, then it is the slaves, not the slave-owners, whose memory should be honoured, as victims but also as the heroes of the Atlantic world. The memory of the slave trade is now intimately bound up in twenty-first-century concerns about race, ethnicity, and human equality. Museum displays are expected to offer an emotional as well as an intellectual response.

But how should France honour men and women whom it had once enslaved and exploited for profit? Were slaves to be honoured as individuals, or dismissed as a faceless mass of humanity, victims rather than people with individual stories and achievements? Toussaint apart, there are few slaves from France's black Atlantic who gained real notoriety in the European world, in part because of the lack of a written record. For, in contrast to the English-speaking world, no former slaves from the French Caribbean left accounts of their experience, and where we have access to the words they spoke, it is from judicial records of their testimonies in court.[35] France had no equivalent of Olaudah Equiano, born the son of a tribal chief in present-day Nigeria, who was shipped at the age of eleven to Barbados on a British slave ship, but who then gained his freedom and travelled the world as a free man, before reaching a wide readership with his *Extraordinary Life*. Equiano was a celebrity in his own right, a campaigner for the cause of abolition, and a sufficiently rich character to warrant a special exhibition in Birmingham in 2007

---

[33] *Le Parisien*, 4 February 2002.   [34] *Le Monde*, 17 September 2017.
[35] Frédéric Régent, Gilda Gonfier and Bruno Maillard, *Libres et sans fers: Paroles d'esclaves français* (Paris: Fayard, 2015), 7–17.

devoted to him and the values that he represented.[36] Thanks to Equiano, the exhibition could move seamlessly from slave ships to the cause of abolition and the men who championed it. As the exhibition catalogue made clear, it was curated in a way that would both celebrate Equiano's life and commemorate British abolitionism, 'the 1807 Act of Parliament to abolish the transatlantic slave trade'.[37] African struggle and British idealism could thus co-exist in apparent harmony, to create a narrative that resonated for many in both the white and black communities. It is a pity that there is no parallel to Equiano in France's memory of slavery, since it makes it much harder to create a black narrative of the French slave trade.

The French government has played its part in encouraging public debate on slavery and in insisting that such issues as the slave trade and France's colonial past have their place in the school curriculum. Indeed, they have become central themes in the classroom, where until recently they were often treated as part of a 'metanarrative of modernity', as collateral damage in the advancement of France.[38] But the transformation is far from complete. If the old stereotype has been challenged, as Françoise Vergès reminds us, the discussion is often limited in scope, focusing principally on the abolitionists and the slave trade, not on slavery itself. This matters, she insists, because slavery and the slave trade, though separate topics for analysis, are intimately connected, two aspects of a system of human degradation to which the merchants and, more generally, the wider communities of the slaving ports owed their prosperity.[39] By focusing too exclusively on the commercial activity of merchants and ship-owners, the extent of this degradation can still be deliberately underplayed.

But even recognizing their debt to the slave trade has been a huge step forward in coming to terms with France's colonial past, both for those who live in the slaving ports and for those whose ancestors were enslaved. In large measure, this reflects the concerns of contemporary French society, a France where many of the descendants of slaves have come to live, French citizens from former colonies and *départements d'outre-mer* who have brought a new level of cultural diversity to the cities of the metropole. It is surely significant that they have been among the most vociferous in demanding to know more about their history and to press for greater recognition and memorialization of the slave trade and of France's slaving past. From the late 1990s, they have shown a new awareness of that past and a greater

[36] 'Equiano: an exhibition of an extraordinary life', Birmingham Museum and Art Gallery, 2007–8; Stuart Burch, 'Equiano: an exhibition of an extraordinary life', *Museums Journal*, December 2007, 48–9.

[37] Arthur Torrington (ed.), *Equiano: Enslavement, Resistance and Abolition* (Birmingham: Birmingham Museums and Art Gallery, 2007), introduction.

[38] Marcus Otto, 'The challenge of decolonization: school history textbooks as media and objects of the postcolonial politics of memory in France since the 1960s', *Journal of Educational Media, Memory and Society*, 5 (2013), 23.

[39] Françoise Vergès, 'Les troubles de la mémoire: traite négrière, esclavage et écriture de l'histoire', *Cahiers d'études africaines*, 179–80 (2005), 1143.

sense of entitlement, insisting that the French state must recognize its part in their historical tragedy in the same was as it had done for other groups in France—most notably the Jewish population over the Holocaust and the Armenian community over the massacres suffered at the hands of the Turks in 1915–17. In 1990, when Holocaust denial became a criminal offence in France, black activists found themselves with a political model to pursue, especially when, in 2000, France went further, complying with the demands of Jewish organizations for financial compensation to those who had suffered loss. In 2001, the state also recognized the Turkish massacres as genocide. Activists from the Caribbean and their political supporters in France felt that their moment for recognition had come, and that slavery, too, would now be given the status of the 'crime against humanity' that it was.[40] Anything less, they believed, smacked of racism and discrimination.

They did not have long to wait. In 2001, under legislation introduced by Christiane Taubira, France became the first nation in the world to declare slavery and the slave trade 'crimes against humanity', and to introduce a national day of remembrance for the victims of slavery, comparable to that with which the French commemorated the victims of the Holocaust. But which date would they choose? There had been criticism from the black community in 1998 when Jacques Chirac had chosen 27 April, the day when Schœlcher's law was passed in 1848.[41] This time they pressed for a more neutral date, one less associated with French initiatives. In the event, the date of 10 May was chosen for the official commemoration, which was simply the day when the new law was passed, and the commemoration has taken place on that date every year since. Politicians regularly take part in parades and ceremonies, the president of the republic is often present, and France's various ethnic communities are invited to take part. The law also sought to improve public education on the slave trade: it attached greater importance to the history of the slave trade in the school curriculum, so that the young should be informed of it. And it increased funding for academic research on slavery, calling for cooperation between scholars in Europe and those in Africa and the Caribbean, and urging that the written records in France be set against the archaeological evidence and oral traditions of Africa, the Americas, and the Caribbean.[42] It did not go as far as some on the left would have liked: unlike the Jews, former slaves were offered no financial compensation for past mistreatment. But it had real significance for the black community. For the first time, France had made it clear that it took its slaving past seriously, and made a point, before the world, of integrating its record of anti-slavery into its republican heritage. The Taubira Law was at the same time a gesture to France's ethnic minorities and a

---

[40] Jean-Yves Camus, 'The commemoration of slavery in France and the emergence of a black political consciousness', *The European Legacy*, 11 (2006), 648–9.

[41] Ibid., 649.

[42] Law of 21 May 2001, the 'Loi Taubira'.

contribution to the nation's politics of memory.[43] It helped to raise public consciousness of the legacy of slavery, and to instil a sense of right and wrong. And interestingly, it was passed without opposition in the French National Assembly.

The mayors of the Atlantic slave ports were stirred to act, often at the instigation of the immigrant communities of their cities. Alain Juppé, for instance, the mayor of Bordeaux for much of this period, has taken a leading role in ensuring that his city has embraced the spirit of the Taubira Law, by enacting a series of measures which, adapting the words of the historian Paul Ricoeur, he termed 'a politics of just memory'.[44] The work had been started by his predecessors in the wake of the 150th anniversary celebrations. In 1999, Bordeaux staged a major exhibition on the Caribbean, 'Regards sur les Antilles'; in 2003, a plaque was placed on the house where Toussaint Louverture's son, Isaac, had spent his final years (he is buried nearby, in the cemetery at La Chartreuse); and a square named in Toussaint's honour was inaugurated on the opposite side of the Garonne, in 2005, in the presence of Haiti's Minister of Culture.[45] In 2008, as Bordeaux prepared to open new galleries in the Musée d'Aquitaine devoted to the city's slaving past, the mayor led a delegation from Bordeaux to Liverpool to take inspiration from the International Museum of Slavery, which had opened the previous year. Bordeaux, he wished to make clear, was sensitive in its treatment of slavery and of issues of colour, and responsive to its own black communities. The curators had learned a lot from Liverpool, even if, as Renaud Hourcade insists, there is an important difference in the way in which they presented their slaving history. 'Whereas Liverpool's museum is mainly a museum about black history,' he explains, 'Bordeaux's museum is mainly a museum about Bordeaux.'[46] And if Saint-Domingue is omnipresent in the museum, it is still presented as a source of riches, as 'L'Eldorado des Aquitains'.[47] The emphasis is highly significant, since it means that the slave trade is not allowed to become the principal focus of the exhibition: it is just one subject among many to be covered in the museum's galleries. As a result, the slaves do not become the principal actors, though, learning from Liverpool's experience, the display makes a commendable effort to link with contemporary issues like racism and cultural diversity.[48]

---

[43] Renaud Hourcade, 'Commemorating a Guilty Past: The Politics of Memory in the French Former Trade Cities', in Ana Lucia Araujo (ed.), Politics of Memory: Making Slavery Visible in the Public Space (London: Routledge, 2012), 131.

[44] Alain Juppé, 'Un message de vérité et d'humanisme', in Musée d'Aquitaine, Bordeaux au XVIIIe siècle, le commerce atlantique et l'esclavage (catalogue of the permanent exhibition on the slave trade, Bordeaux, 2009), 9–10.

[45] Marguerite Figeac-Monthus, 'Bordeaux et la traite', 27.

[46] Renaud Hourcade, 'Commemorating a Guilty Past', 136.

[47] Musée d'Aquitaine, Bordeaux au XVIIIe siècle, le commerce atlantique et l'esclavage, 107–25.

[48] Hourcade, 'Commemorating a Guilty Past', 137.

This was also true, to a greater of lesser degree, of the other museums in France's Atlantic ports which contain important displays of material on the slave trade. All now make some acknowledgement of their slaving past, but—despite the demands of the *Anneaux de la Mémoire* and others—there is no museum devoted to the single issue of the slave trade, and none which, like Liverpool, organizes its narrative around the slave experience. In the Château des Ducs de Bretagne in Nantes, where the city's principal historical museum is housed, much has been done to educate the citizenry on the evils of the slave trade, and to integrate it into the history of both the city and of France. There is an acknowledgement that what was done was morally wrong, particularly the eagerness shown by so many merchants to re-engage with the slave trade after the Napoleonic Wars. The new gallery on the slave trade is richly documented, including in its display the log of a Nantes slaver, the *Bonne Mère*, which sailed from the Loire estuary in February 1815 for the coast of Africa, took on a cargo of slaves, and reached the Caribbean before being seized by the English off Pointe-à-Pitre in September. It is a graphic example of the uncertainties of international law at that time, for between these dates what had been a legal trade had been transformed into a criminal activity. The log recreates the moral dilemma of the moment, one which the visitor is invited to share.[49]

But again, the slave trade is one theme among several given a privileged place in the museum's galleries, and it is presented as part of a wider history of the city and the Nantes estuary across the centuries. The same pattern is to be found elsewhere. In La Rochelle, where, as in the other ports, there is now a permanent display on the slave trade, the obfuscation is perhaps greater, as the city's role in the slave trade is buried in a broader and richer Atlantic narrative. But then, the city's museum, the Musée du Nouveau Monde, does not pretend to focus particularly on the slave trade, nor yet on the Caribbean, as it traces the part played by La Rochelle in a succession of transatlantic contexts: the discovery of the Americas, the opening up of New France and the city's part in the fur trade, and the various indigenous peoples of the United States, all are treated with the same empathy and the same concern for detail as the city's part in slaving. This may seem somewhat perverse, as the museum is housed in the Hôtel Fleuriau, the elegant town house of one of La Rochelle's great slave-owning families, which was purchased by the municipality in 1979.[50] Until then there had been no public acknowledgement in the town of its slaving past, and it was never intended that it should become a museum dedicated to the slave trade. Rather, it aims to explore La Rochelle's multi-faceted presence in the Atlantic world and the interactions between French colonists and the native peoples of the Americas. The opening of the new

---

[49] Musée d'Histoire de Nantes, Château des Ducs de Bretagne, Salle 19, Journal de bord d'un navire négrier nantais, 1815.
[50] *Musée du Nouveau Monde de La Rochelle, plan de visite.*

museum, in 1982, represents something of a first for the port cities of the west. Its inaugural exhibition emphasized its overall theme (*Mémoire d'un port: La Rochelle et l'Atlantique, 16e–19e siècle*), and its opening passed off without protest. It was planned and conceived well before the current wave of interest in the slave trade, and before the whole issue became politicized. By 2002, with the growth of associations dedicated to perpetuating the memory of the slave trade, the display in the Musée Fleuriau came under attack for its discretion and ambiguity, and La Rochelle's memorialization of its past became increasingly contested.[51]

An important line had, however, been crossed. On 10 May 2009, when the official celebration of the abolition of slavery was held in Bordeaux, ministers and dignitaries filed into the Musée d'Aquitaine, and they made it clear that the museum's purpose was central to their goal of fostering education on France's slaving past—education, in Alain Juppé's words, to combat ignorance, 'the ignorance that nourishes fear and the fear that generates hatred', and to spread the values of the republic which slavery insults. His speech was a searing rebuttal of slavery, expressed with a vigour and directness that Bordeaux had not previously heard. But there was a note of caution, and one that those who dreamt of pursuing claims for reparations had no reason to welcome. For if he recognized the need to understand the city's past and its responsibility for the slave trade, Juppé was in no mood to apologize. 'Is it a question of our expressing repentance?' he asked, rhetorically. 'I prefer to speak of it as an acknowledgement of the truth. We, as citizens of the twenty-first century, the sons and daughters of Bordeaux in 2009, we are obviously not responsible for or guilty of actions committed in the seventeenth, eighteenth and nineteenth centuries in a historical context that was profoundly different.'[52] For those clamouring for remorse or compensation, this was an unwelcome answer, but it was one for which Alain Juppé was widely applauded across the city.

In the other slaving ports, too, efforts have been made to give public recognition to the human cost of the slave trade, or to commemorate the leaders of the black insurrection against slavery. In May 2015, La Rochelle sought to rebalance its representation of the slave trade by inaugurating a statue in memory of Toussaint Louverture by the Senegalese artist Ousmane Sow. As in Nantes and Bordeaux, a voluntary association of local people, in this case calling themselves *Mémoria*, played an important part in championing the project and in bringing it to fruition, and Toussaint's statue, in full military uniform, today stands proudly in the courtyard of the city's museum with the Hôtel Fleuriau as its backcloth.[53] Le Havre has done rather less, at least to date. There is a small memorial slab between

---

[51] Mickaël Augeron, 'La mémoire de la traite des Noirs, de l'esclavage et de leurs abolitions à La Rochelle: les initiatives municipales, 1979–2015', *Revue du Philanthrope*, 7 (2018), 78–81.
[52] Journée nationale de commémoration de l'esclavage, speech by the mayor of Bordeaux, Alain Juppé, at the Musée d'Aquitaine, 10 May 2009.
[53] *Sud-Ouest*, 20 May 2015.

the Malraux Art Museum and the entrance to the port, but it struggles to capture the attention of passers-by. By way of contrast, as protestors have noted, five major streets in Le Havre bear the names of merchants and civic dignitaries (Masurier, Begouën, Boulogne, Eyriès, and Massieu) whose fortunes were made trading slaves.[54]

By far the greatest act of commemoration and expiation of the last few years has taken place in Nantes, appropriately perhaps, since it was the city where Serge Daget had done so much to launch the whole memorial movement with his initiative for 'Nantes 85'. In 2012, Nantes inaugurated its own memorial to the abolition of the slave trade on the bank of the Loire close to the merchant quarter which had seen so many slave ships leave for the coast of Africa. The idea of commissioning a simple statue had been swiftly discarded, and the design of the Memorial was carefully planned, with submissions invited from a wide range of international sculptors and artists. The idea of preserving different memories of the slave trade and of providing a place for reflection was prioritized when the jury delivered its verdict and the commission was given to a Polish-American artist, Krzysztof Wodiczko. The memorial lies along the side of the river, looking out on the water; it is shaped like a slave ship, its hull filled with panels that trace the history of the slave trade and remind the visitor of the reality of the Middle Passage and the fight for abolition; and it recognizes the extent of Nantes' responsibility for the slave trade, with the pavement above studded with images representing every slave voyage out of the port in the eighteenth and early nineteenth centuries. But it goes further in linking eighteenth-century slavery with other forms of slavery in the world today, in invoking human rights across the planet, and in inviting reflection on the cost of freedom and on man's inhumanity to man. It is a timely symbol of a new mentality, one which has finally allowed one slaving port to come to terms with the memory of its past.[55]

---

[54] 'The Slave Streets of Le Havre', *Normandy Then and Now* (http://www.normandythenandnow.com/the-slave-streets-of-le-havre/19, June 2018).

[55] Emmanuelle Chérel, *Le Mémorial de l'abolition de l'esclavage de Nantes* (Rennes: Presses Universitaires de Rennes, 2012), 263–8.

Conclusion

The Age of Revolutions was a period of profound crisis across the French Atlantic world. The prosperity that had been generated through colonization in the course of the eighteenth century came to an abrupt end, and it would be many decades before the richest of France's Atlantic ports—Nantes, Le Havre, and Bordeaux—recovered even a fraction of their former dynamism. But it would be misleading to attribute all their ills to the Revolution and Empire. Some ports had suffered grievously in earlier eighteenth-century wars, only to recover and re-establish their primacy in Atlantic markets in the second half of the century; while in the case of others—ports like Bayonne and La Rochelle—their best days were behind them long before the outbreak of revolution in 1789. Revolution, war and blockade during the Napoleonic years, combined with the loss of their most lucrative colony in Saint-Domingue, may have marked a new low for the ports and their merchant elites, the nadir of their commercial fortunes. But they have to be seen in context; they do not explain everything.

That is not in any way to downplay the significance of these years. For the major Atlantic ports, the Age of Revolutions was a turning point from which recovery would prove long and slow. Bordeaux, it is true, would find opportunities to diversify in the course of the nineteenth century, developing trading links with the Far East, the Indian Ocean, and Senegal in West Africa and growing its trade with ports in Central and Latin America, most especially with Cuba. But success in these markets was hard to predict and the merchants found that what had seemed promising outlets were periodically blocked, whether by tariffs imposed by other European states, by English competition in the Americas, or by the French government's own policies in its overseas colonies. Bordeaux would suffer further setbacks, leading to years of slump and to periodic falls in the volume of its wine exports. Prosperity was far from assured. The nineteenth-century port became more dependent on less lucrative internal and coastal traffic—*cabotage*—than it had been in the past. By the time of the Second Empire, Bordeaux seemed destined to make a steady, if unspectacular, recovery from mercantile decay, but that recovery was impeded by the conservatism of the merchant class and its refusal to indulge in risk or speculation. Both owners and workers, indeed, seemed singularly resistant to change, and Bordeaux's commercial fortunes suffered as a consequence.[1] Investors turned away from shipping and colonial commerce in

---

[1] Pierre Guillaume, 'L'economie sous le Second Empire', in Desgraves and Dupeux, *Bordeaux au 19ᵉ siècle*, 192–201.

favour of the more lucrative returns which nineteenth-century industry held out to them. In geographical terms, the Atlantic lands lost out to the heartlands of the French industrial revolution in the north and the east.

Of the other ports, Nantes also turned to its industry and the produce of its hinterland for much of its port activity as Atlantic trade declined. After 1830, even those most involved in the slave trade were forced to look elsewhere as their connections with the sugar islands fell away. Sugar continued to be imported and refined in Nantes, but increasingly it came from the Indian Ocean rather than the Caribbean. The transition came suddenly. Whereas in 1827 around 73 per cent of the sugar unloaded in Nantes came from the West Indies, within a decade, in 1836, 63 per cent originated in the Indian Ocean, and leading Nantes merchants had transferred their attention to Mauritius and especially to Réunion.[2] Renewed prosperity did not come until the second half of the century, until the Second Empire and the Third Republic. By then Nantes had established itself as an industrial city in its own right, with part of the port given over to shipbuilding and the *chantiers navals*. Like Bordeaux, much of its trade was now conducted in Europe and between coastal ports. Just like Bordeaux, too, its population grew only slowly. The eighteenth-century Atlantic world could not be restored.

The Atlantic port which defied the seemingly ineluctable decline following the loss of Saint-Domingue and the damage wrought by the revolutionary years was Le Havre, where industry remained secondary and merchants sought ways to adapt to diminished prospects. At first, many of their initiatives were met with failure and bankruptcy, but by the Second Empire the economy of the port was once again booming. In part this was due to a rapid increase in coffee imports, in part to trade in cotton with the American South, in part, too, to an influx of Californian gold which helped to relaunch mercantile enterprise. Not everything was plain sailing. The American Civil War got in the way of growth in trade with the United States, the Franco-Prussian War, more briefly, with European commerce; and Le Havre suffered, with other ports, from economic recession in the 1880s. But the longer-term trend was one of growth and rapid expansion: if the ships using the port weighed in at 2 million tons in 1856, this doubled by 1878, and grew dramatically in the first years of the twentieth century, hitting 6 million tons in 1901, 9 million in 1907, and 11 million on the eve of the First World War, making Le Havre the second port in France after Marseille. But not all of this tonnage was accounted for by cargo vessels, or by colonial trade. Where Le Havre really prospered was in passenger traffic, as it established itself as the premier port in France for transatlantic liners, vying in sailings to New York with the English Channel port of Southampton. In the century since 1815, the city had reinvented itself.[3]

[2] Pétré-Grenouilleau, *Nantes, histoire et géographie contemporaine*, 145–6.
[3] Jean-Pierre Chaline, 'L'explosion havraise', in Corvisier (ed.), *Histoire du Havre*, 188–92.

Contemporaries argued about which of these elements—revolution, war, or the loss of Saint-Domingue—contributed most to their decline. All posed threats, not least in terms of the huge risks involved in trading on the high seas. In the short term there is no doubt that naval warfare posed the most critical threat, causing severe disruption to the trading patterns which French merchants had established and to partnerships on which their profits depended. The extension of the war into a colonial war with Britain, and the long years of blockade caused by Napoleon's Continental System and Britain's Orders in Council, led to ships being laid up and long-established merchant houses being forced out of business. Markets which the French had nurtured and exploited were lost to foreign competitors. Over more than twenty years of war, the damage and disruption suffered were on a scale unparalleled during the wars of the eighteenth century. But wars end, and periods of peace follow when overseas commerce can again flourish. Revolution, allied to an anti-slavery campaign, would prove more damaging in the long term, inflicting lasting damage rather than temporary disruption, and making it impossible for the Atlantic ports to return to their established ways. The loss of Saint-Domingue, the richest of all European countries, was a blow from which they took decades to recover. Guadeloupe and Martinique, France's remaining Caribbean colonies, could not compensate for the riches that had been lost, and the nineteenth century saw vessels from other countries—Spain, Portugal, Cuba, and Brazil—replacing the French on the trade routes to the Americas.

But the saddest victim of the Age of Revolutions in France's Atlantic world was the country that had been inspired by revolutionary ideas to win its independence: Haiti itself. In the decades that followed the Haitian Revolution, the island would provide political inspiration to anti-colonial campaigners and revolutionaries across the Americas, where it would be held up as an example to other enslaved societies. Slaves could free themselves, the message ran. Black Africans could rise against European masters and win their freedom: the cry was powerful and exhilarating, a battle-cry for the enslaved and oppressed, and it swiftly resonated across Latin America. In the eighteenth-century world's most prosperous colony, 'a world built upon slavery, colonialism and racial hierarchy had been turned upside down'.[4] Saint-Domingue had lit a beacon to the colonized world, and Toussaint's revolution was greeted as a turning-point in race relations between Europeans and Africans in the New World.

But initial enthusiasm quickly turned sour. The gratuitous violence of the uprising spread fear among Haiti's Caribbean neighbours, while back in France the main focus of opinion was on the inhuman cruelty of the insurgents and the obscene tortures which they had inflicted on the white population. Quickly, too, attention turned to economic questions, as Haiti sank into new depths of poverty

---

[4] Ada Ferrer, 'Speaking of Haiti: Slavery, Revolution and Freedom in Cuban Slave Testimony', in David Geggus and Norman Fiering (eds), *The World of the Haitian Revolution*, 223.

in the decades that followed independence. While it is true that France must accept its share of responsibility for the economic failures that followed, crippling the Haitian economy by demanding reparations which it could not possibly afford as the price of diplomatic recognition in the 1820s, this does not wholly explain the transformation of a resource-rich island into the impoverished backwater it became. The sugar plantations that had been at the heart of its prosperity were left untilled as Haitians sought an escape from plantation labour, seeing it as degrading and equating it in their minds with slavery and exploitation. They aspired to economic as well as personal independence as part of a free peasantry.[5] The result, however, was economic devastation. The larger estates were broken up, and Haiti was soon transformed into a land of peasant smallholdings and subsistence agriculture. In political terms, it might claim to have become a liberated society, among the most equal in the Western world, a society inspired by the memory of Toussaint Louverture. But these gains came at a terrible economic cost. An island which in 1790 had been classed among the most prosperous in the world, producing half the world's sugar and more coffee that any other place on earth, sank into poverty and deprivation on an unimagined scale.[6] The hope and optimism that had greeted Haiti's birth in 1804 had been quickly snuffed out, to be replaced by a sense of profound abandonment.

By the end of the nineteenth century, living conditions on the island had deteriorated to such a degree that the mass of the population faced levels of penury and malnutrition that were without equal in other parts of the Caribbean. One nineteenth-century historian, writing in Nantes in the 1880s with all the benefit of hindsight and a knowledge of Haiti's subsequent history, expressed sadness that 'the former colony of Saint-Domingue which could be one of the richest and most prosperous countries on earth has become one of the most miserable'.[7] And that was before the developments of the twentieth century which further ravaged Haiti, and what Jean Casimir refers to as the 'uninvited intervention' of the United States in 1915, bringing other problems in its wake.[8] Haiti's development was no longer one that other nations wished to emulate. And a state whose independent history had started with such promise had come to be seen by many as an economic backwater, still prone to the violence and volatility that had characterized it in the eighteenth century, a nation that seemed to pose a dire warning to the rest of the Atlantic world.

[5]   Paul Cheney, *Cul de Sac: Patrimony, Capitalism and Slavery in French Saint-Domingue* (Chicago: University of Chicago Press, 2017), 222.
[6]   François Blancpin, *La colonie française de Saint-Domingue: de l'esclavage à l'indépendance* (Paris: Karthala, 2004), 7.
[7]   Castonnet des Fosses, *L'île de Saint-Domingue au 18ᵉ siècle* (Nantes, 1884), quoted in Blancpin, *La colonie française de Saint-Domingue*, 222.
[8]   Jean Casimir, 'From Saint-Domingue to Haiti: To Live Again or to Live at Last!', in Geggus and Fiering, *The World of the Haitian Revolution*, xviii.

Bibliography

Aaslestad, Katherine B. and Joor, Johan (eds), *Revisiting Napoleon's Continental System. Local, Regional and European Experiences* (Basingstoke: Palgrave Macmillan, 2015).

Abad, Reynal et al. (eds), *Les passions d'un historien: Mélanges en l'honneur de Jean-Pierre Poussou* (Paris: Presses de l'Université Paris-Sorbonne, 2010).

Adams, Christine, Censer, Jack R., and Graham, Lisa Jane (eds), *Visions and Revisions of Eighteenth-century France* (University Park, PA: Pennsylvania State University Press, 1997).

Adams, Donald R. Jr., *Finance and Enterprise in Early America: A Study of Stephen Girard's Bank, 1812–31* (Philadelphia: University of Pennsylvania Press, 1978).

Aftalion, Florin, *The French Revolution. An Economic Interpretation* (Cambridge: Cambridge University Press, 1987).

Ames, Glenn J., *Colbert, Mercantilism and the French Quest for Asian Trade* (DeKalb: Northern Illinois University Press, 1996).

Angiolini, Franco and Roche, Daniel (eds), *Cultures et formations négociantes dans l'Europe moderne* (Paris: Editions de l'EHESS, 1995).

Araujo, Ana Lucia (ed.), *Politics of Memory: Making Slavery Visible in the Public Space* (London: Routledge, 2012).

Araujo, Ana Lucia, *Reparations for Slavery and the Slave Trade* (London: Bloomsbury, 2017).

Archives Parlementaires de 1787 à 1860: recueil complet des débats législatifs et politiques des chambres françaises.

Armitage, David and Subrahmanyam, Sanjay (eds), *The Age of Revolutions in Global Context, c. 1760–1840* (Basingstoke: Palgrave Macmillan, 2010).

Armstrong, Catherine and Chmielewski, Laura M., *The Atlantic Experience: Peoples, Places, Ideas* (Basingstoke: Palgrave Macmillan, 2013).

Astbury, Katherine and Philp, Mark (eds), *Napoleon's Hundred Days and the Politics of Legitimacy* (Basingstoke: Palgrave Macmillan, 2018).

Augeron, Mickaël, 'La mémoire de la traite des Noirs, de l'esclavage et de leurs abolitions à La Rochelle: les initiatives municipales, 1979–2015', *Revue du Philanthrope*, 7 (2018).

Augeron, Mickaël and Caudron, Olivier (eds), *La Rochelle, l'Aunis et la Saintonge face à l'esclavage* (Paris: Les Indes savantes, 2012).

Augeron, Mickaël, Poton, Didier and Van Ruymbeke, Bertrand (eds), *Les Huguenots et l'Atlantique, vol 1: Pour Dieu, la Cause ou les Affaires* (Paris: Les Indes savantes, 2009).

Augeron, Mickaël and Tranchant, Mathias (eds), *La violence et la mer dans l'espace atlantique, 12ᵉ–19ᵉ siècle* (Rennes: Presses Universitaires de Rennes, 2004).

Auguste, Marcel, 'L'armée française de Saint-Domingue: dernière armée de la Révolution', *Jahrbuch für Geschichte von Staat, Wirtschaft une Gesellschaft Lateinamerikas*, 28 (1991).

Augustin, Jean-Marie, *La Révolution Française en Haut-Poitou et pays charentais* (Toulouse: Privat, 1989).

Aurenche, Marie-Laure (ed.), *Le combat pour la liberté des Noirs dans le Journal de la Société de la Morale Chrétienne* (2 vols, Paris: L'Harmattan, 2011).

Ayrault, Jean-Marc introduction to the catalogue for the exhibition, *Les Anneaux de la Mémoire: Nantes-Europe/Afrique/Amériques* (Nantes : CIM, 1992).

Babb, Winston C., 'French refugees from Saint-Domingue to the southern United States, 1791–1810' (PhD thesis, University of Virginia, 1954).

Ball, Lucy, 'Memory, myth and forgetting: the British Transatlantic slave trade' (PhD thesis, University of Portsmouth, 2013).

Barrière, Pierre, *L'Académie de Bordeaux, centre de culture internationale au 18ᵉ siècle, 1712–92* (Bordeaux: Éditions Bière, 1951).

Bécamps, Pierre, *La Révolution à Bordeaux, 1789–94: J.-M.-B. Lacombe, président de la Commission Militaire* (Bordeaux: Éditions Bière, 1953).

Bécamps, Pierre, *Les suspects à Bordeaux et dans le Département de la Gironde, 1789–99* (Paris: Imprimerie Nationale, 1954).

Belaubre, Christophe, Dym, Jordana, and Savage, John (eds), *Napoleon's Atlantic: The Impact of Napoleonic Empire in the Atlantic World* (Leiden: Brill, 2010).

Belougne, Dominique, 'Un travail d'une année autour des commémorations de 1998 à Bordeaux du 150e anniversaire de l'abolition de l'esclavage', *Institut aquitain d'études Sociales*, 75 (2000).

Benot, Yves, *La démence coloniale sous Napoléon* (Paris: La Découverte, 1992).

Bessel, Richard, Guyatt, Nicholas, and Rendall, Jane (eds), *War, Empire and Slavery, 1770–1830* (Basingstoke: Palgrave Macmillan, 2010).

Bew, John *Castlereagh: A Life* (London: Quercus, 2012).

Binaud, Daniel, *Les corsaires de Bordeaux et de l'Estuaire: 120 ans de guerres sur mer* (Biarritz: Atlantic, 1999).

Binney, Matthew, *The Cosmopolitan Evolution: Travel, Travel Narratives and the Revolution of the Eighteenth-century European Consciousness* (Lanham, MD: University Press of America, 2006).

Black, Jeremy, *France and the Grand Tour* (Basingstoke: Palgrave Macmillan, 2003).

Blancpin, François, *La colonie française de Saint-Domingue: de l'esclavage à l'indépendance* (Paris: Karthala, 2004).

Bolt, Christine and Drescher, Seymour (eds), *Anti-slavery, Religion and Reform: Essays in Memory of Roger Anstey* (Folkestone: Dawson, 1980).

Bonin, Hubert, *Les tabous de Bordeaux* (Bordeaux: Le Festin, 2010).

Bonnet, Natacha, 'Seigneurs et planteurs, entre Ouest Atlantique et Antilles: quatre familles du 18ᵉ siècle' (thèse de doctorat, Université de Nantes, 2006).

Bonnet, Natacha, 'L'investissement colonial au 18e siècle: l'exemple de quatre plantations sucrières à Saint-Domingue', *Entreprises et Histoire*, 52 (2008).

Borucki, A., 'The "African colonists" of Montevideo: new light on the illegal slave trade to Rio de Janeiro and the Rio de la Plata (1830–42)', *Slavery & Abolition*, 30 (2009).

Boulle, Pierre, *Race et esclavage dans la France de l'Ancien Régime* (Paris: Perrin, 2007).

Bourguinat, Nicolas and Venayre, Sylvain (eds), *Voyager en Europe de Humboldt à Stendhal: contraintes nationales et tentations cosmopolites, 1790–1840* (Paris: Nouveau Monde Éditions, 2007).

Bouyer, Christian, *Au temps des Isles: les Antilles françaises de Louis XIII à Napoléon III* (Paris: Le Grand Livre du Mois, 2005).

Bouyer, Murielle, 'Les bassins de main d'œuvre des équipages négriers nantais au 18ᵉ siècle', *Revue du Philanthrope*, 6 (2015).

Bouyssy, Maïté, 'Le Musée négrier', *Lumières*, 3 (2004), *L'esclavage et la traite sous le regard des Lumières*.

Bové, Marie, 'Mémoires présentés à l'Académie de Bordeaux au 18e siècle: « La cause de la couleur des nègres »', *Institut Aquitain d'Etudes Sociales, bulletin*, 76 (2001).

Branda, Pierre and Lentz, Thierry, *Napoléon, l'esclavage et les colonies* (Paris: Fayard, 2006).

Brasseaux, Carl A. and Conrad, Glenn R. (eds), *The Road to Louisiana: The Saint-Domingue Refugees, 1792–1809* (Lafayette, LA: Center for Louisiana Studies, University of Southwestern Louisiana, 1992).

Braun, Juliane, *Creole Drama: Theatre and Society in Antebellum New Orleans* (Charlottesville, VA: University of Virginia Press, 2019).

Brewer, John, *The Sinews of Power: War, Money and the English State, 1688–1783* (Cambridge: Cambridge University Press, 1990).

Bromley, J. S., *Corsairs and Navies, 1660–1760* (London: Hambledon, 1987).

Brouard, Emmanuel, 'Le Premier Empire, âge d'or du commerce du sel à Nantes et sur la Loire', *Annales historiques de la Révolution Française*, 390 (2017).

Brown, Christopher Leslie, *Moral Capital: Foundations of British Abolitionism* (Chapel Hill, NC: University of North Carolina Press, 2006).

Brown, Stewart J. and Tackett, Timothy (eds), *The Cambridge History of Christianity, vol. 7, Enlightenment, Reawakening and Revolution, 1660–1815* (Cambridge: Cambridge University Press, 2006).

Brunschvicg, Léon, *Souvenirs de la révolution à Nantes, ou la mémoire d'un Bleu*, ed. Jean-Clément Martin (Nantes: Reflets du Passé, 1982).

Burch, Stuart, 'Equiano: an exhibition of an extraordinary life', *Museums Journal* 107 (2007).

Butel, Paul, 'L'armement en course à Bordeaux sous la Révolution et l'Empire', *Revue historique de Bordeaux et du département de la Gironde*, NS 15 (1966).

Butel, Paul, 'Le trafic européen de Bordeaux, de la Guerre d'Amérique à la Révolution', *Annales du Midi*, 78 (1966).

Butel, Paul, 'Crise et mutation de l'activité économique à Bordeaux sous le Consulat et l'Empire', *Annales historiques de la Révolution française*, 199 (1970).

Butel, Paul, 'La croissance commerciale bordelaise dans la seconde moitié du 18e siècle' (Lille: Service de reproduction des thèses de l'université, 1973).

Butel, Paul, 'Armateurs bordelais et commissionnaires londoniens au 18e siècle', *Revue historique de Bordeaux et de la Gironde*, 2nd series, 23 (1974).

Butel, Paul, *Les négociants bordelais, l'Europe et les Îles au dix-huitième siècle* (Paris: Aubier, 1974).

Butel, Paul, *Les dynasties bordelaises de Colbert à Chaban* (Paris: Perrin, 1991).

Butel, Paul (ed.), *Commerce et plantation dans la Caraïbe, 18e–19e siècles* (Bordeaux: Presses Universitaires de Bordeaux, 1992).

Butel, Paul, *Histoire de l'Atlantique, de l'Antiquité à nos jours* (Paris: Perrin, 1997).

Butel, Paul and Cullen, L. M. (eds), *Cities and Merchants: French and Irish Perspectives on Urban Development, 1500–1900* (Dublin: Trinity College, 1986).

Butel, Paul and Poussou, Jean-Pierre, *La vie quotidienne à Bordeaux au 18e siècle* (Paris: Hachette, 1980).

Buti, Gilbert and Hrodĕj, Philippe (eds), *Histoire des pirates et des corsaires, de l'Antiquité à nos jours* (Paris: CNRS Éditions, 2016).

Butler, Jon, *The Huguenots in America: A Refugee People in New World Society* (Cambridge, MA: Harvard University Press, 1983).

Cabantous, Alain, *Le vergue et les fers: mutins et déserteurs dans la marine de l'Ancienne France* (Paris, 1984).

Cabantous, Alain, *Dix mille marins face à l'Océan* (Paris: Publisud, 1991).

Cabantous, Alain, *Les citoyens du large: les identités maritimes en France, 17e–19e siècle* (Paris: Aubier, 1995).

Camus, Jean-Yves, 'The commemoration of slavery in France and the emergence of a black political consciousness', *The European Legacy*, 11 (2006).

Canny, Nicholas and Morgan, Philip (eds), *The Oxford Handbook of the Atlantic World, 1450–1850* (Oxford: Oxford University Press, 2011).

Carey, Brycchan and Plank, Geoffrey (eds), *Quakers and Abolition* (Urbana-Champaign: University of Illinois Press, 2014).

Carrier, E. H. (ed.), *Correspondence of Jean-Baptiste Carrier during his Mission in Brittany, 1793–94* (London: Bodley Head, 1920).

Carrière, Charles, *Négociants marseillais au 18ᵉ siècle* (2 vols, Marseille: Institut historique de Provence, 1973).

Carrière, Charles and Goury, Michel, *Georges Roux de Corse: l'étrange destin d'un armateur marseillais, 1703–1792* (Marseille: Éditions Jeanne Lafitte, 1990).

Catterall, Douglas and Campbell, Jodi (eds), *Women in Port: Gendering Communities, Economies, and Social Networks in Atlantic Port Cities, 1500–1800* (Leiden: Brill, 2012).

Caudrillier, Georges, *L'Association royaliste de l'Institut philanthropique à Bordeaux et la conspiration anglaise en France pendant la Deuxième Coalition* (Paris: Société française d'imprimerie et de librairie, 1908).

Cauna, Jacques de, *Au temps des Isles à sucre: histoire d'une plantation de Saint-Domingue au 18ᵉ siècle* (Paris, 1987).

Cauna, Jacques de, 'Architecture coloniale: Haïti, des richesses à découvrir', *Art et Fact: Revue des historiens de l'art, des archéologues, des musicologues et des orientalistes de l'Université d'État à Liège*, 7 (1988).

Cauna, Jacques de, *L'Eldorado des Aquitains: Gascons, Basques et Béarnais aux Îles d'Amérique, 17ᵉ–18ᵉ siècles* (Biarritz: Atlantica, 1998).

Cauna, Jacques de, *Fleuriau, La Rochelle et l'esclavage: trente-cinq ans de mémoire et d'histoire* (Paris: Les Indes savantes, 2017).

Cauna, Jacques de and Beckerich, Richard, 'La Révolution de Saint-Domingue vue par un Patriote', *Revue de la Société haïtienne d'histoire et de géographie*, 46/161 (1989).

Cauna, Jacques de and Graff, Marion, *La traite bayonnaise au 18ᵉ siècle: instructions, journal de bord, projets d'armement* (Pau: Éditions Cairn, 2009).

Cauna Jacques de and Révauger, Cécile, *La société des plantations esclavagistes. Caraïbes francophone, anglophone, hispanophone: regards croisés* (Paris: Les Indes savantes, 2013).

Cavignac, Jean, 'Les Cent Jours à Bordeaux à travers la correspondance de Clausel', *Revue historique de Bordeaux et du Département de la Gironde*, NS 14 (1965).

Centre Méridional d'Histoire, *L'espace et le temps reconstruits: la Révolution Française, une révolution des mentalités et des cultures?* (Aix-en-Provence: Publications de l'Université de Provence, 1990).

Chabannes, Hervé, 'Entre prise de parole et occultation: les intellectuels havrais, la traite des Noirs et l'esclavage', *Revue du Philanthrope*, 4 (2013).

Chabannes, Hervé, 'Les Havrais et la traite des Noirs dans le haut de la Côte d'Or du sieur Amand Le Carpentier', *Revue du Philanthrope*, 4 (2013).

Chaigneau, Steve, 'Un exemple de mobilité sociale dans le monde de l'armement nantais du dix-huitième siècle' (D.E.S., Université de Nantes, 1967).

Charbonnel, Nicole, *Commerce et course sous la Révolution et le Consulat à La Rochelle: autour de deux armateurs, les frères Thomas et Pierre-Antoine Chegaray* (Paris: Presses Universitaires de France, 1977).

Chaussinand-Nogaret, Guy, *The French Nobility in the Eighteenth Century* (Cambridge: Cambridge University Press, 1985).

Cheney, Paul, *Cul de Sac: Patrimony, Capitalism and Slavery in French Saint-Domingue* (Chicago, IL: University of Chicago Press, 2017).

Chérel, Emmanuelle, 'Le Mémorial: enjeux, débats et controverses', *Place Publique Nantes-Saint-Nazaire*, 29 (2011).

Chérel, Emmanuelle, *Le Mémorial de l'abolition de l'esclavage de Nantes* (Rennes: Presses Universitaires de Rennes, 2012).

Chesnais, Robert (ed.), *L'esclavage à la française: le Code noir, 1685 et 1724* (Paris: Nautilus, 2006).

Chira, Adriana 'Le Code noir: idées reçues sur un texte symbolique', *Comparative Legal History*, 4 (2016).

Chivallon, Christine, 'Construction d'une mémoire relative à l'esclavage et instrumentalisation politique: le cas des anciens ports négriers de Bordeaux et Bristol', *Cahiers des Anneaux de la Mémoire*, 4 (2002).

Clark, John G., *La Rochelle and the Atlantic Economy during the Eighteenth Century* (Baltimore, MD: Johns Hopkins University Press, 1981).

Coffman, D'Maris, Leonard, Adrian, and O'Reilly, William (eds), *The Atlantic World* (London: Routledge, 2015).

Colley, Linda, *The Ordeal of Elizabeth Marsh: How a Remarkable Woman Crossed Seas and Empires to become Part of World History* (London: Penguin, 2007).

Cornette, Joël, *Un révolutionnaire ordinaire: Benoît Lacombe, négociant, 1759–1819* (Paris: Champ Vallon, 1986).

Corvisier, André (ed.), *Histoire du Havre et de l'estuaire de la Seine* (Toulouse: Privat, 1983).

Costa, Dominique, *La Révolution à Nantes et la Vendée Militaire. Catalogue des collections départementales* (Nantes: Musée Dobrée, 1967).

Coste, Anne-Laure, 'Étude sur les représentations du passé négrier de Bordeaux: entre oubli et mémorisation' (mémoire de maîtrise, Université de Bordeaux-2, 2001).

Coste, Laurent, 'Bordeaux et la restauration des Bourbons', *Annales du Midi*, 105 (1993).

Coulon, Damien (ed.), *Réseaux marchands et réseaux de commerce: concepts récents, réalités historiques du Moyen Âge au 19ᵉ siècle* (Strasbourg: Presses Universitaires de Strasbourg, 2010).

Courteault, Paul, 'Les impressions d'une Anglaise à Bordeaux', *Revue historique de Bordeaux*, 4 (1911).

Courteault, Paul, 'Bordeaux au temps de Tourny d'après un correspondant de Linné', *Revue historique de Bordeaux*, 10 (1917).

Courtney, Cecil and Mander, Jenny (eds), *Raynal's Histoire des deux Indes: Colonialism, Networks and Global Exchange* (Oxford: Voltaire Foundation, 2015).

Covo, Manuel, 'Commerce, empire et révolutions dans le monde atlantique: la colonie française de Saint-Domingue entre métropole et Etats-Unis, ca. 1778–1804' (thèse de doctorat, EHESS, 2013).

Croix, Alain (ed.), *Nantais venus d'ailleurs: Histoire des étrangers à Nantes des origines à nos jours* (Rennes: Presses Universitaires de Rennes, 2007).

Crouzet, François, 'Wars, blockade and economic change in Europe, 1792–1815', *Journal of Economic History*, 24 (1964).

Crouzet, François, 'Angleterre et France au 18ᵉ siècle: essai d'analyse comparée de deux croissances économiques', *Annales: Economies, Sociétés, Civilisations*, 21 (1966).

Crouzet, François, *De la supériorité de l'Angleterre sur la France: l'économie et l'imaginaire, 18e–20e siècle* (Paris: Perrin, 1985).

Crouzet, François, 'The Second Hundred Years War: Some R-reflections', *French History*, 10 (1996).

Crowhurst, Patrick, *The French War on Trade: Privateering, 1793–1815* (Aldershot: Scolar Press, 1989).

Daget, Serge, *Un document exceptionnel: le 'livre de l'or' d'une troque légitime sur le ravage Akan, en 1827* (Bondoukou: Université d'Abidjan, 1974).

Daget, Serge, 'Long cours et négriers nantais du trafic illégal, 1814–1833', *Revue française d'histoire d'Outre-Mer*, 62 (1975).

Daget, Serge, *La traite des Noirs. Opération « Nantes 85 »* (Nantes, 1982).

Daget, Serge, 'Armateurs nantais et trafic négrier illégal: une histoire sans petite boîte verte', *Enquêtes et Documents*, 13 (1987).

Daget, Serge (ed.), *De la traite à l'esclavage: Actes du Colloque International sur la traite des Noirs* (2 vols, Nantes: Centre de recherche sur l'histoire du monde atlantique, 1988).

Daget, Serge, *Répertoire des expéditions négrières françaises à la traite illégale, 1814–1850* (Nantes: Centre de Recherche sur l'histoire du monde atlantique, 1988).

Daget, Serge, *La répression de la traite des Noirs au 19e siècle: l'action des croisières françaises sur les côtes occidentales de l'Afrique, 1817–1850* (Paris: Karthala, 1997).

Daline, Victor, 'Marc-Antoine Jullien, après le 9 thermidor', *Annales historiques de la Révolution française*, 36 (1964).

Dardel, Pierre, *Commerce, industrie et navigation à Rouen et au Havre au 18ᵉ siècle* (Rouen: Société libre d'émulation de la Seine-Maritime, 1966).

David, Philippe, *Un port de l'océan sous le Directoire: La Rochelle, 1796–1799* (La Rochelle: Pijollet, 1955).

Debien, Gabriel, *Les colons de Saint-Domingue et la Révolution: essai sur le Club Massiac* (Paris: Armand Colin, 1953).

Debien, Gabriel, 'Les colons de Saint-Domingue réfugiés à Cuba, 1793–1815', *Revista de Indias*, 14 (1954).

Debien, Gabriel, *Un colon sur sa plantation* (Dakar: Université de Dakar, 1959).

Debien, Gabriel, 'De Saint-Domingue à Cuba avec une famille de réfugiés, 1800–1809', *Revue de la Faculté d'Ethnologie de Port-au-Prince*, 8 (1964).

Debien, Gabriel, 'Poitevins partis par Nantes pour les Antilles, 1772–1791', *94ᵉ Congrès national des sociétés savantes* (vol.2, Pau, 1969).

Debien, Gabriel, 'Les exilés acadiens après leur départ du Poitou', *La Revue du Bas-Poitou et des provinces de l'Ouest*, 2 (1972).

Debien, Gabriel, 'Une Nantaise à Saint-Domingue', *Revue du Bas-Poitou et des Provinces de l'Ouest*, 6 (1972).

Debien, Gabriel, 'Réfugiés de Saint-Domingue expulsés de La Havane en 1809', *Anuario de Estudios Americanos*, 35 (1978).

Delafosse, Marcel (ed.), *Histoire de La Rochelle* (Toulouse: Privat 1985).

Delobette, Edouard, 'Ces « Messieurs du Havre ». Négociants, commissaires et armateurs de 1680 à 1830' (thèse de doctorat, Université de Caen, 2005).

Delobette, Edouard, 'Mercure et Sosie', *Revue du Philanthrope*, 6 (2015).

Desan, Suzanne, Hunt, Lynn, and Nelson, William Max (eds), *The French Revolution in Global Perspective* (Ithaca, NY: Cornell University Press, 2013).

Descamps, Cyr, 'Gorée au temps de la Compagnie des Indes, 1718–1758', in *Lorient, la Bretagne et la traite, 17e–19e siècles: Cahier de la Compagnie des Indes*, 9/10 (2006).

Desgraves, Louis, *Voyageurs à Bordeaux du dix-septième siècle à 1914* (Bordeaux: Mollat, 1991).

Desgraves, Louis and Dupeux, Georges (eds), *Bordeaux au 19ᵉ siècle* (Bordeaux: Fédération historique du Sud-Ouest, 1969).

Desné, Roland and Dorigny, Marcel (eds), *Les Lumières, l'esclavage, la colonisation* (Paris: La Découverte, 2005).

Dessens, Nathalie, *From Saint-Domingue to New Orleans: Migration and Influences* (Gainesville, FL: University Press of Florida, 2007).

Dessens, Nathalie, *Creole City: A Chronicle of Early American New Orleans* (Gainesville: University Press of Florida, 2015).

Deveau, Jean-Michel, *Le commerce rochelais face à la Révolution: correspondance de Jean-Baptiste Nairac, 1789–90* (La Rochelle: Rumeur des âges, 1989).

Deveau, Jean-Michel, *La traite rochelaise* (Paris: Karthala, 1990).

Dorian, Max, *Un Bordelais: Stephen Girard, premier millionnaire américain* (Paris: Éditions Albatros, 1977).

Dorigny, Marcel (ed.), *The Abolitions of Slavery: from Léger Félicité Sonthonax to Victor Schœlcher, 1793, 1794, 1848* (Oxford: Berghahn, 2003).

Dorigny, Marcel and Gainot, Bernard (eds), *La Société des Amis des Noirs, 1788–99. Contribution à l'histoire de l'abolition de l'esclavage* (Paris: Editions UNESCO, 1998).

Doyle, William, *Aristocracy and its Enemies in the Age of Revolution* (Oxford: Oxford University Press, 2009).

Doyle, William, *The Parlement of Bordeaux and the End of the Old Regime, 1771–1790* (London: Edward Arnold, 1974.

Drescher, Seymour, *Capitalism and Antislavery: British Mobilization in Comparative Perspective* (Oxford: Oxford University Press, 1987).

Dresser, Madge, 'Remembering slavery and abolition in Bristol', *Slavery and Abolition*, 30 (2009).

Dresser, Madge and Giles, Sue (eds), *Bristol and Transatlantic Slavery: Catalogue of the Exhibition 'A Respectable Trade?: Bristol and Transatlantic Slavery at the City Museum and Art Gallery, Bristol, 1999* (Bristol: Bristol Museums & Art Gallery, 2000).

Dubesset, Éric and Cauna, Jacques de (eds), *Dynamiques caribéennes: Pour une histoire des circulations dans l'espace atlantique, 18ᵉ–19ᵉ siècles* (Pessac: Presses Universitaires de Bordeaux, 2014).

Dull, Jonathan R., *The French Navy and American Independence: A Study of Arms and Diplomacy, 1774–1787* (Princeton, NJ: Princeton University Press, 1975).

Dull, Jonathan R., *The Age of the Ship of the Line: The British and French Navies, 1650–1815* (Lincoln: University of Nebraska Press, 2009).

Dun, James Alexander, *Dangerous Neighbours: Making the Haitian Revolution in Early America* (Philadelphia: University of Pennsylvania Press, 2016).

Du Pasquier, Jacqueline, *Raymond Jeanvrot, une passion royaliste: naissance d'une collection bordelaise* (Bordeaux: Musée des arts décoratifs, 2007).

Dupuch, Robert, 'Le parti libéral à Bordeaux et dans la Gironde sous la deuxième Restauration', *Revue Philomatique de Bordeaux*, 1902.

Dupuy, Aimé, *Voyageurs étrangers à la découverte de l'ancienne France, 1500–1850* (Paris: Club du livre d'histoire, 1957).

Ehrard, Jean, *Lumières et esclavage: l'esclavage colonial et l'opinion publique en France au 18e siècle* (Paris: Sofédis, 2008).

Eltis, David, Lewis, Frank D., and Sokoloff, Kenneth L. (eds), *Slavery in the Development of the Americas* (Cambridge: Cambridge University Press, 2004), 3.

Eltis, David and Richardson, David (eds), *Extending the Frontiers: Essays on the New Transatlantic Slave Trade Database* (New Haven, CT: Yale University Press, 2008).

Eltis, David and Richardson, David, *Atlas of the Transatlantic Slave Trade* (New Haven, CT: Yale University Press, 2010).

Even, Pascal, 'Le Congrès et l'abolition de la traite des Noirs', in *Le Congrès de Vienne ou L'invention d'une nouvelle Europe: catalogue d'exposition* (Paris: Musée Carnavalet, 2015).

Falola, Toyin and Childs, Matt D. (eds), *The Yoruba Diaspora in the Atlantic World* (Bloomington, IN: Indiana University Press, 2004).

Ferrer, Ada, *Freedom's Mirror: Cuba and Haiti in the Age of Revolution* (Cambridge: Cambridge University Press, 2014).

Ferrer, Ada, 'Speaking of Haiti: Slavery, Revolution and Freedom in Cuban Slave Testimony', in David Patrick Geggus and Norman Fiering (eds), *The World of the Haitian Revolution* (Bloomington, IN: Indiana University Press, 2009).

Fick, Carolyn E., *The Making of Haiti: The Saint- Domingue Revolution from below* (Knoxville, TN: University of Tennessee Press, 1990).

Fiéran, Jacques, 'Continuités familiales et ruptures dans la construction navale nantaise', *Enquêtes et documents*, 17 (1990).

Figeac, Michel, 'La noblesse aux Antilles: l'exemple bordelais', *Bulletin du Centre d'histoire des Espaces Atlantiques*, 8 (1998).

Figeac-Monthus, Marguerite, 'Bordeaux et la traite', *Revue historique de Bordeaux et du Département de la Gironde*, NS 17 (2011).

Fischer, David Hackett, *Champlain's Dream: The Visionary Adventurer who made a New World in Canada* (Toronto: A. A. Knopf, 2008).

Fladeland, Betty, 'Abolitionist pressures on the Concert of Europe, 1814–1822', *Journal of Modern History*, 38 (1966).

Fleming, Crystal Marie, *Resurrecting Slavery: Racial Legacies and White Supremacy in France* (Philadelphia, PA: Temple University Press, 2017).

Forestier, Albane, 'A "considerable credit" in the late eighteenth-century French West Indian Trade: the Chaurands of Nantes', *French History*, 25 (2011).

Forrest, Alan, *Society and Politics in Revolutionary Bordeaux* (Oxford: Oxford University Press, 1975).

Forrest, Alan, *The Revolution in Provincial France: Aquitaine, 1789–1799* (Oxford: Oxford University Press, 1996).

Forrest, Alan and Jones, Peter (eds), *Reshaping France: Town, Country and Region during the French Revolution* (Manchester: Manchester University Press, 1991).

Forrest, Alan and Middell, Matthias (eds), *The Routledge Companion to the French Revolution in World History* (London: Routledge, 2016).

Forsdick, Charles, 'The Pantheon's empty plinth: commemorating slavery in contemporary France', *Atlantic Studies*, 9 (2012).

Forsdick, Charles and Høgsbjerg, Christian (eds), *The Black Jacobins Reader* (Durham, NC: Duke University Press, 2017).

Forster, Elborg and Forster, Robert (eds), *Sugar and Slavery, Family and Race: The Letters and Diary of Pierre Dessalles, Planter in Martinique, 1808–1856* (Baltimore, MD: Johns Hopkins University Press, 1996).

Foucault, Michel, *Discipline and Punish: The Birth of the Prison* (New York: Vintage Books, 1995).

Fouchard, Jean, *Le théâtre à Saint-Domingue* (Port-au-Prince: Imprimerie de l'État, 1955).

Furstenberg, François, *In the Name of the Father: Washington's Legacy, Slavery and the Making of a Nation* (London: Penguin, 2006).

Gaffield, Julia (ed.), *The Haitian Declaration of Independence: Creation, Context and Legacy* (Charlottesville, VA: University of Virginia Press, 2016).

Gainot, Bernard, *Les officiers de couleur dans les armées de la République et de l'Empire, 1792-1815* (Paris: Karthala, 2007).

Gainot, Bernard, '«Sur le fond de cruelle inhumanité»: les politiques du massacre dans la Révolution de Haïti', *La Révolution française. Cahiers de l'Institut de la Révolution française*, 3 (2011), « Les massacres aux temps des Révolutions ».

Gardey, Philippe, *Négociants et marchands de Bordeaux. De la guerre d'Amérique à la Restauration, 1780–1830* (Paris: Presses Universitaires de Paris-Sorbonne, 2009).

Garnier, Emmanuel and Surville, Frédéric (eds), *Climat et révolutions: Autour du Journal du négociant rochelais Jacob Lambertz, 1733–1813* (Saintes: Le Croît vif, 2010).

Garrigus, John D., *Before Haiti: Race and Citizenship in French Saint-Domingue* (Basingstoke: Palgrave Macmillan, 2006).

Gaspar, David and Geggus, David (eds), *A Turbulent Time: The French Revolution and the Greater Caribbean* (Bloomington, IN: Indiana University Press, 1997).

Gaston-Martin, *Nantes au dix-huitième siècle: l'ère des négriers* (Paris: Karthala, 1993).

Gayot, Gérard (ed.), *La franc-maçonnerie française, textes et pratiques, 18e–19e siècles* (Paris: Gallimard, 1980).

Geggus, David, *Slavery, War and Revolution: The British Occupation of Saint-Domingue, 1793–98* (Oxford: Oxford University Press, 1982).

Geggus, David, *Haitian Revolutionary Studies* (Bloomington, IN: Indiana University Press, 2002).

Geggus, David and Fiering, Norman (eds), *The World of the Haitian Revolution* (Bloomington, IN: Indiana University Press, 2009).

Gemery, Henry A. and Hogendorn, Jan S. (eds), *The Uncommon Market: Essays in the Economic History of the Atlantic Slave Trade* (New York: Academic Press, 1979).

Gerbeau, Hubert and Saugera, Éric (eds), *La dernière traite: Fragments d'histoire en hommage à Serge Daget* (Paris: Société Française d'Histoire d'Outre-Mer, 1994).

Gerbod, Paul, *Voyages au pays des mangeurs de grenouilles: La France vue par les Britanniques du 18e siècle à nos jours* (Paris: Albin Michel, 1991).

Godechot, Jacques, *Les révolutions* (Paris: Presses Universitaires de France, 1963).

Gosnave, Joël, 'Une expédition négrière bordelaise à la fin du 18e siècle, étude du journal de bord du *Patriote* (1788–1791)', *Revue historique de Bordeaux et du département de la Gironde*, 3ᵉ série, 17 (2011).

Grandière, Marcel, 'Les réfugiés et les déportés des Antilles à Nantes sous la Révolution', *Bulletin de la Société d'Histoire de la Guadeloupe* 33–34 (1977).

Greene, Jack P., *Settler Jamaica in the 1750s: A Social Portrait* (Charlottesville, VA: University of Virginia Press, 2016).

Greer, Donald, *The Incidence of the Terror during the French Revolution: A Statistical Interpretation* (Cambridge, MA: Harvard University Press, 1935).

Grindal, Peter, *Opposing the Slavers: The Royal Navy's Campaign against the Atlantic Slave Trade* (London: I.B. Tauris, 2016).

Grosvallet, Christophe, 'Les capitaines négriers bordelais entre 1763 et 1778', *Institut aquitain d'études sociales, bulletin*, 76 (2001).

Gualdé, Krystel, 'Musée versus mémorial?', *Revue du Philanthrope*, 7 (2018).

Guicheteau, Samuel, *La Révolution des ouvriers nantais. Mutation économique, identité sociale et dynamique révolutionnaire, 1740–1815* (Rennes: Presses Universitaires de Nantes, 2008).

Guillet, Bernard, *La Marie-Séraphique, navire négrier* (Nantes: Musée d'Histoire de Nantes, 2009).

Guillot de Suduirant, Bertrand, *Une fortune de haute mer: François Bonnaffé, un armateur bordelais au 18ᵉ siècle* (Bordeaux: Confluences, 1999).

Guilmot, *officier de santé* and Dembowski, *adjudant-commandant, Journal et voyage à Saint-Domingue, 1802* (Paris: Librairie historique F. Teissèdre, 1997).

Guyvarc'h, Didier, 'La construction de la mémoire d'une ville: Nantes, 1914–1992' (thèse de doctorat, Université de Rennes-2, 1994).

Guyvarc'h, Didier, 'Nantes, la traite en mémoire', *Place Publique Nantes-Saint-Nazaire*, 29 (2011).

Hafen, Leroy R. (ed.), *French Fur Traders and Voyageurs in the American West* (Lincoln, NE: Nebraska University Press, 1997).

Hagy, James W. and Van Ruymbeke, Bertrand, 'The French refugee newspapers of Charleston', *South Carolina Historical Magazine*, 97/2 (1996).

Halévi, Ran, *Les loges maçonniques dans la France d'Ancien Régime aux origines de la sociabilité démocratique* (Paris: Armand Colin, 1984).

Hamilton, Andrew, *Trade and Empire in the Eighteenth Century Atlantic World* (Newcastle-upon-Tyne: Cambridge Scholars Publishing, 2008).

Hansard, T. C., *The Parliamentary Debates from the Year 1803 to the Present Time* (London: House of Commons, 1814, 1815).

Hanson, Paul, *The Jacobin Republic under Fire: The Federalist Revolt in the French Revolution* (University Park, PA: Penn State University Press, 2003).

Harper, Marjory (ed.), *Emigrant Homecomings: The Return Movement of Emigrants, 1600–2000* (Manchester: Manchester University Press, 2005).

Harper, Marjory and Constantine, Stephen (eds), *Migration and Empire* (Oxford: Oxford University Press, 2010).

Hartley, Janet M., Keenan, Paul, and Lieven, Dominic (eds), *Russia and the Napoleonic Wars* (Basingstoke: Palgrave Macmillan, 2015).

Haudrère, Philippe, 'La Révolution de 1789 et la flotte de commerce française', *Académie de Marine, communications et mémoires*, 1989/3.

Haudrère, Philippe, *La Compagnie française des Indes au 18e siècle, 1719–1795* (2 vols, Paris: Les Indes savantes, 2005).

Havard, Gilles et Vidal, Cécile, *Histoire de l'Amérique française* (Paris: Flammarion, 2003).

Hector, Michel, 'Colloque de Port-au-Prince, 5–8 décembre 1989', *Revue de la Société haïtienne d'histoire et de géographie*, 46/166 (1990).

Heinl, Robert Debs and Heinl, Nancy Gordon, *Written in Blood: The Story of the Haitian People, 1492–1995* (Lanham, MD: University Press of America, 2005).

Helfman, Tara, 'The Court of Vice Admiralty at Sierra Leone and the abolition of the West African slave trade', *The Yale Law Journal*, 115 (2006).

Hervé, Bruno, 'Noyades, fusillades, exécutions: les mises à mort des brigands entre justice et massacres en Loire-inférieure en l'an II', *La Révolution Française: Cahiers de l'Institut d'histoire de la Révolution française*, 3 (2011).

Higounet, Charles (ed.), *Histoire de l'Aquitaine* (Toulouse: Privat, 1971).

Hourcade, Renaud, *Les ports négriers face à leur histoire. Politiques de la mémoire à Nantes, Bordeaux et Liverpool* (Paris: Dalloz, 2014).

Hourmat, Pierre, *Histoire de Bayonne, vol.1, Des origines à la Révolution Française* (Bayonne: Société des sciences, lettres et arts, 1986).

Ingram, Kenneth, *Sources of Jamaican History, 1655–1838: a bibliographical survey with particular reference to manuscript sources* (2 vols, Zug: Inter Documentation Company, 1976).

Innes, Joanna and Philp, Mark (eds), *Re-imagining Democracy in the Age of Revolutions: America, France, Britain, Ireland, 1750–1850* (Oxford: Oxford University Press, 2013).

Israel, Jonathan, *Radical Enlightenment: Philosophy and the Making of Modernity, 1650–1750* (Oxford: Oxford University Press, 2001).

James, C. L. R., *The Black Jacobins* (London: Penguin, 2001).

Janin, 'Corinne, Les engagés pour les Antilles à partir des rôles d'armement nantais, 1722–1772' (mémoire de maîtrise, Université de Nantes, 1971).

Johnson, Douglas, Bédarida, François, and Crouzet, François (eds), *Britain and France: Ten Centuries* (Folkestone: Dawson, 1980).

Jourdan, Annie, *Nouvelle histoire de la Révolution* (Paris: Flammarion, 2018).

Kaplan, Cora and Oldfield, John (eds), *Imagining Transatlantic Slavery* (Basingstoke: Palgrave Macmillan, 2010).

Keber, Martha L., *Seas of Gold, Seas of Cotton: Christophe Poulain DuBignon of Jeckyll Island* (Athens, GA: University of Georgia Press, 2002).

Kennedy, Michael L., *The Jacobin Clubs in the French Revolution* (2 vols, Princeton, NJ; Princeton University Press, 1982, 1988).

Kielstra, Paul, *The Politics of Slave Trade Suppression in Britain and France, 1814–48* (Basingstoke: Palgrave Macmillan, 2000).

Kimizuka, Hiroyasu, *Bordeaux et la Bretagne au 18ᵉ siècle. Les routes du vin* (Rennes: Presses Universitaires de Rennes, 2015).

King, David, *Vienna, 1814: How the Conquerors of Napoleon made Love, War and Peace at the Congress of Vienna* (New York: Harmony Books, 2008).

Knight, Franklin W. and Liss, Peggy K. (eds), *Atlantic Port Cities: Economy, Culture and Society in the Atlantic World, 1650–1800* (Knoxville: University of Tennessee Press, 1991).

Koest, Françoise, *La Révolution à la Guadeloupe, 1789–1796* (Basse-Terre: Archives Départementales, 1982).

Kouamé, Aka, 'Les cargaisons de traite nantaises au 18e siècle. Une contribution à l'étude de la traite négrière française' (thèse de doctorat, Université de Nantes, 2005).

Kouamé, Aka, 'Les produits des pays traversés par la Loire dans les cargaisons négrières nantaises au 18ᵉ siècle: une approche à partir des archives des armateurs et de la chambre de commerce', *Cahiers des Anneaux de la Mémoire*, 16 (2015).

Koufinkana, Marcel, *Les esclaves noirs en France sous l'Ancien Régime, 16ᵉ–18ᵉ siècles* (Paris: L'Harmattan, 2008).

Kyriazis, Nicholas, Metaxas, Theodore, and Economou, Emmanouil, 'War for profit: English corsairs, institutions and decentralised strategy', *Defence and Peace Economics*, 29 (2018).

Lagrave, Henri, Mazouer, Charles, and Regaldo, Marc, *La vie théâtrale à Bordeaux des origines à nos jours*, vol. 1 (Paris: Éditions du CNRS, 1985).

Lallié, Alfred, *Les sociétés populaires à Nantes pendant la Révolution* (Nantes: L. Durance, 1914).

Lamore, Maria Elena Orozco and Monnar, Maria Teresa Fleitas, *Formation d'une ville caraïbe: Urbanisme et architecture à Santiago de Cuba* (Pessac: Presses Universitaires de Bordeaux, 2011).

Landais, Hervé, 'Une famille de négociants armateurs dans la seconde moitié du 18ᵉ siècle: les Orry de la Roche' (mémoire de maîtrise, Université de Nantes, 1992).

Lastrucci, Marc, 'L'évocation publique à Nantes de la traite négrière et de l'esclavage de « Nantes 85 » aux « Anneaux de la Mémoire », 1983–1994' (mémoire de maîtrise, Université de Nantes, 1996).

Laveau, Claude, *Le monde rochelais des Bourbons à Bonaparte* (La Rochelle: Rumeur des Âges, 1988).

Law, Robin and Strickrodt, Silke (eds), *Ports of the Slave Trade (Bights of Benin and Biafra)* (Stirling: Centre of Commonwealth Studies, University of Stirling, 1999).

Le Garrec, Elodie, 'La place de la Bretagne et des Bretons dans la traite illégale française, 1814–1831', in *Lorient, la Bretagne et la traite: Cahier de la Compagnie des Indes*, 9/10 (2006).

Le Mené, Michel and Santrot, Marie-Hélène (eds), *Cahiers des Plaintes et Doléances de Loire-Atlantique* (4 vols, Nantes: Conseil Général de la Loire-Atlantique, 1989).

Lemonnier, Pierre, 'Les journées des 21 et 21 mars 1793 à la Rochelle', *Bulletin de la Société des Archives Historiques: Revue de la Saintonge et de l'Aunis*, 32 (1912).

Leonard, Adrian and Pretel, David (eds), *The Caribbean and the Atlantic World Economy: Circuits of Trade, Money and Knowledge, 1650–1914* (Basingstoke: Palgrave Macmillan, 2015).

Letertre, Laurent, 'Le consulat de Philadelphie et la question de Saint-Domingue, 1793–1803' (mémoire de maîtrise, Université de Nantes, 2000).

Lhéritier, Michel, *Liberté: les Girondins, Bordeaux et la Révolution Française* (Paris: La Renaissance du Livre, 1947).

Lilti, Antoine, 'Le pouvoir du crédit au 18e siècle, histoire intellectuelle et sciences sociales', *Annales: Histoire, Sciences Sociales* 70, 4 (2015).

Lozère, Christelle, *Bordeaux colonial, 1850–1940* (Bordeaux: Éditions Sud-Ouest, 2007).

Luc, Jean-Noel (ed.), *La Charente Maritime: l'Aunis et la Saintonge des origines à nos jours* (Saint-Jean d'Angély: Bordessoules, 1981).

Lucas, Colin (ed.), *The Political Culture of the French Revolution* (Oxford: Pergamon, 1988).

Lüsebrink, Hans-Jürgen and Tietz, Manfred (eds), 'Lectures de Raynal: l'«Histoire des Deux Indes» en Europe et en Amérique au 18e siècle: actes du colloque de Wolfenbüttel', *Studies in Voltaire and the Eighteenth Century*, 286 (1991).

Lüthy, Herbert, *La banque protestante en France* (2 vols, Paris: SEVPEN, 1959–61).

Maquerlot, Lucie, 'Les résistances au Havre de la Constituante à la Convention', *Cahiers de l'histoire et des mémoires de la traite négrière, de l'esclavage et de leurs abolitions en Normandie*, 2 (2009).

Marchand, Jean (ed.), *Voyages en France de François de la Rochefoucauld, 1781–83* (Paris: Honoré Champion, 1938).

Margadant, Ted W., *Urban Rivalries in the French Revolution* (Princeton, NJ: Princeton University Press 1992).

Martin, Jean-Clément, *La Loire-Atlantique dans la tourmente révolutionnaire* (Nantes: Reflets du Passé, 1989).

Martin, Vanessa, *Pierre-Jean Van Hoogwerff: chronique d'une ascension sociale à La Rochelle, 1729–1813* (Paris: Association pour le développement de l'histoire économique, 2002).

Martinetti, Brice, *Les négociants de La Rochelle au 18e siècle* (Rennes: Presses Universitaires de Rennes, 2013).

Martinetti, Brice, 'Les résistances du négoce rochelais à la première abolition de l'esclavage: les apports des correspondances', *Revue du Philanthrope*, 4 (2013).

Marzagalli, Silvia, *Les boulevards de la fraude: le négoce maritime et le Blocus Continental, 1806–13* (Lille: Presses Universitaires du Septentrion, 1999).

Marzagalli, Silvia (ed.), *Bordeaux et la marine de guerre, 17e–20e siècle* (Bordeaux: Presses Universitaires de Bordeaux, 2002).

Marzagalli, Silvia, *Bordeaux et les Etats-Unis, 1776–1815. Politique et stratégies négociantes dans la genèse d'un réseau commercial* (Geneva: Droz, 2015).

Marzagalli, Silvia and Bonin, Hubert (eds), *Négoce, ports et océans, 16e–20e siècles* (Bordeaux: Presses Universitaires de Bordeaux, 2000).

Marzagalli, Silvia and Marnot, Bruno (eds), *Guerre et économie dans l'espace atlantique du 16e au 20e siècle* (Pessac: Presses Universitaires de Bordeaux, 2006).

Marzagalli, Silvia et al. (eds), *Comprendre la traite négrière atlantique* (Bordeaux: SCÉRÉN-CRDP Aquitaine, 2009).

Mathan, Anne de, Pourchasse, Pierrick, and Jarnoux, Philippe (eds), *La mer, la guerre et les affaires: Enjeux et réalités maritimes de la Révolution Française* (Rennes: Presses Universitaires de Rennes, 2017).

Mathiez, Albert, 'Un procès de corruption sous la Terreur, l'affaire de la Compagnie des Indes', *Annales Révolutionnaires*, 13 (1921).

Maurel, Blanche, 'Une société de pensée à Saint-Domingue, le « Cercle des Philadelphes » au Cap Français', *Revue Française d'Histoire d'Outre-mer*, 48 (1961).

McIntosh, Malcolm and Weber, Bernard (eds), *Une correspondance familiale au temps des troubles de Saint-Domingue: lettres du marquis et de la marquise de Rouvray à leur fille, Saint-Domingue—Etats-Unis, 1791-96* (Paris: Société de l'histoire des colonies françaises, 1959).

McPhee, Peter, *Liberty or Death: The French Revolution* (New Haven, CT: Yale University Press, 2016).

Meaudre de Lapouyade, Maurice, 'Impressions d'une Allemande à Bordeaux en 1785', *Revue historique de Bordeaux*, 4 (1911).

Melchior, Jeanne, 'Histoire du Club National' (thèse de doctorat, Université de Bordeaux, 1951).

Mengeot, Albert, *Le Brassard de Bordeaux: 12 mars 1814* (Bordeaux: Bière, 1912).

Mettas, Jean, *Répertoire des expéditions négrières françaises au 18ᵉ siècle* (2 vols, Paris: Société française d'histoire d'Outre-Mer, 1978-84).

Meyer, Jean, *L'armement nantais dans la deuxième moitié du 18ᵉ siècle* (Paris: SEVPEN, 1969).

Meyer, Jean, 'Le commerce négrier nantais, 1774-92', in *Annales: Economies, Sociétés, Civilisations*, 15 (1960).

Meyer, Jean, *Histoire du sucre* (Paris: Desjonquères, 1989).

Mondot, Jean (ed.), *L'esclavage et la traite sous le regard des Lumières* (Bordeaux: Presses Universitaires de Bordeaux, 2004).

Mondot, Jean and Larrère, Catherine (eds), *Lumières et commerce: l'exemple bordelais* (Berne: Peter Lang, 2000).

Moreau de Saint-Méry, *Description topographique, physique, civile, politique et historique de la partie française de l'isle Saint-Domingue*, Paris, 1796-97, 3 vols, edited by Blanche Maurel et Etienne Taillemite (Paris: Société de l'Histoire des Colonies Françaises, 1958).

Morellet, André, *Mémoire sur la situation actuelle de la Compagnie des Indes* (Paris, 1769).

Morgan, Kenneth, *Bristol and the Atlantic trade in the Eighteenth Century* (Cambridge: Cambridge University Press, 1993).

Morieux, Renaud, *The Channel: England, France and the Construction of a Maritime Border in the Eighteenth Century* (Cambridge: Cambridge University Press, 2016).

Moussa, Sarga (ed.), *L'idée de « race » dans les sciences humaines et la littérature, 18ᵉ et 19ᵉ siècles* (Paris: L'Harmattan, 2003).

Murray, Elsie, *Azilum: French Refugee Village on the Susquehanna* (Athens, PA: Tioga Point Museum, 1956).

Musée d'Aquitaine, *Regards sur les Antilles: Collection Marcel Chatillon* (Bordeaux: Musée d'Aquitaine, 1999).

Musée d'Aquitaine, *Bordeaux au 18ᵉ siècle: Le commerce atlantique et l'esclavage* (Bordeaux: Musée d'Aquitaine, 2010).

Noël, Erick, *Être noir en France au 18e siècle* (Paris: Tallandier, 2006).

Nora, Pierre (ed.), *Les Lieux de mémoire* (7 vols, Paris: Gallimard, 1997).

O'Brien, Patrick, 'The nature and historical evolution of an exceptional fiscal state and its possible significance for the precocious commercialization and industrialization of the British economy from Cromwell to Nelson', *Economic History Review*, 64 (2011).

Oexmelin, Alexandre-Olivier, *Les flibustiers du Nouveau monde: histoire des flibustiers et boucaniers qui se sont illustrés dans les Indes*, introduction by Michel Le Bris (Paris: Phébus, 1996).

O'Reilly, Patrice-John, *Histoire complète de Bordeaux* (6 vols, Bordeaux: J. Delmas, 1857–1858).

Otto, Marcus, 'The challenge of decolonization: school history textbooks as media and objects of the postcolonial politics of memory in France since the 1960s', *Journal of Educational Media, Memory and Society*, 5 (2013).

Pacteau de Luze, Séverine, *Les protestants de Bordeaux* (Bordeaux: Mollat, 1999).

Pagden, Anthony, *European Encounters with the New World* (New Haven, CT: Yale University Press, 1993).

Pagden, Anthony, *Lords of All the World* (New Haven, CT: Yale University Press, 1995).

Palmié, Stephan and Scarano, Francisco A. (eds), *The Caribbean: A History of the Region and its Peoples* (Chicago: University of Chicago Press, 2011).

Parham, Althea de Puech (ed.), *My Odyssey: Experiences of a Young Refugee from Two Revolutions* (Baton Rouge, LA: Louisiana State University Press, 1959).

Pariset, François-Georges (ed.), *Bordeaux au 18ᵉ siècle* (Bordeaux: Fédération historique du Sud-Ouest, 1968).

Peabody, Sue, *'There are no Slaves in France': The Political Culture of Race and Slavery in the Ancien Régime* (Oxford: Oxford University Press, 1996).

Pérotin-Dumon, Anne, *Être patriote sous les tropiques* (Basse-Terre: Société d'histoire de la Guadeloupe, 1985).

Pérotin-Dumon, Anne, *La ville aux îles, la ville dans l'île: Basse-Terre et Pointe-à-Pitre, Guadeloupe, 1650–1820* (Paris: Karthala, 2000).

Perraud, Karine, 'L'armement maritime nantais en période de guerre: étude de la traite et de la course' (mémoire de maîtrise, Université de Nantes, 1999).

Perrot, Jean-Claude, 'Urbanisme et commerce au 18ᵉ siècle dans les ports de Nantes et Bordeaux', in Centre d'histoire économique et sociale de la Région Lyonnaise, *Villes et campagnes, 15ᵉ—20ᵉ siècles* (Lyon: Presses Universitaires de Lyon, 1977).

Pétré-Grenouilleau, Olivier, 'Pour une étude du milieu maritime nantais entres les fins 18ᵉ et 19ᵉ siècles', *Enquêtes et documents*, 17 (1990).

Pétré-Grenouilleau, Olivier, *L'argent de la traite: milieu négrier, capitalisme et développement, un modèle* (Paris: Aubier, 1996).

Pétré-Grenouilleau, Olivier, *Nantes au temps de la traite des Noirs* (Paris: Hachette, 1998).

Pétré-Grenouilleau, Olivier, *Nantes: histoire et géographie contemporaine* (Plomelin: Palantines, 2003).

Pétrissans-Cavaillès, Danielle, *Sur les traces de la traite des Noirs à Bordeaux* (Paris: L'Harmattan, 2004).

Picote, Nolwenn, 'Lorient, la Compagnie des indes et la traite', in *Lorient, la Bretagne et la traite, 17ᵉ–19ᵉ siècle: Cahier de la Compagnie des Indes*, 9/10 (2006).

Pineau-Defois, Laure, 'Un modèle d'expansion économique à Nantes de 1763 à 1792: Louis Drouin, négociant et armateur', *Histoire, économie et société*, 23 (2004).

Pinkard, Susan, *A Revolution in Taste: the Rise of French Cuisine* (Cambridge: Cambridge University Press, 2009).

Planquette, Robert, *Surcouf: Opéra-Comique en 3 Actes et un Prologue* (Paris: Folies-dramatiques, 1887).

Platel, Jean-Philippe, 'La santé à bord des navires négriers de Bordeaux au 18ᵉ siècle' (diplôme d'état de docteur en médecine, Université de Bordeaux-2, 1988).

Pluchon, Pierre, *Toussaint Louverture: un révolutionnaire noir d'Ancien Régime* (Paris: Fayard, 1989).

Polasky, Janet, *Revolutions without Borders: the Call to Liberty in the Atlantic World* (New Haven, CT: Yale University Press, 2015).

Popkin, Jeremy, *Facing Racial Revolution: Eyewitness Accounts of the Haitian Insurrection* (Chicago, IL: University of Chicago Press, 2007).

Popkin, Jeremy, *A Concise History of the Haitian Revolution* (Oxford: Wiley-Blackwell, 2012).

Potofsky, Allan, 'Paris-on-the-Atlantic from the Old Regime to the Revolution', *French History*, 25 (2011).

Poussou, Jean-Pierre, *Bordeaux et le Sud-ouest au 18ᵉ siècle: croissance économique et attraction urbaine* (Paris: Éditions de l'EHESS, 1983).

Poussou, Jean-Pierre, 'Le dynamisme de l'économie française sous Louis XVI', *Revue économique*, 40 (1989).

Poussou, Jean-Pierre, 'Révolution de 1789. Guerres et croissance économique', *Revue économique*, 40 (1989).

Poussou, Jean-Pierre, 'L'immigration européenne dans les îles d'Amérique', in *Voyage aux Iles d'Amérique* (Paris: Archives Nationales, 1992).

Poussou, Jean-Pierre, 'Les activités commerciales des villes françaises de 1789 à 1815', *Histoire, Économie et Société*, 12 (1993).

Price, Jacob M., 'Economic function and the growth of American port towns in the eighteenth century', *Perspectives in American History*, 8 (1974).

Pritchard, James, *In Search of Empire: The French in the Americas, 1670–1730* (Cambridge: Cambridge University Press, 2004).

Proulx, Annie, *Barkskins* (New York: Fourth Estate, 2016).

Quénet, Maurice, 'Le Général du commerce de Nantes: Essai sur les institutions corporatives coutumières des négociants au 18ᵉ siècle (thèse de doctorat, Université de Nantes, 1973).

Rambaud, J., 'L'esprit public dans le Sud-ouest et l'entrée des Anglais à Bordeaux, 1814', *Annales historiques de Bordeaux et du département de la Gironde*, 7 (1914).

Rébuffet, Ferréol and Courdurié, Marcel, *Marseille et le négoce monétaire international, 1785–90* (Marseille: Chambre de commerce et d'industrie de Marseille, 1966).

Régent, Frédéric, *Esclavage, métissage, liberté: la Révolution Française en Guadeloupe, 1789–1802* (Paris: Grasset, 2004).

Régent, Frédéric, *La France et ses esclaves, de la colonisation aux abolitions, 1620–1848* (Paris: Grasset, 2007).

Régent, Frédéric, Gonfier, Gilda, and Maillard, Bruno, *Libres et sans fers. Paroles d'esclaves français* (Paris: Fayard, 2015).

Reich, Jerome, 'The slave trade at the Congress of Vienna', *Journal of Negro History*, 53 (1968).

Renault, Agnès, *D'une île rebelle à une île fidèle: les Français de Santiago de Cuba, 1791–1825* (Rouen: Publications des Universités de Rouen et du Havre, 2012).

Renault, François and Daget, Serge, *Les traites négrières en Afrique* (Paris: Karthala, 1985).

Resnick, Daniel P., 'The Société des Amis des Noirs and the abolition of slavery', *French Historical Studies*, 7 (1972).

Révauger, Cécile and Saunier, Éric (eds), *La Franc-maçonnerie dans les ports* (Bordeaux: Presses Universitaires de Bordeaux, 2012).

Richard, Guy, *Noblesse d'affaires au 18e siècle* (Paris: Armand Colin, 1974).

Richardson, David, Schwarz, Suzanne, and Tibbles, Anthony (eds), *Liverpool and Trans-atlantic Slavery* (Liverpool: Liverpool University Press, 2007).

Robertson, James, *Gone is the Ancient Glory: Spanish Town, Jamaica, 1534–2000* (Kingston: Ian Randle, 2005).

Rollac, J.-S., *Exposé fidèle des faits authentiquement prouvés qui ont précédé et amené la journée de Bordeaux, au 12 mars 1814* (Paris: A. Egron, 1816).

Rolland-Boulestreau, Anne, *Les colonnes infernales. Violences et guerre civile en Vendée Militaire, 1794–95* (Paris: Fayard, 2015).

Roman, Alain, *La saga des Surcouf: mythes et réalités: une famille de marins, de corsaires et de négociants à travers deux siècles de l'histoire d'un port* (Saint-Malo: Cristel, 2006).

Roman, Alain, 'Les représentations de la traite à Saint-Malo (18e–20e siècles), in *Lorient, la Bretagne et la traite, 17e–19e siècle: Cahier de la Compagnie des Indes*, 9/10 (2006).

Rousseau, Jean-Jacques, *The Social Contract* (London: Penguin, 1968).

Roussier, Paul (ed.), *Lettres du général Leclerc, commandant-en-chef de l'Armée de Saint-Domingue en 1802* (Paris: Société de l'histoire des colonies françaises, 1937).

Rouzeau, Léon, *Inventaire des papiers Dobrée, 1771–1896* (Nantes: Bibliothèque Municipale, 1968).

Rowland, Dunbar (ed.), *The Official Letterbook of W.C.C. Claiborne, 1801–1816* (6 vols, Jackson MS, 1917).

Said, Edward, *Orientalism* (London: Routledge, 1979).

Saint-Ruf, Germain, *L'épopée Delgrès. La Guadeloupe sous la Révolution française* (Paris: L'Harmattan, 1988).

Sarrazin, Hélène, 'Comment peut-on défendre l'esclavage?', *Institut Aquitain d'Études Sociales, bulletin*, 76 (2001).

Saugera, Éric, 'Une expédition nantaise sous le Consulat: la *Bonne-Mère*, armement Trottier, 1802–03', *Enquêtes et documents*, CRHMA Université de Nantes, 13 (1987).

Saugera, Éric, 'Une expédition négrière nantaise sous la Restauration: les comptes du *Cultivateur*, 1814–1818', *Enquêtes et Documents*, 16 (1989).

Saugera, Éric, *Bordeaux, port négrier, 18e–19e siècles. Chronologie, économie, idéologie* (Paris: Karthala, 1997).

Saunier, Éric (ed.), 'Villes portuaires du commerce triangulaire à l'abolition de l'esclavage', *Cahiers de l'histoire des mémoires de la traite négrière, de l'esclavage et de leurs abolitions en Normandie*, 1 (2008).

Saunier, Éric and Caillot, Florian, 'Le recrutement des équipages de navires de traite havrais au 18e siècle', *Revue du Philanthrope*, 6 (2015).

Schmidt, Nelly, 'Un témoignage original sur Haïti au 19e siècle: celui de l'abolitionniste Victor Schoelcher', *Jahrbuch für Geschichte von Staat, Wirtschaft und Gesellschaft Lateinamerikas*, 8 (1991).

Scott, Rebecca J. and Hébrard, Jean M., *Freedom Papers: An Atlantic Odyssey in the Age of Emancipation* (Cambridge, MA: Harvard University Press, 2012).

Seeber, Edward Derbyshire, *Anti-slavery Opinion in France during the Second Half of the Eighteenth Century* (Baltimore, MD, 1937).

Sepinwall, Alyssa Goldstein, 'Atlantic amnesia? French historians, the Haitian Revolution and the 2004–06 CAPES exam', *Proceedings of the Western Society for French History*, 32 (2006).

Serna, Pierre, *Comme des bêtes. Histoire politique de l'animal en Révolution, 1750–1840* (Paris: Fayard, 2017).

Shapiro, Gilbert and Markoff, John, *Revolutionary Demands: A Content Analysis of the Cahiers de Doléances of 1789* (Stanford, CA: Stanford University Press, 1998).

Sherwood, Marika, 'The British illegal slave trade, 1808–1830', *Journal for Eighteenth-Century Studies*, 31 (2008).

Shovlin, John, *The Political Economy of Virtue: Luxury, Patriotism and the Origins of the French Revolution* (Ithaca, NY: Cornell University Press, 2006).

Soufflet, Yannick, 'Les négociants nantais et l'architecture: le Quai de la Fosse, 1735–55' (mémoire de maîtrise, Université de Nantes, 2003).

Spang, Rebecca L., *The Invention of the Restaurant: Paris and Modern Gastronomic Culture* (Cambridge, MA: Harvard University Press, 2000).

Sparks, Randy J., 'Blind justice: the United States' failure to curb the illegal slave trade', *Law and History Review*. 35 (2017).

Spierenburg, Pieter, *The Spectacle of Suffering: Executions and the Evolution of Repression from a Pre-industrial Metropolis to the European Experience* (Cambridge: Cambridge University Press, 1984).

Stanwood, Owen, 'From the desert to the refuge: the sage of New Bordeaux', *French Historical Studies*, 40 (2017).

Stein, Robert, 'The profitability of the Nantes slave trade, 1783–1792', *Journal of Economic History*, 35 (1975).

Stein, Robert, *The French Slave Trade in the Eighteenth Century: An Old Regime Business* (Madison: Wisconsin University Press, 1979).

Stein, Robert, *Léger Félicité Sonthonax: The Lost Sentinel of the Republic* (London and Toronto: Associated University Presses, 1985).

Stewart, John, *An Account of Jamaica and its Inhabitants, by a Gentleman, Long Resident in the West Indies* (London: Longman, 1808).

Stewart, John Hall, *A Documentary Survey of the French Revolution* (New York: Macmillan, 1950).

Swann, Julian and Félix, Joël (eds), *The Crisis of Absolute Monarchy: France from Old Regime to Revolution* (Oxford: Oxford University Press, 2013).

Tackett, Timothy, *La Révolution, l'Eglise, la France: le serment de 1791* (Paris: Le Cerf, 1986).

Tackett, Timothy, *Becoming a Revolutionary: The Deputies of the French National Assembly and the Emergence of a Revolutionary Culture, 1789–90* (Princeton, NJ: Princeton University Press, 1996).

Taffin, Dominique (ed.), *Moreau de Saint-Méry ou les ambiguïtés d'un créole des Lumières* (Fort de France: Société des amis des archives et de la recherche sur le patrimoine culturel des Antilles, 2006).

Taïeb, Patrick, Gribenski, Jean, and Morel-Borotra, Natalie (eds), *Le Musée de Bordeaux et la musique, 1783–93* (Rouen: Publications des Universités de Rouen et du Havre, 2005).

Tarrade, Jean (ed.), *La Révolution Française et les colonies* (Paris: L'Harmattan, 1989).

Taylor, Michael, 'British proslavery arguments and the Bible, 1823–1833', *Slavery and Abolition*, 37 (2016).

Terjanian, Anoush Fraser, *Commerce and its Discontents in Eighteenth-century French Political Thought* (Cambridge: Cambridge University Press, 2013).

Thomas, Hugh, *The Slave Trade: The Story of the Atlantic Slave Trade, 1440–1870* (London: Weidenfeld and Nicholson, 2015).

Torrington, Arthur (ed.), *Equiano: Enslavement, Resistance and Abolition* (Birmingham: Birmingham Museums and Art Gallery, 2007).

Touzeau, Nathalie, 'Etude des expéditions négrières nantaises sous la Révolution Française (1789–93) au temps des droits de l'Homme' (2 vols, mémoire de maîtrise, Université de Nantes, 1993).

Tricoire, Damien (ed.), *Enlightened Colonialism: Civilization Narratives and Imperial Politics in the Age of Reason* (Basingstoke: Palgrave Macmillan, 2017).

Trouillot, Michel-Rolph, *Silencing the Past: Power and the Production of History* (Boston, MA, 1995).

Uzureau, François, 'L'évêque de La Rochelle en 1795', *Bulletin de la Société des Archives Historiques de la Saintonge et d'Aunis*, 41 (1926).

Vaissière, Pierre de, *Saint-Domingue: La société et la vie créoles sous l'ancien régime, 1629–1789* (Paris: Perrin, 1909).

Vergès, Françoise, 'Les troubles de la mémoire: traite négrière, esclavage et écriture de l'histoire', *Cahiers d'études africaines* 45: 179/180 (2005).

Vick, Brian E., *The Congress of Vienna: Power and Politics after Napoleon* (Cambridge, MA: Harvard University Press, 2014).

Viennet, Odette, *Une enquête économique dans la France impériale: le voyage du hambourgeois Philippe-André Nemnich, 1809* (Paris: Plon, 1947).

Villepin, Dominique de, *Les Cent Jours ou l'esprit de sacrifice* (Paris: Perrin, 2001),

Villiers, Patrick, 'Le commerce colonial pendant la Guerre de Sept Ans', *Enquêtes et documents*, 17 (1990).

Vivie, Aurélien, *Histoire de la Terreur à Bordeaux* (2 vols, Bordeaux: Feret et fils, 1877).

Vovelle, Michel (ed.), *La Rochelle, ville frontière: actes du colloque des 28 et 29 avril 1989* (La Rochelle: Rumeur des Âges, 1989).

Walvin, James, *The Quakers: Money and Morals* (London: John Murray, 1997).

Walvin, James, *Fruits of Empire: Exotic Produce and British Taste, 1660–1800* (Basingstoke: Macmillan, 1997).

Walvin, James, *A Short History of Slavery* (London: Penguin, 2007).

Ward, William E. F., *The Royal Navy and the Slavers: The Suppression of the Atlantic Slave Trade* (London: Allen and Unwin, 1969).

White, Ashli, 'A Flood of Impure Lava: Saint-Dominguan Refugees in the United States, 1791–1820' (Ph. D thesis, Columbia University, 2003).

White, Ashli, *Encountering Revolution: Haiti and the Making of the Early Republic* (Baltimore, MD: Johns Hopkins University Press, 2010).

Wilson, Ellen Gibson, *Thomas Clarkson: A Biography* (Basingstoke: Macmillan, 1989).

Wilson-Smith, Timothy, Napoleon, White, Ashli, Encountering Revolution: Haiti and the Making of the Early Republic (Baltimore, MD: Johns Hopkins University Press, 2010). Man of War, Man of Peace (London: Constable, 2002).

Wismes, Armel de, *Nantes et le temps des négriers* (Paris: Éditions France-Empire, 1992).

Wright, Philip and Debien, Gabriel, 'Les colons de Saint-Domingue passes à la Jamaïque, 1792–1835', *Bulletin de la Société d'Histoire de la Guadeloupe*, 26 (1975).

Yacou, Alain, 'L'émigration à Cuba des colons français de Saint-Domingue au cours de la Révolution' (thèse de 3e cycle, Université de Bordeaux-3, 1975).

Yacou, Alain, 'Francophobie et francophilie au temps des révolutions française et haïtienne', in *Cuba et la France: Actes du Colloque de Bordeaux* (Pessac: Presses Universitaires de Bordeaux, 1983).

Yacou, Alain, *Journaux de bord et de traite de Joseph Crassous de Médeuil. De La Rochelle à la côte de Guinée et aux Antilles, 1772–76* (Paris: Karthala, 2001).

Young, Arthur, *Travels in France during the Years 1787, 1788 and 1789* (Cambridge: Cambridge University Press, 1929).

Index

For the benefit of digital users, indexed terms that span two pages (e.g., 52–53) may, on occasion, appear on only one of those pages.

Abolition 11–12, 129, 238
  abolitionist voices in merchant community 118
  and liberal elite 128
  as a Christian cause 241
  attacks by *colons* on 153
  attributed to white liberals rather than black activists 270
  call on black population to take up arms 162
  concerns of the various slaving powers 245
  Convention votes to abolish slavery 179–80
  international pressure for 240–49
  lack of moral outrage over 108–09
  law of 1817 and 250
  Napoleon decrees abolition of slave trade 239
Académie de Bordeaux 29, 62, 112
  debates on race in 114
  membership of 112
Acadians 5–6, 33, 205
African peoples, diseases among 73
  hot climates and 79–80
  rights of Africans 104–06
  strengths and weaknesses as field workers 106
African merchants, trade with 72–73, 118, 260
Age of Revolutions, crisis years for Atlantic ports 286
Agents and plantation managers 93–95
  chosen from home regions in France 93
Agriculture, condition of 36–37
Aix-en-Provence 132
Albert, Maurice 144
American Civil War 239, 287
American Revolution 126
Amiens, Treaty of 40, 220, 222, 224, 247
Amis des Noirs 110–11, 120, 123, 128, 146, 147–50, 155–56, 250
Amnesty International 276
Amsterdam 18
Anglo-French Treaty of Abolition 251
Angola 71–72, 106
Angoulême, duc d' 229, 234, 237
  popularity of duchess in Atlantic ports 237
Anjou 82, 88
Anneaux de la Mémoire 277, 283

Anse-de-Veau 86
Antwerp 18, 267
Archangel 45
Archives Départementales, Gironde 273
Argenson, René Louis de Voyer, marquis d' 3
Aristocracy, attitudes to commerce of 50–52
Artois, Charles-Philippe, comte d' 235
Assistance 164
  compensation to *colons* 193–94
  from the French state 192–93
  to refugees arriving in the United States 208–10
  workers in receipt of 224
Atlantic port cities, assessment of causes of crisis in 288
  strengths and weaknesses of 25–33
Atlantic world 15–16
  decline of smaller ports in 23
French expansion in 5–9
Audin, Jean-Baptiste 208
Augsburg, Treaty of 47
Augustin, Jean 208
Aunis 28, 122, 132, 134
Ayrault, Jean-Marc 273
Azilum, refugee community in Pennsylvania 209

Baco de La Chapelle, René-Gaston, mayor of Nantes 131
Badagry 73
Bailly, planter 163
Balguerie, Pierre 62, 275
Balguerie-Stuttenberg, Pierre 278
Baltic, trade with 26, 31, 44, 46, 52, 146, 226
Baltimore 123, 207
Banking 26
  Paris banks 65–66
  weakness of 218
Bankruptcy, fears of 17
Bany 74
Baour, Pierre 62, 278
Baracoa 204
Barbados 9, 239, 279

Barbary coast 70
   pirates 22
Barnave, Antoine 158
Bart, Jean 54, 57
Basle, Treaty of 180
Basse-Terre (Guadeloupe) 20, 51, 55, 90, 175
Bastille, assault on 129
Baton Rouge 123
Baux, Balguerie, *négociants* 70
Baux, Jean-Louis 145
Bayonne 24–25, 40, 233, 286
   as centre of privateering 58, 222
Bearn 4
Benin, Bight of 23, 73, 79, 258, 260
Beresford, William 234
Bergasse, Nicolas 147
Berlin 35
   Berlin Decree 225, 227–28
Berquin-Duvallon, Pierre-Louis 206
Bethmann, Jean-Jacques 45–46, 70
Bétrine, Jean-Paul 134
Biassou, slave leader on Saint-Domingue 179
Biafra, Bight of 73, 103, 260
Biens nationaux 218
Blanchelande, Philippe-François
   Rouxel de 170, 174
Blaye 31, 137
Bois-Caïman, secret meeting at 175, 189
Bologne, Joseph, Chevalier de Saint-Georges 279
Bonaparte, Joseph, King of Spain 202
Bonaparte, Napoleon, *see* Napoleon I, emperor
Bonnaffé, François 30, 113, 144–45, 216
Bonnet, Natacha 88
Bordeaux 9, 15, 20, 23, 25, 26, 27, 32, 41, 67, 93,
   97, 115, 126–27, 156, 163, 174, 194, 200,
   207, 211
   American ships in 45
   Arthur Young impressed by 37–38
   debates on slave trade in 111–14
   collective memory of slave trade in 270–85
   development of new trading links after
      1815 286–87
   economic decline of 211–30
   eighteenth-century wealth of 29–31
   emigration through 83
   exports to Saint-Domingue from 44
   fragility of merchant economy of 212–13
   German merchant community in 39
   illegal slave trade in 258
   Journal de Commerce de Bordeaux 218
   merchant population of 50
   merchants stopped trading 215–16
   offer to send troops to Saint-Domingue
      161–62

population growth in 31
   range of trading destinations 44
   real estate sales in 217–18
   refugees to 191–94
   religious tolerance of 46
   Restoration in 233–37
   revolution in 124–46
   Saint-omin[gue] refugees originating in 201
   speculation in real estate in 30
   wine growing in 29
Boston 195
Bounties for landing slaves 61
Bourbons, restoration of 41, 233–39
Bourg 31
Bourges, transfer of government to 139
Bourgneuf 25
Boyer-Fonfrède, Jean-Baptiste 137
Boze, Jean 206
Brazil 248, 250, 255, 287
   treaty with Britain outlawing slave trade 256
Brest 28, 97, 192, 214–15
Brissot, Jacques-Pierre 128, 135, 147, 158
Bristol 66, 109, 271
   commemoration of slave trade in 277–78
   joint conference with Bordeaux 273
Britain 3, 19, 30, 167, 178
   abolition a populist issue in 242
   access to credit 18
   accused of turning abolition to its
      advantage 121–22
   and slave trade 60
   beneficiary of reforms in French colonies 159
   claims right of arrest of foreign vessels 261
   engagement in slave trade 23
   France declares war on 59
   invasion of Guadeloupe by 190
   naval supremacy of 52–53
   obligation to respect maritime law by 262–64
   threat of privateers from 58
British Act of Abolition 243
   bicentenary of 275
   slaving continues after 243
British blockade, effects of 219–20
   Orders in Council 225–26, 288
British High Court of Admiralty, acquittals
   by 263
British North America 6–8
Brittany 4, 30, 68, 72, 82, 139
   and Newfoundland fisheries 52
   exodus to the commercial cities from 51
   nobles engaging in colonial trade 51–52
Brooks, English slave ship 111
Brumaire, coup of 18, 181
Buenos Aires 224

Buffon, Georges Louis Leclerc, comte de 79, 107
Butel, Paul 31, 127

Cahiers de doléances 115, 124–27
Canada, French loss of 19
Canning, George 226
Cap Finisterre 22
Cape Mesurado 263
Cape Verde Islands 106, 260
Capital, needed to fit out slave ship 69–70
    prospectus to raise 73
Caribbean, colonial imports from 4
    decline of France's position in 20–21
    direct commerce (*en droiture*) with 32, 47,
      60–61
    insurance rates quoted 217
    trade with 23–25.
Carrier, Jean-Baptiste 141, 143
Carrière, Charles 24
Carteaux, François, planter 177
Casamayor, Prudencio 200
Casimir, Jean 289
Castlereagh, Robert Stewart, viscount 226,
    240–45
Catholicism, and anti-slavery 108–09
Catlin, George 6
Cayenne 5, 29, 216, 228, 246–47, 259, 260
Chaigneau, *colon* in Santiago 201
Chambers of commerce 46, 66
    caution in addressing Emperor 227–28
    created in leading commercial centres 49
    debates in 112
    dilemmas faced by 155
    extreme sensitivity during Bourbon
      Restoration 237–38
    interpretation of merchant interests
      by 150–52
    lobbying by Bordeaux chamber 148
    mobilized against the threat of abolition 120
    questions about status of neutrals 220
    view of decree on free men of colour 159
    voices of the merchant community 115–116
Chambres de lecture 134–36
Champlain, Samuel de 7
Charleston 123, 170, 195, 207–09
    birth places of French refugees in 207
Chartrons (Bordeaux) 29–30, 38, 95, 112, 278
Chatillon, Marcel 111, 274
Chaurand frères, *négociants,* Nantes 65–66, 68,
    69, 71
Chaurand, Honoré 66
Chavannes, Jean-Baptiste 170
Chile 54
China, colonial trade with 18, 24, 239

Chirac, Jacques 276, 281
Cholet 72
Civil Constitution of the Clergy 141
Claiborne, William 204–05
Clarkson, Thomas 108–11, 170, 240–41,
    252–53, 271
Clausel, Bernard, marshal, governor of
    Bordeaux 237
Clavière, Étienne 147
Clérisse, Dominique 93
Climate, as justification for slavery 81
    effects on health of 92
Clubs and political societies 133–38
    Amis de la Constitution de La Rochelle 134
    Amis de la Constitution de Nantes 135
    Amis de la Liberté et de l'Égalité, Bordeaux
      (Club des Récollets) 136–37, 161
    Club National, Bordeaux 136, 161
    Jacobin Club, Paris 136
    Société Patriotique de la Merci, Bordeaux 136
    Surveillants de la Constitution, Bordeaux 136
Club Massiac 12, 122, 146, 153, 155
Code noir 96, 272
Coffee 80
    coffee houses 5
Colbert, Jean-Baptiste, marquis de Torcy 13, 279
Colley, Linda 80
Colonies, as source of wealth 4–5, 15, 22
colonial goods 15
colonial rivalries 167
Colons, committee of 152–53
    compensation payments to 193–94
    decision to leave in the face of
      violence 163–64
    grands blancs and *petits blancs* 167
    laws could not be imposed without consent
      of 157
    lingering bitterness of 268
    lobbying in favour of the slave trade
      by 119, 153
    negotiations with Britain 178
    on return to France 95
    returning to their homes after the
      insurrection 178
    *Société des colons franco-américains de La
      Rochelle* 122
Commerce, attacks on commercial
    privileges 124
    trade fluctuations 41
Committee of Public Safety 220
Compagnie d'Afrique 23
Compagnie des Indes (French East India
    Company) 13–15, 39
    liquidation of 14

Condorcet, Nicolas de Caritat, marquis de 105, 128, 270
Continental System 214, 224–29, 288
  as a form of protectionism 227
Corsairs, see Privateers
Cotton 4
Coucy, Monseigneur de 141–42
Couraye, Léonor-François 58
Couturier, merchant 278
Covo, Manuel 20
Coyer, Gabriel François 50
Craddock, Mrs, English visitor to Bordeaux 38
Crassous, Joseph 117–118
Credit, availability of 66, 69–70
  credit from other Protestant and Jewish merchants 70
Creoles 10, 13, 147, 151, 155, 176, 190
  and cultural life 85–86
  complexity of Creole society 82
Croix, Alain 97
Cuba 161, 165, 177, 195, 248–49, 255, 260, 266, 286, 288
  as a destination for colons from Saint-Domingue 198–204
  French colons expelled from 202
  vigilance committees established in 203
Cuizeau, colon and pamphleteer 186
Cul-de-sac 91, 201
Curaçao 195
Currency, shortages of 70–71

Daget, Serge 77, 251, 255, 258, 260, 271, 285
Damiens, Robert-François 107–08
Danton, Georges 15
Debien, Gabriel 90, 153, 201
Decrès, Denis, minister for the Navy 184
Delanoë, Bertrand 279
Delaunay, Jean 201
Delaville, planter 160
Delgrès, Louis 187, 270
Demissy, Samuel 134, 146
Demouy, François 265–67
Denmark 58, 213, 239
Dérogeance, threat of 51
DeSaussure, Daniel 208
Descourtilz, Michel-Étienne 182–83
Desfourneaux, General 187
Dessalines, Jean-Jacques 185–86, 190, 192
Dessalles, Pierre 96
Diaspora from Saint-Domingue 189–210
Diderot, Denis 105
Dieppe 9, 27, 54, 90
Diseases, deaths from tropical 225
  in the Antilles 92–93

DiversCités 276, 278
Division into departments and districts 132
  prejudice against Atlantic ports 132–33
Dobrée, Thomas 239–40
Domestic servants 98
  black boys as 108
Drescher, Seymour 81
Drouin, Louis 94
Dubocage de Bléville, Michel-Joseph 63
Ducos, Jean-François 137
Ducs de Bretagne, Château des 129, 283
Duguay-Trouin, René 54
Dunkerque 54, 156, 159
Dupaty, Jean-Baptiste Mercier 89
Dupleix, Joseph-François 14
Dupouy, Madeleine 190–91
Dutch colonies 13, 195

Economic stagnation in Revolution 211–30
  critical effect on cities 223–4
Eden Treaty 121
Edict of Nantes, revocation of 27, 46
Egypt 59, 106
Ehrard, Jean 107–08
Emigrants from France 10, 87
  accompanying families 90
  discrete groups among 89
  halted by revolution in Caribbean 189
Émigrés, return of 237
Encyclopédie,106
Engagement, system of 10–11, 80–82
English Channel 22, 58
Enlightenment, challenge of 103
  rejection of 141
Equiano, Olaudah 279
  exhibition in Birmingham to honour 279–80
Estates-General, elections in colonies to 152
Exclusif 20, 148
  abandonment of 219
Executions 107–08

Fashion, importance of 5
Federalism 138–40
Fernandes, François 264, 268
Fick, Carolyn 174
Fiscal-military state 18
Fischer, David Hackett 7
Fisheries 9, 25, 26, 48
Fleming, David 274
Fleuriau, Aimé-Benjamin 91–92
Flour mills 32
Foäche, Stanislas 88
Fontainebleau, Treaty of 238
Forced migration 79–80

Forster, William 252
Fort Dauphin 83
Fosse, quai de la (Nantes) 33
Fourche, Madame, planter 196
Franco-Prussian War 287
Free people of colour 59, 167
    increasing French reliance on 179
    legal restrictions on 168–70
    National Assembly's support for 170
Free trade, calls for 116
Freemasonry 66
    and the merchant community 114–115
    in small country towns 134
    masonic lodges 43, 84, 115, 133
Free men of colour 156–59
    white planters' fears of 161
Freetown 263, 264
French army, cost in lives to 190
French colonies, administration of 6
French navy 28
French Revolution 13, 14, 276
    and business confidence 59
    and new waves of migration across the
        Atlantic world 123
    and tourism 40
    clubs 133–38
    in the Atlantic ports 124–46
    Jacobin coup in Paris 138
    merchants' initial response to 127–28
    recovery from 34–35
    refractory priests and 140–41
    role of *Commission Militaire* 139
    split between Girondins and Jacobins 137–39
French Revolutionary Wars 57
    declaration of 59
    global impact of 59
    impact on trade 215–16
    traditional character of 214
Fur trade 5–6

Gaillac 212–13
Galbaud, François-Thomas, General 162, 177
Garesché, Daniel 127, 134
Garrigus, John 169
Gascony 4
Geggus, David 42, 180
General Maximum 213
Geneva 70
Gensonné, Armand 113, 137
George III, oaths of loyalty to 178
Géraud, Edmond 234
Germany 44
Gibraltar, Straits of 22
Girard, Stephen 209–10

Giraud, estate manager on Reiset's
    plantation 94–95
Girauld and Raimbaud, *négociants*, Nantes 64
Girondins 137–39
Glasgow 246
Goguet de la Sauzet 131
Gold Coast 73, 260, 266
Gondrecourt, Charles-Gabriel 175–76
Gorée Island 19, 29, 71, 111, 254, 261
Gournay, Jacques Claude Marie Vincent,
    marquis de 3
Gradis, David 62, 278
Grand Tour 34, 40
Grande Tabagie 7
Grangeneuve, Jean-Antoine 137
Graslin, quartier (Nantes) 30
Grégoire, Henri-Jean-Baptiste (abbé) 158, 270
Greer, Donald 142
Grenada 9
Grindal, Peter 243, 256
Grovellet, Christophe 67
Guadalajara 141
Guadeloupe 9, 19, 41, 43–44, 53, 56, 62,
        76, 83, 95, 158, 168, 180–81, 192, 194, 213,
        228, 238, 249, 256–57, 259–60, 262, 268,
        270, 288
    Gazette de la Guadeloupe 43
    series of slave revolts in 175–76
    military force sent to 183–84
    Napoleonic policy in 187–88
    restoration of slavery to 184, 247
Guadet, Marguerite-Élie 113, 137, 162
Guillaud, planter 160
Guillet de la Brosse, merchant 268
Guinea 74, 103
Guinea Company 58, 60
Guinebaud, Jacques-Nicolas 127
Guyana 62, 195, 238, 247
Guyenne 68

Habitation, see Plantation
Haiti, diplomatic recognition by other
    nations 269, 289
    effects of intervention from the United
        States 289
    Minister of Culture of 282
    misery after independence 268, 288–89
    treatment by France 269
Haitian Revolution, causes of 166
    Haitian independence 186, 218
    resonates across Latin America 288
Hallman, Swedish merchant 38
Hamburg 45
Hanseatic ports 30, 45, 213, 226

Hanson, Paul 138–39
Haudrère, Philippe 77
Havana 123, 196, 199, 224, 260, 264–65
Henri, Jacques 144
Henry, Mathurin 86
Higounet, Charles 112
Holland 3, 30, 58, 70, 239, 264
Holocaust, commemoration of 281
Honfleur 22, 26, 61, 73, 89, 224, 257, 262
Hong Kong 253
Hopkins, Richard 34
Hourcade, Renaud 282
Huguenots 7, 198, 209
    turning to the slave trade 118–19
Hugues, Victor 187
Hundred Days 236–37, 247
Hunt, Lynn 17
Huntington Library 265

Île Feydeau (Nantes) 30, 95, 127, 272
Illegal slave trade 250–69
    allegations of political connivance 254
    three main periods of 257
    under foreign flags 243, 260
    vessels involved in 259–60
India 59
    colonial trade with 18, 24, 53
    French trading posts in 14
Indian Ocean, trade with 24, 61, 216, 286–87
    colonies in 181, 238
    slave trafficking in 257
Indiennes 95, 223
Industry, impact of Revolution on 223–24
Inflation 213
Inscription Maritime, registers of 259–60
Institut Philanthropique 235
Insurance rates, in wartime 216
    premiums for different voyages 216–17
Interest rates, for government 16–17
Ireland 30, 44, 46

Jacmel 83, 85
Jacobins, and Terror 137–40
Jacquette, African king and slave trader 267
Jamaica 161, 165, 177, 239, 248
    as destination for refugees 195–98
    British governor of 178
    British occupation of 3
Java 59
Jean-François, slave leader on
        Saint-Domingue 179
Jefferson, Thomas 105
Jérémie 83, 85, 165, 177
Jews 125

Jones, John Paul 58
Journal de Guienne 113
Journu frères, merchants 212
Jullien, Marc-Antoine 143
Juppé, Alain, mayor of Bordeaux 274, 284

Keber, Martha 51–52
Kervégan, Daniel, mayor of Nantes 131
Kindelán, Sebastian 198
King, David 244
Kingston 195–97, 203

Lacombe, Benoît 212–13
Lacombe, Jean-Baptiste 145
La Croix-des-Bouquets 86, 91
Laffon de Ladebat, André-Daniel 113, 118,
        134, 278
Lambertz, Jacob 145–46
Langouran, Jean 206
La Réole 137
La Rochelle 9, 23, 25, 46, 49–50, 61, 67, 91–92,
        97, 115, 118–19, 122, 127, 131, 139, 149,
        163, 192, 207
    decline in prosperity of 27–28, 218–19, 286
    impact of the Vendée 140–43
    limited value of hinterland 28
    optimism in 1814 230
    role of protestants in 27, 63, 125–26
La Salle, René-Robert Cavelier, sieur de 6
Lebourg, Jeanne-Eulalie 90
Le Cap (Le Cap français) 12, 42–43, 51, 63, 76,
        83, 84, 85, 89–91, 99, 123, 144, 162–65, 170,
        175, 184, 195, 209
    in flames 177
    plot to burn 150
    renamed Cap Haïtien 268
Le Chauff de Kerguenec, plantation owners 88
Leclerc, Charles-Emmanuel, General 182–84,
        190, 199
Lefebvre, Élie 164
Lefebvre, François-Joseph, marshal 233
Légions de l'Égalité 172
Le Havre 15, 20, 23, 25, 32, 47, 50, 61, 63, 67, 73,
        93, 97, 108, 115, 127, 132, 155, 163, 200, 219,
        224, 262, 271
    as a military city 26–27
    revival of economy after 1815 287
Lenormand de Mézy, plantation 175
Léogane 85
Le Pouliguen 25
Les Cayes 51, 85
Lesage, merchant in Cayenne 246–47
Lestapis, colon in Santiago 201
Letestu, Pierre 89, 164

Lettres de marque 53–54, 221
  issued in eighteenth-century wars 57
Levant trade 70
Libourne 132, 137
Liège, Marie-Anne-Suzanne 91–92
Ligue des Droits de l'Homme 276
Lille 49
Limoges 31, 35
Linnaeus, Carl 38
Liverpool 66, 75, 109, 122, 243, 246, 271
  as a slave port 23
Liverpool, Robert Jenkinson, earl of 242
Loire 67
  drowning of prisoners in 142–43
  Loire valley 82, 134
  Pays de Loire 72
London, City of 18
  conference on slave trade in 245
  investors in 243
Lorient 23, 28, 32, 39, 97, 192, 257
Louis XIV, King of France 3, 26, 48, 279
Louis XV , King of France 103
LouisXVI, King of France 39
Louis XVIII, King of France 229, 233, 236, 241,
  244–47, 261
Louis-Philippe, King of France 245
Louis, Victor, architect 29
Louisiana 5, 19, 197–98, 269
  as destination for refugees from Saint-
    Domingue 203–04
  sale of 186
  status of slave trade in 205
Lynch, Jean-Baptiste, mayor of
    Bordeaux 234
Lyon 31, 38, 49, 175, 223

Madeira 260
Madrid 202
Mallet, Nicolas-Pierre 187
Marans 140
Marcé, Louis de, General   140
Marie-Galante 9, 194
Markoff, John 125
Marmande 32
Marmont, Auguste- Frédéric-Louis,
    marshal 233
Maroons 172–73
Marriage, as a commercial arrangement 66
Marsh, Elizabeth 80
Marseille 27, 38, 47, 50, 61, 70, 97, 132, 138, 192,
  211, 219, 224, 262, 287
  commercial links with the Levant and North
    Africa 24, 258
Martin, Jean-Clément 142

Martinique 9, 19, 41, 44, 53, 56, 62, 76, 83, 89,
  95, 152, 158, 180, 192, 194, 213, 224–25,
  228, 238, 249, 256–57, 259–60, 268, 288
Marzagalli, Silvia 60
Mather, James 204
Maurepas, Jean-Frédéric Phélypeaux, comte
    de 52–53
Mauritius (Île-de-France) 14, 216, 247, 287
McIntosh, Duncan 209
Memory of slave trade 270–85
  Memorial to the Slave Trade in Nantes 285
Mendès, Jacob 278
Mercantilism 19–21
Merchants, passim
  and risk-taking 44–45
  and Terror 144–45
  arrest for bringing slaves into Louisiana 206
  assume municipal offices in 1790 130–31
  aversion to risk in wartime 56
  colony of French merchants in
    London 46–47
  defence of slavery by 153
  differences from interests of colons 154–55
  immigration to Nantes 33
  lobbying in Paris by 147–49
  networks 27
  support for Bourbon Restoration 235
Mexico, Gulf of 6
Meyer, Jean 47, 48, 64
Meyer, Lorenz 191, 222–23
Meyer, merchant in La Rochelle 246
Middle Passage 10, 75–76, 98, 105, 166,
  225, 277
Migrant labour, attraction of 28, 31
Milan Decree 225, 227–28
Mirabeau, Honoré Gabriel Riqueti, comte
    de 110–11, 149
Mississippi, river 6
Mixed Prize Commissions 264
Monroe Doctrine 269
Montaigne, Michel de 39, 112, 273
Montesquieu, Charles-Louis de Secondat, baron
    de 39, 103–04, 112, 273
Montivilliers 132
Moreau de Saint-Méry 12, 84, 88
Morellet, André 14
Morris, Robert 209
Mosneron, Jean-Baptiste, baron de
    Launay 129, 161
Mulhouse 70
Musée de Bordeaux 62, 112–13
Museums, exhibitions on slave trade in 273–75
  Birmingham Museum and Art Gallery 279–80
  Château des Ducs de Bretagne, Nantes 283

Museums, exhibitions on slave trade in (*cont.*)
  International Museum of Slavery,
    Liverpool 274, 282
  Malraux Art Museum, Le Havre 285
  Musée d'Aquitaine, Bordeaux 274, 282, 284
  Musée du Nouveau Monde, La Rochelle
    (Musée Fleuriau) 283–84
  National Museum of African American
    History, Washington 274
Mutiny on slave ships 77

Nairac, Jean-Baptiste 149, 275
Nairac, Paul 113, 130
Nantes 9, 15, 25–27, 41, 47–52, 67, 82, 93, 122,
    156, 163, 174, 200, 207, 211, 257, 262
  slave voyages from 17, 23, 77
  architectural splendour of 36–37
  development of new trading links after
    1815 287
  economic decline in Revolution 222
  emigration through 83
  growing economy of 31–33
  hinterland of 72
  illegal slaving in 251–52, 255
  losses in wartime 56
  memory of slave trade in 270–85
  refugees to 191–92
  reluctance to create a chamber
    of commerce in 49
  resumption of slaving after American
    War 61
  revolution in 124–46
  sensitivity during Restoration 237–38
  speculative frenzy in 30
'Nantes 85', conference 272, 285
Napoleon, First Consul then Emperor 5, 166,
    181–82, 214
  attitude to abolition of slave trade 181
  during the Restoration 233–40
  encouragement to trade 228–30
  exile to Elba 233
  hostility in Bordeaux to 234
  invasion of Spain 202
  last stand against Allies 233
  reinstitution of the slave trade 109, 224,
    229, 247
  visit to Nantes 227
Napoleonic Wars 57–58
National Assembly, *passim*
  decree of 15 May 1791 156, 174
  decrees on colonial governance 168
National Guards 130, 140, 144, 146,
    161, 172
Naval warfare, Britain's advantages in 214–15

Navigation licences, issuance of 225–26
Necker, Jacques 16
Nemnich, Philippe-André 222
Neutral shipping 20–21, 219–20
Newfoundland 6, 9, 25, 52, 54
Newspapers, revolutionary press 133
New Bordeaux 8
New France 6–7
  exhibition on 283
New Orleans 123, 197, 204–06, 216
New World, colonization of 3–5
New York 195, 264
Ney, Michel, marshal 233
Nicholson, John 209
Nine Years' War 54, 56
Nobles, and overseas commerce 89
  and slave plantations 88–89
  ending of privileges of 130
Norfolk Virginia 123, 190, 207
Normandy 4
  and Canada trade 52
Nugent, Sir George, governor of Jamaica 197

Oexmelin, Alexandre-Olivier 54–55
Ogé, Vincent 170
Orleans 82
Orry de la Roche 65
Oudinot, Nicolas, marshal 233
Ouidah 71, 73

Page, Pierre-François 159
Paimboeuf 25, 265
Pamphlet campaigns 115–16
Pantheon, transfer to 270
Papin, royalist 236
Paris 4, 25, 31, 35, 38, 41, 97, 130
Paris, Peace of (1763) 19–20, 33, 119, 148
Paris, Treaty of (1814) 238, 242
Parkman, Francis 6
Parlement, of Bordeaux, magistrates as slave
    owners 89
  in revolutionary politics 126
Pays de Lathan, plantation owners 88
Peace, merchants' desire for 236
Pellet, Jean 47
Peninsular War 35
Pérotin-Dumon, Anne 43
Peru 54
Pétré-Grenouilleau, Olivier 87
Philadelphes, Cercle des 84
Philadelphia 12, 123, 150, 152, 163, 195, 206,
    208–09, 217, 219
Physiocrats, ideas on slave trade of 104
Pince, Welsh sea captain 253

Pinkard, Susan 4
Piracy, in the Caribbean 55
  threat of 22
Planquette, Robert 58
Plantations, nostalgia for 96
  owners of 88
  plantation burning 160–64
  purchase by free people of colour 174
  running plantations from France 94–95
Planters 32
  absentee owners targeted 176
  anguish on return 182
  circulation of pamphlets from 116
  demand for slaves 64
  lobbying in favour of slave trade by 149–50
  opposition to rights for free men of colour
    by 156
  legacy of fear among 164–65
  thriving planter community established in
    Cuba 198–99
Pleuvri, Jacques-Olivier 108
Pluchon, Pierre 181
Pointe-à-Pitre (Guadeloupe) 20, 51, 283
Poitiers 31
Poitou 87
Poland 35
Polverel, Étienne 129, 162, 174, 178
Pont-Charrault, battle of 140
Population 27–28
  expansion of 27
  black population of French cities 97
  decline in La Rochelle 28
  decline during Revolution and Empire 223
  different classes in the French Caribbean 82
  occupations of 98
Pornic 25, 258
Port-au-Prince 42, 51, 75, 83, 90–92, 99, 123,
    145, 173, 184, 192, 199, 216
  torching of 189
Port-Louis 14
Portier de Lantimo, Marie 66
Porto Novo 73
Portugal 3, 23, 44, 58, 60, 250, 264, 287
  abolition of slave trade by 244
Potofsky, Allan 4
Poussou, Jean-Pierre 83, 223
Praslin, duc de 29
Presents, for African rulers 74
Price, Jacob 195
Prison hulks, in Portsmouth and Chatham 193
Privateers 22, 48, 265
  expedient in Revolutionary Wars 220–22
  use of during maritime wars with
    Britain 53–58

Protestants 125–26
  and freemasonry 134
  and political clubs 134
Proulx, Annie 6
Prudhomme, Louis 5
Puerto Rico 248, 256–57

Quakers 109
'Quasi War' of 1800 18
Quebec 5, 19, 33

Race, and identity in the Caribbean 167–70
  and revolution in the Caribbean 178
  debates about 107
  issue that united white population 173
Raimond, Julien 162, 171–72, 181
Randolph, Edmund 208
Raynal, Guillaume-Thomas, abbé 103,
    105, 270
Refugees, from Saint-Domingue 163–64,
    189–210
  colonies of refugees in American cities 207
  destinations in the Americas 195–207
  entry ports into the United States 207
  misery of 191–92
  prejudice against men of colour 204
  range of skills among 200
  those returning to France 191–94
Régent, Frédéric 168
Reiset, Jacques 94
Religion 46
  Christianity and abolitionism 109–11
  Christianity and pro-slavery groups 110
  religious persecution 6–8
Restaurants 5
Réunion (Île Bourbon) 14, 212, 247, 253, 257,
    260, 268, 287
Richard, Guy 50
Richepanse, Antoine 183, 279
Rigaud, André 180
Rights of Man, Declaration of 128–29,
    167, 172
  application to colonies 162
  debates over meaning of 158
Rio de Janeiro 260, 264
Robespierre, Maximilien 144
Rochambeau, Donatien-Marie-Joseph de
    Vimeur, vicomte de 184, 186
Roche, madame de la 39
Rochefort 28, 139, 214–15
Rochefoucauld, François de la 38
Rochefoucauld-Liancourt, duc de la 38
Roland de la Platière, Jean-Marie 136
Rollac, J.-S., royalist pamphleteer 235–36

Rouen 22, 25–26, 35–36, 49, 132
Rousseau, Jean-Jacques 104–05
Rouvray, marquis de 150
Roux, Georges, armateur 71
Royal Navy 16, 48, 180, 252, 265
  claimed right to board and arrest slave
    ships 243–44
  focus on capturing colonies 53
  off Sierra Leone 250, 256
  infrequency of searches 260
  patrols along French coastline 221
  work of the Jamaica and Leeward Islands
    squadrons 256
Royalism, in Bordeaux 235–36
  succession of royalist clubs in city 235
Rural poverty 35–36
Rush, Richard 245
Ryswick, Treaty of 3

Saige, François-Armand 62, 275
Saint-Barthélemy 9, 253, 259
Saint-Christophe 9
Saint-Domingue 3, 9–1, 12–13, 19, 41–44, 62,
    71, 73, 75, 89, 94, 147, 153, 158, 167, 189,
    224, 269, 270
  dreams of wealth from 87
  French troops sent to 172
  impact on Atlantic ports of loss of 218, 251,
    286–89
  nostalgia for 165
  panics leading to exodus of whites 190
  proposed constitution for 182
  revolution in 59, 160–65, 166–88
  slave insurrection in 129
  urban culture of 42–43
Saint-Eustache 259
Saint-Jean 52
Saint-Lucia 158, 194, 238
Saint-Malo 9, 23–24, 32, 47–48, 54, 57–58, 82,
    127, 156, 159, 200
  profits from privateering in 221
Saint-Marc 83, 85, 94
Saint-Martin 9, 195
Saint Napoleon, festival of 227
Saint-Pierre and Miquelon 9
Saint-Thomas 259
Sainte-Croix 9, 52
Sainte-Gême, Henri de 206
Saintes 132, 139
Saintonge 28, 68, 122, 132, 134
Santiago de Cuba 123, 198–204, 260
  population growth of 200
  transformation by colons from Saint-
    Domingue 201–02

Santo Domingo (Spanish) 3, 177, 195, 203
St Lawrence river 6
St Petersburg 45, 128
Saugera, Éric 225
Saumur 82
Saunier, Éric 68
Sauton, Marie 208
Savannah 207
Savary, Jacques 76
Scandinavia, trade with 26, 30, 44
Schœlcher, Victor 248, 268, 270, 281
Schopenhauer, Arthur 39
Scott, Rebecca 199
Scott, William 263
Scurvy, spread of 212
Senegal 19, 79, 106, 111, 253, 254, 261
Sepinwall, Alyssa 269
September Massacres 138
Seregambia 260
Sers, Jean-Pierre 134
Sers, Pierre 137
Seven Years' War 14, 18, 47–48, 55, 57–58,
    122, 155
  French losses in 53, 56
Shapiro, Gilbert 125
Shipbuilding 16–17, 32
Ships' captains, importance of 66–67
  deaths on slave voyages 67
Shovlin, John 16
Sierra Leone, Court of Vice-Admiralty
    in 243, 263
  Court disbanded 262
  governor of 261
  reports of French slave ships in 250
Simon, Albert 86, 173
Slave Coast 258
Slave insurrection 77–78, 175–78
  first reports of 159–60
  levels of support for 177
Slave ships 66–68
  anonymous appearance of 99
  arrested by British warships after the war
    ended 262–64
  captains 66–67
  conditions on board 76–77
  crewmen 67–68
  geographical origins of crews 68
  journal of 74–75
  inaccurate records on 264
Slave trade 4, 11, 23
  arguments in favour of 120
  ceremonials attached to 74
  declared a crime against humanity 281
  French involvement in 60–78

merchants demand exclusive rights to 68
reduced French dependence on 258
refusal to issue papers for 246
regulation by monarchy 62
role of Spain, Portugal and Brazil 249
royal decrees on 245
Slavery, collective memory of 270–85
call for changes to street names 278
official amnesia 271
role of Communist Party and of voluntary
associations 276
role of people of African and Caribbean
descent 276
Slavery, moral questions relating to 11–12, 62,
103–123
campaign in National Assembly 111
change in moral climate 239
dominant image of 108
slaves seen as a source of profit 63
value of anniversaries 275
Slavery Abolition Act (Britain) 248
Slaves, attitude of Louisiana to slaves from
Saint-Domingue 206
claims of humane treatment 106
controls on entry into France 96–97
religious instruction of 106
Slaving voyages, by naval vessels 28–29
costs of fitting out 65–66
dangers incurred in crossing 64
deaths of slaves on board 63, 212, 266
in first years of the Revolution 211–12
preparing ship for a slaving voyage 71–72
profits from 64–65
provisions on board 72
reduced profits from 224–25
spreading of risk 70
the illegal voyage of the *Jeune Louis* 265–68
weaponry on board 72
Smith, Adam 3
Smith, Robert 204–05
Smuggling 20
Société de la Morale Chrétienne 109
during Restoration 252–53
Société Française de Bienfaisance 209–10
Society for the Abolition of the Slave Trade
(Britain) 110
Sonthonax, Léger-Félicité 129, 162, 174,
178, 181
Southampton 287
Sow, Osmane 284
Spain 3, 19, 35, 44, 46, 58, 60, 167, 178, 250,
264, 287
abolition of slave trade by 244
declaration of war on 162

no interest in assisting abolition 257
slaves taking up arms for 179–80
wars with 22
Spanish Town 195–97
Standing army, need to maintain 16
Stapleton, plantation owner 88
Stein, Robert 69, 167
Steiner, Philippe 104
Stuart, William 92
Sugar, trade in 4, 41–42, 47, 53, 80
processing 33
sugar production 19, 88
Suicides 76
Surcouf, Robert 57–58
Surinam 260, 264
Switzerland 70

Tackett, Timothy 124
Tadoussac, treaty with Native Americans 7
Tallien, Jean-Lambert 143
Tarbes 132
Tariffs, hindering growth 218
Taubira, Christiane 281
Taubira Law 282
Terror 139–46
Revolutionary Tribunal 140, 143
scale of repression 142–44
Textile industry 32–33
Theatre in France 39
Théâtre Graslin, Nantes 33
Grand Théâtre, Bordeaux 39
Theatre in Saint-Domingue 85–86
Creole drama 86
and theatre in New Orleans 86
Third Estate, demands of 125
Thomas, Hugh 64
Thomas, Theodore. 46–47
Thorpe, Robert 243, 263–64
Tobacco 4, 47, 80
Tobago 238
Tonneins 32
Tornézy, Jacques-Philippe-Guillaume 201
Tortue, Île de la 55
Toulon 28, 215
Toulouse 31, 49
Tournon, Camille, comte de 237
Tours 72, 82
Toussaint, François-Dominique (Toussaint
Louverture) 146, 166, 179–82, 270,
288–89
memorial slab in Le Havre 285
square named in honour of in Bordeaux 282
statue of in La Rochelle 284
Travellers to Atlantic ports 34–40

Triangular trade 27, 98
  increasing dependence on 61
  more complex versions of 211–12
Trinidad 195, 248
Trois-Rivières 175
Trottier, Mathurin 225
Turgot, Anne-Robert-Jacques 4

United States 20, 124, 161, 195, 213
  as destination for refugees 201–09
  maintenance of slavery in 248
  public hypocrisy over slaving 255–56
Uruguay 256
Ustaritz 132
Utrecht, Treaty of 4

Van Hoogwerff, Pierre-Jean 63, 93–94,
    128, 134
Vannes 25
Vauban, Sébastien Le Prestre, marquis de 26
Vaucluse, répression in 175
Vendée, insurrection in 139–43, 175
Vergès, Françoise 280
Vergniaud, Pierre-Victurnien 113, 137
Verne, Jules 272
Versailles 4, 126, 130
Vertières, battle of 185
Vienna, Congress of 240–49, 256, 260
  abolitionist pressure at 241–42
Villeneuve, Geoffrey de 111
Violence, as initiation rite 77
  following attempts to restore slavery 184
  on the plantations 160–62, 170–79
  on slave ships 76–77
Volney, Constantin François de Chassebœuf,
    comte de 107
Voltaire (François-Marie Arouet) 50, 103

War, destruction caused by 9
  effects of war with Britain in the
    Caribbean 213–17
  renunciation by National Assembly of 121
  and revolution in the Caribbean 166–88
War of 1812 55
War of American Independence 16–18, 48, 53,
    56, 57–58, 61, 65, 68, 155, 219
War of the Austrian Succession 32, 52–53, 57
War of the Spanish Succession 17, 47, 54, 57, 60
Washington, George 105
Watier de Nantes 33
Wellington, Arthur Wellesley, duke of 234
West Africa 22, 27
  expeditions to 61
  gift culture in 75
  perils of 74
  slaves' nostalgia for 78
  traders in 32
  voyages to 262–63
  West Africa Station 244
Whitbread, Samuel 240–41
Wilberforce, William 108, 240–41, 244, 252,
    271, 274
Windward Islands (Lesser Antilles) 9–10, 52, 55
Winegrowing 31–32
  in the Médoc 50
  wine trade 215
Wodiczko, Krzysztof 285
Women, civilizing role of 10
  liaisons with slave women 91
  reputation for libertinage 90

Yellow fever, death rate among French 185–86
Yoruba, religious legacy to Haiti of 73
Young, Arthur 35–40
Ysabeau, Claude-Alexandre 143